Wish Were Here!

A Guide to Baltimore City
for Natives and Newcomers

To Linda—
Enjoy Baltimore &
The book!

Carolyn Males
Carol Barbier Rolnick
Pam Makowski Goresh

WOODHOLME
HOUSE
PUBLISHERS

Baltimore, Maryland

©1999, Carolyn Males, Carol Barbier Rolnick,
Pam Makowski Goresh

All rights reserved. No part of this book may be reproduced or
transmitted in any form or by any means, electronic or mechanical,
including photocopying, recording, or by any information storage
and retrieval system without written permission from the publisher.

Printed and bound in the United States of America.

First Printing, First Edition

Library of Congress Cataloging-in-Publication Data

Males, Carolyn.
    Wish you were here! : a guide to Baltimore City for natives
and newcomers / Carolyn Males, Carolyn Rolnick, Pam Goresh.
—1st ed.
            p.   cm.
    Includes bibliographical references and index.
    ISBN 1-891521-05-5
    1. Baltimore (Md.)—Guidebooks. I. Rolnick, Carol Barbier,
    1951- . II. Goresh, Pamela M., 1953- . III. Title.
F189.B13M35 1999
917.52'60443—dc21   98-55255
                                                        CIP

Woodholme House Publishers
1829 Reisterstown Road
Suite 130
Baltimore, Maryland 21208
Orders: 1-800-488-0051
e-mail: whp@ix.netcom.com

Cover and book design: Lance Simons
Interior photographs: Carolyn Males, Pam Makowski Goresh
Maps: Carol Barbier Rolnick
Additional photos: Dr. Samuel D. Harris National Museum of
Dentistry, pg. 160; Carol Barbier Rolnick, pg. 162; US National
Park Service, pg. 217; St. Mary's Seminary, pg. 394.

Special thanks to Pamela Foresman for dolling up as "Miss Hon"
for the book's spine.

Contents

Uptown

Entertainment

Catching Some ZZZZs   428

Just the Facts   435

Suggested Reading   440

Index   441

Acknowledgments

Thanks to Jamie Hunt of the Mount Vernon Cultural District, Frances Zeller of Harbor City Tours, Alice Torriente and Tom Saunders of African American Renaissance Tours, Harriett Goldberg of Concierge Plus, D. Randall Beirne, Frank Shivers, Romaine Somerville, Dean Krimmel, Walter Schamu, Father Peter E. Hogan S.S.J., Andi Swift, Cindy Kelly, Ellen Sybor, Dorothy Dougherty, Jeff Jerome, Carol Warner and Greg Schwalenberg, Jimmy Rouse, Margaret Footner, Martha Dickey, Gia Blattermann, Pamela Foresman, Mary Pat Andrea, Sharon P. Gill, Rafael Alvarez, Herb Howard, Helynn Garner, Ron Harvey, Tessa Hill-Aston, George Gilliam, Bob Oliver, Bill Larson, Andy Goresh, Laurie Hay, Ed Wojnowski, Melvin Laszczwski, Bob Wall, Dan Van Allen, Mary-Margaret Stepanian and Fran and Deb Rahl, Art Koch, Susan Lowe, Stephen Rubin, Julie McCallister, Barbara and Mike Noonberg, Louise and John Titchener, Terri Diener, Clay Welch, Linda Kemp, Anna Harbom and Pam Taylor, JoAnn Marshall.

Many thanks to all our writers' groups, on-line as well as in real time, who offered a listening ear. We especially appreciate the Enoch Pratt staff of the Maryland Room and the library's research department and the librarians of the Maryland Historical Society who assisted us in our research, and all helpful people around town who answered all our many questions. And a special thanks to our editor Gregg Wilhelm and our book designer Lance Simons who made this guidebook possible.

And most of all, we'd like to thank our families for their patience and support: Dick, Rich, Guenevere, and Beowulf Males; Michael, Tim, and Tessa Rolnick; and Andy, Samantha, Alexandra, and Chili Goresh.

Welcome to Baltimore, Hon

He was a man with a mission. Armed with three large laminated letters, he braved the traffic on the Baltimore-Washington Parkway. His target: the "Welcome to Baltimore" sign. Motorists honked their horns and shouted encouragement as he walked the center median and stapled his precious letters to the wooden board. H-O-N. He stood back and admired his handiwork: Welcome to Baltimore, Hon.

Anyone who's ever cracked a jimmie in a Baltimore crab house, eaten in a deli on Corned Beef Row, or downed a Natty Boh has met up with the proverbial Baltimore waitress who says, "What can I getcha, Hon?" It doesn't matter what your age, gender, or color—in Baltimore's folksier establishments, you are "Hon." So naturally, the intrepid one-man "Bawlmer Welcome Wagon" became "The Hon Man."

Alas, the State Highway Administration did not see the humor. A road crew was dispatched to tear down the illegal lettering only to have The Hon Man strike again and again. Indeed, Baltimore's secret admirer had a trunk full of Hs, Os, and Ns.

The identity of the man who dared to pin Baltimore's term of endearment to the staid wooden sign remains a mystery. But maybe that's just as well. The Hon Man symbolized all of us who view this port city with affection.

The Hon Man is only one of Baltimore's wacky and endearing institutions. What other city could have grown bizarro movie auteur John Waters and his 300-pound drag queen leading lady, Divine? What other city annually commemorates the death of one of the strangest writers who ever put pen to paper—Edgar Allan Poe? And we've got culture.

The serious stuff: the Peabody Institute with its renowned classical music curriculum; the Baltimore Symphony Orchestra and the Baltimore Opera; the Walters Art Gallery and the Baltimore Museum of Art with their Old Masters counterbalanced by the American Visionary Arts Museum with its mavericks who view the world through their own unique lenses; top-notch research departments at Johns Hopkins and the University of Maryland; and captains of industry who created great commercial empires during the Gilded Age.

And the colorful: Blaze Starr and the Two O'clock Club; Barry Levinson and *Homicide*; Anne Tyler and her quirky characters; Wild Bill Hagy, Cal Ripken, Brooks Robinson, Jim Palmer, and Johnny Unitas; the late James Rouse, city revitalizer and developer of Harborplace; former mayor William Donald Schaefer—touted as best mayor in the country by his peers and *Esquire* magazine.

For background music: Cab Calloway, Ethel Ennis, Billie Holiday, Eubie Blake.

For sustenance: pierogies, pasta, schnitzel, barbecue, and moussaka from the city's ethnic neighborhoods.

So come with us on a rollercoaster ride through Baltimore's fascinating, and sometimes very peculiar, history and culture.

Where else but Baltimore, Hon?

Key to the City

ALERT!!!

Good! We've got your attention. Nobody ever reads keys but if you take the time to look at this now, it will save a lot of head-scratching, not to mention hassle, later.

PLAN OF THE BOOK

The book is divided by geographic area, starting with the Inner Harbor, moving on to Downtown areas and ending with the Neighborhoods and Uptown. The last sections list area tours, performing arts, sports and recreation, and hotels.

RESTAURANTS AND SHOPS

Here today, gone tomorrow. It's a fact of life. We've tried to include shops and restaurants with staying power. But even so, it's best to call first. Ditto for hours and days of operation. To give you a general guideline, we've noted what meals restaurants serve (see symbols below). However, for the most part, we've not listed what days they're open since restaurants are notorious for shifting their schedules.

Restaurant Symbols:

B=Breakfast

L=Lunch

D=Dinner

Br=Brunch

☽=open until 11 pm or later

Prices:

$= inexpensive

$$= moderate

$$$= expensive

SITES

Whenever possible we've included visiting hours and days. But at the risk of repeating ourselves, we'll mention that bugaboo: **things change**. Don't like surprises? Call first.

What Makes Baltimore "Bawlmer"

What's in a name? Sure, Baltimore's got its serious side—the financial district near the harbor, the Baltimore Museum of Art, the symphony, and the opera. It's got glitz at Harborplace and elegance in Mount Vernon. But venture out into the old blue-collar neighborhoods where Baltimore becomes "Bawlmer" and you'll find folksy charm and humor along with unique architecture and art, kitsch, and plenty of characters.

Rowhouses and Marble Steps

Mention the word "house" and "Baltimore" together and most people think of blocks of two and three-story red brick rowhouses with marble steps at their front doors. Indeed the city is lined with these practical no-nonsense rows. The first of these affordable red brick houses sprang up in the population surges of the early 19th century. Plain, with gable roofs and dormers, these houses provided shelter for artisans, merchants, and maritime workers. Pascault Row, at 651-665 West Lexington Street, is a good example of these flat-front buildings.

By mid-century developers were constructing the flat-roofed Italianate rowhouses with cornices and marble steps, the kind of rows many people associate with Baltimore. In middle and upper class neighborhoods, alley houses for servants were built behind the main streets. As the Industrial Age brought in an influx of immigrants, attached homes proved a practical housing solution and the number of rows swelled. To sweeten the pot, a system of ground rents, where homeowners leased the land their houses sat on, cut purchase costs by a fifth.

As the century progressed and turned, other styles cropped up: the cottage-style Queen Anne (seen at Belvidere Terrace in the 1000 block of North Calvert Street); turreted swell fronts (along North Avenue); Philadelphia porch-fronts (in Charles Village); daylight houses built wide and shallow with a window in each room (Park Heights Avenue); and the half-timbered gabled Tudors of the Jazz Age (Ednor Gardens near Memorial Stadium).

Baltimore's famed marble steps were often used as a sales gimmick, providing a dash of the deluxe to otherwise plain dwellings in immigrant and working-class neighborhoods. Coupled with marble transoms and tops of window frames, these architectural details resulted in buyers so satisfied that ladies of the house took pride in scrubbing their steps weekly. One of the largest stretches of these marble step rowhouses is in the 2600 block of Wilkens Avenue, but others can be seen all over East and South Baltimore.

Formstone

It was the "Stone of Ages," or so the little plaques on one brand of these simulated stone facades read. This miracle "stone" would cover that unsightly red brick—the stuff you've been painting every two years, sometimes painstakingly brushing in white over each line of mortar—and deliver you from the evils of intensive maintenance. And so in the 1940s and '50s salesmen came to you and your neighbors' door, extolling the fake stone's no-upkeep-necessary qualities, its insulating protection, hand-sculpted beauty, and inexpensive price. Rowhouse Baltimoreans lapped this progressive product up, transforming the streets of Canton, Highlandtown, Federal Hill, Hampden, and beyond from lines of red to lines of gray. You could pick your pattern—wide block, narrow block, textured, or flat. Then up went the galvanized wire nailed into the brick and over that went wet cement. On the last coat, the mason sculpted in your stone design. A day or so later you'd be Formstone-proud with a brand-label plaque embedded in your "little castle's" facade, a photo of the finished job, and a certificate from Baltimore Gas & Electric patting you on the back for installing a modern energy-efficient material.

To understand Formstone's allure, you have to look back at the 19th century when the population boomed and Baltimore became a rowhouse city. Brick, the material of choice, didn't burn like wood and the red clay needed to make the block was plentiful. To meet demand, kilns baked up brick—good quality for well-to-do homes, inferior for everyone else. Inferior meant needing to seal up the porous material, which in turn meant painting every few years, generation after generation.

In 1938, Albert Knight invented Formstone, a kind of stucco that could be hand-fashioned into stone. For Baltimore it was love at first sight. Formstone swept industrial neighborhoods with companies like Stone King, Fieldstone, and Romanstone in its wake. The craze moved across the country, skipping only the Pacific Northwest and Rockies, which, presumably, had enough rock already.

Formstone met its doom by the early '60s as charlatans sneaked in with the good guys. These hucksters would blow into town, fan out into neighborhoods, put up an inferior job, and then skip out. The faux faux stuff popped off walls. Burned customers complained and a home improvement commission convened, putting the industry on trial and cleaning it up. Also tipping the balance of the product's fate was its very virtue—its permanence. With the market saturated, masons packed up their trowels.

Nowadays few of these craftsmen remain, and those left spend much of their time tearing theirs and everybody else's old handiwork down. In Federal Hill and Fells Point, the imitation stone is rapidly disappearing. Some of the best examples left are in Highlandtown around Clinton, Gough, and Bouldin Streets.

Alas, what will happen to what film maker John Waters calls "the polyester of brick"?

Should Baltimore preserve a row or two as a kind of a "Formstone Williamsburg" as Waters has suggested? Or maybe we should find new uses for this lost art, as did one SoWeBo wag when he Formstoned his car in yet another Baltimore aesthetic statement.

For a good look at the Formstone craze scout out Lillian Bowers and Skizz Cyzyk's documentary *Little Castles*. The Maryland Historical Society (410-685-3750) has shown it on occasion.

Screen Paintings

Legend has it that in 1912 when secretaries at an air-compressor firm in Newark, New Jersey, groused about passers-by ogling them, company draftsman William Oktavec took the window screen down, painted it with a still life of a jardiniere of flowers, and reinstalled it. Now no one could see in, but the secretaries could still gawk all they wanted at the passing parade.

A year or so later Oktavec was running a Baltimore grocery and fretting about his outdoor produce display. The lettuce, tomatoes, and grapes were wilting and rotting in the sun. Forced to move the lot inside, the grocer came up with a new advertising plan—paint pictures of veggies and fruit on his screen door. A second career was launched. Neighbors, delighting in the decorative touch, besieged him with requests and he complied, ornamenting East Baltimore's screens with bucolic scenes of red mills, country cottages, and placid lakes. Now folks could sit with their doors and windows open and keep their privacy. Other painters took up the business and at one point thousands of these wire mesh masterpieces dotted the city. Sad to say, many screens landed on the scrap-heap when air-conditioning took over, although you can still find some on houses in Highlandtown and Canton. Recently the art has experienced a revival and painters like Dee Herget, Tom Lipka, and Chrissy Maxwell have exhibited their craft at the Canton Gallery on O'Donnell Square.

Window Shrines

How to dress up those long rows of brick and Formstone houses? Sure, there's screen painting, but East Baltimoreans, moved by the quest for individuality and artistic expression, also like to set up little tableaux in their windows. Old-time residents of Little Italy go in for Madonnas and artificial flowers. In Highlandtown and Canton, however, Infants of Prague get thrown into the mix with conch shells, ceramic kitties, and bowling trophies. (All this religious display in a town that gave the world atheist activist Madalyn Murray O' Hair!) Naturally, bunnies, pumpkins, and Santas step up to the plate-glass stage on holidays. In-season and out, baseball fans proclaim their loyalty with pictures of Cal, Orioles' hats, and other memorabilia. Several years back, elsewhere in the city, a shrine to Barbie arose in one creative soul's window. But it wasn't Barbie skipping off to go skating or shopping. Instead it was Barbie-in-bondage, complete with ropes, leather, and all accoutrements. Well, no matter whether sacred or profane, "these little gifts to the street," as local historian Dean Krimmel calls them, are genuine Baltimore folk art.

Wall Art

Anyone who's done any driving around Baltimore has seen them—vast colorful murals on the sides of buildings, often where neighboring structures have long departed. In Little Italy, it's people dressed in their Sunday Best going to church. On 36th Street in Hampden, it's a war veteran's memorial. Catty-corner to the Walters Art Gallery on Cathedral and Centre, artist Mary Carfagno Ferguson and the homeless clients of My Sister's Place created a message of hope in "My Sisters' Garden," a fairy tale Victorian house with a carpet of flowers. And painted alligators amuse motorists along the 28th Street Bridge. These outdoor "canvases" now cover about 100 buildings throughout the city. Some works are privately funded; others are sponsored by the Mayor's Advisory Committee on Art and Culture.

While you're on the lookout for wall art, note the "whiskey walls," advertisements painted directly on brick buildings. Many of these ads, touting merchants and manufacturers, tobacco and food products, and, of course, whiskey, went up in place of billboards from the '30s into the '70s. Vestiges of them can  still be seen all around the city today.

John Waters

In 1972, John Waters took a borrowed camera and $10,000 of his father's money and made film history. *Pink Flamingos* would splash across America's movie screens with the biggest gross-out sequence ever filmed—the doggie doo-doo scene. In the ultimate one-upmanship to keep her family's title as "Filthiest People Alive," the Mack Truck-sized drag queen Divine scoops the poop and lifts it to her luscious lips...and chomps down!

The roots of this culinary cinematic coup reach back into Waters' childhood. Now oddly enough, the Waters family appeared pretty normal—two parents, siblings, a house in woodsy Lutherville. But the auteur of the awful was another story. Born in 1946, Waters had a dual fascination with villains like the wicked queen in *Snow White* and car accidents, the gorier the better. So naturally, by the time he was 10, Waters was producing creepy puppet shows, charging neighborhood kids for the thrill of getting bitten by a vicious dragon puppet.

For his seventeenth birthday, his grandmother gave him a camera and he climbed on top of the roof to record little dramas enacted by his pals. Film school at New York University followed, or at least it tried to—Waters got kicked out for smoking pot. However, the budding filmmaker had already abandoned his professors for movie house masters—Fellini, schlockmaster Russ Meyer, and underground filmmakers the Kuchar Brothers and Kenneth Anger. Armed with an education in film and the bizarre, Waters lensed the 8-mm suburban trash epic *Roman Candles*.

Now when you've got a three-reel "orgy" featuring a sexually depraved nun and priest, S&M foreplay, supplemented by news footage of the Pope, and a soundtrack of Lee Harvey Oswald's mom giving a press conference, where do you debut it? Hey, we're in Baltimore, Hon. So why not the Emmanuel Episcopal Church hall? The film's three shows sold out and the *Baltimore Sun* reeled off the first of Waters' many bad reviews. That day stars were born: Mink Stole, Pat Moran, David Lochary, and the brightest light in the Waters' firmament Glenn Milstead a.k.a. Divine. Other Waters classics:

Multiple Maniacs (1970). "A new high in blasphemy," proclaimed film censor Mary Avara, reacting perhaps to the scene with Lobstora, the 15-foot broiled lobster raping Divine, and to those rosary jobs Mink Stole was trawling for in the church pews. The eccentric Edith Massey and artist Susan Lowe made their debuts here.

Polyester (1981). Filmed in Odorama. A scratch-n-sniff card came with the ticket and at key points viewers were prompted to take whiffs of roses, air freshener, dirty socks, and, well, let's not spoil the fun. Divine plays a troubled housewife wooed by a devilish rake played by former teen heart-throb Tab Hunter.

Hairspray (1988). Against a background of segregated Baltimore in the early '60s, this nostalgic trip dropped Ricki Lake, a Hon with a haystack 'do, onto "The Corny Collins Show," a fictitious twist on the old real-life *Buddy Deane Show*, which was Baltimore's version of *American Bandstand*.

Serial Mom (1994). In this Donna Reed-turns-Psycho flick, Beverly Sutphin (Kathleen Turner) dispatches recycling scofflaws, parking space hogs, and other etiquette-impaired folks.

Pecker (1998). Hampden sandwich shop worker Pecker (Edward Furlong) is catapulted to art-world stardom when an art dealer (Lili Taylor) flacks his photos of a talking Virgin Mary, a girl shaving her legs on a city bus, and other Bawlmer characters.

Water's diva Divine died in 1988. "I wrote those movies for him," Waters said. "He was my Elizabeth Taylor." Steve Yeager's *Divine Trash*, which won the 1998 Sundance Filmmakers Trophy for Best Documentary, offers an in-depth look at Waters' early career, the creation of *Pink Flamingos*, and the ever divine Divine. Yeager's 1999 sequel, *In Bad Taste*, documents Waters' career from *Female Trouble* to *Pecker*. For additional reading, pick up a copy of Waters' autobiographical *Shock Value* and his musings-filled *Crackpot*.

Gone *but not* Forgotten

She came. She saw. She snipped. Mary Avara was once Maryland's and the country's most famous movie censor. While she kept local eyes pure by scissoring the smut, Avara made the talk show rounds from Carson to Cavett, expounding her views about full frontal nudity, explicit on-screen couplings, and, well, stuff you wouldn't talk to your mother about. Not unexpectedly, John Waters' cinematic efforts were particularly vexing to the upright Avara. She pronounced *Pink Flamingos* "filth" and gave the heave-ho to the artificial insemination, blow job, and the chicken humping scene.

She did leave in the doggie doo-eating finale, which Waters thought, "says a lot for the community standards of Baltimore." Alas, Maryland's morals now stand in peril, for the State took the shears to the censor board in 1981.

Barry Levinson

While Waters walks on the wacky side of town, filmmaker Barry Levinson takes the historic route with his films of Baltimore Past. The grandson of Jewish immigrants, the Forest Park native grew up in a tight-knit extended family much as he would depict in his 1990 *Avalon*, a semi-autobiographical account of two generations of Jewish families trying to live the American dream.

Levinson began his career performing comedy and writing scripts for television programs like the *Carol Burnett Show* before hooking up in 1976 with Mel Brooks to co-script and act in the films *Silent Movie* and *High Anxiety*. In 1982, Levinson debuted as director in *Diner*, the first of his Baltimore films that includes *Avalon*, *Tin Men*, and *Liberty Heights*. *Diner*, set at the tail-end of the Eisenhower era, is a slice of life about former high school buddies who cling to the safety of their chrome Fells Point hangout as they stand one foot on the threshold of manhood. Many feel that *Tin Men* (1987), Levinson's tale of aluminum siding salesmen who bamboozled Baltimoreans into redoing their houses in the early '60s, was really the story of the imposter Formstone hustlers. Levinson's fourth Baltimore movie, *Liberty Heights*, which centers on gambling and the underworld, began filming here in 1998.

Other Levinson-directed flicks include: *The Natural* (1984); *Young Sherlock Holmes* (1985); *Good Morning Vietnam* (1987); *Rain Man* (1988), which won four Oscars—best picture, director, actor, and screenplay; and *Wag the Dog* (1998). In 1992, his Baltimore Pictures production company ventured into the gritty side of the city with *Homicide: Life on the Street*, a contemporary cop show based on David Simon's electrifying book about the inner workings of the homicide squad (see *Fells Point*).

Did You Know?

"Hollywood on the Patapsco" might not have been wishful thinking if the Warner brothers had stayed in Baltimore. That's right...Jack, Harry, Sam, and Albert lived here as children for a short time in the 1880s. Their Polish-born father, Benjamin, a cobbler and devout Jew, moved the large family around the East Coast and Canada before settling in Youngstown, Ohio. It was there that the four brothers first forayed into the movie business in 1903, buying a projector and showing *The Great Train Robbery* under a tent in their backyard—for a fee, of course. (It is not known if they served drinks and popcorn.) The brothers expanded their cinema enterprise, eventually earning big bucks, made the move into production, and settled in Los Angeles. They never looked back.

"Romper bomper stomper boo, tell me, tell me, tell me do, magic mirror tell me today, did all my friends have fun at play?" From 1953 until 1964 *Romper Room*'s original Miss Nancy, Nancy Claster, uttered these words as she looked into her magic mirror and saw all of the city's preschoolers who'd tuned in to her show. She sang them songs and taught them manners and responsibility in her "Do-Bee" games, as in "Do-Bee a milk drinker." At its height, Claster and her husband Bertram, the Baltimoreans who created the show, franchised *Romper Room* to 160 licensees across the country, with the last episode signing off in 1994.

Festivals and Fun Stuff

Oh, how Baltimore loves to party. Whether it's celebrating its seafaring history, ethnic diversity, or cultural heritage, the city's festivals offer fun and activities that are uniquely Baltimore. Birthday bashes for Edgar Allan Poe to Babe Ruth,

ethnic festivals honoring African American to Ukrainian heritage, Billie Holiday vocal competitions to the Night of a 100
Elvises—all these and scores more take place here every
year. Additionally, many of the city's attractions hold special
seasonal events and festivities, most of which are listed in
the *Baltimore Sun* and the free weekly *City Paper*. Contact
the Baltimore Area Visitors' Center (410-837-INFO) for seasonal updates of Baltimore festivities, or the State Office of
Tourism (1-800-MD-IS-FUN) for a free copy of Maryland
Celebrates, which also lists festivals and events throughout
the state.

Hons

You've seen them in the movies—the ultimate John
Waters fantasy girl. You may have even spotted them on the
street—although they're a dying breed. But a true Baltimore
gum-snapping, hip-swaying, high-haired babe is a national
treasure—to be preserved and admired for generations to
come. Happily some foresighted gals are keeping the heritage alive. In Hampden each spring, gals with Bawlmer
souls compete for the honor of wearing the "Best Miss Hon"
banner across her bosom. The winner gets to ride in the
Hampden Christmas Parade past illuminated candy canes
and hubcap holiday trees to greet her fans with a Queen
Elizabeth wave.

So in the interests of preserving this bit of Bawlmerana,
we offer you tips from Hons past and present, for moving
you beyond the ordinary world into the realm of Hondom.

1. WARDROBE First you got to dress the part—get yourself a mini skirt or capri pants, form-fitting to show off your
Marilyn Monroe wiggle. A sweater, tight enough to show
you're a girl and loose enough to show you're a lady, is best.
Accessorize with the mandatory long scarf, preferably patterned with leopard spots, and high-heeled mules. And don't
step off your marble stoop without cat's eye sunglasses and
a wad of gum between your teeth.

2. HAIR Always invest in the proper tools—big rollers (or
empty frozen orange juice cans), teasing comb, and Aqua
Net. When it comes to styles, you got your choice: lacquered into a beehive; poofed into a bubble-head flip; or, for
special occasions, whipped into a mushroom cloud atomic

'do. And if you're gonna tint the locks, go for strong color—Priscilla Presley shoe polish black, Marilyn platinum, or "I Love Lucy" red.

3. COSMETICS Makeup is *de rigueur*. Bubble gum pink on the lips, if you're into the movie star look. Dead man's white if you're into the high fashion model scene. Getting the blue eye shadow right is a real art, but luckily Hons are the Michelangelos of makeup. Long polished nails complete the make-over but get little pictures of wedding bells, Christmas trees, or fireworks painted on top for special occasions.

4. LIBATIONS As for drinks, there used to be Natty Boh, cheap suds brewed right here in Bawlmer. You'd drink it while watching an O's game on the tube or with a bunch of your girlfriends at the local watering hole, where Mr. Boh winked at you from the sign above the bar, points out "Miss Pam," Best Hon of 1997 (a.k.a. Pamela Foresman). But those days are gone along with your '75 Corvair. The sad truth is that Stroh Brewing Company spirited little Natty off to Pennsylvania and now Hons often settle for a Bud.

5. NUTRITION Well, at least food hasn't let hometown honeys down. When the temperature rises sno-ball stands pop up. The sno-ball men grind the ice right in front of you, then spritz flavored syrup all over top. Coddies (deep fried fish and potato cakes to you newcomers), gravy fries, sauerkraut with turkey on Thanksgiving, and, of course, crabs—soft shell sandwiches or hard shells steamed in Old

Bay—are dietary staples. Buy your hardshells by the dozen at Obrycki's where they spread 'em on brown paper and you whack away with mallets, picking out the meat. When you have cravings for crab cakes—which, by the way, you *always* eat with crackers—drive up to Angelina's on Harford Road or go to Faidley's at Lexington Market.

6. ELVIS WORSHIP Miss Bonnie's Elvis Shrine and Bar was where some Hons used to pay homage. But now Miss Bonnie's gone to Heaven to be with the King. So we buy our very own bust lamps of Big El at the Hampden Bargain Center and hip-wiggling clocks at Herb's Bargain Center in Federal Hill. And we never miss Night of 100 Elvises at the Lithuanian Hall in December.

7. ATHLETIC PURSUITS To keep in shape, Hons go duck-pin bowling—which, you know, was invented right here. Years ago some fuddy duddy bureaucrat in Annapolis picked jousting as the official state sport, but as "Miss Pam" likes to point out, "Who goes jousting in Bawlmer?"

8. PROPER DICTION We've saved the best for last and that's using your proper diction. Hons don't say "Okay, dear." They say "A-Kay, Huhn." And they don't go to the ocean either. They go "downy ayshen." We don't ask our boyfriends how the Orioles are doing—those are birds that chirp in trees. We say "How 'bout dem O's?" By the way, Hons like to stroll in "Droodle Park" (Druid Hill Park to you) and a drive down I-95 is going to "Wurshington on bizness." And, of course, Hons, as we all know, are "bee-yoo-ti-ful" and set men's hearts on "fayr."

So time to get out that jar of Dippity-Do and make yourself over. Think of the advantages. "Men want you," points out "Miss Sharon," Best Hon of 1998 (a.k.a. Sharon P. Gill). Just the hair alone, she exclaims, sends your sex appeal quotient sizzling. And who knows, maybe if John Waters catches sight of you at the duckpin lanes, movie stardom could be just around the corner, Hon.

Inner Harbor

Pratt Street sweeps east along the harbor catching sight of Oriole Park at Camden Yards, outdoor cafes, historic brick buildings and new skyscrapers, abstract sculptures, and fountains. At the Inner Harbor, the scenery explodes into a kaleidoscope of color and activity. The green-roofed pavilions of Harborplace spring into view. Flags dance in the wind. Shoppers, sightseers, and strollers crowd the brick promenade overlooking a waterway filled with paddleboats, sails, and cruisers. Cutting through the profusion of vessels, water taxis and shuttles ferry passengers to museums, restaurants, and other points of interest along the harbor. Meanwhile, in front of the Light Street Pavilion, tall ships, skipjacks, and navy boats hold open houses, giving visitors opportunities to poke around their decks.

Over at Planet Hollywood, cutouts of Baltimore filmmakers John Waters and Barry Levinson ride their submarine through Baltimore's own little Hollywood on the Patapsco. Down below in a small outdoor amphitheater onlookers cheer a fire-eating juggler riding a unicycle backwards. While all this is happening, thousands more people are exploring the harbor's other attractions. History buffs board the submarine *Torsk* and the lightship *Chesapeake* for glimpses of life at sea. Over  at the Maryland Science Center, families watch mountaineers tackle Mt. Everest on a five-story-high movie screen. And at the National Aquarium toddlers clutch mom's hand as they walk through the humid rain forest with squawking macaws.

As the sky darkens, the red neon intertwined hula hoops that encircle the Science Center's IMAX theater light up. To the east the geometry of the National Aquarium—all angles and red, blue, and gray—juts out against the darkening sky. And from the Power Plant, dormant for so many years, a gargantuan guitar on the rooftop smoke stacks announces the Hard Rock Cafe. At the other end of the old brick Power Plant, a bronze shish-kebab of balls and a flaming pit grill trumpets the country's first ESPN Zone, an indoor playground of sports-themed television, amusements, and eateries. Beyond that at Pier 6 Concert Pavilion, funky blues wrung from B.B. King's guitar issue from the scalloped canvas tent.

Contrast this exuberance with the sleepy waterfront back in 1974—before the Maryland Science Center, Harborplace, and all the hoopla. The *Constellation*, the submarine *Torsk*, and tour boats docked at the otherwise desolate brick promenade. Over on Light Street, McCormick & Company, one of the few industries left from the harbor's boom times, perfumed the often fishy air with scents of cinnamon and other spices it manufactured. On Pier 4, Connolly's, an old shack of a restaurant, served up local fare. Cruising the harbor, sightseers on the *Patriot* saw only a fading industrial town with rotting docks and warehouses.

Harbor History

In the 18th century, docks covered the area where Harborplace and The Gallery now sit, the most famous being Cheapside Wharf, named after the busy trading area in London. With its harbor extending further inland than any other regional port and its relatively mild winters, Baltimore's piers drew farmers with wagonloads of tobacco and grain to be sold in Europe. In 1818, Cheapside Wharf was filled in and commerce moved onto Pratt and Light Streets. A variety of maritime industry services such as shipping agents, chandlers, and coopers joined grocers and craftsmen along the waterfront. By the mid-1850s warehouses and wholesalers gobbled up the smaller businesses that had moved further into the city. For nearly a century after, the harbor bustled with boats unloading produce and fish for the city markets, and with ferries, steamboats, freighters, and processing plants. The harbor also became a dumping ground for waste and garbage. As Baltimore sage H.L. Mencken observed, the city "smelled like a billion pole cats."

By the end of World War II, port business had shifted east to deeper water and the harbor here lay neglected and blighted by dilapidated warehouses and wharves, flophouses, hulks of rusting cars, rats, and water full of gunk. In 1950, Mayor Thomas D'Alesandro, Jr., tore down the Light Street piers and established Sam Smith Park where the city later held ethnic festivals. During this time business leaders formed the Greater Baltimore Committee, which spearheaded plans to revive the city's business and residential areas with new buildings and with restoration of old ones.

The Renaissance

Some Baltimoreans mark one of the first visible shifts toward the Inner Harbor's Renaissance as the arrival of the Tall Ships during the Bicentennial when people gathered at the promenade to greet the windjammers as they sailed in. By the late '70s, the Maryland Science Center and World Trade Center opened, the clipper *Pride of Baltimore* had been launched, and the new Convention Center had started drawing visitors. Meanwhile, local developer James W. Rouse offered a new centerpiece for the harbor. His Rouse Company had transformed abandoned buildings in Boston into the very successful Faneuil Hall Marketplace. Could he do the same for Baltimore? He proposed European-style pavilions filled with shops and restaurants.

Baltimoreans have always been notorious for foot-dragging when it comes to new projects, so it was no surprise this proposal drew naysayers who wanted to maintain a tranquil waterside park and skeptics who believed the city would be throwing away taxpayers' money. In many cases, Baltimore's conservatism had worked to the city's benefit, keeping officials from leveling historic areas for highways and mediocre modern buildings. But in this case, luckily, the visionaries led by Rouse and Mayor William Donald Schaefer prevailed.

Harborplace was launched on July 2, 1980, to much fanfare, crowds of people, and boats, fireworks, and the thunderous "1812 Overture" played by the Baltimore Symphony Orchestra. It was quickly followed by the opening of the National Aquarium, the Hyatt Regency Hotel, and the Science Center's Imax Theater. Over the years new hotels, offices, restaurants, shops, museums, and condominiums have filled in the harbor perimeter. The spot that once drew mostly hearty sailors now pulls millions of visitors a year.

And what of the harbor's future? Lots of projects are in the works: more hotels and restaurants, a facelift for Rash Field, and more innovative attractions like Disney's Port Discovery. Events are scheduled year round: St. Patrick's Day in March, the CitySand sand sculpture contest in June, Merry Tuba Christmas and the Lighted Boat Parade in December to name a few. So go play at the Harbor, but don't miss the rest of the city with its fascinating history, interesting architecture, ethnic neighborhoods, and lively arts scene.

Sights & Sites

THE PROMENADE

This red brick pedestrian footpath runs along the harbor and will eventually link the waterfront from Canton, Fells Point, and Little Italy on the east to the Inner Harbor, west to Federal Hill and the Baltimore Museum of Industry. The 7½ mile walkway is scheduled to be completed in the year 2000. As of this writing, a few stretches in Fells Point and Federal Hill are still under construction.

HARBORPLACE

Pratt and Light Street Pavilions. 410-332-4191
www.harborplace.com

Mayor Schaefer and local developer James W. Rouse wanted to bring people back into the city and they did just that with the opening of these two European-style glass pavilions in 1980. The centerpiece of the harbor's Renaissance, this festive marketplace boasts 130 shops and restaurants along with open verandas and floor-to-ceiling windows that keep an eye focused on the harbor. Inside the airy two-story structures, exposed pipes and beams hint at the area's industrial past. In addition, the second floor of the Light Street Pavilion contains a food court and pushcarts—the latter reminiscent of late

19th and early 20th century peddlers' carts that were wheeled or horse-drawn through Baltimore's immigrant communities. Skywalks link the Light Street Pavilion with the Hyatt Regency Hotel's garage and the Pratt Street Pavilion with The Gallery, another shopping mall developed by Rouse (see Browse and Buy).

AMPHITHEATRE

Between Harborplace's Pratt and Light Street Pavilions
800-HARBOR-1 (800-427-2671)

Jugglers and jokesters, *a capella* singers and rock groups, reggae and Andean folk musicians, pop groups, military and concert bands, and contests, too. In good weather, there's always something happening in this small outdoor amphitheater. Free.

Robert K. Strong's parents think he's in law school, but he's traveling the world making folks laugh from Japan to Baltimore's Inner Harbor with his off-beat style of juggling, fire eating, interactive magic, and pickpocketing (the latter for entertainment only). It all started in 1985 when little Robert, on a day trip to Harborplace, was mesmerized by a magician. The next day he tried out several tricks at his summer camp's talent show. A star was born.

BALTIMORE AREA VISITORS' CENTER

Next to Phillips, Light Street Pavilion
800-282-6632 or 888-BALTIMO
www.baltimore.org

The most often asked question the staff of the Visitors Center gets asked is, "Where's the closest restroom?" The folks here can answer that and just about any other tourist inquiry about Baltimore. In addition, they give out telephone numbers, recommendations, and brochures on attractions, accommodations, and services. Daily. Free.

BALTIMORE TICKETS

Baltimore Area Visitors' Center Ticket Kiosk
410-752-TICS (8427) Groups: 410-727-4569
Avoid lines of cranky kids and frustrated parents by purchasing tickets here for area attractions, including the
National Aquarium, the Maryland Science Center, Babe
Ruth Museum, Water Taxi, and more. Seasonal packages and weekender packages are also available.
Offered in conjunction with TicketMaster. Daily 10 am-
4 pm. Cash only.

USS CONSTELLATION

Pier 1. 410-539-1797 (Reopening July 1999)
One thing this grand old lady of the sea isn't is a frigate.
Welcome aboard the former US naval sloop of war, the
USS Constellation, launched from Norfolk, Virginia, in
1854. Now on long-term loan to Baltimore, the craft
has been recently restored and is scheduled to return to
her permanent berth at Pier 1 in July 1999. For most of
her years on display at the Inner Harbor, the
Constellation was touted by Baltimoreans as a frigate
built and launched in Canton in 1797 as part of the
original US Navy. In truth, that noble frigate was
decommissioned and dismantled in 1853, and only her
name was carried over to the current ship—although
historians acknowledge there may be a few boards of
the original in the 1854 sloop's construction, in keeping with naval traditions of passing along a ship's
name.

The *Constellation* does have a naval history to be
proud of, regardless of her age. She was the Navy's
largest sloop of war and the last full-sail warship. Prior
to the Civil War, as flagship of the Navy's African
Squadron, she captured a slave ship, saving 700 from
bondage in the States. In May, 1861, the *Constellation*
seized the slave brig *Triton* near Charleston, South
Carolina, the first naval capture in the Civil War, and
went on to serve in battle. After distinguished service
on the high seas lasting into the 1870s, she became a
training boat for US Naval Academy midshipmen.
During World War II, the *Constellation* served as both

the relief flagship for the Atlantic fleet and the flagship for Battle Group 5.

The Constellation Foundation, which oversaw the ship's most recent restoration, has returned the ship, canons, and portholes as much as possible to its original 1854 condition. Call for days, hours open. Admission.

TOP OF THE WORLD OBSERVATION LEVEL AND MUSEUM—WORLD TRADE CENTER

401 E. Pratt St. 410-837-8439

Step inside and you've entered the tallest pentagonal structure on the globe. Renowned architect I. M. Pei designed the $22 million 28-story tower, one of six such trade centers in the United States and one of 250 in the world. The Maryland Port Administration has its headquarters here along with other local firms dealing in international trade and commerce. Take the elevator to the 27th floor for a panoramic view of the harbor and to see a small exhibit on Baltimore history and its port. Sunset jazz programs feature local musicians. At the base of the tower waterside is a bronze plaque commemorating Baltimore's own *Exodus 1947* of movie fame (see *Jonestown*). Observation level: Daily. Admission.

PADDLEBOATS AND ELECTRIC BOATS

On the Promenade near the World Trade Center
Paddleboats: 410-563-3901
Trident Electric Boats: 410-539-1837

Want to get out there on the harbor with the big guys and the ducks? Paddle or putt around in the water between the Aquarium and the *Constellation*. Summers daily. Weekends only, spring through fall.

NATIONAL AQUARIUM IN BALTIMORE

Pier 3, 501 E. Pratt St. 410-576-3800
www.aqua.org

The tilted, off kilter glass pyramid catches the eye of the first-time visitor to the National Aquarium. There are trees growing at the top of the pyramid, more than one hundred feet above ground. Loud, rasping grunts draw the visitor's attention back to ground level and the Seal Pool where staff trainers are tossing the gray, harp, and harbor seals pieces of fish. A few regulars in the crowd spot their favorite pinnipeds and call out to them by name as a trainer answers questions from the crowd.

In the two pyramidal buildings a one-way self-guided tour transports visitors through a variety of aquatic habitats from Maryland to the South Pacific, then to the world of dolphins in an entertaining, educational show. Throughout the two facilities volunteer guides are available to answer questions about the exhibits and the more than 10,000 animals (covering 600 species) living here.

Level One—The Wings in the Water exhibit contains dozens of sting rays, small sharks, and a large Hawksbill turtle named Pita (ask an exhibit guide how that turtle got its name). Twice a day, trained volunteer divers enter the tank to feed the critters by hand.

Level Two—Maryland: Mountains to the Sea comprises four exhibits demonstrating the variety of aquatic life in the state.

Level Three—Temporary exhibits like Venom: Striking Beauties (continuing until January 2000) are displayed here along with the permanent Surviving through Adaptations.

Level Four—Talks by staff complement a display of live puffins. Also featured are a Pacific kelp forest and coral reef, and a touch pool called the Children's Cove.

Level Five—Enter a living Rain Forest. The temperature and humidity are tropical, as are the many birds, sloths and monkeys, fish, and small reptiles who live in this recreated habitat under the peaked glass pyramid.

Atlantic Coral Reef—Back on Level Four take the descending ramp through the circular 335,000 gallon tank, where divers feed the thousands of tropical fish several times a day. Continue down to the Open Ocean tank in which large sharks, sawfish, and pelagic fish swim lazily.

Marine Mammal Pavilion—Across the indoor pedestrian footbridge, the Marine Mammal Pavilion is home to several bottle nose dolphins, two of which were born here. Both levels of the pavilion contain high-tech attractions, including interactive exhibits and videos. A large cafeteria and the Aquarium gift shop occupy the bottom level.

Beat weekend and summer crowds by visiting weekdays before 11 am and after 3 pm, and during Friday evening extended hours October through March. Note: Families planning on returning to the Aquarium within the year should consider buying a money-saving membership, which also lets you skip the long lines.

Free or discounted admissions: Friday after 5 pm October-March and Dollar Day in December. Maryland students pre-kindergarten through 12th grade are admitted free September-February with advance reservations. Call for seasonal hours and show times.

Did You Know?

Dressed in an 1890s swimsuit, Mayor William Donald Schaefer went for a dip in the seal pool at the National Aquarium along with his rubber ducky, as promised, when that facility failed to open on time. But Schaefer in his 40 years' public service as a City Council member, mayor, and then state governor almost singlehandedly turned Baltimore back into a world-class city. Strong-willed and pragmatic, stubborn and autocratic, Schaefer pushed the concept of Inner Harbor revitalization through to its completion. In 1982, the US Conference of Mayors lauded him with the Michael A. diNunzio Award for outstanding personal leadership which was followed by the National Urban Coalition's Distinguished Mayor Award. Two years later, *Esquire* magazine labeled him the "best mayor in America."

BALTIMORE MARITIME MUSEUM

Ticket Booth at Pier 3. 410-396-3453
(Sites not wheelchair accessible.)

A visit to the Baltimore Maritime Museum reveals the grueling work and reality of shipboard life in cramped and often wet quarters. Before satellite communications, automated beacons, and 24-hour weather stations, vessels entering the Chesapeake Bay relied on lightships like the 133-foot *Chesapeake* to mark safe channels, warn them of navigational hazards, and provide weather updates. From 1933 to 1971 the *Chesapeake*, with her bright red hull and a 1,000-watt "beacon" lamp burning from her mast, rode the bay in storms and calms, prepared to signal warnings or perform rescues.

The submarine *Torsk* roamed the Pacific in search of Japanese subs and the Atlantic looking for German U-boats. She has made more dives than any other sub and is credited with sinking the last enemy warship in World War II. The 311-foot vessel also saw  service during the 1960 Lebanon Crisis and took part in the 1962 naval blockade of Cuba. Touring the claustrophobic quarters of this small submarine, which carried a crew of 8 officers and 71 enlisted men, gives a taste of the non-too-private life of sailors beneath the seas.

The US Coast Guard Cutter *Taney* is the only survivor still afloat of the 101 US warships at Pearl Harbor during the Japanese surprise attack on December 7, 1941. During the invasion of Okinawa, where it served as the Admiral's flagship, the vessel endured despite the Kamikaze assault. Named for native Marylander and former Chief Justice of the Supreme Court Roger B. Taney, brother-in-law of Francis Scott Key, the ship saw over 50 years of service before being decommissioned in 1986. The *Taney* also displays photographs and memorabilia from its World War II service and a small exhibit on Amelia Earhart.

Enter the Seven-Foot Knoll Lighthouse for exhibits on Maryland maritime history, the boats of the Chesapeake, and life in a lighthouse. Before it was moved here, the red 1855 screwpile lighthouse, the oldest in the state, had welcomed ships at the entrance to the harbor for 135 years.

One ticket gives access to all three vessels plus the lighthouse. Allow 1½ hours for a self-guided tour. Daily April-Dec. Fri-Sun only, Jan-Mar. Closed major holidays. Admission. A National Historic Seaport ticket offers discounts on a multi-attraction package.

Did You Know?

Conceived as a link between the city's rich maritime history and today's modern port, the National Historic Seaport of Baltimore, debuting in May 1999, enables sightseers to visit several attractions around the harbor on a three-day passport ticket. Included in the package is transportation by Harbor Shuttle around the waterfront and to participating attractions like the Museum of Industry, the steam tugboat *SS Baltimore*, city fireboats, the *Constellation*, and the Baltimore Maritime Museum. Tickets available at the Baltimore Maritime Museum, the Museum of Industry, and the ticket kiosk left of the Light Street Pavilion. 410-396-3453.

POWER PLANT
Pier 4. Pratt St.
For years while crowds surged past on the way to the Aquarium this huge brick hulk sat empty and forlorn. Opened in 1895 as a power generating station for the city's streetcars, the Beaux-Arts structure is topped by four huge smokestacks which belched coal exhaust. In 1973

Baltimore Gas & Electric shut down operations here. After abortive runs as a Six Flags amusement center and a nightclub, the building recently reopened with a Hard Rock Cafe, Barnes & Noble Bookstore, the ESPN Zone, and offices. Today the building's smokestacks sport the Hard Rock's gargantuan red guitar.

ESPN ZONE

Power Plant. Pier 4. 410-685-3776
www.ESPN.Sportszone.com
The first of its kind in the nation, this football field-sized sports emporium allows fans to eat upscale stadium food, test their skills at virtual sports, and watch a remote control surfer's heaven of sports videos and live games playing simultaneously on a sea of TV screens. The downstairs is a veritable shrine to sports with items like a Colts mascot head signed by 34 former players. Amidst the restaurants and bars, dining tables at the Screen Bar face a 16 x 16 foot TV with six other monitors on either side tuned to different sporting contests and videos. Meanwhile at mezzanine level sits an operator commanding the Zone's 204 monitors. Upstairs, sports enthusiasts play at virtual baseball, hang gliding, skateboarding, surfing, and more.

Note: Upstairs, kids under 18 must be accompanied by an adult after 9 pm weekdays and 10 pm on weekends. No cover charge. Daily.

PIER 6 CONCERT PAVILION

731 Eastern Ave. 410-625-3100
The sounds of live rock, Motown, blues, jazz, reggae, and country issue from the large white scalloped tent-like structure. Pier 6's open-air concert "hall" has been rockin' since 1981 with nationally known acts like Ray Charles, Aretha Franklin, Clint Black, and Patti La Belle. The evening concerts seat 3,200 music lovers in permanent seats under the tent, and a thousand more on the lawn (bring blankets and/or chairs). Seasonal. Admission.

COLUMBUS CENTER HALL

Piers 5 and 6. 701 E. Pratt St.
www.umbi.umd.edu

Planned as a combined public exhibition hall and a marine research institute, the Columbus Center got seasick the first year it was launched. What does remain beneath the fiberglass-and-Teflon roof, however, is the Center of Marine Biotechnology, part of the University of Maryland Biotechnology Institute, which does research into marine life with applications for health care, the environment, and industrial and economical development.

BALTIMORE PUBLIC WORKS MUSEUM

751 Eastern Ave. at President St. 410-396-5565

When the rubble was cleared after the Great Fire of 1904, and the city began to rebuild, civic leaders saw to it that Baltimore's first municipal sewage system was laid along with water pipes and cables. This 1912 Edwardian brick structure, now housing the Museum of Public Works, was the city's earliest pumping station and still operates as one. Today the museum, located in one end of the Eastern Avenue Pumping Station, offers photographic, video, and artifact displays on water supply, waste water disposal, and bridge, road, and tunnel building. View exhibits of old valves, cast iron hydrants, surveying and earth moving equipment, 18th and 19th century wooden water pipes, water meters, and other related items. Small children will also find hands-on activities to learn about public works operations. Tues-Sun 10-4. Admission.

PORT DISCOVERY

34 Market Pl. 410-727-8120

Housed in the historic Fish Market, the main theme of this children's museum is to challenge and develop the imagination of kids ages six through twelve. Among the interactive world-class exhibits designed by Walt Disney Imagineering are: Adventure Expeditions, which takes kids on an Egyptian time-trek; a television studio for kids to produce shows; Miss Perception's Mystery

House where children play Sherlock, solving the disappearance of a family of characters; an R & D Dream Lab using real tools to make things; and KidWorks—a three-story Rube Goldberg-type obstacle course challenging the mind as well as the body. Open daily. Closed major holidays. Admission.

HOLOCAUST MEMORIAL

Located between Gay, Lombard, and Water Sts.

The image is of railroad boxcars—those coffins-on-wheels in which Nazis herded and transported many of the six million European Jews like cattle to their deaths in World War II. An inverted triangle on the ground leads visitors past a statue of people being consumed by fire, over railroad tracks toward the box cars inscribed with chilling words from a survivor of Auschwitz describing the experience of arriving at the camp. The Holocaust Memorial was commissioned by the Baltimore Jewish Council and dedicated in 1997, replacing an older memorial built on the same site.

UNITED STATES CUSTOMS HOUSE

40 S. Gay St. 410-962-7611
(General Services Administration.)

Lovers of ships and art will find plenty in common when visiting the Customs House. The Call Room where ships' captains once conducted business features an immense ceiling painting and dozens of murals by Francis Davis Millet. These famous paintings have been called "the finest decorative art of any public building in the country." Indeed, it can be dizzying to stand in the middle of the room, surveying the paintings and decorative plaster moldings, trying to assimilate both the maritime history and symbolic significance of Millet's work.

The entrance wall holds five large lunettes illustrating prominent ships in maritime history. The middle painting is of the *Mauritania*, a contemporary of the *Titanic*, on which Millet died in April, 1912 on its catastrophic maiden voyage. Other paintings include the clipper ship *Empress of the Seas* and the steam-yacht *Corsair*. The recently renovated Beaux-Arts Customs House replaces an earlier customs building on the same site.

The public can view the murals with certain restrictions. All visitors must pass through a metal detector upon entry, and if the Call Room is in use visitors will be unable to gain access. Groups of 10 or more are requested to call before visiting. Weekdays, 8-5. Free.

Did You Know?

At the turn of the century when foundations for the current Customs House were being excavated, workers discovered subterranean passages and rooms containing skeletons beneath the remains of an earlier customs house. Legend has it that prior to the construction of the old building, a Frenchman had operated an inn on the same spot. Renowned as a great cook, he became rich quite rapidly. Oddly, he forbade his wife and children who lived nearby to ever enter the inn. The wife was curious about both her husband's sudden wealth and reasons why the inn was off-limits, and there was the other little matter of several guests suddenly disappearing. One night she hid in the inn to observe the goings on, and to her shock, saw her husband kill and rob a guest. The woman quickly gathered her children and fled. Fearing his wife might turn him over to the police, the Frenchman also ran off, never to be seen again.

SAIL BALTIMORE
On the waterfront near the Light Street Pavilion.
410-837-4636
A regatta's worth of visiting tall ships, international naval vessels, and educational and environmental craft dock at the harbor during the year. Tour a Navy tank landing ship, an Australian tall ship, or whatever vessel has pulled up alongside the Promenade. Come aboard and learn about search and rescue missions, ship rigging and sails, navigational aids, naval weapons, and get a glimpse of shipboard life. Days and hours of visiting vessels vary. Admission.

MARYLAND SCIENCE CENTER

Intersection of Light St. and Key Hwy. 410-685-5225

From a distance, it appears as a giant's handful of metal pick-up sticks frozen in mid-air, suspended for eternity. Up close, the silvery tubes, braced together with cables, more closely resemble a crazily rigged cluster of masts. This 1967 sculpture by Kenneth Snelson fits the name, "Easy Landing," with its unique vision of an object in flight in search of ground. This theme carries over to the three-level atrium of the Science Center where an asteroid, space satellites, and a pterosaur suspended from the ceiling beams compete for air space.

The interactive exhibits and fun attractions can keep children of all ages mesmerized, and if hands-on activities don't wear the little ones out, there's the K.I.D.S. room where children three to seven can let off some steam and romp while they create scientific masterpieces. Several times a day, live presentations at the second floor Demonstration Stage illustrate the concepts and use of sound, electricity, chemical reactions, and other scientific processes.

Permanent displays on all three floors of the Center include visual, textual, as well as interactive exhibits on a variety of topics. The Chesapeake Bay features live aquatic animals and summarizes the historic and present status of the Bay. The Science Arcade contains multiple hands-on experiments to teach children about light, magnetism, mechanics, sight, and sound. The Hubble Space Telescope National Visitors Center explains how the Hubble contributes to scientific knowledge of galactic events past and present, and displays frequently updated information and photographs transmitted from this orbiting telescope.

The Davis Planetarium and IMAX theater schedule several shows each day, all of which are included in the ticket price. Additionally, NightMax on weekend nights features IMAX movies on subjects ranging from the Rolling Stones to volcanoes. The Science Center offers several temporary exhibits each year so there's always something new to do or explore. The gift shop carries an extensive number of science-themed items. Friendly's

Restaurant provides snacks and meals. Advance tickets for IMAX shows are available at the Center or from TicketMaster (410-481-SEAT). Daily. Admission.

RASH FIELD

Formerly the playing field for Federal Hill's old Southern High School, this park is named after Joseph H. Rash, a food company executive who once headed the city's Board of Recreation and Parks. In the past, sporting events and ethnic festivals were held here. Nowadays a miniature golf course (see below) uses the green in the summer and in the winter a public ice rink draws more than 40,000 skaters a season. Special programs like the annual Winterfest are also staged here.

ART LINKS BALTIMORE

Rash Field. 410-962-8565

Sink a putt in the Crab Feast Hole, or drive a ball up Cab Calloway's piano at the Hi-De-Hi-De-Ho-Hole. A William Donald Schaefer Fill-the-Pothole Hole, and even Poe and Mencken make an appearance on this whimsical miniature golf course. Artists in collaboration with Maryland Art Place, a local arts organization, designed these 18 holes celebrating the state's cultural and historical inheritance. Daily 10-10 May-Sept. Admission.

Did You Know?

Some people are awed by it. Newcomers wonder why it's there. Some find it romantic. But Baltimoreans love the Domino Sugar Corporation sign. Its red glow has brightened the Inner Harbor since 1951, with only a short hiatus during the oil crisis of the '70s. And brighten it does with the 32-foot "D" and 13-foot-high letters in "Sugars." The 70 x 120 sign, powered by 113 transformers and nearly 40 circuits, uses 3,200 feet of neon tubes, all handmade. In other words, this sign is biiiiiiig.

PRIDE MEMORIAL

Pride of Baltimore II. 410-539-1151
www.pride2.org

Pride of Baltimore, a modern re-creation of the early 1800s Baltimore clippers and built here at the harbor by the city in the 1970s, made her maiden voyage in May 1977. The *Pride*, which logged 150,000 miles traveling to 125 ports as a goodwill ambassador, was lost at sea on May 14, 1986, during a freak squall 240 miles off Puerto Rico. This memorial depicting submerged mast and rigging is dedicated to the captain and three crew members who went down with the topsail schooner. (Eight sailors miraculously survived.) Launched in 1988, *Pride of Baltimore II* now carries on the role of Maryland's roving ambassador of the high seas. With her sleek body and twin masts at full sail, the *Pride II* cuts a pretty picture when she sails back into her home port several times each year, docking at the Finger Piers off Light Street.

"The Pride of Baltimore" was the nickname given to one of the most famous early clipper ships, *Chasseur*, which gained notoriety on both sides of the Atlantic as the most successful privateer during the War of 1812.

McKELDIN FOUNTAIN

Light and Pratt Sts.

In steamy weather this delightful cascade adjacent to Harborplace draws children and older folks alike to luxuriate in its spray. Designed to portray Maryland's hills and waterways, this concrete sculpture is named after former Baltimore Mayor and State Governor Theodore Roosevelt McKeldin, an avid supporter of the Baltimore Renaissance.

BALTIMORE CONVENTION CENTER

100 W. Pratt St. 410-649-7000
www.baltimore.org

Each day thousands of conventioneers throng this hall's vast space. Spanning three city blocks, the center consists of two buildings, a 1979 three-level and a 1996 four-level structure. The facility has 50 meeting rooms, a ballroom, offices, and seven exhibition halls (covering 300,000 square feet). A steel truss system extruding from its white concrete exterior sets off the newer building (some say quite overpoweringly) from its neighbors. Aside from helping with convention and tour groups, the Baltimore Area Convention and Visitors Association, located at 100 Light Street, sends out visitor information packets (800-343-3468).

GETTING AROUND

ED KANE'S WATER TAXI *410-563-3901*
HARBOR SHUTTLE *410-675-2900*

These zippy little boats offer a quick, convenient way to get around the harbor. Both services stop at major attractions and landings along the waterfront. An all day ticket will save shoe leather and parking hassles.

NOTABLE QUOTABLE

"No matter where I go, Baltimore will always be the place that I am proud to call 'home.'"

Pam Shriver, tennis champion and sports commentator

Browse and Buy

HARBORPLACE
410-332-4191
Concierge: 410-332-0060
www.harborplace.com
While a handful of shops have stayed on since the marketplace's opening, Harborplace's management likes to keep a changing, eclectic mix of boutiques and peddlers'

carts. What carts you see one day may be gone a few weeks later or just may move into a more permanent spot. Peddlers might range from Ms. Venus' Zodiac Astrology Gift Cart to a stuffed animal menagerie to a body lotion vendor. A concierge is on call to offer advice on restaurants, shopping, and other attractions at Harborplace and The Gallery. Valet parking available in front of the Pratt Street Pavilion daily from 5 pm to midnight and weekends and holidays from 11 am to midnight. Open daily.

Among the more interesting shops in the Light Street Pavilion are: American Sports Classics (410-528-0011), general sports memorabilia; Celebrate Baltimore! (410-752-3838), unique Baltimore souvenirs; and Next Stop, South Pole (410-659-0860), penguin-themed gifts. In the Pratt Street Pavilion check out: Fire and Ice (410-332-1334), one-of-a-kind jewelry and gifts; Hats in the Belfry (410-528-0060), hats for every occasion; and The Irish Country Store (410-659-9304), wares straight from the Emerald Isle.

THE GALLERY

410-332-4191

www.harborplace.com

This airy shopping mall offers three levels of mid-to upscale chains like Ann Taylor, Brooks Brothers, Banana Republic, J. Crew, Godiva, and other clothing, shoe, jewelry, kids, and gift stores. Along with these familiar retailers are several quick food eateries and a few homegrown shops. Two interesting shops to visit: Amaryllis (410-576-7622), antique to contemporary jewelry and crafts; Night Goods (410-625-5081), bedtime accessories.

Epicurean Bites

HARBORPLACE, THE GALLERY, AND THE POWER PLANT

The Pratt and Light Street Pavilions offer a variety of eateries ranging from theme restaurants like Planet Hollywood, The Cheesecake Factory, and Hard Rock Cafe to chains like Paolo's to homegrown restaurants like Wayne's Bar-B-Que. Most have outdoor verandas for dining. In addition to carry-outs and a small "diner" on its lower level, the Light Street Pavilion features an upstairs food court that's a grazer's delight with a variety of ethnic and fast foods. Don't miss The Fudgery where candymakers sing "Buy Some Fudge" in *a cappella* harmony while performing synchronized dance steps. Among the sit-down restaurants:

PAOLO'S

Light Street Pavilion. 410-539-7060

With its blond wood booths and chairs and its marble floors, this informal restaurant leans toward gourmet Italian with specialty pizzas, Mediterranean soups and salads, seafood pastas, and Northern Italian fish, beef, and veal dishes. L, D. $$

PHILLIPS HARBORPLACE

Light Street Pavilion. 410-685-6600
www.phillipsfoods.com

This Eastern Shore-based restaurant serves 150,000 pounds of crab meat, 125,000 crab legs, and 150,000 pounds of shrimp each year. Join the nightly sing-a-longs by the grand piano. Send a taste of the Chesapeake to friends and neighbors. 1-800-782-CRAB. L, D. Weekends until 11. $$

PLANET HOLLYWOOD

Pratt Street Pavilion. 410-685-7827

The 76th "planet" in this chain's constellation of restaurants, the Baltimore version offers a touch of hometown moviemaking mingled with the rest of the genre. Enshrined in glass are artifacts like Charlie Sheen's baseball uniform from *Major League II* and Harrison Ford's Hawaiian shirt ensemble from *Mosquito Coast*—both from movies filmed in part here. A diorama of pink flamingos celebrates hometown filmmakers John Waters and Barry Levinson with cutouts of Divine, Ricki Lake, Sonny Bono, and Deborah Harry mixing it up with Michael Douglas and Tom Cruise. While John Travolta sweats away a Saturday Night Fever on the video screen above your head, dine on salads, fajitas, pastas, sandwiches, and pizzas. L, D. 🌙 $½

WAYNE'S BAR-B-QUE

Light Street Pavilion. 410-539-3810

Chow down on ribs, burgers, and an award-winning chicken BBQ sandwich beneath antlered hanging lamps in this western lodge-style restaurant. Codfish cakes, a.k.a. coddies, used to be sold more than 50 years ago in neighbors' backyards in Fells Point. Wayne has 'em, too. L, D. Weekends until 11. 🌙 $½

BEYOND HARBORPLACE

Escape the chains and the crowds—and get in a little exercise to boot—by walking to these nearby restaurants. All are located just off the Promenade.

HAMPTON'S

Harbor Court Hotel. 550 Light St. 410-347-9744

Vivaldi plays as candlelight flickers over tables adorned with a gardenia floating in a bowl at one of the city's most romantic restaurants. The menu features New American cuisine *à la carte* and *prix-fixé* four-course meals reflecting seasonal menus. The sinfully opulent champagne Sunday brunch offers entrees ranging from

traditional eggs benedict to grilled medallions of beef.
D. Br Sun. Reservations recommended. $$$

LENNY'S CHOP HOUSE
Harbor Inn Pier 5. 410-843-5555
This classy chop house with its dark wood appoint-
ments serves steaks, lamb chops, pork, veal, and
seafood to perfection and on request will plank them
with a bouquetier of seasonal vegetables. The lounge
features a pianist Tues-Sat. D. Restaurant open until 11.
Reservations recommended. ☽ $$$

McCORMICK & SCHMICK'S SEAFOOD RESTAURANT
Harbor Inn Pier 5. 410-234-1300
The forest green carpeting, dark wood booths and paneling, and the Tiffany-style lamps set a comfortable
atmosphere for dining on fish specialties like mahi mahi
with macadamia nuts and coconut as well as jumbo
lump crab with seafood Newburg. In good weather, the
outdoor tables offer a great view of the harbor. L, D.
Open late except on Sun. ☽ $$

MORTON'S OF CHICAGO
Sheraton Inner Harbor Hotel. 300 S. Charles St.
410-547-8255
Forget intimacy. In Morton's the spirits get as high as the
cholesterol levels. While steaks sizzle on the open
kitchen's grill, waiters wheel out the dinner "menu"—a
trolley of shrink-wrapped meats, vegetables, and fish.
The steak knife, one that would do Jim Bowie proud, is
a harbinger of the prodigious portions. Everything is big,
à la carte and pricey, so plan on sharing side dishes. D.
Open until 11 except on Sun. Reservations recom-
mended. ☽ $$$

PISCES
Hyatt Regency Hotel. 300 Light St. 410-605-2835
Come to the top of the Hyatt for one of the best city
views in town. Stay for the plantain crusted snapper
filets, Chesapeake paella, or grilled portobellas with
vidalia onion tartlet. Couples dance to a jazz band and

pianist in the lounge Thurs-Sat. D. Call ahead for reservations and complimentary valet parking. $$$

RUTH'S CHRIS STEAK HOUSE

The Brokerage. 600 Water St. 410-783-0033

In May 1965 when Ruth Fertel mortgaged her house to buy Chris' Steak House in New Orleans, it proved a good investment. Today there are more than 60 Ruth's Chris Steak Houses, including this elegant-warehouse version on Water Street. Bring a big appetite. Generous portions of US Prime steaks come sizzling to the table and vegetables, served *à la carte*, can feed two or three. Afterwards head up to the Havana Club to boogie with Baltimore's beautiful people. Dress code requires men to wear a collared shirt. D. Reservations recommended. Complimentary valet parking. Weekends until 11. $$$

VICTOR'S CAFE

Pier 7. Inner Harbor East Marina. 801 Lancaster St. 410-244-1722

What better place to be on a summer night than Victor's outdoor deck overlooking the harbor and the lit-up downtown skyline? Indoors, the windowed pavilion presents dramatic views as well. An eclectic menu runs from pastas and pizzas to tequila-barbecued pork to teriyaki-flavored snapper. L, D. Weekends until 11. $$

WINDOWS

Renaissance Harborplace Hotel. 202 E. Pratt St. 410-685-8439

With one of the most spectacular views of the Inner Harbor, it's easy to ignore the staid hotel dining room decor. Windows' New American cuisine leans heavily on seafood with outstanding dishes like seared ahi tuna in plum sauce and wood-fired rockfish. B, L, D. $$$

EXPLORER'S LOUNGE

Harbor Court Hotel. 550 Light St. 410-234-0550
Sip martinis on plush sofas under a ceiling worthy of Versailles in this elegant African-themed lounge. Live piano music weeknights and jazz by the Lou Rainone Trio weekends.

HAVANA CLUB

Ruth's Chris Steak House. 600 Water St.
410-468-0022
Ah, was Cuba ever this glamorous? Cherry wood humidors, leather couches, and vibrant music attracts a stylish crowd. Even Demi Moore and Arnold Schwarzenegger have dropped in—and have their names engraved on their humidor boxes to prove it. Members can take the private elevator up to drink, dance, or eat dessert any time and Ruth's Chris Steak House patrons get preferential entry, as well. For the rest, it's first-come-first-served. As might be expected, cigars are *de rigueur* so non-smokers enter at your own risk. Doors open at 6 pm, but the place doesn't start swinging until after 9:30 or so. Closed Sun.

Inner Harbor

Inner Harbor

N E S W

N

E

S

W

10 Market

Water

11

12

Gay

Commerce

South

Calvert

Redwood

Baltimore

Lombard

Pratt

Charles

Conway

Lee

Light

13

3

1 2

4

6

5

7

8

9

16

15

14

1. *USS Constellation*
2. Pratt Street Pavilion
3. Light Street Pavilion and Baltimore Area Visitors' Center
4. World Trade Center
5. National Aquarium
6. Baltimore Maritime Museum
7. Power Plant
8. Pier 6 Concert Pavilion
9. Baltimore Public Works Museum
10. Port Discovery
11. Holocaust Memorial
12. US Customs House
13. Baltimore Convention Center
14. Maryland Science Center
15. Rash Field
16. *Pride of Baltimore Memorial*

Downtown

Business District

Baltimore Town began with three streets—the north-south running Calvert and Forest (later called Charles) crossed by Long (eventually renamed Baltimore) and a grid of alleys. In front of wood frame houses pigs and other animals mucked about in garbage littering the dirt roads. Sanitation, to put it kindly, left much to be desired. Several years earlier in 1729 the state legislature had granted a group of prominent Marylanders the official right to establish the town on the northwest branch of the Patapsco. A county surveyor divided the town into 60 one-acre lots, the first of which went to the Carroll family on whose land the town was founded. Meanwhile to the east, across Harrison's Marsh and the falls, merchants and other craftsmen settled into what would be called Jones' Town. Soon a bridge linked the villages, and by 1745 the two towns had merged.

Over the next 30 years, industries like flour milling and brick manufacturing grew up, and trade with surrounding counties and states boomed as wagon routes were carved out. Europe began craving Maryland tobacco, leading to the erection of public wharves and an inspection shed on Charles Street. By the 1750s wheat wrested tobacco's spot as top export and ships laden with grain took off for New England, Britain, Spain, Portugal, and the West Indies. In return they brought back dry goods, wines, sugar, molasses, and other food stuffs and wares as well as servants and slaves. Taverns, craft workshops, a church, and even a school went up so fast that newcomers complained of the shortage of workmen and servants.

By the end of the Revolutionary War, Baltimore was bursting at the seams, spawning businesses and commercial ventures and taking in immigrants who arrived with each passenger ship. Calvert Street was extended further northward and the city opened three public markets—Marsh Market on the former Harrison's Marsh, Broadway Market in Fells Point, and Hanover Market on the west side. A 1790 census counted 13,503 residents. Private libraries, theaters, and schools run by religious and benevolent societies opened to meet the town's growing needs.

Back in 1773 Baltimore had wisely annexed Fells Point, a hub of shipbuilding, and, as a result, by the outbreak of the War of 1812, the town had become a force on the high seas. There was good cause for the Brits to tag Baltimore "that nest of pirates" as city businesses helped finance privateers sailing out of Fells Point on the famed and swift Baltimore clippers.

Throughout the 19th century, the boom periods continued and the city fanned out from its crescent around the harbor, increasing its boundaries in 1816 to North Avenue and further north and west in 1888. As industry took over the waterfront and poor immigrants packed into rowhouses, slums and pollution ate away at the central city driving wealthier families northward to Mount Vernon. The business district with its collection of shops, taverns, churches, and service industries, however, remained concentrated in the rectangle north of the Inner Harbor bounded by Jones Falls on the east, and what is now Martin Luther King, Jr. Boulevard on the west.

Growth of the Business District

In the latter part of the 1800s, retailing got a boost from German Jewish merchants who lived and worked around the city markets. In 1894, Hamburger's, a clothing manufacturer who sold by catalog and in its small shops, opened a department store on Howard Street. Hochschild, Kohn & Co. followed with a four-story 36,000 square-footer at the corner of Howard and Lexington. The store pioneered an innovative one-price policy that eliminated the bargaining that marked most retail transactions up until then. Hutzler's got its start just before the Civil War as a dry goods business on the first floor of a house on Howard Street. Flushed with success, the Hutzler brothers moved their operation into "The Palace," five stories of fashion and fine merchandise in the 1880s.

To the east, Charles Street garnered fashionable cachet in 1882 when Thomas O'Neill opened O'Neill & Co., which offered the finest in clothing, imported linens, and other dry goods. The enterprising red-headed Irish immigrant provided his best advertising as he stood at the front door in black frock coat and striped trousers greeting customers. Charles Street soon became Baltimore's swankiest shopping district catering to those whose tastes ran to fine art and china, silk garments, and other upscale merchandise.

Very little of downtown Baltimore was to change appreciatively for decades. Then in the space of 30 hours, the business district was transformed forever by the Great Fire of 1904 (see below). After the fire, the city rebuilt, widening and paving streets, improving sanitation, and installing utilities. Many department stores expanded and folks took streetcars downtown to shop and then lunch in Hutzler's Colonial Tea Room. And in its last major annexation, Baltimore extended its borders, pulling in pieces of Baltimore and Anne Arundel counties in 1918.

After World War II, many forces contributed to the deterioration of the inner city: a growing number of cars on the road and its attendant urban flight, the riots following Martin Luther King, Jr.'s assassination, and increasing crime. One after another, the big department stores closed and the retail district shrunk as shoppers switched their allegiance to suburban malls.

The Baltimore Renaissance

In 1961, groundbreaking for Charles Center heralded the start of Baltimore's Renaissance. On its 33 acres, plazas surrounded by new and old office buildings, shops, hotels, the Mechanic Theatre, and apartment houses injected new life into the decaying downtown and provided a springboard for the ensuing Inner Harbor development. In recent years, however, like the pretty new girl on the block, the glitzy revitalized Inner Harbor drew attention, grabbing the spotlight away from Charles Center which, over the decades, began losing its luster. That should all be changing with Johns Hopkins University's plans to rebuild the old Hamburger's clothing store on Charles and Fayette Street along with a proposal by Jimmy Rouse (son of late developer James Rouse) and Kemp Byrnes for transforming Charles Plaza into "an urban entertainment center" with art movie houses, upscale shops, and restaurants. Recently the Downtown Partnership and the city have teamed up to plant trees, set out planters of flowers, replace sidewalks with pavers, and redo roads so by the turn-of-the-century Baltimore should be looking a lot spiffier.

Did You Know?

Stand near the intersection of Calvert and Redwood Streets, and you're visiting the hottest spot in Baltimore's history. Temperatures here during the Great Fire of 1904 reached an estimated 2,500°F. Even more amazing is the reddish brown building on the northeast corner of the intersection, the old Mercantile Safe Deposit and Trust building, which survived the blaze. Although its exterior was hardly damaged, the interior was gutted by flames coming through a skylight.

The fire began, most likely, with a carelessly tossed cigarette or cigar that fell through a low casement opening at street level into the basement storage area of the Hurst Building at the corner of Liberty and Redwood Streets. It ignited a bale of cotton and within minutes the building was on fire with flames so intense they exploded through the roof and spread rapidly among the old buildings in the financial district.

Despite their quick response, firefighters found their efforts ineffectual against the spreading blaze. (Ironically, there was no firehouse located in the entire area now known as the Burnt District.) Shortly before midnight, the winds shifted, turning the conflagration away from its eastward march toward the City Hall district, thus sparing several government buildings and residential areas, but now pushing the roaring fire toward the harbor. The glow in the midnight skies could be seen over 100 miles away.

Fire companies from the counties, the District of Columbia, and states as far away as New York poured into the city attempting to help. However, because hose and pump couplings were not yet standardized, most of the equipment brought in was rendered useless. By late afternoon on Monday, February 8, the fire had spread to the Jones Falls where the expressway stands today. Thirty-seven fire engines and their crews pitched a final effort to contain the blaze. By dusk, the fire was under control.

The rebuilding of the Burnt District turned Baltimore into a modern city. Most of the streets were widened and paved, underground electrical cables, and, thankfully, a public sewer system was installed. The city acquired large sections of the waterfront for municipal piers and began implementing a plan by Frederick Law Olmsted to link city parks and acquire additional green spaces next to major boulevards. Baltimore, like a phoenix from the ashes, was on her way to the 20th century.

Sights & Sites

CHARLES CENTER

Charles, Lombard, Saratoga, and Liberty Sts., and Hopkins Place.

As urban blight swept through downtown in the 1950s, groups of business leaders (the Committee for Downtown and the Greater Baltimore Committee) and city planning and housing organizations came up with plans to revitalize the commercial district by erecting Charles Center, a 33-acre complex of office and apartment buildings, hotels, shops, a theater, and parking garages connected by walkways and plazas. In 1962 the anchor of this urban renewal project, the Mies van der Rohe-designed One Charles Center, an eight-sided glass, aluminum, and concrete tower arose. Two nearby statues of Thomas D'Alesandro, Jr., one sitting and one standing, commemorate the former mayor's push to start the Baltimore Renaissance.

Diagonally across from One Charles Center, the new Blaustein Building at One North Charles Street opened in 1964 as corporate headquarters for Crown Central Oil and American Trading and Production Company, which encompassed tanker manufacturing, real estate, oil refining, and development firms. Russian-Jewish immigrant Louis Blaustein had gotten his start hawking oil from a horse-drawn tank on the city streets in the early 1900s. He and his son Jacob eventually parlayed the business into what became Amoco. After losing control of the American Oil Company, the Blausteins bought Crown. The lobby of this building features Barbara Hepworth's *Single Form*, a smaller version of her sculpture at the United Nations in New York, symbolizing Dag Hammarskjöld's pursuit of peace.

The hexagonal Charles Center South (1975) sits at the edge of the Inner Harbor development while the two northern anchors, Two Charles Center's apartment buildings at Charles and Saratoga, stand over Charles Plaza. At night when the upper half of the Baltimore Gas & Electric Company building at 39 West Lexington is lit up, it resembles a Greek temple. It overlooks Center Plaza, a large oval patterned on Siena, Italy's famed Palio.

MORRIS A. MECHANIC THEATRE

25 Hopkins Plaza. 410-625-4230
www.themechanic.org
It's not a pretty sight unless you happen to be a fan of Brutalist architecture. However, although it resembles a big bunker, when the sun hits its concrete form sides, the theater looks like a piece of sculpture. Ironically, the playhouse was named for Morris Abel Mechanic, a man in the habit of tearing down old theaters for more lucrative enterprises. Mechanic redeemed himself with Baltimore playgoers when he agreed to Mayor J. Harold Grady's entreaties to build a new theater. Architect John M. Johansen produced his "functional expressionism" design much to the dissatisfaction of some of the citizenry. Mechanic died six months before its 1967 opening of *Hello Dolly*. Today national touring companies of hits like *Rent* and *Chicago* along with pre-Broadway try-outs come to the 1,604-seat theater. The theater sits in Hopkins Plaza, named after merchant Johns Hopkins of his name-sake university and hospital fame.

THURGOOD MARSHALL STATUE

Corner of Pratt St. and Hopkins Plaza.
Thurgood Marshall, the first African American justice on the Supreme Court of the United States, was born and raised in West Baltimore a few blocks west of this

statue. Prior to his appointment to the Supreme Court, Marshall headed the NAACP's legal team where, among other cases, he successfully argued *Brown v. the Board of Education*, which led to the desegregation of schools across the United States (see *West Baltimore*).

BALTIMORE ARENA

201 W. Baltimore St. Event hotline: 410-347-2000
Ticket information: 410-347-2010
Whether you're coming to cheer the Baltimore Blast, hurl insults or encouragement at your favorite pro wrestler, or laugh with the Muppets, you'll be rubbing elbows with more than 11,000 other enthusiasts at the area's largest indoor sporting and entertainment venue. Just a short walk from the Inner Harbor, the Arena is also accessible via Light Rail and bus, and has an 840-car garage.

HANSA HAUS

S. Charles and Redwood Sts.
Constructed for the North German Lloyd Line's offices in 1912, this half-timbered building features the coats of arms of Hanseatic League members lining the base of its second story windows and a tile picture of a Viking ship beneath the gable. In the 19th century, North German Lloyd's steamers shipped tobacco and other Maryland products to Hamburg and Bremen. Then in 1868, the company joined with the B&O Railroad, offering combination ship-rail tickets to would-be German immigrants who landed at the Locust Point wharves and hopped the railroad west. Among the building's past tenants have been Swedish and German consulates and a French cafe. First Maryland Bancorp, which recently acquired the landmark, plans to restore it for brokerage offices.

Did You Know?

Since 1983, Beauregard, a peregrine falcon, has made his nest with several mates on a windy ledge of the 33rd floor of the Legg Mason building at 100 Light Street. Beauregard and his numerous progeny have played a key role in the comeback of peregrine falcons, which are on the Endangered Species List. Scarlet, a captive-born peregrine released to the wild, was the first falcon to nest on the building, and went through a series of suitors before settling on Beauregard, a wild falcon. After Scarlet died in 1984, Beauregard, ever the ladies' man, maintained the nest, luring females and siring dozens of young over the years.

NATIONSBANK BUILDING
10 Light St.
You can't miss the distinctive gold leaf and green copper roof of this Art Deco building on the southern approach to the city from I-95. When constructed in 1929, the former Baltimore Trust Building was the tallest skyscraper in the city. The main entrance, a monument to the city's commercial success, includes arches adorned with carvings representing major local industries like railroading, medicine, textiles, and shipping. The bronze double doors and frieze also contain symbolic figures pertaining to Baltimore and Maryland. (Look for the crab.) Inside, the cavernous main banking floor has intricate mosaic floors, marble columns, and a rich multi-colored ceiling. Names of the other 49 states and US territories in the iron grill work surround the entrances and tellers' counters

Above the second tier gallery, four murals painted by Baltimore artist R. McGill Mackall overlook the main room. They depict four key events in Maryland history: the 1634 arrival of its first colonists on the *Ark* and *Dove*; a 1730 view of the harbor and construction of a pier; the famed clipper *Anna McKim* circa 1830; and a view of Baltimore in 1930. The bank personnel are used

to folks wandering around the main room, so feel free
to gawk.

When the sign is red, warm weather's ahead.
When the sign is blue, cooler weather's due.
An amber light means no change in sight.
When a color moves in agitation,
there's going to be precipitation.

This little ditty imprinted itself on the collective Baltimore brain
from 1971 to 1994 as the interpretative code for the weather forecast
flashing from the former Maryland National Bank tower's promotional
letters. The 18 x 38 foot wide letters *mn* on the east and west facades
of the tower could be seen for 30 miles, and thousands of Baltimoreans
depended on their accurate forecast, updated eight times daily from the
US Weather Service at BWI Airport. Alas, the letters were deep-sixed
when NationsBank took over the building in 1993.

FIRST UNION NATIONAL BANK OF MARYLAND

1 E. Baltimore St. 410-244-3400

Baltimore's own 1907 "Temple of Thrift" is patterned
after the Erechtheum on Athens' Acropolis. Passing the
Ionic columns and walking through the portico, a
depositor would enter a huge banking floor with Italian
marble wainscotting and a two-story coffered ceiling.
Although growing business resulted in the installation
of a second floor over the lobby in the '50s and a tower
addition in the '80s, the building still exudes grandeur.

MACHT BUILDING

11 E. Fayette St.

This fanciful facade—with lions' heads, cartouches,
Greek fretwork, and bare-chested babes—was built for
Russian immigrant Ephraim Macht's real estate company. With savings from his wife Annie's hatmaking business (her showroom was a pushcart in Fells Point),

Macht commissioned architect Alfred Lowther Forrest to do the design. Despite Macht's success in buying up old houses and renovating them, he felt anti-Semitism was hurting his business, so in 1911 he borrowed the name "John Welsh" and renamed his firm, Welsh Construction Company. Local historian Frank R. Shivers, Jr. likes to point out that keeping the two topless nymphs company are two similarly unclad lads on the Hotel Junker across the street.

ONE EAST LEXINGTON STREET

The Great Fire of 1904 licked at, but didn't bring down, Charles Carson's Romanesque Revival building. Originally the brick-and-brownstone building (circa 1890) housed the Central Savings Bank. Today the five-story structure holds commercial businesses and offices, including that of a violin maker. The tiny lobby displays a few photos of old Baltimore. Take the elevator up to see the light court and look down four stories to the open former banking floor. Note the oak paneling installed with pegs and the ornamental metal railings that circle each level.

FIDELITY BUILDING

210 N. Charles St.

When the Fidelity & Deposit Company of Maryland constructed the original eight-story granite building in 1894, they wanted it to symbolize the solidity of the company. Indeed the building weathered the Great Fire which stopped a half-block from its door. During downtown reconstruction, Fidelity's vault, one of the few surviving the fire, became the banking center for the city. In its heyday, ladies doing their banking were served in a reception room, paneled in mahogany with Chippendale furniture, oak flooring, and oriental rugs. The ladies' reception room has long vanished and the building, now 15 stories high, houses bank, insurance, law, and other offices. Do stop in and look at the lobby with its white Mycenaean marble floor and walls, brass railings and elevators, and grand chandelier.

DOWNTOWN PARTNERSHIP OF BALTIMORE

217 N. Charles St. 410-244-1030

The Downtown Partnership likes to take care of business, that is, "the business of keeping Downtown safe, clean, and prosperous." In addition, the organization promotes area businesses and coordinates First Thursdays (see *Mount Vernon*), monthly festivities featuring art openings and extended gallery and shop hours.

Clad in purple baseball caps, black slacks, and jackets with diamond-shaped insignia, the **Public Safety Guides,** funded by a surcharge paid by local businesses, cover **106** blocks of the central business district, lending helping hands, giving directions, assisting with auto trouble and other emergencies, and serving as ``eyes and ears'' for the police. Give them a call **(410-244-8778)** and they'll escort you to your car during their hours of operation.

MASONIC TEMPLE

223-225 N. Charles St.

This seven-story building, constructed in 1869, had ten large meeting rooms evoking historic eras such as a Tudor Gothic room resembling Roslyn Chapel in Edinburgh, a hall in the style of an Egyptian temple, and a marble room right out of Ancient Rome. Valuable furnishings like Tiffany benches, Rococo chandeliers, and stained glass filled its vast space. In 1997 the Masons decided to sell the building and stripped it of its treasures. An uproar ensued and most of the fixtures were reinstalled. In 1998 the owners of the Tremont hotels bought the building and plan to use it as banquet facilities.

BROWN'S ARCADE

326 N. Charles St.

This collection of 1820s rowhomes was named after Governor Frank Brown whose claim to fame was ending the Frostburg coal miners' strike of 1894. After purchasing the buildings following the Great Fire, Brown along with architect Henry Brauns transformed them into storefronts. Today Brown's Arcade houses speciality shops and restaurants.

WOMAN'S INDUSTRIAL EXCHANGE

333 N. Charles St. 410-685-4388

The Woman's Industrial Exchange began after the Civil War as a way for destitute women to support themselves through selling their needlework, quilts, and other handcrafted items. Later these early social activists added a dining room serving afternoon tea and light suppers to Baltimore's society matrons. At one point there were 72 such exchanges in the country. Of those left, Baltimore's is the oldest. Over the years celebrities like Katharine Hepburn have dined here and a scene in the movie *Sleepless in Seattle* was filmed here. Along with inexpensive meals, the shop sells chef Dorothea's cakes, cookies, and pies as well as crafts like potholders, puzzles, wood toys, and rag dolls made by women-in-need. With rising costs and falling revenue, the charity has fallen on hard times so her supporters have launched a campaign to save this "damsel in distress" (see Epicurean Bites). Weekdays 7-3.

Did You Know?

Baltimore-born Upton Sinclair once lived at 415 N. Charles Street (where the American Heart Association building stands today). He didn't hang around town for long even though H.L. Mencken published him in *The Smart Set*. The Socialist reformer penned more than 80 books including *The Jungle*, a graphic 1906 novel exposing the meat industry.

CATHEDRAL HILL

This hill, rising just above the harbor, was the cradle of Baltimore's Christian heritage. Early city planners had set aside land for a church and St. Paul's, which was looking for a centrally located spot, got the blessing. By 1739 the Anglicans were singing their first hymns in their new brick home which sat so high that sailors could see it from the harbor. In July 1806, Bishop John Carroll led a procession from the harbor up the slope to lay the cornerstone for what would be the United States' first Roman Catholic Cathedral. (One had already been built in New Orleans, however, Louisiana did not join the union until 1812.) The Classical building, consecrated in 1821, changed the skyline of Baltimore with its grand dome and later additions of Saracenic towers. Baltimore's religious choices continued to expand and soon sermons issued from the hilltop churches of Unitarians, Presbyterians, and other denominations. The congregants, Baltimore's movers and shakers, took up residence in the shadow of the spires and fancy stores opened to serve them. Historian Frank Shivers has called this area the seat of Baltimore's first golden age.

OLD ST. PAUL'S EPISCOPAL CHURCH
N. Charles at Saratoga Sts. 410-685-3404
Maryland's early Anglican churches were fueled by tobacco. Spurred on by anti-Catholic feeling in England, in 1692 the Maryland General Assembly had passed a law taxing freeholders 40 pounds of tobacco a year to pay for Anglican churches and their clergy. Even those of different religious persuasions were forced to fork over the leaves until the Revolution set them free. Meanwhile, the colony was divided into 30 Anglican parishes, one of which was St. Paul's. A log church went up near what would later be Fort Holabird; however, as the population drifted westward, St. Paul's found higher ground in the newly established Baltimore Town. From that vantage point, in 1739 St. Paul's became the town's first religious establishment. As Mother Church of the Episcopal community, it spun off several others over the years.

Three different St. Paul churches sat on this spot until the present day building, designed by Richard Upjohn, celebrated its first service in 1856. The Romanesque red brick church, fronted by a triple arched portico, is embellished by two bas-stone reliefs of Christ and of

Moses, carved by Antonio Capellano for the previous church. Inside the basilica-style building, the green, maroon, and gold leaf chancel contains Maitland, Armstrong, and Company stained glass windows and a reredos of Tiffany Studio's mosaic tiles. Patterned clerestory windows line the nave. Tours by appointment. Mon, Wed & Fri Eucharist 12:15 pm. Sunday morning services 8 and 10:30 am.

OLD ST. PAUL'S RECTORY
Cathedral and Saratoga Sts. 410-685-2886
Wealthy landowner and Revolutionary War hero John Eager Howard chipped away at his holdings, donating a half-acre on a hill overlooking the city and harbor to St. Paul's for a rectory in 1785. The financially strapped church held a lottery to pay for the new building. It was bad timing. The city had just issued a lottery to pay for a public wharf which cut into the church's fund-raising. Eventually the house was completed in 1791, but not before a second lottery and an additional land donation by the generous Howard bailed St. Paul's out. Dr. William West, the rector for whom the house had been built, died before he could unpack his clothes.

Over the years, a back porch, a new kitchen, and west wing have been added. Today the house, which serves as the verger's home and the office of Preservation Maryland, has been restored with 19th century antique furnishings and reproduction wallpapers. The house is available for party rental and many a bride has leaned over the winding staircase to toss her bouquet. Mon-Fri 10-4.

ST. ALPHONSUS CHURCH
Saratoga and Park Sts. 410-685-6090
This brick church with its tiered steeple harkens back to Baltimore's immigrant roots. Built by the German Redemptorists in 1845, the "German Cathedral," as it was called, was designed by Robert Cary Long, Jr. in Gothic Revival-style. The large rectangular interior features stenciled ceilings, an ornate altar, and marbleized ribbed columns. Between the Great Fire of 1904 and

World War I, the church lost its Teutonic base as the original parishioners moved further out and anti-Kaiser sentiment flourished. Meanwhile, an influx of Lithuanians emigrated down from New York to work Maryland's iron forges, garment industry sweatshops, sugar refineries, and tobacco plantations. In 1917, a Lithuanian parish bought St. Alphonsus.

Healing is a major theme of this church. Folks suffering from arthritis come to pray to St. Alphonsus, the 18th century Italian founder of the Redemptorists, whose statue, head bent to his chest in arthritic pain, stands over the altar. The church also holds a perpetual novena in honor of Our Lady of the Miraculous Medal commemorating the Virgin Mary's 1830 appearance to St. Catherine of Labouré during which she'd given the sister a design for a medallion offering improved health and other blessings. Today, worshippers can buy these medals, along with candles, rosaries, and healing water from the Grotto of Lourdes at the church's front office.

Daily 6:30 am-2 pm; Thurs and first Fridays until 5. Lithuanian mass: Sun 8:30 am. Tridentine (Old Latin rite): Sunday 11:30 am. English masses: Sun 10 am; weekdays 7 & 8 am and 12:10 pm. Blessings for the sick follows all masses.

MARYLAND ART PLACE

218 W. Saratoga St. 410-962-8565
www.MDartplace.org
This nonprofit was established in 1982 to promote the arts, stir up new ideas, and to offer Mid-Atlantic artists in all media a venue to exhibit their works. Along with a gallery, workshops, resource center, critics' residency program, newsletter, and bulletin, MAP offers a slide registry and biographical information on more than 1500 regional artists. Several times a month it presents jazz and other live music while 14Karat Cabaret hosts a line up of eclectic acts such as stand up comedy, music, and animated films. The annual Out of Order is a free-for-all style art show. The fall benefit, however, is a curated exhibition and auction with an after-show party. Tues-Sat 11-5.

LATROBE HOUSE

11 W. Mulberry St.

In 1833 John H. B. Latrobe, son of architect Benjamin Latrobe and inventor of the Latrobe stove, sat here with two other judges over a bottle of port, considering entries in a literary contest. The prize was publication in the weekly *Baltimore Saturday Visitor* plus $50 for the winning short story and $25 for best poem. Edgar Allan Poe captured top honors for his story "Ms. Found in a Bottle." His poem "The Coliseum" won kudos, too, but not first place because the judges felt it unfair to award one writer both prizes. Latrobe's fireplace stoves or "Baltimore heaters," efficient successors to the old Franklin stoves, were precursors to modern central heating. Not open to the public.

BASILICA OF THE NATIONAL SHRINE OF THE ASSUMPTION OF THE BLESSED VIRGIN MARY

Cathedral and Mulberry Sts. 410-727-3565
www.baltimorebasilica.org

Maryland's Catholic roots stretch back to 1632 when Charles I granted Cecil Calvert a royal charter and opened the territory up to Catholics fleeing persecution. During much of the 17th and 18th centuries, worshippers gathered at mass houses or private homes for devotions. As Protestantism grew stronger in England,  prevailing anti-Catholic sentiments discouraged building of Catholic churches here and wealthy parishioners often converted to Anglicanism to avoid discriminatory inheritance laws. With the Revolution came a new openness. In 1790, Baltimore had been appointed diocese for all the United States from Canada to Florida. Bishop John Carroll, capitalizing on the fledgling country's new freedom of religion, embarked on a successful quest to fund the nation's first Roman Catholic cathedral.

In 1803, the church purchased a prominent hill from Revolutionary War hero John Eager Howard for $20,000. After a few false starts, architect Benjamin Henry Latrobe (who also worked on the US Capitol) was commissioned to draw up plans. He obliged, offering both a Gothic and a Roman design. The latter won Carroll's approval and Latrobe's masterpiece—inspired by grand buildings like London's Bank of England and St. Paul's Cathedral, Paris' Pantheon, and Lulworth Castle Chapel in Dorchester, England—was dedicated in 1821. Latrobe, who died a year earlier, never saw the completed cruciform-shaped building with its huge dome. Nor was he around to settle the century-plus-old debate about whether he had designed the controversial 1830s addition of two Saracenic or Islamic towers.

In 1808, the pope split the United States into six dioceses, making Baltimore an archdiocese. Even so, two other cathedrals in the country were deemed minor basilicas before Baltimore was granted that distinction by Pious XI in 1937. In 1959, when the Cathedral of Mary Our Queen opened uptown, the Basilica began sharing co-cathedral status. Pope John Paul II visited here in 1995, followed by Mother Teresa of Calcutta in 1996.

Today, walking through the Cathedral's columned portico of New Brunswick freestone into its cool gray granite interior, you can see echoes of Latrobe's work on the Capitol building. The great dome, originally ringed with clear glass skylights, had allowed sunlight to filter down, creating a *lumiere mysterieuse*, or holy gloom. In the 1940s its skylights were covered and the sanctuary's original colonial style windows replaced by stained glass depicting Christ's life, Old Testament stories, and the history of the American Catholic Church. Beneath the sanctuary a crypt houses the remains of the archbishops of Baltimore.

Behind the Basilica, the Archbishop's Residence (1829) is an interesting bit of Baltimorana. Once stuccoed brick, the Greek Revival facade got swept up in the home improvement craze of the mid-1900s and was Formstoned to look like the Basilica. Self guided tours of the Basilica weekdays 9-5. Guided tours Sun noon. Mass daily.

OUR DAILY BREAD

411 Cathedral St. 410-659-4000

Every day, 900 poor and often homeless men and women stand in line for a meal at this soup kitchen. Catholic Charities first started handing out food from a storefront pantry on Franklin Street in 1981. After brokering a deal with the Downtown Partnership, it shifted operations to this new $1.1 million brick building by the Basilica and was favored by a visit in 1995 from Pope John Paul II who ate here among his destitute brethren. From its beginnings, controversy has swirled around the charity's location and recently there have been discussions about moving the soup kitchen to a campus where the poor could would have access to a variety of services like health care, job training, and child care.

ENOCH PRATT FREE LIBRARY

400 Cathedral St. 410-396-5430
TDD: 410-396-3761
www.pratt.lib.md.us

This three-story Modified Italian Renaissance library sprawls across one acre of downtown real estate. At the time of its construction, Chief Librarian Joseph Wheeler insisted the building be "characterized by friendliness rather than aloofness." Hence, instead of the traditional flights of steps, the entrance sat at ground level flanked by department-store type windows featuring book displays and notices of upcoming events. The interior is appointed with marble, bronze, and dark wood as well as grillwork forged in Baltimore.

Enoch Pratt was a hardware and dry goods merchant who in 1886 gifted the city with its library—one of the first in the United States. The original building sat on this site, facing Mulberry Street. The new building, opened in 1933, houses over 2.2 million volumes, along with periodicals, computer work stations, and audiovisual equipment. The Maryland Room on the second floor is a research and reference center for Maryland history and also contains the Pratt's considerable African American collection. Originally designed to be the Humanities department, this room has murals of Edmund Spenser's *The Fairie Queen* painted above the windows. The Poe Room contains first editions and an uncataloged collection of his work and the Frederick P. Stieff Collection houses 2,000 volumes on international and American cookery. These latter two rooms are not open to the public, but can be booked for research and meetings. The H.L. Mencken Room on the third floor houses the author's memorabilia, newspaper and magazine pieces, books, family documents, clipping books, research materials, and a file of his correspondence with prominent Marylanders. The room is not open to the public but arrangements can be made for scholarly research. Every year, the Saturday closest to Mencken's September 12th birthday, the library throws the late author a fête complete with displays, films and talks. In the hall, a bas-relief honors Baltimore poet Lizette Woodworth Reese, whose lyrical "Tears" is often called one of the greatest sonnets in the English language.

The Pratt offers readings and signings by authors and talks by community leaders, and free film series and lectures. Audio cassette tour of the building available. Open Mon-Wed 10 am-8 pm. Thurs & Sat 10 am-5 pm. Sun. 1-5 pm Closed Fri. Closed Suns from May to September.

Did You Know?

The phones start ringing at 10 am at the Enoch Pratt Free Library Centralized Phone Reference with questions about stain removal, business information, homework, and queries about all things under the sun. Librarians armed with more than 1,500 reference books ferret out answers. Calls are limited to five minutes, but these paper Sherlocks will phone back if the search takes longer. For nocturnal souls seeking answers to the universe, a Night Owl Service, operating after business hours on Mon-Thurs until 11 pm, provides quick answers. 410-396-5430 Night Owl: 410-396-3557 or 1-800-325-6483.

BREAD OF LIFE AT THE CATHEDRAL

Franklin and Cathedral Sts. 410-783-5020
www.bolcathedral.org

This 1847 Tudor building designed by Robert Cary Long, Jr. has witnessed many incarnations: first as the Franklin Street Presbyterian Church in 1847; then as New Psalmist Baptist Church in the '70s; and today as the nondenominational Bread of Life at the Cathedral. At the time it was built, the twin-towered brick building (then painted to resemble stone) broke the Neoclassical mold that city churches followed. Today a look inside the large sanctuary reveals red carpeting, faux stone painted walls, oak paneling and pews—enough to hold 900 people—adorned with finials in the shape of poppies. Stained glass windows by Charles J. Connick of Boston depict biblical stories like the Good Samaritan and the Prodigal Son. Tours Sun 1 pm following services or by appointment Tues-Fri.

FIRST UNITARIAN CHURCH OF BALTIMORE

Charles and Franklin Sts. 410-685-2330

In 1817 a group of liberal-minded Congregationalists, dissatisfied with the standard Trinitarian version of Christianity, banded together to form the First Independent Church of Baltimore. The religious rebels, many of them former New Englanders, hired noted French architect Maximilian Godefroy to design their meeting house. Modeled after the Pantheons of Rome and Paris, the 1818 church is a white stucco box with sculptor Antonio Capellano's terra cotta Angel of Truth above the entrance. Unfortunately the dome at the church's center resulted in poor acoustics and after 75 years of the congregation straining to hear the preachers' words, a false ceiling was added to capture the sound. Hidden above this false ceiling are pews where slaves of church members once sat. In 1819, Reverend Dr. William Ellery Channing gave his famous "Baltimore Sermon," which marked the formal beginning of Unitarianism in the United States. Service 11 am Sun.

HAMILTON STREET HOUSES

W. Hamilton St. between Charles and Cathedral Sts.

This block of early 19th century Federal houses is believed to have been designed by Robert Cary Long, Sr. who once owned the row and lived here. While several of the houses have been altered, numbers 12, 16, and 18 still retain the big tripartite windows situated in the middle of the second and third floors.

Browse and Buy

In its day, Charles Street was a street of mercantile dreams as shoppers came to buy furs, linens, china, art, and other luxuries. Today you'll find small shops selling fine art, ethnic clothing, beading, unique home furnishings, cameras, records, books, and boutique items. On First Thursdays, some stores stay open until 8 pm.

AN DIE MUSIK

407 N. Charles St. 410-385-2638

An die Musik, taken from a Schubert lieder, means "to the music." Peabody students and faculty search here for the best of classical, opera, jazz, New Age, and world music along with a smattering of more popular fare. And if you're looking for that esoteric recording, the staff will do a search. An Avid Listener Club membership offers 10% discounts.

BEADAZZLED

501 N. Charles St. 410-837-2323

More than 4,000 different types of beads from every continent glitter from this jewelry crafters' heaven. Along with stringing materials, crafting tools, how-to books, as well as ready-made pieces, Beadazzled offers classes for all levels of beaders.

C GRIMALDIS GALLERY

523 N. Charles St. 410-539-1080

You need big bucks to buy here, but there's no charge for looking. C Grimaldis launches 11 shows a year featuring art luminaries like Sukey Bryan, Anthony Caro, John Ruppert, Costas Varotsos, and Baltimore artists Raoul Middleman and Grace Hartigan.

CRAIG FLINNER GALLERY

505 N. Charles St. 410-727-1863

Flinner credits the fine arts books in the Enoch Pratt Free Library for providing him with most of his art history education. He buys and sells antique prints and maps, old etchings and lithographs, watercolors, and vintage French posters.

FIRMA

521 N. Charles St. 410-547-1124

Delgardo A. Darby stocks his menswear store with Euro-style lines like Mondo Di Marco, Cavelli, and Mani. Royal shirts and Tino Cosma ties complete the professional image.

NOUVEAU CONTEMPORARY GOODS

517-19 N. Charles St. 410-962-8248

Go ahead, buy that Hollywood-style overstuffed couch and lounge around like Harlow. Need a lava lamp to light up your Jimi Hendrix posters? Here's the most eclectic and interesting line of contemporary and retro-influenced giftware, jewelry, housewares, and furniture in the city.

A PEOPLE UNITED

516 N. Charles St. 410-727-4471

The store's collection of textiles, handicrafts, hand knitted and woven ladies' clothing is made by women's cooperatives and home businesses throughout the Third World. Marie Payzant designs several of the clothing lines and prices them at 10% discount.

THE RECORD ROOM

416 N. Charles St. 410-528-8327

THE MUSICAL EXCHANGE

422 N. Charles St. 410-528-9815

The Record Room sells vintage and contemporary vinyl from a top-priced James Brown album ($150) to bargain buck disks (a favorite of DJs for sampling). A sister store, The Musical Exchange, offers a selection of used CDs for $9.99 or less.

STEVEN SCOTT GALLERY

515 N. Charles St. 410-752-6218

The gallery offers solo and group exhibitions of contemporary art—original oils, watercolors, etchings, lithographs, and prints. This is the place to buy Tom Miller's painted furniture and his charming color screen prints of the city.

TARLOW FURS, LTD.

337 N. Charles St. 410-539-1931

"My customers know I can do anything with a fur coat," says David G. Tarlow who's been selling, making, remodeling, repairing, and cleaning furs and leathers here for almost six decades. Tarlow's loyal customers are folks who know exactly what they want and don't glance at price tags.

CARIBBEAN KITCHEN

218 N. Liberty St. 410-837-2274

An old fashioned diner counter serves Jamaican fare, including the best meat patties north of Kingston. The

Kitchen, which also cooks up standard American eats, has limited seating so plan your orders to go. L, D. $

JAVA JOE'S GOURMET CORNER
222 N. Charles St. 410-727-4007
Drink your java along with Hopkins students, high pow-ered attorneys, businesspeople, and a gaggle of shop-pers. When hunger strikes, there's muffins, tarts, bagels, sandwiches, and salads to go with the joe. B, L from 7 am weekdays. $

SASCHA'S DAILY
5 E. Hamilton St. 410-659-7606
Line up cafeteria style for eat-in or take-out sandwich-es, salads, platters, and the not-to-be missed finale, homemade desserts. L. Weekdays. $

THE STRAND
105 E. Lombard St. 410-625-8944
www.thestrandcafe.com
The Strand Cybercafe has two menus: one for food; the other for software. With eight computer work stations, a dining area with tables and stuffed sofas, this is a pleas-ant spot to catch up on e-mail, type your novel, or snack on sandwiches, muffins, and salads. B, L, D. Open until 11 pm weekends. $

WOMAN'S INDUSTRIAL EXCHANGE
333 N. Charles St. 410-685-4388
You could be dining at Granny's. The food is basic—eggs, pancakes, cereal for breakfast; soup, sandwiches, sweet potato pie for lunch. It's all served in a tea room outfitted with wood-grain Formica tables, red leatherette banquettes, and murals of Old Baltimore. The waitresses, long time veterans of the Exchange, call everyone "Hon." B, L weekdays. $

Epicurean Bites

In the mood for ethnic food? Lower North Charles Street offers Japanese, Ethiopian, Thai, Irish, Afghan, as well as good old American food. Listed below are a few of the choices.

AZEB'S ETHIOPIAN RESTAURANT
322 N. Charles St. 410-625-9787
At Azeb's one eats Ethiopian communal style, tearing off pieces of spongy enjera bread and scooping up chicken in tangy barbarre sauce, lamb marinated in awaze, and other North African delicacies. Dine downstairs on white tablecloths. Upstairs pull up a stool to coiled basket tables atop animal-skin rugs. D. $½

KAWASAKI!
413 N. Charles St. 410-659-7600
Tucked in a lacquered cabinet, Kathleen Turner's chopsticks await her return. So do Nicholas Cage's. Many famous folk have sat on low cushions and dined Japanese style on sushi, teriyaki, and tempura. If you like you can plop down $20 and join the 700 other folks who keep their very own chopsticks in storage. Or, opt for the free-issue ordinary wooden variety and just enjoy. L, D. Open late Sat. $½

LOUIE'S THE BOOKSTORE CAFE
518 N. Charles St. 410-962-1224
Bookstore: 410-962-1222
Back in the 1980s former owner Jimmy Rouse transformed this furniture store into a combo bookstore-cafe with high ceilings, a classy bar, and an upstairs loft. The bookstore features small press publications,

contemporary literature, greeting cards, and an eclectic selection of newspapers and magazines. Behind it the restaurant dishes up gourmet vegetarian selections, seafood, lean burgers, Okonomo-yaki—a Japanese pancake—and Middle Eastern dishes. Live jazz or classical music nightly. L, D. Br, Sun. 🌙 $½

MAISON MARCONI

106 W. Saratoga St. 410-727-9522
Marconi's, which served its first meal in 1920, remains old Maryland from its tuxedoed waiters to its pre-cholesterol-conscious menu. Old-standbys like lobster Newberg, veal cutlet with spaghetti, and chicken *à la king* can seem heavy-handed, but diners come here for the nostalgia, not *haute cuisine*. Men will need a jacket to dine in the front room, but there's a back room for the less-formally attired. L, D. Reservations recommended. $$$

MARTICK'S RESTAURANT FRANCAIS

214 W. Mulberry St. 410-752-5155
Customers must ring the bell to get into this eccentric house with its blue and white chevron striped door, broken shutters, and gingerbread trim. Inside, a dining room and lounge with walls made of aircraft aluminum scavenged from a junkyard awaits along with blue tablecloths, Tiffany-style lamps, a large partially nude "Venus," and a hand-written photocopied menu featuring dishes like bouillabaisse and lamb tangine. Jazz plays softy in the background. In its beatnik-era incarnation, Martick's drew a stellar crowd. Even Leonard Bernstein came around to tickle the ivories. L, D. $$½

SOTTO SOPRA

405 N. Charles St. 410-625-0534
A mural of a woman preparing for an evening at this sleek Euro-style restaurant is enough to make even the romantically challenged loosen up. Its chic Northern Italian cuisine focusing on pastas, seafood, and veal may just turn your life around, or maybe even "sotto sopra" upside down. L, D. Reservations recommended. Open until 11:30 pm weekends. 🌙 $$

TIO PEPE'S

10 E. Franklin St. 410-539-4675

The festive atmosphere in this cellar warren of white-washed rooms fueled by pitchers of sangría and outstanding food has made Tio Pepe a Baltimore favorite for more than 30 years. The paella for two is chock full of shellfish, chicken, veal, and chorizo. The suckling pig accompanied by black beans and applesauce is moist and tender. And for the finale there's the famous pine nut roll. L, D. Reservations recommended. $$$

NIGHT LIFE

BUDDIES PUB & JAZZ CLUB

313 N. Charles St. 410-332-4200

Jazz and Po' Boys? Nope, you're not in New Orleans but in Buddies, a classic neighborhood pub that just happens to have its own house band, the Bing Miller Quartet, jazzing up the joint Thursday through Saturday nights. In addition to the N'Awlins po' boys, this family-owned club also offers up seafood, pasta, and burgers. L, D. $$

MICK O' SHEA'S IRISH PUB AND RESTAURANT

328 N. Charles St. 410-539-7504

Lift that draft of Guinness Stout. Mick O'Shea's has gifted Baltimore with the most rollicking Irish pub this side of the Patapsco. Homesick Irishmen mingle with Emerald Isle lovers. Corned beef and cabbage and Irish stews share the culinary spotlight with burgers and crab cakes. Bands like the Flying Cows of Ventry and the Irish Accents alternate nights with impromptu jam sessions and open mikes. And the politically minded will find leaflets galore about Irish causes. L, D. Open late weekends.

Business District

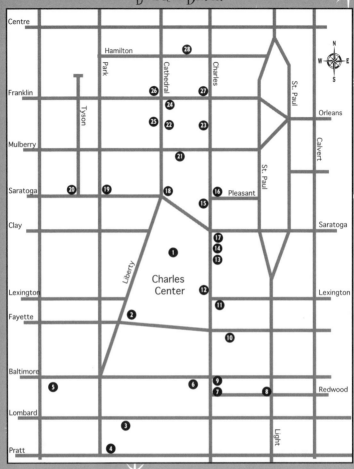

1. **Charles Center**
2. **Baltimore Gas & Electric Building**
3. **Hopkins Plaza**
4. **Thurgood Marshall Statue**
5. **Baltimore Arena**
6. **Morris A. Mechanic Theatre**
7. **Hansa Haus**
8. **NationsBank Building**
9. **First Union National Bank of Maryland**
10. **Macht Building**
11. **One East Lexington Street**
12. **Fidelity Building**
13. **Downtown Partnership of Baltimore**
14. **Masonic Temple**
15. **Brown's Arcade**
16. **Woman's Industrial Exchange**
17. **Old St. Paul's Episcopal Church**
18. **Old St. Paul's Rectory**
19. **St. Alphonsus Church**
20. **Maryland Art Place**
21. **Latrobe House**
22. **Basilica of the National Shrine of the Assumption**
23. **Archbishop's Residence**
24. **Our Daily Bread**
25. **Enoch Pratt Free Library**
26. **Bread of Life at the Cathedral**
27. **First Unitarian Church of Baltimore**
28. **Hamilton Street Houses**

Mount Vernon

In the early 1800s, in what was then called Howard's Woods, gentlemen, hot to defend their honor, fought duels. Those preferring healthier competition stuck to playing ball. A few years before, in 1784, crowds had gathered to watch the nation's first hot air balloon rise above the hilltop. In 1809, Baltimore patriots proposed erecting a monument honoring George Washington downtown where the Battle Monument now stands. Immediately cries of fear rose up from folks living near the intended site. The tower, they worried, would collapse onto their houses. So the memorial was moved northward into this then no-man's-land where if it did tumble down, it wouldn't do any damage. When the monument was completed in 1829, it stood 100 feet above sea level, making it a landmark for ships coming into the harbor.

The monument was a boon to the area as four garden squares were installed to set off the obelisk, making Mount Vernon one of the first planned open spaces in the country. Yet when Charles Howard, son of Colonel John Eager Howard who owned the area, wanted to build his house here, people scoffed. "It is too far out," they pooh-poohed. "In a few years you will be turning it into a beer garden." Undeterred, he finished his home. Later on the Howard family sold off building lots and stylish folk moved in. The suds never materialized.

During the 19th century's Gilded Age, grand houses arose and galas filled the dreary winter months. By the 1920s, however, the automobile began changing the landscape. With more mobility, society headed uptown for quieter, larger spaces and non-gasoline fumed air. Businesses and institutions settled into Mount Vernon and many houses were carved up for apartments and offices.

The area also became a rallying point for protests. In the 1920s angry citizens bickered over plans to install the

Lafayette statue which would block a clear view of the monument from the south. Later, during the '60s, hippies staged May Day protests over Vietnam and what they labeled "establishment crimes." Happier events like the annual Flower Mart in May and in recent years the Baltimore Book Festival in September found their place on the green.

For the most part the neighborhood survived it all. Although some buildings are gone, Baltimore's conservative attitude toward change and its citizen involvement has left much of 19th century Mount Vernon intact. The Mount Vernon Improvement Association, a neighborhood and business coalition founded in the 1930s, spearheaded efforts to preserve, clean up, and cultivate the area while the more recent Mount Vernon Cultural District promotes foundations and cultural institutions in the vicinity.

This section is organized around the Washington Monument which stands at the center of the north-south running Washington Place and east-west Mount Vernon Place. Starting with the North Square on Washington Place, the tour moves counter-clockwise around the monument. Afterwards we fan out into each neighborhood ending with Belvedere.

On First Thursdays, the first Thursday evening of each month, the Walters Art Gallery, the Washington Monument, the Maryland Historical Society, and the Mount Vernon Museum of Incandescent Lighting offer extended hours and free admission. Small galleries host artists' openings and the Peabody and Enoch Pratt Library often hold concerts.

For walking tours of the area contact the Baltimore Architecture Foundation (410-625-2585) or the Mount Vernon Cultural District (410-605-0462) for Literary and Romantic Legends tours.

Sights & Sites

WASHINGTON MONUMENT AND MUSEUM

Mount Vernon Pl. 410-396-1049

Washington, D.C.'s may be bigger, but ours was first—by nearly 55 years. In 1815, Baltimore began constructing the country's first monument to George Washington. Arising from a square in the soon-to-be-fashionable Mount Vernon district, the 178-foot high column took 14 years to construct at a cost of $200,000. Even though the city raised nearly half the funding by lottery, financial setbacks along the way compromised Robert Mills' more elaborate concept, resulting in the lopping off of its tiers of ornamental galleries. The result was a simple classical shaft of Cockeysville marble, topped by a statue of the president (whom Italian sculptor Enrico Causici portrayed as Cincinnatus) submitting his resignation as commander-in-chief of the Continental Army. Mills later returned to design the monument's cast iron fence. His patriotic creation is ornamented with fasces symbolizing the Union; ax heads, the nation's defense; and 13 stars, the original states. Mills, it should be noted, went on to design Washington, D.C.'s own Washington Monument several years later.

Today the base of the monument contains a tiny museum featuring illustrations of the monument-as-work-in-progress accompanied by notes on its construction. There are no elevators—only a guaranteed huff-and-puff 228-step spiraling climb to the top. At the top four cutouts offer views of the harbor, the city streets, downtown office buildings, and the rooftops of industrial-area warehouses. Open 10-4 Wed-Sun and First Thursdays until 8 pm. Admission.

NORTH WASHINGTON PLACE

It's only fitting that the man who gave so much to the city should have a statue here. Yes, Revolutionary hero Colonel John Eager Howard rides his mount northward, urging his troops into a charge, much as he moved his fellow Baltimoreans to expand the city beyond the harbor. Frenchmen Emmanuel Fremiet cast the bronze sculpture.

Another Marylander, US Chief Justice Roger Brooke Taney, sits contemplating the monument. Taney, a remnant of Maryland's divided past, was famous for his recognition of states' rights in the 1857 Dred Scott Decision, which decreed that slaves had no rights as citizens and that Congress had no authority to stop slavery in the territories. His controversial rulings helped ignite the Civil War although as a lawyer he'd represented abolitionists and had freed most of his own slaves. The statue is a copy of one done by local sculptor William Henry Rinehart for the Maryland State House in Annapolis.

The square is flanked on the west by an odd collection of residential structures. With its witches' cap turret, bay windows, marble columned portico, and pediment the Graham-Hughes House at No. 718 N. Washington Place is a confection of late 19th century whimsy. The 1893 high society French Chateau home is somewhat overpowered by its contemporary next door, a brick and brownstone former hotel, The Stafford. The American Psychoanalytic Association was founded at the hotel in 1911, and 20-some-odd years later F. Scott Fitzgerald wrote and boozed in one of its rooms while Zelda underwent therapy for her mental illness at Johns Hopkins' Phipps Clinic. Over the years, many well-to-do visitors occupied the hotel's beds but by the 1970s the clientele had long disappeared and the city turned the aging building into subsidized housing for the elderly.

Anchoring the south-west end of the block, the Washington Apartments (700 N. Washington Place) radiate a sense of European tradition and formality. Built in 1906, the multi-storied Beaux-Arts building came close to threatening the vertical superiority of the Washington Monument.

MOUNT VERNON PLACE UNITED METHODIST CHURCH
Mount Vernon and Washington Pl. 410-685-5290

In 1872 this "Cathedral to Methodism" was built on the site of Charles Howard's home. The mansion, demolished in the transition, had been where Francis Scott Key died while being cared for by his daughter Elizabeth who was married to Howard. A plaque on the church's south front commemorates Key.

The church's American Romantic Gothic architecture celebrates the glory of creation. Flowers, vines, and fanciful creatures peek out from an ornate facade built with six types of stone including green serpentine sandstone quarried off Falls Road. A stained-glass rose window crowns the entranceway. Inside, the nature theme is carried out in carved grape vines above the altar, on the ceiling beams, and in the tall stained glass windows. The leaves adorning the ends of the walnut pews took seven years for the carver to fashion. Each Sunday the Gospel is read from the pulpit used by Francis Asbury (1745-1816), the first Bishop of the American Methodist Church, when he preached at earlier churches in Baltimore. A 1988 renovation lightened up the dark interior by faux painting the walls to resemble granite block. Among its many community services, the congregation sponsors services for AIDS patients, runs The Carpenter's Kitchen that feeds 400 needy folk each Saturday, sells inexpensive clothing and furniture at The Goodbye Shop thrift store, and houses artists' studios and children's spiritual art programs. Tours Mon-Fri 9:30-2:30. Services Sun 11 am and Wed noon.

ASBURY HOUSE
10 Mount Vernon Pl. 410-685-5290

This mid-19th century Italianate Mansion was once the home of Albert Schumacher, a prosperous German merchant. The second floor library features walls lined with German Baroque mahogany bookcases and a ceiling painted with a copy of Guido Reni's "Aurora." Now serving as offices for the Mount Vernon Place United Methodist Church, Asbury House can be visited during church tours.

MOUNT VERNON MUSEUM OF INCANDESCENT LIGHTING

717 Washington Pl. 410-752-8586

How many dentists does it take to turn visitors on to a basement of 8,000 light bulbs? One, if it's Baltimore's Dr. Hugh Francis Hicks.

Back in the '20s, when Dr. Hicks was a baby, his mother found that giving him a bulb to play with would quiet him. From that simple act grew a lifelong obsession, and by the time he was practicing dentistry, Hicks was a renowned expert. In 1960, wanting to share his bounty, Hicks put a selection of his 60,000-piece collection on public display in the basement of the townhouse where he treats patients.

And what a collection! Glass mould Christmas lights from the 1880s and later, shaped like Santa, Betty Boop, fish, sheep, grapes. A cockpit bulb from the Enola Gay. The world's second largest light bulb—50,000 watts with filaments that resemble mattress springs. Built in 1929 to commemorate the 50th anniversary of Edison's invention, the 30-inch globe was powered by two generators and could only be burned for 30 seconds at a time. Then there's the Branston Violet Ray display. Back in the late 1800s medical quacks inserted tubes into patients' orifices to heal cancer or combed tubular rakes across scalps to rid dandruff. The electric controller was turned on and zap—all healed. By appointment. Also open on special weekends and during First Thursdays. Admission.

WEST MOUNT VERNON PLACE

Two of French sculptor Antoine-Louis Barye's four "strong government" bronzes, those representing War and Peace, sit at the monument end of the square. Behind them a lion, also by Barye, lazily watches the cars round the monument. On the other end of the square stands Paul Dubois' statue of Military Courage, a winged dragon on his helmet and sword in hand. Oblivious to all the war imagery around him, the figure of a young boy with a turtle, perhaps a legacy of the area's pastoral legacy, romps mid-park in the fountain. When benches were added years ago, it fomented an uproar among gentle folk who were sure men would use them as a vantage point for ogling ladies.

The houses facing the square on West Mount Vernon Place present a marvelous 19th century tableaux. The Romanesque Revival House at No. 6, now a private home, once quite fittingly housed the Italian consulate. Designed by George Archer in 1889, the marble mansion's three stories bow outward to form a gallery on the fourth level.

John Eager Howard's heirs sold merchant William Tiffany the two lots at numbers 8-10 Mount Vernon Place on which he built his Greek Revival mansion in 1842. After he died, his family rented out the flat fronted brick house to various occupants, the most intriguing being the Allston Association, an arts organization named after a South Carolina painter. The group, which gave lectures and art exhibits, had no sooner settled in when Union Troops cleaned out "that nest of rebels" and carted its Southern sympathizers off to jail. After the war the family chose a less troublesome girls' school as tenant. A parade of owners followed, including a lawyer named Fisher who contributed the second half of the building's present day moniker, The Tiffany-Fisher House. The Mount Vernon Club, a private women's organization, took over in 1942.

Fierce lions' heads guard the door and a window of at No. 14, the Marburg Mansion. Once home to Theodore Marburg, a US ambassador to Belgium, it's believed that he and President Woodrow Wilson worked on the League of Nations Charter in the upstairs library. Today the 1847 Niernsee and Neilson-designed mansion serves as headquarters for Agora Publishing, Inc., which has rescued several architecturally significant buildings around town.

GARRETT-JACOBS MANSION
ENGINEERING SOCIETY OF BALTIMORE, INC.
11 W. Mount Vernon Pl. 410-539-6914
Baltimoreans had always turned up their noses at what they considered vulgar excess, yet throwing money around in a tasteful manner won their approval. And there was no one whose approval they sought out more than that of Mary Frick Garrett Jacobs, Baltimore's First

Lady of the city's Gilded Age and mistress of Baltimore's grandest mansion.

Samuel George purchased the lot at what would be 11 West Mount Vernon Place from the John Eager Howard clan and built a typical Baltimore home there around 1853. Over the years the square drew more and more wealthy residents. And when B&O Railroad magnate John Work Garrett bought the house for his son Robert and wife Mary Frick Garrett, the neighborhood's prestige went up another ratchet. Mary Garrett then embarked on one of the longest, most expensive remodeling jobs in Baltimore history, enlarging the home to 40 rooms and annexing three adjoining homes in the process.

With the renovation came controversy. When the Garretts announced they were adding brownstone and a large vestibule onto the original house, Henry Janes, who lived next door, sued the Garretts, complaining that "the monstrous vestibule" would cut off his light and view of the monument. Janes lost and the hammering continued.

Meanwhile Robert Garrett had taken over the reins of the B&O, expanding the railroad into Philadelphia. However, heavy business responsibilities and financial problems broke his health and Mary Garrett hired a private physician Dr. Henry Jacobs who came down from Massachusetts. After Robert died in 1896 at age 49, Jacobs hung around, joining the staff at Johns Hopkins Hospital. In April 1902, Mary and Henry walked over to Grace and St. Peter's Episcopal Church and exchanged wedding vows.

The remodeling continued until finally with great satisfaction, the Jacobs bought out the disgruntled Henry Janes in 1915, tore off the back of his building, leaving it one-room deep, thus allowing more light into No. 11's foyer Tiffany windows.

After Mary Jacobs died in 1936 and Dr. Jacobs in 1939, Baltimore's great mansion was sold at public auction to William Cook who wanted to use it as a funeral home. Ironically, in earlier years Dr. Jacobs had helped establish a zoning board which now turned

Cook down flat, so in 1941 he sold it off to the Boumi Temple, who tore out some of the prized stained glass windows, placed acoustical tile over the ornate gilded ceilings, and on at least one occasion reportedly rode horses into the entrance hall.

In 1958, the city bought the house in hopes of expanding the Walters Art Gallery. When that came to nought, the Engineers Club of Baltimore stepped in and restored the mansion. The Engineers Club had grown out of the Great Fire of 1904 when a foresighted water engineer, Alfred M. Quick, gathered a group of engineers to make and implement plans for redeveloping the city and with that, the club was born. Today the private club provides seminars, meeting space, and other services for its membership. Movies like *Accidental Tourist*, *Diner*, *Twelve Monkeys*, *Her Alibi*, as well as *Homicide* have been filmed here. Tours by appointment. The club's annual Fire Ball is open to the public.

702 CATHEDRAL

Across Cathedral Street at the west end of the square stands the former home of 19th century businessman William J. Albert. Albert hosted Abraham Lincoln overnight on April 18, 1864, after the president had spoken at the Maryland Institute, then located near today's Port Discovery. Afterwards Lincoln met with fellow civil rights supporters here. The 1856 brick and block building was later converted into a Christian Science Reading Room and church. Today Agora Publishing, Inc., owns the building and has restored the 400-seat auditorium with its Moeller pipe organ as a corporate and community meeting room.

704 CATHEDRAL

During the early 1930s in a third-floor apartment, writer and critic H.L. Mencken edited the *American Mercury* magazine while his wife Sara, ailing from tuberculous, penned fiction. Upon looking out his front window at the church towers of Cathedral Street, the irreverent wordsmith, notes author Frank Shivers, jested that they dwelt among angels. Private.

SOUTH WASHINGTON PLACE

That old curmudgeon Mencken once eyed the distance from the statue of Washington atop the monument to the south fountain and pronounced the limestone bowl "Washington's spittoon." Let's hope Washington doesn't oblige, for that young nymph ("Sea Urchin" by Henry Berge) might not appreciate a wad of presidential spit aimed her way. But hark! Another danger lurks, this one from Lafayette who seems intent to gallop over her. The statue, by Andrew O'Connor, was erected in 1924 to commemorate both Lafayette's and France's aid to American forces during the Revolution. Neither H.L. Mencken nor a host of critics could stop the city from erecting the "aesthetically offending" monument.

WALTERS ART GALLERY

600 N. Charles St. 410-547-9000

What a fortunate day it was for Baltimore when William Walters, his wallet bulging with cash from liquor and railroad businesses, bought his first piece of sculpture. He'd started off collecting works of local artists like William H. Rinehart, but as the Civil War broke out Walters shifted his attentions to Europe. With heavy investments in Southern railroads and his support of states' rights, he, like many other similarly-minded Baltimoreans, sat out the war in France.

Paris provided the springboard for expanding Walters' tastes and collection. He bought up works by artists like Couture and Gérôme then, growing more daring, he plunged into Delacroix, Rousseau, and Honoré Daumier. He also developed an admiration for the work of Antoine-Louis Barye whose sculptures he'd later place in Mount Vernon Square. At the same time he began dabbling in oriental porcelains and within 20 years had amassed 4,000 pieces.

During their time abroad, his wife Ellen died of pneumonia, leaving William to raise their teenaged son Henry and young daughter Jennie. When the war ended, the family returned to their Mount Vernon Place home where they would spend the winter months. In spring 1874 Walters began opening his collection and Mount Vernon home to the public, charging them 50¢, which he donated to the poor. Later he built a gallery behind his house and began printing collection catalogs.

William died in 1894 and son Henry, no slouch in amassing money and collecting, expanded the art holdings, shelling out millions for everything from Egyptian mummies to illuminated manuscripts to medieval armor to old Masters and Art Nouveau jewelry. However, with his collection languishing in boxes and crates, Walters needed a showcase. The showcase he opened in 1909, the main building of today's Walters Art Gallery, was a grand Italianate and Baroque palace with a courtyard patterned after Genoa's 17th century Palazzo Balbi.

Even though he'd gifted Baltimore with this magnificent museum, Walters spent most of his time elsewhere. His personal life caused some eyebrow lifting, too. The life-long bachelor had been fast friends with wealthy rice farmers Pembroke and Sarah Jones, to the point of moving in with them in New York. After Pembroke died, Henry, then 74, took Mrs. Jones as his bride. On his death in 1931, Henry, who'd been on the board of the Metropolitan Museum of Art in New York, shocked his fellow directors by leaving his massive collection and its gallery to Baltimore.

The collections are housed in three buildings: the 1904 building, a 1974 wing, and the Hackerman House. Currently, the 1974 building is undergoing renovations and is scheduled to reopen in March 2001. As a result, some of its treasures are on display in the older building.

The 1904 Building

Arms and Armory—Brass rubbings of crusaders greet visitors to this dark, block walled space, featuring 16th to 19th century European arms. Items on display include chain mail helmets, Turkish rifles, halberds, armor, and swords.

Renaissance Sculpture Court—Modeled after a 17th century Genoese Palazzo's open air courtyard, this magnificent columned space holds 16th century roundels depicting ancient Roman rulers, della Robbia altar pieces, 15th to 18th century sculptures, and other early works.

Renaissance and later Decorative Arts Galleries—Exhibits feature European porcelain, Baroque and Renaissance bronzes, 17th century Flemish paintings, Limoges enamels, religious triptychs, and wood sculptures. A corner room illuminated by a 16th century stained glass window displays shelves of majolica ewers, plates, bottles, and other faience pottery—all categorized by workshop.

The Treasury—Devoted to the art of goldsmithery, this gallery dazzles with 16th century Italian pendants and Spanish crucifixes, 18th century French enameled pocket watches, snuff boxes, and Italian mosaic jewelry. But the exhibits drawing the biggest oohs and aahs are the Tiffany broaches, Lalique Art Nouveau necklaces, and Fabergé eggs which open to reveal palaces.

Old Master Painting Galleries—Here in rooms with damask wallpaper, carved moldings, and skylights, hang works by Raphael, El Greco, Veronese, van Dyck, Reni, and other master painters.

Note: Because of special installations and renovations of the 1974 wing, exhibits are sometimes shifted.

The 1974 Building

The 1974 wing tripled the Walters' size and gave it an ultramodern showcase for its ancient, medieval, Islamic art and artifacts; 19th century American and European art; and an illuminated manuscript collection. Along with added gallery space, the Brutalist concrete structure provided more room for conservation activities as well as offices, classrooms, an auditorium, and library. When it reopens after renovations in spring 2001, visitors will enter through a four-story atrium featuring a grand staircase leading to the upper floors. The exhibit space will be updated and enlarged, with art displayed in the context of its time and culture.

Note: For an in-depth look at the collection, buy a catalog at the museum store before going through the exhibits. Also, available at the shop are reproduction jewelry, Chinese porcelain, art books, postcards, and other gift items.

The Hackerman House

In this 1851 Greek Revival house, designed by John R. Niernsee and J. Crawford Neilson, owners Dr. John Hanson Thomas and his wife Annie threw lavish balls to which the *crème* of Baltimore society flocked. Even the Prince of Wales, later King Edward VIII of England, once walked beneath its columned portico and crossed its marble hallway to party in the grand double parlor. The lavish affairs came to an abrupt halt when Dr. Thomas' Southern leanings earned him a prison stint at Fort McHenry during the Civil War.

The next occupants, Francis and Elizabeth Jencks, gave the house an overhaul, widening the spiral staircase, installing a Tiffany skylight in place of plain glass, and removing much of the Victorian embellishment. By the 1950s, when the house became vacant, Mount Vernon society had already moved on. Homes were converted into apartments or offices while others succumbed to the wrecker's ball. In 1963 Harry Lee Gladding stepped in, rehabilitated the house, and filled it with Louis XIV and Louis XV furniture. After Gladding left in the 1980s, the mansion once again stood in peril, but philanthropists Mr. and Mrs. Willard Hackerman came to the rescue, purchasing the house for the city. After renovation, Walters' prized Asian collection was moved to its new home in 1991.

The Indian and Southeast Asian Art Gallery—This small gallery features a display of early Buddhist art.

The Foyer—A century ago, you might have cozied up to a begowned Mount Vernon matron here; today you'll find yourself next to a display of late 18th century Japanese armor. In the opposite case, tomb sculptures from the T'ang and Han dynasties provide a fitting counterpoint.

Great China Room—It's been said that the Hackerman's greatest challenge has been to provide a fitting western setting for eastern art. With its mix of Baltimore pier tables, Hepplewhite and Empire furniture, and display of 16th to 18th century Chinese and Japanese porcelains, enamels and glass, the museum has succeeded.

The Library—People choked when William Walters purchased a peach blow vase for $18,000 in 1878. Gawk at this eight-inch string vessel through a glass case in the Elizabethan Revival-style library. The Ch'ing dynasty's peach bloom glazed wares range from a pink to a gray-green and are much prized among collectors.

The Japanese Study—At the time Henry Walters was collecting, Japan was starting to modernize. Among the items he picked up were a brush rest in the shape of a praying mantis, carved elephant tusks, and 19th century swords and daggers. A room off the study displays colorful woodblock prints, many of military battles.

Chinese, Japanese, and Korean Galleries—Sword guards, Samurai helmets, and swords are exhibited here. Also displayed are *netsuke*, cord holders shaped like dogs, rabbits, sea creatures, and other fanciful creatures, and *inro* boxes used to carry pills, tobacco, coins, and other necessities.

The Walters and Hackerman House are open Tues-Fri 10-4; Sat-Sun 11-5. Admission. Open until 8 pm on First Thursdays when admission is free. Docent lead tours available on Wed & Sun.

Did You Know?

The Contemporary (410-333-8600), founded in 1989 by George Ciscle to foster exchanges between artists and the community, has displayed everything from ceramics to Jewish art to found-art sculptures, screen painting, folk art, photography, and even Internet graphics. You never knew just where an exhibit from this "museum without walls" would show up—an abandoned bus garage, an ex-Buick dealership, a 1959 Chevy pick-up, a vacant shopping mall. The museum acquired a permanent home at 104 W. Centre St., but will continue to mount off-site exhibitions.

EAST MOUNT VERNON PLACE

Force and Order, the two remaining Barye bronzes celebrating good government, flank the monument side of this square. A statue of George Peabody, sitting in a chair, seems to be listening for the sounds of an orchestra emanating from the institute he started next door. Meanwhile all around him, people relax on benches eating lunch, dozing, reading, or catching a few rays. To George Peabody's north stands a row of brownstone houses, built on speculation in the 1850s. Many of these homes have been broken into apartments, some housing Peabody students.

In the center of the park, a naiad by Baltimore sculptor Grace Turnbull arches her back to revel in the water spraying from her fountain. And on the east end, Severn Teackle Wallis prepares to rally against the Know-Nothings who'd infiltrated the fire and other city departments with their anti-immigrant propaganda in the mid-1800s. When the Know-Nothings nominated Millard Fillmore for president in 1856, the only state Fillmore carried in the election was Maryland.

PEABODY INSTITUTE

1 E. Mount Vernon Pl. 410-659-8165
www.peabody.jhu.edu
This Renaissance Revival temple of learning, now one of the country's top music schools, stands in the heart of Mount Vernon, a testimony to the generosity of one of Baltimore's most prosperous 19th century business-men—and one of the era's most successful school dropouts.

When family financial difficulties forced the Massachusetts-born George Peabody to put aside his books at age 11, he went to work as a grocer's assistant. After a series of jobs and a stint in the military, the enterprising 19-year-old opened a dry goods wholesaling business bankrolled by partner Elisha Riggs. In 1815 the company moved into Baltimore's old Congress Hall at Liberty and Baltimore Streets where the Continental Congress had met during the winter of 1775-76. Business boomed and the firm opened branches in New York and Philadelphia, becoming one of the largest mercantile houses in the United States.

In 1836 Peabody, a confirmed bachelor and Anglophile, decided to move to London, the financial capital of the world. But he didn't shut the door on Baltimore. At the urging of his friend—Baltimore lawyer, novelist, and former US Navy secretary John Pendleton Kennedy—Peabody agreed to fund an institute that would "improve the moral and intellectual culture" of the city. Although completed in 1861, the dedication of this marble edifice was delayed by the Civil War. Five years later, the septuagenarian Peabody returned for the grand opening ceremony.

The Peabody, part of the Johns Hopkins University system, consists of a Conservatory, offering undergraduate and graduate degrees focusing on classical music, and a Preparatory, a pre-college program for gifted children and adolescents. Concerts and operatic performances are open to the public (see *Standing Ovation*).

The Library—The original plan for the library was to include the best works on every subject ranging from the sciences, philosophies, fine arts, to authoritative encyclopedias and dictionaries. The Institute would also sponsor lectures and contain an art gallery and a music salon. However, the collection grew exponentially and a new library was added in 1878. This grand "Cathedral of Books," one of the most magnificent public spaces in the city, features an open court surrounded by six tiers of stacks embellished with Neo-Grec style cast-iron and topped by a skylight. H.L. Mencken had a reserved desk in the library while he worked on his book *The American Language*, and author John Dos Passos spent many an hour here, too. Sidney Lanier, the poet, lectured at the Institute and played flute in the Conservatory orchestra open Mon.-Fri. 9 am-3 pm.

SCHAPIRO HOUSE

609 Washington Pl.

This four-story white-washed house with its iron work gallery looks as if it could have been shipped up from New Orleans. In the 19th century Jerome Napoleon Bonaparte, Betsy's son, lived here. Today it houses administrative offices for the Peabody Institute. Many buildings in the city once sported similar iron work, all manufactured in Baltimore, but much of it was stripped off in 20th century wartime scrap metal drives and in frenzies of overzealous renovations.

Did You Know?

Nipper, part of the RCA Victor record company's logo, has long been Baltimore's larger-than-life pet. The real-life Nipper was a fox terrier in England who often sat, ears cocked, listening to his master's gramophone. An artist friend painted the charming scene and sold it to the Gramophone Company in London who adopted the picture of the terrier as the company logo. RCA eventually acquired the US rights to the symbol, and Nipper crossed the Atlantic.

Baltimore's Nipper kept watch for 22 years on top of the old D&H Distributing Company on Russell Street and was one of the first sights visitors to Baltimore laid eyes on as they entered the city. When the D&H Company, a distributor for RCA records, moved in 1976, Nipper was carted off to Virginia by a private collector who set him out on his front lawn. The former Baltimore City Life Museum brought Nipper back home in 1995, and when the museum went bankrupt (no fault of Nipper's), the Maryland Historical Society acquired the pooch, washed his coat and refurbished him, and sat him on his perch on the rooftop of the Heritage Wing in 1998.

MARYLAND HISTORICAL SOCIETY

201 W. Monument St. 410-685-3750

If digging for your genealogical roots or researching Maryland's rich history is of interest, the Maryland Historical Society is the place to go. Once encrusted with stuffiness, the MHS is now one of the preeminent boosters of all things Baltimore and Maryland, from the truly historical, such as the original manuscript of "The Star-Spangled Banner," to the nostalgically Bawlmer, as in Nipper—that dawg sitting on his haunches perched on top of the Heritage Wing, (formerly the Greyhound bus terminal).

The Historical Society owns an impressive collection of artifacts and objects representing Maryland's past, including paintings by the Peale family and Joshua Johnson (see below), portraits of prominent Baltimoreans, silver, period costumes, quilts, and other needlework. Additionally, the Society gained an impressive slice of Baltimore history when it took over the defunct Baltimore City Life Museums' collection in 1998.

Included among the permanent galleries and sections of the Society are: the library, renowned for its genealogical holdings; the Radcliffe Maritime Museum; a special hands-on center and gallery for children; exhibits on Maryland during the Civil War and the War of 1812; and the Symington Sporting Arts Library. One of the Heritage Wing's two permanent galleries displays exhibits from the MHS's Baltimore City Life collection; the other, the new Claire McCardell Costume and Textile Gallery, has rotating exhibits on textiles and fashions. The third gallery features temporary displays from the Society's collection or visiting exhibits from other institutions.

The cornerstone of the museum, the former home of Baltimore merchant and philanthropist Enoch Pratt, is decorated with period furniture and art much in the way Pratt would have lived in his day, although only a few items of furniture in the library actually belonged to Pratt. The fine china on display in the dining room once belonged to Betsy Patterson Bonaparte.

Museum galleries and library: Tues-Sun. Admission. Free admission to museum First Thursdays.

Did You Know?

As a saddle maker in Annapolis, Charles Willson Peale (1741-1827) yearned to become a painter like Pennsylvanian Benjamin West, the first American artist to earn an international reputation. Peale got his wish when Charles Carroll the Barrister and other wealthy Maryland gentlemen paid his way to London to study with the great West himself. Upon his return to the American colonies, Peale established himself in Philadelphia where he garnered fame painting the portraits of George Washington and several other revolutionary or civic leaders of post-war America. Best known for his portraiture, Peale also organized the first artists' society in the country, was an inventor, and collected indigenous specimens which formed the basis of the first museum of natural history in the Western Hemisphere. He led the first scientific expedition in America in 1801 which excavated the first complete fossil skeleton of a mastodon, then assembled it and put it on display in his museum. Later, the mastodon was exhibited at the Peale Museum in Baltimore, founded by son Rembrandt (see *City Hall District*). Currently, a replica of the fossil skeleton is on display in the Historical Society's Heritage Wing.

Several of Peale's children, particularly Rembrandt, achieved fame as painters, and a niece, Sarah Miriam Peale, was America's first professional female portrait painter. The Peale family lived several years in Baltimore where it is believed they extended a considerable influence upon a young African American named Joshua Johnson.

Little is known about Joshua Johnson, the nation's first professional black painter, whose style clearly shows the influence of the Peales. Recent research indicates Johnson, who most likely had been brought to America from the West Indies as a slave, was owned by Charles Willson Peale and grew up in the Peale household, exposing him to the artist's craft. By the late 1790s Johnson was a free man earning his living as a portrait painter, advertising himself as a "self-taught genius." For over thirty years, Johnson painted the portraits of wealthy Baltimoreans. He lived in several locations in central Baltimore as well as on Strawberry Alley (now Dallas Street) in Fells Point. Paintings by Joshua Johnson and three generations of Peales are on display at the Maryland Historical Society.

GRACE AND ST. PETER'S EPISCOPAL CHURCH

707 Park Ave. at Monument St. 410-539-1395

This 1852 Gothic Revival church holds the distinction of being Baltimore's first brownstone. Sitting amongst its gardens, the building, which began life as Grace Church, resembles a rural English church. Inside, its persimmon-colored walls and blue trim set off the dark walnut pews and stained-glass windows from England and Germany. More than 50,000 English mosaic tiles inlaid on the floor lead up to a high stone altar carved with Old Testament stories of sacrifice and figures of John the Baptist and Luke the Evangelist. A copy of daVinci's "The Last Supper" is the centerpiece of the reredos.

In 1912, St. Peter's Episcopal left its Druid Hill Avenue location and merged with Grace. The combined church has maintained its Anglo-Catholic traditions and its masses are filled with incense, bells, and the voices of its marvelous choir. Grace & St. Peter's was also one of the first churches in the country to have a healing ministry. During its Tuesday noon masses, the priest does "laying on of hands" for the sick and prays for their recovery.

Nearly one-third of the parish are of Chinese descent, a legacy of the church's depression-era outreach work done among Cantonese immigrants who settled on lower Park Avenue. Come February a huge dragon prances in the street to the beat of drums as the church celebrates Chinese Lunar New Year. Note that many of the bronze plaques inside the church reflect its Asian heritage.

Grace & St. Peter's also holds organ recitals featuring critically acclaimed musicians. Masses daily.

FIRST AND FRANKLIN STREET PRESBYTERIAN CHURCH

210 W. Madison St. 410-728-5545

Let it be noted that this church is *not* on Franklin Street. First Presbyterian Church started out in private homes in 1761, progressed to a log cabin, then on to two other buildings. However, in the 1840s in a spirit of "colonizing" or spreading their beliefs, a group splintered off, starting their own house of worship at the corner of Cathedral and Franklin. In 1859, First Presbyterian took up residence in this Gothic Revival building on Madison Street. Then with storm clouds of war on the horizon, the two congregations realigned, breaking along political lines, with Southern sympathizers occupying the Franklin Street pews and Northern, those of First Presbyterian. By 1973 the divided congregation reunited, merging into this building, and combining both names much to the confusion of would-be attendees.

The New Brunswick freestone-faced exterior is dominated by a 273-foot spire, the tallest in the city. While the stained glass windows donated by the congregation's families are stunning, the most notable feature of the magnificent rose-colored interior is the ornate plaster pendants that hang unsupported from the fan-vaulted ceiling. Preservation consultant C. Dudley Brown has called the church "the finest Victorian Gothic plaster interior in North America." Services Sun 11 am. Tours by appointment.

BALTIMORE SCHOOL FOR THE ARTS
712 Cathedral St. 410-396-1185
In years past, debutantes in white gowns swirled across the then-Alcazar's ballroom floor with gentlemen in white tie and tails. The event was the Bachelors Cotillion where 60 or so 18-year-old women danced their dainty feet into the ranks of upper-crust society. There was much weeping among those not receiving invitations. The Lyric Opera House and the Sheraton-Belvedere also hosted these balls. In 1980 the building was converted into the city's high school for the arts, one of the top such preparatory schools in the country.

EMMANUEL EPISCOPAL CHURCH
811 Cathedral St. 410-685-1130
While the Civil War raged on battlefields, Emmanuel Episcopal parishioners waged their own political skirmishes. Whenever the rector, a Northern sympathizer,

prayed for Lincoln, the congregation's pro-Southern contingent refused to kneel. The rift even extended to the graveyard where the rector buried Union dead; his assistant did the honors for the Confederates. So high was the level of animosity, that the church paid a security guard 50¢ to keep order during Sunday services.

In those days, Emmanuel Episcopal was a square box of Indiana limestone. Poorer folks sat up in the balconies while those who could pay pew rents, many of whom were the *crème* of Baltimore society, sat below. In October 1896, Bessie Wallis Warfield, the future Duchess of Windsor, was baptized here.

During World War I the original 1854 structure was Gothicized, the galleries removed and stone columns, arches, and a chancel added. Later, in the 1920s, the old tower was replaced with a new one, popularly called the Christmas Tower, but in reality an Epiphany Tower. John Kirchmayer of Oberammergau carved the limestone and granite structure with the story of the wise men's visit to Jesus as a heavenly orchestra of angels trumpets tidings of Christ's birth.

Inside the arched and columned nave, Tiffany (the first three on the north side) and English stained glass windows lead to the chancel with its massive rood suspended over the choir. Above the marble altar, the Great East Window depicts Christ surrounded by figures of church history—among them St. Anselm, St. Paul, and Phillips Brooks, a popular 19th century bishop from Massachusetts. Bathed in blue light from John La Farge's stained glass windows, the octagonal baptistery to the right of the chancel encases a kneeling marble angel clasping a baptismal bowl, carved by Lincoln Memorial sculptor Daniel Chester French in 1904. On the opposite side of the chancel, the Chapel of Peace commemorates the end of World War I. Its Gothic archway guarded by the figures of Joan of Arc and St. George (representing allies France and Britain) leads into a room with an open canopy of whimsical animals—among them an elephant with a trumpet, a rabbit gunning for hunters, a pelican with her young.

The Eccleston Chapel in the lower part of the church had its fifteen minutes of fame when George C. Marshall, author of post-World War II European recovery program the Marshall Plan, married a Baltimore widow here. Crowds thronged to Penn Station and stood outside the church to see best man General "Black Jack" Pershing. The church's moment of infamy came, however, when young filmmaker John Waters persuaded the church fathers to screen the world premiere of his suburban teenage shocker *Roman Candles* in 1966. The "trash epic" played to sold out crowds. Services: Sun 8:30 and 10:30 am. Tours following the latter. Self-guided tour brochure available.

Did You Know?

Long before Wallis Warfield Simpson, the future Duchess of Windsor, ever lay eyes on King Edward VIII, Betsy Bonaparte sent shock waves through Europe. Daughter of William Patterson, Baltimore's second richest man, Betsy infuriated Napoleon by catching the eye of the French dictator's younger brother Jerome at a party in September 1803. Jerome, a spoiled youth taken to wearing flashy uniforms, had come to the gala. As he approached Betsy and her friend Henriette Pascault, Henriette pointed to a member of Jerome's retinue and announced, "I will marry that one." "Then I will marry the other," Betsy reportedly countered, eyeing Jerome. They both kept their promises and Betsy became Bonaparte on Christmas Eve.

Baltimore society was scandalized. First, Betsy's father had opposed the match but reluctantly acquiesced. Then there was the gown, a clingy form revealing thin sarcenet with white crepe. The ladies of Baltimore harrumphed that the new Madame Bonaparte would have to don more clothes if she wanted the pleasure of their company.

Meanwhile Napoleon, who planned to strengthen his position by marrying his wayward sibling off to European royalty, threw an imperial fit, denying Betsy entry into France. Jerome, swearing his eternal love, swept off to Paris, leaving his unhappy wife to give birth to their son in London. The ill-fated duo never spoke again. Napoleon annulled the marriage and Jerome wound up with the kingship of Westphalia.

Betsy reluctantly returned to Baltimore in 1840. When she died at age 94 she was living alone in a rooming house on the corner of Cathedral and Read.

BELVEDERE

A few years after the Revolutionary War, John Eager Howard stood on his 700-acre Howard's Woods estate and envisioned his dream house. From the mansion that arose, a fine Georgian with two wings, Howard could see the harbor. Inspired, he called his home Belvidere or "beautiful view." Over the years, a legion of famous guests like Washington and Lafayette journeyed out to visit.

Meanwhile Howard, who'd served as a Revolutionary War commander, Maryland governor, and US senator, sold or gave his land away to churches like the Basilica, Mount Vernon Methodist, and Old St. Paul's Episcopal, as well as to public institutions like the Washington Monument and Lexington Market. Howard died in 1827. John McKim owned Belvidere during the Civil War but in 1875 urbanization and the extension of Calvert Street doomed the mansion.

Homes of Famous Women...

As an orphaned teenager, Gertrude Stein came from California to stay with her aunt in Reservoir Hill. She moved to this brownstone and brick house at 212 E. Biddle during her Hopkins medical student days. When academics no longer appealed, she turned to writing experimental poetry and prose, some of it based on her Baltimore experiences. Following her Bohemian instincts, she moved to Paris in the early 1900s and established a famous salon frequented by upcoming art and literary luminaries like Hemingway, Fitzgerald, Picasso, and Matisse. It was Stein who introduced sisters Claribel and Etta Cone to modern art and helped inspire their collection now in the Baltimore Museum of Art.

Across the street at 215 E. Biddle, Wallis Warfield Simpson—the future Duchess of Windsor—grew up. Her father, the socially prominent Teackle Wallis Warfield, died shortly after her birth, forcing her mother Bessie to move to this modest mansard-roofed rowhouse. Smart and attractive, Wallis collected admirers, among them Navy Lt. Earle Winfield Spencer who she married in 1916. By 1928, Spencer was history and Wallis went off to wed shipping businessman Ernest Simpson in England. Wallis dazzled London society, particularly with her culinary masterpiece Chicken à la Maryland. Whether it was her mysterious ways with poultry that sent the Prince of Wales' heart aflutter or her non-culinary charms, the future king was hooked. Gossip swirled around the enraptured couple, especially when the Prince took the throne as Edward VIII in 1936. In December of that year the King announced over the radio that he was giving up his kingdom for "the woman I love." They married the following June, taking the title Duke and Duchess of Windsor. On October 13, 1941, business in Baltimore halted and thousands jammed Charles Street as the waving royal twosome rode in their convertible from City Hall to a reception at the Baltimore Country Club.

...and Illustrious Men

Samuel Shoemaker, who lived at 901 N. Calvert, ran the Adams Express Company, which transported anything and everything, including dead bodies and one live one (see "The Baltimore Civil War Museum" in *Little Italy*) by river, coach, and rail to the West and South during the 19th century. At No. 915, John O' Donovan conceived and founded the Maryland Hunt Cup, a point-to-point horse race that first ran in 1894 out in Green Spring Valley. Several doors down No. 937 was the home of pathologist Dr. William H. Welch, one of the founders of Johns Hopkins School of Medicine and Hospital.

MARYLAND CLUB

1 E. Eager St. 410-727-2323
Baltimore society men found their escape at this elite private club. Founded in 1858, the social club, then located at Franklin and Cathedral, chose Betsy Bonaparte's boy Jerome as its first president. With the outbreak of Civil War, the Club's pro-South sentiments got it in a

passel of trouble. General Ben Butler put it on notice, training his cannons up on Federal Hill in its direction, and General Lew Wallace, who'd later author *Ben Hur*, opened a center for homeless ex-slaves there in 1864. The club moved to its new quarters here, a Romanesque Revival behemoth of Beaver Dam marble in 1891. Despite its charter charging the club to extend hospitable courtesies to strangers, non-members who walk beneath that green awning today and step inside onto those fine oriental rugs will be ushered outside posthaste.

THE BELVEDERE

1 E. Chase St.

A young Wallis Warfield, the future Duchess of Windsor, sipped tea here with a gaggle of girlfriends. Mencken downed a few at the German-style bar. Presidents stopped by for dinner and Clark Gable and Carole Lombard stayed on to sleep.

Beneath its mansard roof crown, the Belvedere (now spelled with an "e") reigned as Queen of Society. The construction of the $1.7 million Beaux-Arts hotel had attracted crowds who gawked at its 188-foot height. On its opening in December 1903 the hotel immediately drew a galaxy of guests. Local ladies sat among the Tea Room's potted palms in front of the large ornate fireplace sipping India's finest imports. Visitors who wanted to chat or read gravitated to the Palm Room with its lattice-work walls, Tiffany skylights, and chandeliers shaped like bunches of grapes. Business meetings, shows, and even children's dance recitals were held in the 12th Floor assembly room with its stage and musicians' balcony. However, the jewel in the crown was the ballroom where couples dined and danced among masses of flowers, caged canaries, and other lavish decorations.

One of Baltimore's favorite haunts was the Bar at The Belvedere. The bar was for manly men—guys who liked to aim a wad at the spittoons, slug back Maryland rye, and when the mood struck them, brawl. Ladies, naturally, were not allowed. Businessmen wheeled and dealed, gentlemen told jokes, and bookmakers collected bets.

When the intellectual "discussions" got physical, occasionally even the waiters resorted to fisticuffs. Of course, the owls, two large bronzes that sat watch over the bar, were the most famous feature. Legend goes that Colonel Consolvo who owned the hotel from 1917 to 1936 used the creatures as a signal during Prohibition. If whiskey was available, they'd blink. Other wags deemed them a sobriety test. If you saw them flutter their lids, you'd had too much.

The Depression sent the hotel into receivership and enterprising manager John Folger, looking for a new draw, decided to give the Tea Room a make-over. He renamed it The John Eager Howard Room and hired artist Verna Rogers to paint murals of old Baltimore over the Japanese rice paper wallpaper. Several changes of ownership marked the hotel's downhill tumble. At the hotel's nadir, in the 1970s, it was rented as a college dorm. Students indulging in collegiate sports like beer spilling, spray paint obscenity art, hallway roller tournaments, and impromptu demolition derbies left the old grand dame dangling another foot in the grave. At the auction block, Baltimore entrepreneur Victor Frenkil pulled an 11th hour rescue and restored the building to its former splendor. Unfortunately, the owls, those bar mascots, had flown the coop years earlier. Then in April 1977, the owls mysteriously flew back through locked doors and past the watchman.

Nowadays the Belvedere is a condominium and home base for Truffles, a catering company. Weddings, parties, and business meetings are held here. The 13th Floor nightclub (see Night Life) and the Owl Bar (see Epicurean Bites), a florist, and other shops are open to the public. By the way, if you stop by the Owl Bar for a drink and dinner and see the birds blink, don't drive!

WILLIAM P. DIDUSCH MUSEUM OF THE AMERICAN UROLOGICAL ASSOCIATION

1120 N. Charles St. 410-727-1100

The displays of urologic instruments and contraptions used in days of yore to plunge the urinary system may make stout-hearted men weak. But those with a yen for bygone eras of medical practice should find this small museum's displays fascinating as they trace urologic progress from the 14th century to present day. Included in the artifacts is a replica of a 1782 catheter, devised by Benjamin Franklin for his brother. By appointment. Free

EMILY POST'S CHILDHOOD HOME

14 E. Chase St.

America's etiquette queen Emily Post spent her childhood here in the late 19th century. In 1922 she wrote her *Blue Book of Social Usage*, which set the tone for polite society and she continued to set mannerly matters straight in a syndicated column until her death in 1960. Her father, architect Bruce Price, helped design several buildings in Baltimore including the Albion Hotel and the nearby Christ Church, now New Refuge Deliverance Cathedral. Private.

NEW REFUGE DELIVERANCE CATHEDRAL

Chase and St. Paul Sts. 410-752-6524

This old stone church began life in 1872 as Christ Protestant Episcopal Church and drew a congregation of Gilded Age society. Twenty-year-old Wallis Warfield married her first husband, Navy man Lt. Earle Winfield Spencer, here in 1916, a matrimonial stepping stone to her ascent to Duchess of Windsor a little more than two decades later. Today the Gothic structure houses the New Refuge Deliverance Cathedral. Services Sun and Wed.

ROSS WINANS' HOUSE

1217 St. Paul St.

This huge French Chateau fired fevered imaginations of Baltimore when it went up on this corner in 1883. Folks dubbed it "the house of mystery," perhaps owing to its eccentric owner Ross R. Winans, who sunk a chunk of the family fortune in its 46 rooms. Winans, whose wealth derived from his grandfather's and father's railroad car building empire, hired the famous Stanford White to design the residence. White gave him a four-story brownstone and brick fantasy with towers, dormers, chimneys, and a steep roof. Inside, grand ornamentation—oak paneling, carved plaster-work, leaded glass—festooned the surprisingly modest-sized rooms. In 1914 Girls' Latin, a prep school, occupied the building, followed by William Cook's funeral parlor, which, in addition to its mortuary ser-vices, rented rooms to those who cared to spend a night beneath the same roof as the deceased. Next, doctors offices bumped out the corpses, and in 1995 that white knight of preservation, Agora Publishing, took over, restoring White's gem for offices.

ST. IGNATIUS CATHOLIC CHURCH
740 N. Calvert St. 410-727-3848

In 1855, the Jesuits opened their new Loyola College and High School building on Calvert Street. A year later, the second building of the Loyola compound, St. Ignatius Church, opened its iron doors to overflow crowds of worshippers, which included many promi-nent Baltimoreans. The lower church in the basement served African American parishioners until they started their own congregation several years later (see *Washington Hill*). In 1921, the college moved to Charles Street and the high school to Towson in 1934. By the late 1960s the parish had dwindled and the archdiocese considered closing the church. However, after Center Stage moved in (see below) to the old seminary build-ing, the neighborhood started turning around and St. Ignatius got a reprieve. Today the Jesuits maintain an active social ministry and run Saint Ignatius Loyola Academy, an educational program for culturally diverse, low-income middle school students.

The interior of the brick church features ornate plas-terwork and a marble altar flanked by pillars and topped by an elaborate arched cornice. Among its trea-sures are an ivory crucifix donated by John Eager Howard's wife and paintings of St. Ignatius, The Sacred Heart, and St. Aloysius. The church is open during the Sunday 10:15 am mass, which features a Peabody

Institute-trained choir. Other masses are held below in the Chapel of Grace.

CENTER STAGE

700 N. Calvert St. 410-332-0033
In 1974 two disgruntled ex-employees of Pappy's Beef and Beer Bar planned revenge by burning down the North Avenue establishment. The perps, no Einsteins, crawled into the wrong basement and torched Center Stage instead. Like a phoenix, the theater group rallied. *Who's Afraid of Virginia Wolf* went on the next night at the Baltimore Museum of Art. From there the group moved on to the College of Notre Dame to finish out their season. Meanwhile Loyola College came up with an offer the theater group couldn't refuse. They donated their vacant seminary on North Calvert. The mid-19th century building, however, was falling apart and infested with rats. From the ruins, architects James R. Grieves Associates fashioned the 541-seat Pearlstone Theater, offices, and work areas. In 1991 a second stage, the Head Theater, was added. The new space offers great flexibility with moveable two-tier seating modules that can be rearranged to fit various productions and a stage that can convert from proscenium to thrust to theater-in-the-round. Playgoers stopping for coffee or other libations in the Chapel Bar will find vestiges of the building's seminary past like painted glass windows and niches for shrines (see *Standing Ovation*).

WATERLOO ROW

West side of 600 block Calvert St.
When Robert Mills, architect of the Washington Monument, proposed developing a row of houses here overlooking a swamp, Baltimoreans, ever the disbelievers, scoffed and called the project Mills' "Waterloo." Undeterred, he forged ahead and built his houses— three-and-a-half stories with marble steps, and iron work railings on the outside, double parlors with elaborate plasterwork on the inside. Despite the early skepticism, Mill's little row hung around until 1969 when

the heavy foot of urban renewal crushed them into oblivion. Today the site holds luxury apartments and the remnants of Mills' "folly" can be seen at the Baltimore Museum of Art.

Browse and Buy

Perhaps this area's proximity to the Walters has attracted stores that appeal to artsy types. On First Thursdays, galleries sponsor art openings and several stores extend evening hours until 8 pm.

ATOMIC BOOKS

1018 N. Charles St. 410-625-7955
www.atomicbooks.com
"Literary find for mutated minds" proclaims the sign and indeed this store delivers. Books on fetishes, tattooing, and piercing along with Sizzlin' Sisters comic books, Betty Page bondage photos, and French girlie trading cards. For further viewing pleasure, there's a small cabinet of curiosities containing a stuffed four-legged chicken, a two-headed fetus (a fake once used to illustrate the dangers of incest, alcoholism, or nuclear fallout), and other Ripley's-Believe-It-Or-Not-type oddities.

DREAMLAND

1005 N. Charles St. 410-727-4575
Just a glance at the Silver Glitter Dreamland sign says it all. Inside it's Ricky Ricardo smoking jackets, 1950s Ralph Kramden bowling shirts, Jackie O. pillboxes, Theda Bara vamp bracelets. Rows of crinolines and hats dangle from the ceiling. There's a slew of James Dean black leather jackets and enough fake leopard to outfit

a stuffed animal petting zoo. No wonder film and TV costumers shop here—not to mention drag queens and the terminally hip.

FINDINGS

1011 N. Charles St. 410-783-9393

Interior designer Rita St. Clair scours the world to find unique home furnishings like antique Indian jugs, carved tables from Thailand, sleek sidechairs from Italy, and Indonesian picture frames. It's all displayed in her jewel of a showroom, an 1860s townhouse with its paneled library and stained glass windows.

McLAIN WIESAND

1013 Cathedral St. 410-539-4440

McLain Wiesand custom-designs and fabricates wonderful decorative art metal and wooden furniture. For the impatient, there's a small selection of handcrafted pieces for sale in the front of the shop.

MEREDITH GALLERY

805 N. Charles St. 410-837-3575

A chair that's made out of giant sponges? A tall chest with triangular drawers? Every two months Meredith Gallery launches a new exhibition of Furn-Art-Ture—artists' unique, and often whimsical, takes on home furnishings.

QUESSIE LEATHER

827 N. Charles St. 410-625-8214

Owner Quessie Natibu has been hand-tooling leather bags and belts for more than three decades. Several years ago he added African art—mudcloth from Mali, Senegalese dance bags, kente cloth vests, asanti stools, and verdite sculptures—to his inventory.

Epicurean Bites

AKBAR

823 N. Charles St. 410-539-0944

The smell of curry wafts up as you step beneath the yellow awning and enter this basement level Indian restaurant. Tandori specialties, paneers, vindaloos and curries, a bargain lunchtime buffet, and an attentive staff have made this a Charles Street classic. L, D. $½

BRASS ELEPHANT

924 N. Charles. 410-547-8480

Originally a private residence for a branch of the John Eager Howard family, today the four-story building exudes romantic elegance. Dine on Continental dishes like cioppino, cashew-crusted chicken, and Idaho brook trout stuffed with crab, shrimp, and mushrooms in the Elephant's many dining rooms—a front parlor with elaborate plaster moldings, a middle room with carved Moroccan teakwood doorways, and the glass-roofed Atrium with doors of bull's-eye glass encased in lead. For lighter, less expensive fare, head for the upstairs lounge. D. Reservations recommended. $$$

THE BREWER'S ART

1106 N. Charles St. 410-547-6925

This eclectic restaurant, located in a fine old townhouse, is one of the few brew-pubs in the country that makes Belgian beer. The brewing takes place in the big copper vats located to the rear of the dining room. Entrees and appetizers span the European continent: steak-frites, bouillabaisse, tapas—and the desserts are not to be missed. D. $$

DONNA'S COFFEE BAR

2 W. Madison St. 410-385-0180

Just steps from the Washington Monument and the Walters, Donna's offers a small but marvelous menu of salads, sandwiches, pastas, desserts—and most importantly, good coffee. In warm weather, sipping iced cappuccino and people watching are a favorite activity from the sidewalk tables. B, L, D. $

HELMAND

806 N. Charles St. 410-752-0311

Culinary masterpieces such as aushak (leek-filled ravioli served on minted yogurt) or kaddo borawni (pumpkin on yogurt garlic sauce) have earned this Afghan restaurants a place among Baltimore's best. It's all served in an intimate brick-and-white dining room with displays of turbans, ethnic dresses, and oriental rugs. D. Reservations recommended. $$

MINATO/CAFE VIET

800 N. Charles St. 410-332-0332

Japanese and Vietnamese food come together in two restaurants with different menus sharing the same space. Confused? Let's put it this way: you can order sushi and teriyaki from Minato while your tablemate orders bun thit nuong, skewered pork served over rice noodles, from Cafe Viet. No matter which part of the continent you choose, save room for the plum wine ice cream. L, D. $½

OWL BAR (THE BELVEDERE)

1 E. Chase St. 410-347-0888

Mencken drank at the big oak bar. When prohibition threatened to put a damper on the camaraderie, owner Colonel Consolvo hid barrels of booze in the basement (see "The Belvedere"). Today's patrons need not fear a shortage. Twenty beers on tap complement the regional American menu. A pizza oven and raw bar serve both lounge and table patrons in the patterned brickwork restaurant. L, D. $$

113

THE PRIME RIB

Horizon House, 1101 N. Calvert St. 410-539-1804

With slabs of thick beef that cover entire dinner plates, Baltimore's premier steak house offers an *à la carte* menu geared toward carnivores. The dark paneled dining room and the bar with its leopard skin base and rug exude a masculine sophistication. And, by the way, there's fish on the menu for the cholesterol-impaired. D. Reservations recommended. $$$

THE RUBY LOUNGE

802 N. Charles St. 410-539-8051

This sophisticated and sleek urban bistro offers an eclectic menu. Through the open kitchen, you can watch the chef prepare grilled salmon, fajitas, or whatever seasonal delicacy has seized your fancy. In keeping with its arts location, there's an ever-changing display of paintings in the dining rooms. D. Open Late Thurs-Sat. ☽ $$$

TONY CHENG'S SZECHUAN RESTAURANT

801 N. Charles Street. 410-539-6666

Tony Cheng's lacquered furnishings and white table cloths offer a serene setting to enjoy Mongolian pork, fresh squid saute Michael, or old standbys like chow mein and vegetable fried rice. L, D. Open late Fri & Sat. ☽ $½

The city may appear to be sleeping, but night owls will find kindred souls at area restaurants and bars, as well as the clubs listed below.

CLUB CHARLES
1724 N. Charles St. 410-727-8815
ZODIAC RESTAURANT
1726 N. Charles St. 410-727-8815

This two-decade-old lounge is a favorite hang out for students, twenty-somethings, artists, theatergoers, and hip locals who crowd the narrow room and spill into the upper area on weekend nights. A Wurlitzer, lights bubbling, plays Fiona Apple, Frank Sinatra, the Pet Shop Boys, the Gipsy Kings, and yes, Brigitte Bardot. And in honor of patron John Waters there's a *Pink Flamingo* sound track CD. When hunger pangs strike step next door into the Zodiac restaurant for comfort food like crab cakes, hot turkey and gravy, or vegetarian specials.

Club Charles: nightly 6 pm- 2 am.

Zodiac: D. 🌙 $½

HIPPOPOTAMUS
1 W. Eager St. 410-547-0069

Gay or straight, folks have fun at the Hippo. Up front there's the Saloon Bar with its pool tables and pinball machines where every other Tuesday night Sinatra and Streisand wannabes take a turn at the karaoke mike. A smokey video bar pulsates with MTV-type videos on some nights and transforms into a piano bar on others. Thursday through Saturday the main action takes place in the Dance Room where beneath the glint of a mirror ball, couples and singles alike gyrate on the sunken dance floor to the DJ's choice. Not to be missed are theme parties like Bonnet Ball when outlandish chapeaux are *de rigueur*, Amazon night when Tarzans along with Janes of both sexes cavort among the grass hut bars, and the 4th of July when Uncle Sams and Lady Libertys boogie. Or just sit back and be entertained by the Hippo's occasional drag show. Ladies tea dances first Sunday of the month. Saloon bar daily. Dance Room: Thurs-Sat.

115

13TH FLOOR AT THE BELVEDERE

1 E. Chase St. 410-347-0888
Hotline: 410-783-1332

Ride the elevator up to the 13th Floor and boogie to live bands. Rock 'n' roll to Jr. Cline and the Recliners, groove to Jump Street's blues, reggae to the Kelly Bell Band and well, mambo to Mambo Combo and rhumba to Rhumba Club. Wallflowers and the lead-footed can opt for gazing at the panoramic views of downtown, Mount Vernon, and Penn Station. Wed-Sat. Music at 9:30.

H.L. Mencken, F. Scott Fitzgerald, and a good many of Baltimore's literary lights lifted glasses here at the **Peabody Book Shop and Beer Stube at 913 N. Charles St.** Siegfried Weisberger, wanting to recreate the cafes of his native Vienna, opened The Stube at the rear of his bookstore in 1933 and crammed it with tables and chairs and personal mementoes. A stag head gazed in amusement on walls cluttered with paintings, framed poems, and photographs. When new owner Rose Hayes took over in 1957, she installed vaudevillian Dantini the Magnificent, a fumbling magician who never did perfect his tricks, and added a second floor lounge with a large television set for those occasions when conversation lagged. Alas, when Hayes died in 1986, the sounds of laughter and tingling glass faded away. Eleven years later the wreckers' ball did the rest.

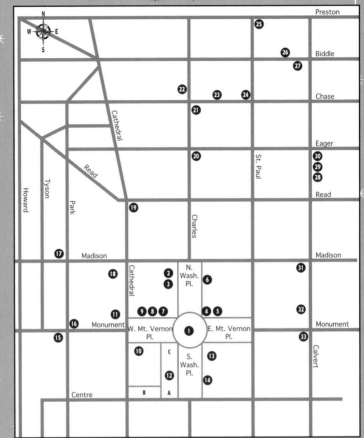

Mount Vernon

1. Washington Monument and Museum
2. Graham-Hughes House
3. Stafford Hotel (former)
4. Mount Vernon Place United Methodist Church
5. Asbury House
6. Museum of Incandescent Lighting
7. Romanesque Revival House
8. Tiffany-Fisher House
9. Marburg Mansion
10. Garrett-Jacobs Mansion
11. 702-704 Cathedral St.
12. Walters Art Gallery
12A. 1904 Building
12B. 1974 Building
12C. Hackerman House
13. Peabody Institute
14. Schapiro House
15. Maryland Historical Society
16. Grace and St. Peter's Episcopal Church
17. First and Franklin Street Presbyterian Church
18. Baltimore School for the Arts
19. Emmanuel Episcopal Church
20. Maryland Club
21. The Belvedere
22. William P. Didusch Museum
23. Emily Post's Childhood Home
24. New Refuge Deliverance Cathedral
25. Ross Winans' House
26. Gertrude Stein's House
27. Wallis Warfield Simpson's House
28. Samuel Shoemaker's House
29. John O'Donovan's House
30. William H. Welch's House
31. St. Ignatius Catholic Church
32. Center Stage
33. Waterloo Row (former site of)

Cultural Center and Bolton Hill

Institutions associated with education, culture, and travel mark the Cultural Center, as the Mount Royal area to the north of Mount Vernon is often called. The Pennsylvania Railroad built a succession of train terminals here, culminating in its paean to the locomotive, the grand Pennsylvania Station on North Charles Street in 1911. Its rival, the B&O, had already seized a big hunk of the passenger trade with its classy Mount Royal Station and its north-south connections 15 years earlier. The automobile, too, vied for the traveling Baltimorean's dollar, and dealers like Kelly's Buick (now the Academic Center for the University of Baltimore) and The Monumental Motor Car Company at Mount Royal and Maryland Avenues offered cars as an easy escape from the confines of city life.

In the late 19th and early 20th century, academies like Friends School at Park Avenue and Boys' Latin on Brevard arose. The Bryn Mawr School, which opened in 1888, was fueled by feminist goals of giving girls a good preparatory education. It had a track, swimming pool, and gym—most unusual amenities for that era. Two decades later the Maryland Institute moved into its palazzo on Mount Royal Avenue, followed by the University of Baltimore over on St. Paul in 1925. The district also became a cultural hub as the Lyric (1894) and its 20th century companion-in-performing-arts the Meyerhoff brought in the show and concert crowds. Sitting on the edge of the action is Bolton Hill, a 170-acre historic neighborhood of 19th century houses.

Annually, in July, Mount Royal Avenue and Cathedral Street burst into Artscape, a three-day festival of song, art, literature, theater, food, and poetry. The corridor's stages resonate with music from African to folk rock to zydeco as the sounds of sitars, zithers, drums, vibraphones, and horns fill the air. Celebrity performers like Gladys Knight add star glamour while courageous bards face their critics in poetry slams or just sit back and listen to readings and one-act plays. Even John Waters has shown up to expound on his unique brand of movie making. A car show, films, videos, literary contests, exhibits of paintings, sales booths of photographs, weaving, and art galore round out the festivities.

Sights & Sites

EVERYMAN THEATRE

1727 N. Charles St. 410-752-2208

The seed for one of Baltimore's newest professional acting companies was planted when then-college student Vincent Lancisi visited the Everyman Theatre in Liverpool and saw a Shakespeare for the masses. Lancisi carried the idea of an affordable, accessible theater into graduate studies at Catholic University where he sought a venue to establish such a theater. Charm City didn't win an audition until 1988 when the artistic director of D.C.'s Woolly Mammoth Theatre put in a plug. Two years later, Lancisi made the move up I-95 and debuted the Everyman Theatre at St. John's Church, where a lack of heat had the company handing out blankets along with the playbills. In 1994, Everyman settled into its Charles Street home where it produces dramas like *The Trip to Bountiful, Cat on a Hot Tin Roof*, and comedies like *All in the Timing*.

CHARLES THEATRE

1711 N. Charles St. 410-727-3456
www.thecharles.com

Moviegoers watched Japanese kamikaze pilots dive-bomb ships and US troops slash through jungles back in the early 1940s at the city's first all-newsreel playhouse, then called the Times Theatre. But as television came in with its faster news coverage, the management switched to features from B movie studios like Republic and Monogram. *Donovan's Brain* flickered across the screen along with classics like *When Strangers Marry*. By 1979 the Charles had found its niche. First run art movies like *The Last Temptation of Christ* and *Howards End*, the second coming of *Pink Flamingos*, and other artsy gems now grace its 486-seat theater. Its new addition includes a cafe along with four new smaller screens showing first run art and repertory programs.

PENNSYLVANIA STATION

1500 N. Charles St. Amtrak 800-USA-RAIL

Anywhere from 3,000 to 7,000 passengers cross these terrazzo floors daily, making this the Amtrak station with the fifth largest ridership in the country. When the station opened in 1911, replacing two previous terminals, the Pennsylvania Railroad, ever cognizant of the B&O's beautiful Mount Royal Station, must have felt it was giving its former competitor a final *coup de grâce*. With its mahogany benches, Sicilian marble walls, Rookwood tiles, and leaded glass skylights, the grand Beaux-Arts-Neoclassical structure outmassed and outclassed its less flamboyant rival. Even nowadays at night, its terra cotta-and-granite facade bathed in light, the station sits on a rise like an old Greek temple.

Today Penn Station services Amtrak, MARC, and Light Rail passenger trains. Come Fall 1999 a new high speed line traveling at 150 mph promises to whittle the interminable trek to Boston down to a more manageable five-and-a-half hours. An underground garage provides parking. The city is redoing the Charles Street entrance and bridge and is building a ramp to the Jones Falls Expressway.

UNIVERSITY OF BALTIMORE

1420 N. Charles St. 410-837-4200
www.ubalt.edu

Back in 1925 civic leaders banded together to start a private school for working Baltimoreans who wanted to study law or business at night. The fledgling college opened at the corner of St. Paul and Mount Vernon Place with 62 law and 114 business students making up its first class. Today the 4,600-student school, now part of the University System of Maryland, offers a full-time liberal arts day program along with its law and business curriculum. Over the years, UB has purchased a variety of buildings like the Baltimore Athletic Club and Kelly Buick and converted them into classrooms and offices. Among the university's graduates were former vice-president Spiro Agnew and former mayor and governor William Donald Schaefer. Edgar Allan Poe didn't go here but he does have a statue in the student plaza inscribed with this line from "The Raven": Dreaming dreams no mortal ever dared to dream before.

LYRIC OPERA HOUSE

Mount Royal Ave. and Cathedral St. 410-685-5086

On Halloween 1894 the Lyric Opera House made its debut. Australian soprano Nellie Melba collected cheers from the orchestra, balcony, and boxes for her rendition of Handel's "Sweet Bird." Over the years bravos followed for Enrico Caruso in the Metropolitan Opera's production of *Marta*, Leopold Stokowski, Eugene Ormandy, through hundreds of musical comedy stars to tenor Chris Merritt and bass James Morris who've starred in Baltimore Opera Company productions. Mike Sullivan and Joe Gans boxed here. William Jennings Bryan delivered an oration. Charles Lindbergh and Amelia Earhart told their adventures, Will Rogers cracked jokes, and Aimee Semple McPherson won converts. Somewhat plain on its modern outside, the house's interior, designed after the Gewandhaus in Leipzig, Germany, is Baroque with ornamentation like angels, lattice work bronze railings, and names of famous composers encased in gilt above the balcony portals. Along with being home to the Baltimore Opera, the theater hosts Broadway show road companies and other events.

REVOLUTIONARY WAR MONUMENT

Mount Royal Ave. and Cathedral St.

On this sliver of a triangle the allegorical figure of Liberty stands atop a slender column, grasping a laurel wreath of victory in one hand and a scrolled

Declaration of Independence in the other. Better known to locals as The Maryland Line Monument, this memorial was erected in 1901 by the Sons of the American Revolution to honor all Marylanders who fought in the Revolutionary War and, in particular, the Maryland Line. Also known as "the Bayonets of the Continental Army," the Maryland Line fought in almost every American conflict with the exception of the Civil War. (See "Fifth Regiment Armory and National Guard Museum.")

MOUNT ROYAL STATION
MARYLAND INSTITUTE COLLEGE OF ART

Mount Royal Ave. and Cathedral St. 410-669-9200

In the late 1890s passengers embarking from their trains entered one of the most up-to-date railroad stations in the country. The station, a long horizontal granite building with arched windows that could have graced a palazzo, sat on a lawn landscaped with shade trees and flowers. A Romanesque clock tower announced "B&O" in electrified letters.

The station was born out of a vexing problem—the B&O Railroad was missing a link between its southern and northern Baltimore terminals. The solution was a tunnel beneath Howard Street. Royal Blue Line train number 514 chugged through the completed tube on May 1, 1895, and four months later the new station opened its ticket counters. In 1966 the Maryland Institute College of Art bought the building and converted it into sculpture studios, offices, a foundry, auditorium, and gallery space. Also located here is the Rinehart School of Sculpture, a graduate program named in honor of famous alumnus William Henry Rinehart whose statues stand in the Walters and Mount Vernon Square.

MARYLAND INSTITUTE COLLEGE OF ART

1300 Mount Royal Ave. 410-669-9200
www.mica.edu

When the grand Italianate Maryland Institute downtown melted away in the Fire of 1904, Andrew Carnegie and the state of Maryland contributed funds to build this Renaissance Revival palazzo. A grand marble staircase stage center anchors a large two-story court with marble and mosaic floors. Below the frosted skylight is a ring of friezes embellished with the names of Italian Renaissance artists like Bernini, Giotto, and Raphael. Around the room, sculptures provide models to sketch. The Institute, one of the country's top art schools, has studios, darkrooms, and administrative offices here. The lower level holds a small student gallery.

Across the street, past the metal rooster—one of several sculptures that brighten the Mount Royal median strip and sides—stands the Fox Building. Along with classrooms, the former shoe factory contains galleries exhibiting work by renowned artists, faculty, and students. Next door, the Bunting Center houses the visual communication and illustration departments, new library, and more gallery space. Needless to say, all this talent on display offers a golden opportunity for art lovers to purchase works of up-and-coming artists.

JOSEPH MEYERHOFF SYMPHONY HALL

1212 Cathedral St. 410-783-8000

In an auspicious moment in 1965, developer Joseph Meyerhoff became president of the Baltimore Symphony Orchestra. Seventeen  years later, thanks to Meyerhoff's generosity and leadership, the BSO moved into this modernistic curved sculpture of glass and brick. The hall, with its sleek blonde wood interior, is renowned for its acoustics enhanced by a ceiling of precast concert "clouds" or sound-diffusing baffles over the orchestra seating and by 18 curved plaster sound-reflecting disks suspended above the stage itself. The 2,462-seat theater replaced an 1888 Romanesque Revival building that once housed the Bryn Mawr School, a young ladies' prep school established by B&O heir Mary Garrett and her friends, and the later Deutsches Haus, a German-American social center. The hall, currently undergoing renovation, will have an even more enhanced acoustical system in place by Summer 1999.

GREEK ORTHODOX CATHEDRAL OF THE ANNUNCIATION

Maryland Ave. and Preston St. 410-727-1831

In 1937 a Greek Orthodox congregation rescued this 1889 Romanesque Revival building, formerly a Congregationalist church, from being razed for a gas station. The Cathedral's graceful rounded exterior belies the interior's structure. Inside one first notices the lack of a domed ceiling. The flat overhead surface was installed in the 1960s as a result of water damage and to hide lights and other mechanicals in the conical dome. A large balcony curves around the rear of the nave and a wrought-iron and brass chandelier hangs near the entrance. The iconostasion, a wooden screen of painted and carved icons opened during parts of the Divine Liturgy, separates the altar from the nave. Four Tiffany windows, three beneath the balcony and a circular one near the altar, grace the recently renovated interior. In 1978 the Cathedral added The Annunciation Orthodox Center at 25 West Preston Street (410-528-0154), which holds a 15,000-volume library and archives plus a ballroom. Divine Liturgy: Sun 10 am. Tours by appointment.

FIFTH REGIMENT ARMORY
AND THE MARYLAND NATIONAL GUARD MUSEUM

29th Division St. at Dolphin and Howard Sts.
410-576-1441

Tucked into a corner of the Fifth Regiment Armory, the Maryland National Guard Museum is a treasure house of Maryland military memorabilia, especially that of the state's premier volunteer fighting force, the Fifth

Regiment. Known throughout much of its history as "the Dandy Fifth" for its colorful dress uniforms and elite status, the Regiment traces its ancestry to a small militia formed in 1774, later absorbed into the Fifth Regiment of the Continental Army. These Marylanders developed a reputation as a ferocious fighting unit in the 1776 Battle of Long Island where they stood as the last line of defense between the British and Washington's beaten, retreating army. Their courageous action saved thousands of lives and earned them the title, "The Maryland Line." During the War of 1812 at the Battle of North Point, the land-based portion of the two pronged British attack on the city, the Maryland Line battled enemy land forces while the invading fleet bombed Fort McHenry in a vain attempt to capture the Port of Baltimore.

The Fifth Regiment fought in every American war with one exception. As went the country in 1861, the unit found its loyalties divided between North and South. The majority joined the Confederate Army while the remainder fought under the Union flag. In several battles, including Gettysburg, former Fifth Regiment members found themselves fighting against their former comrades. After the war, the regiment reformed in 1867, adopting a conciliatory emblem, a circle half blue and half gray. The Fifth Regiment fought in both World Wars, most notably as part of the 29th Division, landing at Normandy Beach on June 6, 1944. Much of the museum collection is from both World Wars, including uniforms, arms, flags, and photographs. The museum's smaller Maryland Room houses an array of uniforms and other memorabilia from the Fifth's Union soldiers. There are also some rare photographs of John Wilkes Booth which the actor used as calling cards in the custom of the day. By appointment. Donations accepted.

ARENA PLAYERS
801 McCulloh St. 410-728-6500
Back in 1953, when this African American acting troupe started, Baltimore was a segregated city where blacks and

whites didn't share stages or auditorium seats. Working on volunteer power, the company began mounting productions, over the years offering everything from *Pygmalion* to the recent *The Servant of the People: The Rise and Fall of Huey P. Newton and the Black Panther Party*. Persevering through thin times, when there were only a handful in the audience, the company had to scrounge for a stage to present their shows. The players solved that problem in 1961 when it took over an empty church hall where it found itself sharing space with caskets and mortuary supplies. Eight years later the players bought the building and renovated it into a 300-seat theater. Today the Players, now the country's oldest African American theater company still in operation, feature a variety of plays from musicals to dramas.

TYSON STREET HOUSES
Between Park and Howard Sts. off W. Read St.
These tiny houses, originally part of the estate of Elisha Tyson, a Quaker farmer and activist, were built in the 1820s and later inhabited by Irish immigrants who wove rugs in their tiny backyards. After the Civil War, African American laborers moved in. By the end of World War II, the small dwellings needed facelifts along with major repairs. Urban homesteaders, wanting to live in central city, rescued the small row in the '50s and painted it in a rainbow of colors. Look for the rare 18th and 19th century fire marks above or near the front doors (see "Fire Museum of the Baltimore Equitable Society" in *University Center*). Private.

EUBIE BLAKE NATIONAL JAZZ INSTITUTE AND CULTURAL CENTER
847 N. Howard St. 410-625-3113
A cascading tinkle of the ivories, a driving, thumping boogie-woogie bass. Close your eyes and you're transported to...New York? Harlem when the Cotton Club and jazz were king? Wrong. Welcome to turn of the century Baltimore, the home of Eubie Blake and other jazz greats. And though the focus of the Eubie Blake Center is, of course, on the man who honed his musical talent

in East Baltimore, wrote "Wild About Harry," and co-authored the Broadway musical *Shuffle Along*, the center also commemorates several of Blake's contemporaries and other Baltimore jazz luminaries like Cab and Blanche Calloway, Billie Holiday, and Chick Webb. Among the Blake memorabilia are recordings, original scores, photographs, playbills, and movie clips documenting this prolific composer's life. The Center also acts as a regional resource for both established artists and aspiring students of the performing arts. Every February the Center commemorates Blake's birthday. Call for exact date and location.

Browse and Buy

ANTIQUE ROW
800 Block N. Howard St.
Antique Row grew out of the cabinetmaking workshops and artisans' studios that dominated this section of North Howard Street in the 1800s. Craftsmen built and sold tables, chairs, and other wares on the lower levels of their homes and lived upstairs. This is where John and Hugh Finlay made their famous Baltimore furniture—fine English-style pieces with pictures of mansions like Belvidere and Rose Hill and even St. Paul's carriage house. It's rare to find these or any of the distinctive Baltimore bell-flower design furniture here nowadays (although E.A. Mack recently had one of the latter with a five figure price tag), as museums and wealthy collectors have snapped them up. To view examples of Baltimore furniture, visit the Baltimore Museum of Art.

With the demolition of the old buildings for Maryland General Hospital, the district which once flanked Howard has been reduced to the east side.

AMOS JUDD & SON, INC.

841-843 N. Howard St. 410-462-2000

The Judds have been retailing fine 18th and 19th century Continental art, accessories, and furniture for more than two decades and are one of the area's premier refinishers and restorers of brass.

ANTIQUE TREASURY

809 N. Howard St. 410-728-6363

The shop features a variety of dealers, including Richard Sindler, offering a trove of Russian icons, bronze statuary, Chinese antiquities, and other *objets d'art*; dealer Alice S. Marks, specializing in Staffordshire-transferware china; and Thelma Hilger, selling porcelain, art, silver, and jewelry. For collectibles and larger pieces of furniture, try the top floor.

BOGART'S ANTIQUES AND RESTORATION

861 N. Howard St. 410-728-4517

Bogart's is a hospital for wounded antiques. Whether it's a porcelain ballerina figurine with a shattered foot, a torn portrait of Great-Aunt Millie, or ruined mirror, Bogart's can restore it. They also have a small selection of antiques for sale.

CROSSKEYS ANTIQUES

801 N. Howard St. 410-728-0101

This is Nirvana for serious collectors who can afford a carved 17th century English canopy bed or an elaborate German Baroque sideboard. Tucked among the exquisite furniture on this former circa 1830 flower shop's three floors are wonderful old paintings, lamps, and other home accessories. By the way, if some of the antiques look familiar, that's because they've been used as props in movies.

DRUSILLA'S BOOKS

817 N. Howard St. 410-225-0277

Nostalgic for Nancy Drew, Tom Swift, or a set of Little Golden Books? Drusilla Jones specializes in antiquarian children's books for collectors. She also carries vintage volumes on Victoriana, leather-bound sets of literary classics, as well as books on art, antiques, and book collecting. In addition she offers a book search, appraisal, and collection development service.

E.A. MACK ANTIQUES

839 N. Howard St. 410-728-1333

Big time antique dealers and serious collectors make E.A. Mack a must-stop on their buying tour. The shop specializes in the best of period American furniture with some period English and related decorative accessories. Occasionally museum-quality Baltimore pieces grace the showroom floor.

HARRIS AUCTION GALLERIES, INC.

875 N. Howard St. 410-728-7040
www.harrisauction.com

Since 1955 Harris Auction Galleries has been offering antiques, art, and collectibles to the public as well as dealers. Auctions are held on various Sundays throughout the year and sale items are available for examination during auction week from Wednesday through Sunday. Call or check the website for information and catalogs.

IMPERIAL HALF BUSHEL

831 N. Howard St. 410-462-1192

American antique silver and hollowware is lovingly displayed and well-labeled here. Look for "Baltimore Silver," with its *repoussé* or relief pattern hammered in from the reverse side, crafted by artisans like Samuel Kirk in the early 1800s. The shop also carries some English and Continental pieces.

REGENCY FINE ART AND ANTIQUES

895 N. Howard St. 410-225-3455

There's enough gilt in these showrooms to furnish Versailles. Reproductions of Continental chandeliers, furniture, bronzes, and paintings go for a fraction of the real thing.

R. MARK MITCHELL FINE ANTIQUE CLOCK RESTORATION

206 W. Read St. 410-837-7055

For more than two decades, R. Mark Mitchell, C.M.C., has been repairing antique clocks in his workshop. He also does appraisals and makes house calls for grandfather clocks and other large timepieces. By appointment.

ZAKIYYAH'S ETHNIC VIBE

223 W. Read St. 410-383-9141

Zakiyyah packs this little gem of a store with carvings, cloth, and jewelry from countries like Zaire, Liberia, Cameroon, and the Ivory Coast. Many of the masks and figurines date from the early part of the century. You'll also find Bob Marley portraits, appliqued greeting cards, beaded earrings, and silver bracelets all made by local African American craftspeople.

Epicurean Bites

On Lyric and Meyerhoff show nights, these restaurants get crowded so it's best to phone ahead for reservations. Charles Street eateries (see *Mount Vernon*) are another nearby option.

LA TESSO TANA

58 W. Biddle St. 410-837-3630

Located in the basement of Abacrombie Badger Bed & Breakfast—just steps from the Meyerhoff and Lyric— Tesso Tana (The Badger's Den) is a favorite of opera and symphony patrons. While its menu is packed with traditional Italian favorites like veal *saltimbocca* and *penne alla Bolognese*, specials run to more interesting fare like lamb dijonaise and horseradish-encrusted salmon. L, D. Reservations recommended. $$$

SPIKE & CHARLIE'S

1225 Cathedral St. 410-752-8144

Brothers Spike and Charles Gjerde bring diners savory delights like roast boar chops, duck cassoulet, and oven-roasted monkfish wrapped in applewood smoked bacon. Without a doubt, the warm chocolate tart with homemade kirsch ice cream is worth driving through a snowstorm for. The decor, in colors of sherbet offset by filmy white drapings, evokes visions of sophisticated ladies and dapper gents sipping martinis. Reservations recommended. D. $$$

VICCINO BISTRO

1317 N. Charles St. 410-347-0349

Viccino began as an offshoot of its neighboring pizza and deli shop. As such it offers creative pizzas in addition to antipasto, salads, pastas, and *piatto forte* like *osso bucco* in its quiet softly-lit dining room. L, D. $$

BOLTON HILL AND EUTAW PLACE

Author and resident Frank Shivers likes to point out that Bolton Hill has the ambience of a sleepy, charming late 19th century Southern city. Indeed if one ignores the cars parked along the streets, one could be fooled. Classic red brick rowhouses share the stage with their more ornate neighbors that sing with turrets, elaborate cornices, wrought iron balconies, and mansard roofs. There's even the occasional house with gingerbread trim. But no Formstone. Trees, small gardens, and tiny parks, tucked off alleys or even sometimes in the middle of a street, provide greenery. Come warm weather up go the yard sale signs as residents haul out bric-a-brac and other household goods to sell from their marble steps or makeshift tables. Arabbers or street vendors lead horse-drawn carts down the street, stopping to sell fruits and vegetables to customers who rush out of their houses to buy produce for dinner.

Wedged between North Avenue, Mount Royal on the east, Dolphin on the south, and Eutaw on the west, Bolton

Hill stands on two hills surrounded by a mix of state office buildings, the Cultural Center, and some iffy neighborhoods. The historic district is and has been an enclave for the upper middle class—the wealthy, with the exception of the Jewish merchants on Eutaw, having preferred the loftier climes of Mount Vernon, Belvedere, and points north.

Bolton Hill was carved out of pieces of several former country estates: Mount Royal, an 18th century stone house near Jones Falls; Rose Hill, part of which became Eutaw Place; Lanvale Farm, a produce concern; and Bolton, a grand three-story Federal home owned by merchant George Grundy. The latter, from which the area took its name, stood where the Fifth Regiment Armory is located today. The mansion was razed to build the structure, which in 1912 held the Democratic  National Convention. Coincidentally Woodrow Wilson, a former Bolton Hill resident, won the nomination for President.

In the early 1800s the first streets were laid out west of today's John Street across farms and along where Irish mill workers lived. However, development really took hold when horse-drawn trolleys came out to Druid Hill Park in 1859, and later by the opening of Mt. Royal Avenue. Henry Tiffany, of stained-glass family fame, plotted the grand boulevard of Eutaw Place in the mid-1850s and embarked on constructing its grander homes.

The outbreak of the Civil War evoked an outpouring of Southern sentiment with many residents joining the ranks of the Confederacy. Afterwards, the area became a magnet for former rebels fleeing the ravages of the postbellum South. For instance, Mississippi cotton planter Thomas Dabney, his fortune ruined, took in boarders at his John Street house and even Colonel Charles Marshall, Lee's *aide-de-camp*, took up residence in the neighborhood.

Many settled in the famous red brick rowhouses along Lanvale and adjoining streets. "Simple flat surfaces with holes cut in them," says Shivers, speaking of the three-story structures' classic cornices, white marble trim and their occasional narrow width—sometimes as little as 15 or 20 feet. From the upper windows of their homes, residents could see the harbor and a line of masts, but up here they were cushioned from its smells and grime. In the late 1880s and early 1890s, more elaborate siblings, notably along Park Avenue, went up drawing a more monied crowd. Soon institutions like the Lyric Opera House and the Maryland Institute College of Art moved in, adding a cultural dimension to the enclave.

Did You Know?

By the time F. Scott Fitzgerald and family moved to Baltimore in 1932, their once glitzy life with its French Riviera interludes and New York Jazz Age celebrity was on a downward spiral. The year before, the novelist had written to H.L. Mencken requesting the name of a psychiatrist for Zelda and a bootlegger for himself. Wracked by financial difficulties, Fitzgerald guzzled gin and attempted to write during his five-year stint in Baltimore while Zelda was treated at the Phipps Psychiatric Clinic at Johns Hopkins and Sheppard-Pratt Hospital. Throughout the chaos, daughter Scottie attended Bryn Mawr School. *Tender is the Night* (1934) was published after the Fitzgeralds moved to 1307 Park Avenue that same year. While living at Park Avenue, the author plunged into a frenzied madness which he would chronicle in *The Crack-Up*, a series of essays in *Esquire* later published as a book.

The area had its first setbacks during two depressions in the late 19th century that forced some owners to convert their homes into rooming houses, setting up the odd situation of having prosperous families next door neighbors to clerks. By the 1920s and '30s, the Jazz Age brought the moniker "Gin Belt" and a bit of literary glamour as luminaries like F. Scott Fitzgerald and classicist Edith Hamilton moved in. However, World War II wreaked havoc on the real estate. The demand for Liberty ships created a need for inexpensive worker housing and mansions and rowhouses, especially near Eutaw Place, were hacked into apartments. West Virginians flocked in and for a while the area was dubbed "Little Appalachia." As city dwellers defected to the suburbs, residents, determined to keep their enclave from degenerating into slums or leveled by the steamroller of urban renewal, fought back. They formed a private corporation to buy up properties, rehab and then sell them to responsible buyers. Later the neighborhood, originally called Mount Royal, garnered cachet when resident activists dubbed it Bolton Hill, after Grundy's mansion. Today the neighborhood is a national and city-registered historic district.

Did You Know?

Among Bolton Hill's notable neighbors: F. Scott Fitzgerald struggled with his demons while Zelda descended deeper into madness (a tiny park at Wilton and Bolton commemorates the troubled writer, who was a descendant of his namesake, "Star-Spangled Banner" composer Francis Scott Key); Edith Hamilton, author of *The Greek Way* (1930) and *The Great Age of Greek Literature* (1942); novelist James M. Cain (*The Postman Always Rings Twice* and *Mildred Pierce*); author Gertrude Stein (*The Autobiography of Alice B. Toklas*); Pulitzer Prize-winning journalist Russell Baker; novelist Christopher Morley who penned *ThoroFare*, which incorporated scenes from his Park Avenue youth; early television personality Gary Moore, then Garrison Morfit, grew up across the street from Memorial Episcopal rectory; Ottmar Mergenthaler, the inventor of Linotype, typesetting machines that revolutionized newspaper printing, called 159 W. Lanvale "home"; 127 Lanvale housed bacteriologist Dr. Jesse Lazear, who while working with Dr. Walter Reed on testing Carlos Juan Findlay's theory that yellow fever was transmitted by mosquitoes, got bitten by one of his specimens and died a few days later; and neighborhood tongues were sent awagging when Alger Hiss, who grew up here, was convicted of spying for the communists in 1950.

Bolton Hill is best explored on foot. Resident Frank Shivers' book *Walking in Baltimore* offers an intimate glimpse of this neighborhood.

ROLANDO-THOM HOUSE

204 W. Lanvale St.

Built in 1848, this two-and-a-half story Gothic cottage is one of the oldest houses in Bolton Hill. A bay window, two rooms flanking the entrance, and Georgian details were later additions to Robert Cary Long, Jr.'s painted-brick structure. In 1937, Family and Children's Services of Central Maryland (then Family and Children's Society) bought the house and today use it as offices.

BROWN MEMORIAL PARK AVENUE PRESBYTERIAN CHURCH

1316 Park Ave. 410-523-1542

In 1802, 15-year-old George Brown stepped off the boat from Ireland. His father had founded Alex. Brown & Sons, an importing company that later evolved into the famous investment firm. After becoming a partner, George joined his father and 23 other businessmen in founding the Baltimore & Ohio Railroad in 1827. After the younger Brown died, his wife Isabella honored him by building a "country" church.

The Gothic limestone church was dedicated in a morning and an evening gaslight service in December 1870. In the early 1900s, ten Tiffany windows were installed, two of them reputedly some of the largest ever made. The Chancel window was given as a memorial for US Postmaster General James A. Gary and his wife Lavinia by the Gary family. Tours weekdays 9-1 and by appointment. Sun services: 9 and 11 am.

MEMORIAL EPISCOPAL CHURCH

1407 Bolton St. 410-669-0220

In a city of locked doors, this is one of the few houses of worship that keeps its open. The church's inspiration was the fiery Reverend Henry Van Dyke Johns, rector of the earlier Emmanuel Church, who spurred his parishioners to start a mission for Northern Central Railroad workers near the Bolton freight yards. Upon Dr. Johns' death in 1859, the ladies' auxiliary lobbied for a church commemorating their late pastor.

Although work on the new building began in 1860, its progress was delayed by the Civil War. The 1864 structure is simple in design: a stone facade, a dark wood ceiling resembling an inverted ark, bulls-eye glass windows, and a baptismal fount by the front door. In recent times, Memorial has drawn its congregation from the suburbs as well as the city and continues its outreach legacy with a food pantry and other community services. Open daily. Weekday and Sun services.

JOHN STREET PARK

1300 block John St.

In the 1950s residents coaxed this little park out of the city, turning this lovely block of semi-detached 19th century houses into a pedestrian street. Other Bolton Hill folks took note and more of these green spaces followed.

RUTTER'S MILL PARK

1400 block Rutter St.

Yet another example of good urban renewal, this gem of a passive park with its shade trees, flowers, and brick walls displaced a decaying row of alley houses. Named after 19th century mill owner, the park is maintained by residents.

CORPUS CHRISTI CHURCH

Mt. Royal Ave. and Lafayette St. 410-523-4161

On New Years Day 1891, Cardinal Gibbons and a cadre of robed assistants walked through the early morning mists up the steps of this grand Gothic building to consecrate what was then called the Jenkins Memorial Church. Nearly four hours later, an invitation-only crowd of worshippers stood at the pews as a cross-bearer led a procession of 100 Catholic priests, six bishops, and the ermine-caped cardinal up the aisle to the altar. The church had been built at the deathbed request of Louisa Carrell Jenkins who wanted to honor her late husband, banker and railroad magnate Thomas Courtney Jenkins. In keeping with her wishes, the Jenkins children hired architect Patrick Charles Keeley who'd designed Holy Name Cathedral in Chicago.

The resulting Woodstock granite structure with its subsequent embellishments has echoes of old Italian churches with its magnificent Florentine wall and floor mosaics, symbolic of the communion theme, and its carved marble walls and altars. Stained glass windows in the sanctuary and chapels by John Hardman and Co. contain hand-painted figures from biblical stories, while along the aisles windows emblematic of the Eucharist display vines, golden crowns, and thorns. Side chapels devoted to St. Thomas Aquinas and St. Joseph hold Jenkins family crypts.

The church fell upon hard times in the '70s. The roof was leaking, a tree was growing from a turret, the interior paint was peeling, and the lead was loose on the windows. What's worse, the diocese was threatening to shut the big wooden doors forever. An activist priest Fr. Francis X. Callahan, working with preservation-minded supporters, turned the church around, restoring it to its former splendor. Today, along with services, weddings, organ and piano recitals, concerts are held here during Artscape. Mass Sat 4 pm & Sun 10:30 am.

CONFEDERATE SOLDIERS AND SAILORS MONUMENT

1400 block Mount Royal Ave.

"Gloria Victis. To the soldiers and sailors of Maryland in the service of the Confederate States of America 1861-1865" reads the inscription on this monument as an angel clutches a youth fallen in battle. At the statue's dedication in May 1903, the crowd sang "Dixie."

EUTAW PLACE

Like the Champs Elyseés of Paris, upon which it was modeled, Eutaw Place once housed some of the most prosperous citizens of Baltimore. Conceived in the 1850s by city developer Henry Tiffany, Eutaw Place was constructed in waves that typified Baltimore's architecture and people. The majority of the dwellings are typical of the city's rowhouses in that they have long, vertical lines. However, most also have ornate, custom-designed facades and stand three stories tall unlike the simpler two-story rowhouses in older sections of the city.

The first residents of Eutaw Place and neighboring Madison Avenue were affluent merchants and manufacturing families followed by German Jews in the 1880s. By the turn of the century, the northern sections of Eutaw and Madison were predominately Jewish, and many of the older synagogues had relocated here from downtown and East Baltimore. Among some of the notables were Claribel and Etta Cone whose apartment at the Marlborough at 1701 Eutaw Place displayed their vast collection of 20th century art (see "Baltimore Museum of Art" in *Uptown*).

As America prepared for war in the 1940s, landlords chopped up many of the once-elegant mansions into small apartments for the tide of Appalachian migrants who poured in to work the factories and shipyards. The rich merchants and German Jews had already exited the neighborhood in successive waves along the northwest corridors towards the suburbs. What the landlords did by hacking up the houses, the newcomers completed by trashing the interiors. In the mid-1950s, African Americans began to move into the area from burgeoning neighborhoods along Pennsylvania and Druid Hill Avenues to the west. Today the neighborhood remains racially and economically mixed with many homes individually owned and under restoration.

PRINCE HALL GRAND LODGE AND MASONIC TEMPLE

1307 Eutaw Pl. 410-669-4966

Rejected by a lodge of white Masons in Boston, Barbados-born Prince Hall, a free black immigrant to colonial Massachusetts, instead joined a lodge of British soldiers in March 1775. Yet, when the Revolutionary War erupted, Hall fought for his adopted country, then devoted himself to battling slavery and racial discrimination. Today, however, he is most remembered for organizing the first Masonic Lodge for African Americans at Boston in 1787.

Black Freemasonry spread rapidly in the United States. By 1825, the First Lodge of Colored Masons in Maryland was established in Baltimore, and remains the headquarters of Black Freemasonry in the state. In 1960 Prince Hall Lodge purchased the former Oheb Shalom synagogue for their temple. The Byzantine-style landmark, constructed in 1893 with white Beaver Dam marble, copper roofs, and yellow tiled domes, was truly one of the most beautiful buildings in the city. Rabbi Benjamin Szold, father of Zionist educator Henrietta Szold, led congregations here from 1859-92. The Prince Hall Masons have restored the breathtaking 2,200-seat sanctuary with its original pews, balconies, lighting fixtures, and stained glass windows. The adjoining building houses the Masonic offices as well as those of its sister organization, The Order of the Eastern Star.

The Masons have perpetuated the work of Prince Hall in striving for racial equality. Martin Luther King, Jr. drew thousands when he spoke at the temple on

January 5, 1964, in the lodge's annual commemoration of the Emancipation Proclamation.

KEY MONUMENT
Eutaw Pl. and Lanvale St.
This tribute to Francis Scott Key, a sculpture of the composer in a boat extending his manuscript of "The Star-Spangled Banner" to the triumphant Columbia, was a gift to Baltimore by Theodore Marburg in 1910. Community groups are working with the city to clean up and fix the monument's fountain.

LILLIE MAE CARROLL JACKSON MUSEUM
1320 Eutaw Pl.
Also known as the Civil Rights Museum, this rowhouse belonged to activist and Baltimore NAACP director Lillie Mae Carroll Jackson. The museum, temporarily closed, contains documents, photographs, personal papers, and belongings of Ms. Jackson from the civil rights era. Morgan State University recently acquired the facility and plans to reopen it, after renovation, in 2000. The museum will chronicle the national Civil Rights Movement with a focus on Jackson and other prominent Baltimore leaders.

Browse and Buy

H. LEWIS GALLERY
1500 Bolton St. 410-462-4515
Leave it to a bunch of current and former Maryland Institute students to open an art gallery named after rock star Huey Lewis. They've offered exhibits by *City Paper* cartoonist Tim Kreider, print maker Bill Fick, and other regional artists. Along with paintings, photographs, and

sculptures, shows often freewheel into video. The brass plate under the doorbell lists the name of former tenant The London Shop where First Lady Jackie Kennedy picked up an antique or two for the White House.

MARYLAND INSTITUTE COLLEGE OF ART STORE
1200 W. Mount Royal Ave. 410-225-2276
The tattooed, pierced, and pink mohawked mingle with their less conspicuously-clad peers to purchase art books, discounted studio materials, and supplies in the art college's student store. Happily you don't have to be taking a course to buy here.

THE HIDDEN BEAN
1431 John St. 410-225-9667
Along with the turkey clubs, veggie burgers, and tuna melts, this four-table coffee shop offers carry out specialities that reflect co-owner Patricia Vargas' Latina heritage. In a nod to Bolton Hill's Southern roots, grits are on the menu. B, L.

Cultural Center and Bolton Hill

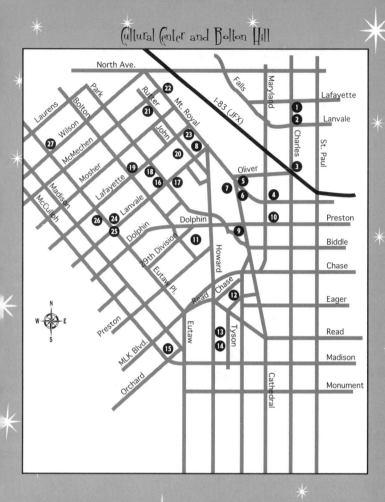

1. Everyman Theatre
2. Charles Theatre
3. Pennsylvania Station
4. University of Baltimore
5. Lyric Opera House
6. Revolutionary War Monument
7. Mount Royal Station
8. Maryland Institute College of Art
9. Joseph Meyerhoff Symphony Hall
10. Greek Orthodox Cathedral of the Annunciation
11. Fifth Regiment Armory
12. Tyson Street Houses
13. Eubie Blake National Jazz Institute and Cultural Center
14. Antique Row
15. Arena Players
16. Rolando-Thom House
17. Otto Merganthaler House
18. Brown Memorial Park Avenue Presbyterian Church
19. Memorial Episcopal Church
20. John Street Park
21. Rutter's Mill Park
22. Confederate Soldiers and Sailors Monument
23. Corpus Christi Church
24. Prince Hall Grand Lodge and Masonic Temple
25. Key Monument
26. Lillie Mae Carroll Jackson Museum
27. The Marlborough (Cone Sisters' apartment)

City Hall District

Historically, the area now known as the City Hall District has been the center of government since colonial days. More recently, in this century, The Block sprawled down Baltimore Street, less than a stripper's runway's distance from City Hall and the courthouse, convenient for the ladies of the night should they need legal representation or to grease bureaucratic palms in those days of yore. Today, The Block, now a tawdry section of strip joints and peep shows, is a mere shadow of its previous pre-television-era self when vaudeville and burlesque reigned.

Slightly less colorful, yet richer in history, are the buildings and monuments around the Clarence M. Mitchell, Jr. Courthouse, City Hall, the War Memorial Plaza, and along Redwood and Calvert Streets. It was a twist of a breeze and fate that prevented many of these buildings from burning in the Great Fire of 1904, when a shift of the prevailing winds turned the raging fires southeast toward Jones Falls and the harbor. To many Baltimoreans at the time, it was an act of Providence that their beloved Battle Monument, official symbol of the city and a testament to the city's victory over the British in 1814, was spared during the conflagration that burned much of downtown. Here's a rundown of what was spared and has been built since then.

CITY HALL
Holliday St. between Lexington and Baltimore Sts.
This imposing 1875 French Second Empire style building with its white marble facade, mansard roofed wings, and 227-foot high dome was renovated in 1975

to create six levels from the original four. Walk to the center of the main floor surrounded by marble columns with an outer circle of marble wall. Look up at the stained glass rotunda crowning the building several stories above. In the Council Chambers on the fourth floor, original brass spittoons still sit at the foot of each member's seat. As an innovative protest against this symbol of male expectoration rituals, former Council woman Barbara Mikulski,

now a United States Senator, planted flowers in her spittoon. The mayor's ceremonial room, not accessible to the public if in use, displays the original chandeliers as well as some original furniture. Look for the brass doorknobs with the city's seal depicting the Battle Monument. In each wing off the rotunda on the main floor, small galleries host rotating displays of local artists and the Circle Gallery, located in the basement, features exhibits of Baltimore school children's artworks. Tours of City Hall can be arranged through the Women's Civic League (410-837-5424).

Did You Know?

City Council Chairman Clarence "Du" Burns was the first African American Mayor of Baltimore, appointed in 1989 when outgoing mayor William Donald Schaefer was elected Governor. That same year Kurt Schmoke became the city's first elected black mayor.

ZION CHURCH OF THE CITY OF BALTIMORE
400 E. Lexington St. 410-727-3939
The German church services held here each Sunday and the concerts that fill the sanctuary with Bach fugues are a reminder of Baltimore's Teutonic past.

German immigrants founded Zion Lutheran Church, as it is known to most Baltimoreans, in 1755 when Baltimore was little more than a hamlet. The present sanctuary, reminiscent of medieval architecture, was started in 1807, and the parish hall and tower added in 1913. The Rev. Julius Hoffman, pastor and guiding light of the church for 60 years, designed the stained glass windows of both upper balconies. The church library of more than 15,000 volumes, several of which are printed from wood-cuts and date to the 16th century, is named after Hoffman.

Zion Lutheran Church maintains its German identity while actively participating in Baltimore life. The church hosts parish festivals and a variety of musical events. The Baltimore Bach Society, founded at Zion, still holds concerts at the church on a regular basis. In a neighborly act of good faith, the church keeps its delightful walled garden open to the public, and many a tired city employee or tourist has found a few moments' respite there. Sun. services: 9:45 German; 11:15 English. Tours by appointment.

PEALE MUSEUM
225 Holliday St.

Rembrandt Peale, one of several sons of noted Maryland-born painter Charles Willson Peale, gave Baltimore several of its most notable "firsts." In 1814 he commissioned this building, the first erected specifically as a museum in the United States (his father earlier established the first public museum in Philadelphia's Independence Hall). Two years later the enterprising artist demonstrated the country's first commercial use of gas illumination here (brother Rubens Peale first developed gas lighting in Philadelphia). Then with several backers, Rembrandt organized the Baltimore Gas Light Company, the first in the country, and in 1817, erected the nation's first gas street lamp at the intersection of Holliday and Baltimore Streets.

The museum floundered financially, however, and in 1830 the building was sold to the city and used as the first City Hall until 1875. The facility then served as the

"Number One Colored Primary School" beginning in 1876, and when higher grades were added in 1883, held the distinction of being the first public high school for African Americans in Baltimore. The building was used for a variety of other civic functions after the school closed in 1887, then reopened in the 1930s as the Municipal Museum of Baltimore. In the 1990s the museum was incorporated with other historical facilities to form the Baltimore City Life Museums, which, unfortunately, ran up insurmountable debts and closed in 1997. Not open to the public.

WAR MEMORIAL

101 N. Gay Street, Room D. 410-685-7530

The exterior of this 1925 Greek Revival building does little to divulge its function and interior elegance. But ask to see the second floor auditorium and you'll find an impressive monument to the Marylanders who gave their lives in World War I. Beneath the auditorium's vaulted ceiling stands a dais and behind it a wall inscribed with names of Baltimoreans who died during the war. Above the names, a niche holds the eternal flame. The remaining three marble walls display emblems of wartime military units and below them, by county, the names of other state veterans who gave their lives. (Scan the roster for some of the more unusual occupations of the war dead.)

The main lobby and first floor halls display photographs depicting these support personnel in the field. While most of the pictures were shot by the War Department, others were taken by soldiers in the field and later donated along with firearms, uniforms, flags, and other memorabilia. The memorial was rededicated in 1977 to honor those who died during World War II and the Korean and Vietnam Wars. Memorabilia and photography from those conflicts are on display as well. The building also houses veterans' organizations. Weekdays 9-3:30. Large groups by appointment. Free.

THE BLOCK

300-400 Blocks E. Baltimore St. and adjacent streets.

"Come on in," beckons the doorman. "Sixteen beautiful girls." Hormones surging, the fraternity boys take the bait. Sailors and soldiers, guys sneaking around on their wives, the occasional slumming couple, and lonely guys cruise these grubby blocks of strip joints, peep shows, and adult video shops. Big Top, Stage Door, Norma Jean's, The Jewel Box. The lights entice with unspoken offers of all-you-can-get voyeurism and cheap sex.

Oh, for the days of Gypsy Rose Lee and Blaze Starr when stripping was an art. In its early 20th century heyday The Block's vaudeville, burlesque, and movie houses spanned more than three blocks of East Baltimore Street. Doormen greeted locals and out of towners flocked in to see entertainers like Jackie Gleason, Red Skelton, and Martha Raye. Ordinary folks along with nobs in tuxes and furs stepped into a Damon Runyonesque world peopled with baggy pants comics, big-bosomed babes, live bands, bookies, boxers, tattoo artists, street hustlers, and military guys celebrating their leaves. Over at the Gayety, Gypsy Rose Lee oh so slowly peeled off her gown and gloves. Blaze Starr blew rose petals off her legendary bosom at the Two O'Clock Club and Busty Russell showed off her 44s. It was entertainment mingled with the forbidden.

By the late '60s, however, the sizzle had fizzled and The Block was edging its way toward the fate of the dinosaur. Vaudeville and burlesque were dead and go-go dancers, peep shows, and drug dealers muscled in along with panhandlers. Meanwhile a new police station at the east end of The Block and later a city office building knocked out several clubs, ripping holes in the red light district. What's more, the sexual revolution had rolled in and Baltimoreans found their amusements elsewhere—in television, X- and R-rated movies, and in their own freer lifestyles.

So what's left on The Block these days? Sure, there's lots of pretty girls (and some pretty boys, too) who step up onto the bar counter, chuck their clothes, and slither along poles to canned music. Other "dancers," as they like to be called, strip with an "it's a job" attitude. They undulate along bar tops and runway stages, shedding bikini tops and bottoms. Even as The Block's club owners talk about installing gas lights and prettying up the old gal, lots of obituaries are being inked. The Internet, cable TV, and the availability of X-rated videos have conspired against The Block. Yet it hangs on, kind of like a washed up chorus girl needing to take another bow.

BALTIMORE INTERNATIONAL COLLEGE
17 Commerce St. 410-752-4710
www.bic.edu
BIC offers a variety of certification, associate degrees, and baccalaureate programs in its School of Culinary Arts and in its School of Business and Management, the latter of which focuses on hotel, food, and beverage management. Besides its 19 buildings in Baltimore (including the Mt. Vernon Hotel and Washington Cafe), the college has a 100-acre campus on an 18th century estate in Ireland. BIC also sponsors Elderhostel programs in ethnic cuisines, wine and beer making, horticulture, holistic medicine, and other related fields. An edible art gallery on the fifth floor features sculptures of flowers, buildings, and other objects created from nonperishable foods. Gallery hours: Mon-Fri 7:30-6:30 pm. Call ahead for entry.

MONUMENT SQUARE
Calvert Street between Fayette and Lexington Sts.
In the center of the square stands the majestic Battle Monument, the emotional heart of Baltimore, built to commemorate the victory over the British in 1814, and now the city's official emblem. Designed by French architect Maximilian Godefroy, the monument is unusual in that it reflects Egyptian architecture, extremely popular in France where Godefroy was trained, and it honors all the men who died in the defense of Baltimore, regardless of rank.

The marble monument's base, meant to symbolize an Egyptian tomb, supports the shaft which represents fasces, the Roman symbol for unity, bound by bands engraved with the names of those who lost their lives at Fort McHenry or North Point. The classic female statue at the top, carved by Antonio Capellano, stands for Baltimore, and displays several symbolic objects: on her head a crown of victory; in her right hand a laurel wreath (glory), in her left a rudder (representing either navigation or steadiness); and at her foot a cannon ball.

Toward Lexington Street stands the Black Soldier Statue, sculpted in bronze by Baltimorean James E. Lewis. Dedicated to the memory of all African American heroes, its inscription reads, "Sleep in peace, slain in thy country's wars." Additional works by the sculptor can be seen at the James E. Lewis Museum at Morgan State University (see *East of Charles Street*).

Did You Know?

Visiting the city in 1827, President John Quincy Adams, duly impressed by the number of monuments in the city, exclaimed that Baltimore truly was "a monumental city." Baltimore has worn this nickname proudly ever since.

CLARENCE M. MITCHELL, JR. COURTHOUSE
100 N. Calvert St. 410-396-5080
To fully appreciate the Courthouse, one should stroll around the building and first take in some of its exterior features. Built in the Beaux-Arts style in 1900, the building occupies a full city block. Its grandeur and elegance are a fitting tribute to Clarence M. Mitchell, Jr., one of Baltimore's leading civil rights activists, to whom the Courthouse was rededicated in 1985. The upper stories of the building are faced with marble from Beaver Dam in Cockeysville while the base is of granite quarried from (where else?) Granite, Maryland. Eight Ionic columns form the facade's loggia. At 31 feet and 35 tons each and cut from single blocks of marble, these are the largest

columns in the world. A decorative balustrade borders the roof's perimeter and is worth an examination for even the undersides of the eaves are intricately carved.

The statue of Lord Cecil Calvert at the St. Paul Street entrance serves as a tongue-in-cheek footnote to local history. Calvert, Second Lord Baltimore and Proprietor of Maryland, organized the first colonial settlement in the state at St. Mary's in 1634 and is remembered for establishing religious tolerance—a concept both noble and novel for the times. The model for the statue of this upstanding first citizen of Maryland was Hollywood's Francis X. Bushman, the Baltimore-born star of the silent film era and previously an artist's model in New York.

During the 1950s the interior of the Courthouse was radically altered, expanding the original three floors into six and eliminating the interior's open atrium—and much of its beauty— in the process. Thankfully, many elegant features of the Courthouse remain. The St. Paul Street Lobby, comprised of Numidian and Sienna marbles and a beautiful mosaic floor, contains a small exhibit honoring the late Clarence M. Mitchell, Jr. and includes mementoes of his accomplishments. The Criminal Court Lobby (Second floor, Calvert St. side), is a marbled room with ornate balustrades, columns, and murals depicting Maryland history. (Barry Levinson filmed the ballroom scene from his movie *Avalon* here with musicians playing from a balcony overlooking the lobby.)

With the combined atmosphere of a French parlor and an English taproom, The Museum of Baltimore Legal History, located in the former Orphans Court, is considered the most beautiful courtroom in Maryland. Parquet floors, a mahogany bench and finishes, plus a mural over the bench, "The British Surrender at Yorktown" by French painter Jean-Paul Laurens, provide an elegant backdrop to the museum's collection of artifacts dating to colonial times. In this small museum you can learn the origin of the term "cutting through the red tape," the history of Baltimore's courthouses, and many of the famous firsts for women and minorities in Maryland law. For tours of the museum and the Mitchell Courthouse, call the offices

of Judge James F. Schneider, 410-962-2820. By appointment. Donations to museum accepted.

FORMER SITE OF SUN IRON BUILDING

Baltimore and South Sts., SW corner

The first major commercial cast-iron-front building constructed in the United States (and probably the world),
was the Sun Iron Building, home for over 50 years to the
Baltimore Sun until it burned in the Fire of 1904. The
structure's success resulted in a building boom of cast-
iron buildings in the late 19th century and the city's
foundries produced and shipped thousands of the iron
facades, precursors of the modern, steel-frame skyscraper, to other cities in the US and abroad.
Regrettably, only a few of these magnificent buildings
remain in Baltimore today, the majority of which are in
the vicinity of the University of Maryland (see "Iron-
Front Buildings" in *University Center*).

ALEX. BROWN & SONS BUILDING

135 E. Baltimore St.

The former headquarters of Alex. Brown & Sons, the
oldest investment and banking institution in the nation,
made it through the Fire of 1904 with a few scars and
burns, only to fall prey to 20th century expansion when
the company moved to new quarters in the city. Now a
branch office of Chevy Chase Bank, the building was
restored to its original grandeur by its new owners in
1996, and it's worth a peek to see, if nothing else, the
original Tiffany glass dome.

The teller's cage replicates one from the early part of
the century, but much of the interior including the marble walls, brass-railed balconies, and rich plaster trim
inside this small bank date back to its construction in
1901. Several portraits decorate the walls, including an
original of King Charles I of England with his son, the
future Charles II. Another depicts company founder
Alexander Brown with his four sons. Also of interest is
the original vault in the basement of the building which
remained locked when the combination was lost for several years. During the 1996 renovations a locksmith

151

finally managed to open the vault, uncovering unopened wedding presents belonging to the Griswold family, descendants of George Brown, one of the original sons. Better late than never.

EQUITABLE BUILDING
10 N. Calvert St.
Before this Romanesque building arose in 1894, Barnum's City Hotel occupied this corner. Opened in 1826, the luxurious seven-story hotel was visited by President John Quincy Adams, Charles Dickens, William Thackeray, Washington Irving, Sarah Bernhardt, Swedish songstress Jenny Lind, and other luminaries. During the Civil War, John Wilkes Booth and co-conspirator Samuel Arnold plotted against Lincoln in the basement barbershop. In 1889, wreckers demolished the aging grand dame and in her place arose the ten-story granite and brick Equitable Building complete with Turkish baths and a rooftop garden. While the building, designed to be fireproof, did survive the Great Fire of 1904, the wooden floors burned and sent safes on one-way journeys to the basement.

MERCANTILE SAFE DEPOSIT AND TRUST BUILDING
Calvert and Redwood Sts.
Not only did this red brick building survive the fire, it withstood the conflagration's hottest flames, estimated at 2,500°F on this corner. Its Romanesque style incorporates broad arches and carved details, such as the "spy holes" several feet above the pavement on either side of the front doors. In the years before high tech security systems, policemen patrolling the street would grasp the iron rings below these small windows and haul themselves up to peer through the narrow openings to see if all was well inside the bank's central room.

Did You Know?

On the front of 206 E. Redwood is a plaque noting this site as the birthplace of the Methodist Episcopal Church in America. The Lovely Lane Meeting House, a simple, one-room structure built in 1774, was one of the first places of worship for the fledgling Methodist Society of Baltimore. In 1784, the Methodists held the Christmas Conference at which the Methodist Episcopal Church of America was formed and elected Francis Asbury, pastor at Lovely Lane, as its first bishop. The Lovely Lane congregation soon outgrew its small meeting house and a larger one was dedicated in 1786 at Light Street and Wine Alley. Over the course of time the church moved to several locations before settling in its permanent home on N. St. Paul St.

LUNCH BREAK

There are several lunch counters in the area offering a variety of sandwiches and light fare. Just follow the crowds or your nose.

HOLLYWOOD DINER
400 E. Saratoga St. 410-962-5379

This 1954 diner may look familiar to movie fans. Originally the Mountain View Diner in Long Island, it was moved to Baltimore in the early '80s to be the centerpiece for Barry Levinson's movie, *Diner*. The small courtyard outside bears the star-studded titles of the films in which the Hollywood Diner has been featured, including the locally filmed television series, *Homicide*. The interior has a cinematic theme for both decor and the menu, which is, after all, fairly typical greasy spoon fare. B, L.

OTTOBAR

203 E. Davis St. 410-752-OTTO (6886)

#%$*^#!%!!!! You can say that or a whole lot more at Ottobar's Cursing Contest. Or you can go eyeball to eyeball with another patron as a cadre of distracters try to break your gaze in the Staring Contest. Perverse Poetry Night, an anti-folk evening, towel fight championships, the Death of Vaudeville (tap dancing violinist, anyone?)—they're all part of the freewheeling fun of this events bar. Ottobar also features touring and local bands playing jazz, punk rock, alternative, and other music. Daily from 9:30 pm. Events and bands Tues-Sun.

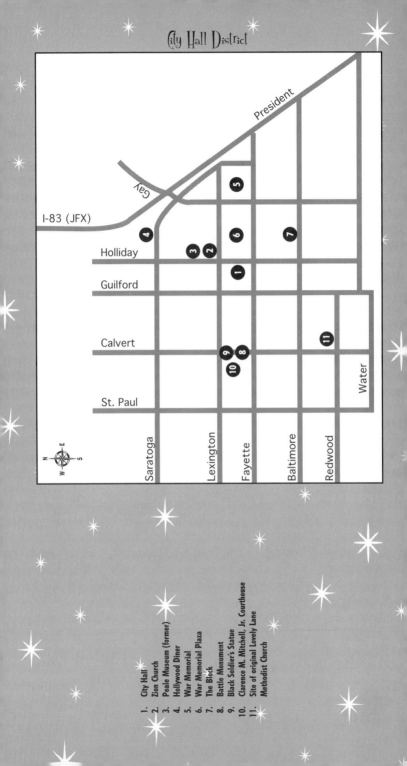

City Hall District

President

Gay

I-83 (JFX)

Holliday

Guilford

Calvert

St. Paul

Saratoga
Lexington
Fayette
Baltimore
Redwood
Water

N
W E
S

1. City Hall
2. Zion Church
3. Peale Museum (former)
4. Hollywood Diner
5. War Memorial
6. War Memorial Plaza
7. The Block
8. Battle Monument
9. Black Soldier's Statue
10. Clarence M. Mitchell, Jr. Courthouse
11. Site of original Lovely Lane
     Methodist Church

University Center

Ninety years ago, a whirring clatter spilled from the windows of several garment factories along Paca and Redwood Streets, the clamor of sewing machines clacketing nonstop 12 hours or more each day. Hundreds of laborers, most of them immigrant women, bent over these machines, stitching and piecing together clothing in factories clustered in this section of Baltimore. The city's garment industry, second only to New York during its heyday from the 1870s through World War I, had modernized by the turn of the century as manufacturers built huge plants stocked with cutting edge technologies that promised increased production. While these new factories eliminated many sweat shops and provided improved working conditions, the men and women who operated the machines or cut thick layers of fabric still labored long hours in settings that would make a modern garment worker shudder. Over in East Baltimore, however, dozens of sweatshops remained, employing hundreds of immigrant men, women, and children in crowded, poorly lit, and unsanitary environments (see *Jonestown*).

Today the same stretches of Paca and Redwood hum with the voices of hundreds of health professionals and University of Maryland graduate students. Several times a day, the drone of a helicopter eclipses all other sounds as critically injured patients are flown from all parts of the state to the university's renowned Shock Trauma Unit, the first to open in the nation. Up the street, Lexington Market, which has sold produce, meats, and baked goods to city residents since 1803, still bustles with crowds of shoppers, especially at lunch time. Some of the old factory loft buildings, now offices and luxury apartments, remain standing amid the university's soaring concrete and glass buildings, reminders of the once great garment industry. Another architectural wonder of 19th century Baltimore, the iron-front buildings, once numbering over a hundred, have not fared so well. Today, only a handful of these buildings remain in the city, the majority of them in or adjacent to University Center.

UNIVERSITY OF MARYLAND, BALTIMORE

520 W. Lombard St. 410-706-7820
www.umaryland.edu

Since its modest beginnings in 1807 as the College of Medicine, the University of Maryland, Baltimore (UMB) has evolved into a 38-acre campus housing the state university's professional graduate schools in medicine, dentistry, law, nursing, pharmacy, and social work. Indeed, the school of medicine was the founding campus for the university, now headquartered at its College Park campus just north of Washington, D.C.

The focus of UMB has always been medical care, teaching, and research. Even today it remains on the cutting edge of medicine and dentistry with its many research institutes, Health Sciences Library, and primary teaching affiliates University Hospital and Baltimore Veterans Affairs Medical Center. The School of Medicine has one of the country's fastest growing research facilities, which has produced numerous medical breakthroughs in the diagnosis and treatment of illnesses like diabetes, AIDS, cholera, and typhoid fever, to name a few (see "Did You Know?" p. 158). The School of Nursing ranks among the top six nursing schools in the country, while the Law School is a national leader in clinical and public service law. UMB currently has over 5,000 graduate students in its 42 masters and Ph.D. programs in health, medical, and social sciences.

Did You Know?

Below is a listing of some of the many medical firsts accomplished at the University of Maryland, Baltimore:

The 1823 Baltimore Infirmary was the first hospital founded by a medical school specifically for clinical instruction. The School of Medicine was also the first to open its hospital wards for bedside teaching, a significant advance in medical education. In 1833, the School of Medicine introduced the world's first preventive medicine course. The Dental School established in 1840 was the first dental college in the world. Dr. David Stewart became the first professor of pharmacy in the country in 1844. In 1853, Dr. Francis Donaldson became the first physician to advocate the biopsy and microscopic diagnosis of malignant tumors. Dr. B. Olive Cole became the first female professor at a School of Pharmacy in 1948, then the first female Dean (1948-49). The R. Adam Cowley Shock Trauma Center, opened in 1961, was the first such specialized trauma facility in the world.

DAVIDGE HALL, SCHOOL OF MEDICINE
522 W. Lombard St. 410-706-3658

Named for Dr. John B. Davidge, the founder and first dean of the University of Maryland School of Medicine, the 1812 Davidge Hall is the oldest medical school building in continuous use in the country. Don't let the age or stature of this National Historic Landmark fool you, however. Davidge Hall has a history of controversy.

At the turn of the century, Dr. Davidge, an Edinburgh-educated surgeon, and two other physicians held lectures in their homes for a handful of students and performed dissections in a small anatomical hall that Davidge built in 1807. When Davidge, needing a body to dissect, acquired the corpse of a man hanged for murder, an outraged mob attacked the hall and destroyed the building. The three physicians sought protection from the State, which created the College of

Medicine of Maryland in 1807, and granted the school protection to dissect corpses for medical instruction. These safeguards did little to quell mobs who attacked anyone even suspected of smuggling corpses into the school, or, worse, robbing graves. Nevertheless, Davidge rebuilt his anatomical hall in 1812 on land purchased from Baltimore mega-landowner John Eager Howard, and carried on with his work despite persistent protests.

A second controversy concerns the architectural plan of Davidge Hall. Until a few years ago the design was attributed to Baltimorean Robert Cary Long, Sr. Recent discoveries suggest, however, that Long was only the builder and French architect Maximilian Godefroy may have designed the building with assistance from Baltimorean Benjamin Henry Latrobe and President Thomas Jefferson, whose Monticello home closely resembles Davidge Hall. The neoclassical building, whoever the architect, is beautiful for its simplicity and functionality, with two circular, interior lecture halls for chemistry and anatomy. The front portico has eight Doric columns reminiscent of the Pantheon of Athens, and the domed roof is borrowed from the Pantheon of Rome. The lecture halls contain prints, early medical instruments, and memorabilia of medicine as practiced in the late 18th and early 19th centuries. Contrary to legend, there are no tunnels leading from Davidge to the Westminster Burying Ground, but the two narrow circular staircases may have been designed to allow corpses to be brought in covertly through the back entrance of the building so as not to incite mob violence. Tours by appointment.

Did You Know?

Riots, jeers, and general rowdiness have long characterized early Baltimore, which has borne the nefarious nickname "Mobtown" since

the early 1800s. By 1812 the British press liberally referred to Baltimore by this title, earned in their eyes when rabble-rousers attacked the printing office of a publisher who had editorialized against America's recent declaration of war against Great Britain. The enraged crowd tore down the offending office and smashed the press. Publisher Alexander Hanson promptly fled town. Surprisingly, he, along with political cronies, returned days later to set up a new press and publish yet another criticism of the incipient war. Again, protesters attacked, attempting to tear down the house and crush the press. This time, Hanson and friends fired back, killing an attacker. The militia came out to control the rioting crowd, and Hanson and his supporters surrendered on the condition they be granted safe haven to the city jail. But as soon as night fell and the militia returned to their barracks, the mob stormed the jailhouse, killing one prisoner and beating the others senseless. Although several rioters subsequently faced trial, all were acquitted.

DR. SAMUEL D. HARRIS
NATIONAL MUSEUM OF DENTISTRY

31 S. Greene St. 410-706-0600
Debunked Myth #1: George Washington never wore wooden teeth. Debunked Myth #2: Tooth worms do not cause cavities. Discover these and many other tooth facts by visiting this colorful, kids-oriented museum on, yes, teeth. But there are exhibits that will charm adults as well. Remember Bucky Beaver and Ipana toothpaste? That classic commercial is displayed here in a giant tooth video box.

The museum's primary theme, how people have sought throughout history to improve the health and appearance of their teeth and gums, is illustrated with fascinating exhibits of instruments, tooth powders and pastes, false teeth, and the evolution of the dental chair. Among the many displays are dentures from Washington (they're ivory) and Mrs. Tom Thumb, the circus midget (hers were porcelain), and a set of instruments made for Queen Victoria's dentist to use on the royal enamel.

160

The museum is named for Dr. Samuel D. Harris, a pediatric dentist from Detroit, who donated $1 million to the construction of the facility. The museum conducts school programs for students pre-K through 12th grade, and offers seasonal, family-oriented programs. Wed-Sat 10-4; Sun 1-4. Closed major holidays. Admission.

The Loft District

The Loft District earned this name because of the large number of lofted garment factories that once existed in the area. The manufacturers turned out everything from men's clothing to straw hats to BVDs and umbrellas, making Baltimore second only to New York City in the needle trade. This historic district roughly comprises the area between Baltimore and Pratt Streets, with Howard on the East and Greene on the West. Most of the lofts have been converted now to apartments, although others, such as the University of Maryland School of Law (the former Schloss Bros. factory) and the Paca and Pratt Building (the former Henry Sonneborn & Co.), function as offices.

The major garment-producing companies, almost exclusively owned by German Jews, were far from desirable work places, but definitely a vast improvement over the notorious sweat shops. The garment industry in Baltimore reached its zenith in World War I, fueled by government contracts to provide uniforms for the military forces. The garment industry never completely rebounded from the post-war slump and by mid-century many of the factories had relocated to countries with low-wage, nonunion laborers.

For additional information on the garment industry in Baltimore, read *A Stitch in Time*, by Philip Kahn, Jr., and *The Baltimore Book, New Views of Local History*, edited by Elizabeth Fee.

WESTMINSTER HALL AND BURYING GROUND
Fayette and Greene Sts. 410-706-2072

The Westminster burying ground bears the remains of dozens of prominent Baltimore citizens, yet no single grave site in the entire city is as well known or visited as the final resting spot of Edgar Allan Poe. His memorial, just inside the gate to the cemetery, was paid for by pennies collected by Baltimore school children in the 1870s. Originally buried in 1849 in his family plot, the author's remains were reinterred, along with those of his wife Virginia and his aunt (and Virginia's mother) Maria Clemm, under this memorial 26 years later. At any given day of the year, visitors place an international mix of coins along with flowers and

wreaths at the monument's base. Japanese aficionados bring incense—Poe being much revered in their country. Yet it is on this master of the macabre's birthday, January 19, that Baltimore's special mystery unfolds.

For nearly 50 years a solitary man slipped into the cemetery in the wee hours to lay three red roses and a half-empty bottle of Martel cognac on Poe's grave. On the author's birthday in 1999, a note left with the annual tribute stated that the Toaster, as he was dubbed, had recently passed away, but not before passing the torch to relatives to carry on the tradition. The rationale behind this half-century old memorial ritual remains unknown, or, at least, unrevealed to the public. Whatever his reasons, the original Toaster held a deep reverence for Poe. A *Life* magazine photographer using infrared lights and camera captured an ethereal photograph of the elderly gentleman, cane at his side, kneeling at the grave in one of his last visits. This photo and other Poe memorabilia are on display at the Poe House and Museum on North Amity Street (see *Camden Yards*).

The burial grounds originally belonged to the First Presbyterian Church, which purchased the land for the cemetery in 1786, and reburied the remains of congregants previously interred at an earlier gravesite on the east side of Jones Falls. When the Jones Falls flooded the old cemetery, a frequent occurrence in those days, the staid Presbyterians were horrified and dismayed to find the coffins of their beloved floating out from underground. The catacombs were formed in 1852 when the Westminster Presbyterian Church was built on arches over the various family plots and crypts in the original graveyard. Many of the crypts still have padlocks on the doors, a leftover from the days when grave robbers raided them for fresh bodies to sell to the nearby University of Maryland Medical School for dissection. Although not officially designated as a stop on the Underground Railroad, it is believed that runaway slaves often hid in the cavernous crypts beneath the church.

The Poe Birthday Celebration is held here each January and a Halloween event honors Poe in the fall. Tours are conducted the first and third weekend April-Nov.

Did You Know?

Is it Poe...or someone else? Try as they might, ghost seekers can't agree whether the elusive apparition seen near Poe's grave is the wisp of the tormented poet or that of a young girl kneeling to pay her respects. Whoever the spirit, no one should be surprised this cemetery is flush with ghosts. Westminster was infamous for its grave robbers, particularly "Frank the Body Snatcher," who by day worked as a handyman at Davidge Hall, but by night, delivered freshly dug up corpses to the anatomy students. Frank became so adept at his nocturnal profession that soon he had a plethora of stiffs, and began shipping them to other medical schools. To preserve the bodies so they would be fresh for the dissection table, Frank shipped them in barrels filled with cheap whiskey, hence the term "rot gut whiskey."

While it is hard to fillet fact from fiction when it comes to Frank, grave robbing did occur, as well as "burking," a practice which dispensed with digging for corpses. Instead, the burkers would suffocate a victim then bustle the fresh body straight to the dissection rooms.

Baltimore's infamous burking case occurred in 1886 when an elderly woman was killed in Pig Alley—now part of Oriole Park at Camden Yards—and her body sold to the medical school. The witless murderers didn't suffocate their victim, but stabbed her and smashed her over the head with a brick. Suspecting the bloody goner lying on their dissection table might not have died by natural means, the doctors notified the police. The furor over the blundered burking resulted in legislation prohibiting trade in cadavers, though citizens tended to give the local medical institutions a wide berth for fear of falling prey to scalpel-wielding medical students.

BROMO SELTZER TOWER
Eutaw and Lombard Sts.

Back in the late 1880s, entrepreneur and eccentric Isaac E. Emerson, a chemist who owned three drug stores, concocted a compound of sodium bicarbonate, citric acid, and acetaminophen. It fizzed and bubbled and brought relief from hangovers and upset stomachs. Emerson, a world traveler, thought back to the effervescent Mt. Bromo, a Javanese volcano, and *voilà*, Bromo Seltzer was born.

The overeaters and drinkers of America sent sales skyrocketing and Emerson, cash burning in his pocket, commissioned architect Joseph Evans Sperry to design the tower and headquarters for his Emerson Drug Company. This time the peripatetic entrepreneur drew upon Florence, Italy, for inspiration. The crowning touch for his business complex was to be a 288-foot high copy of the Palazzo Vecchio. Not only would the tower be the loftiest on the Baltimore skyline but topping the edifice would be a 51-foot tall reproduction of a blue Bromo Seltzer bottle that would rotate twice a minute. But there was more. When it opened in 1911, 596 lights illuminated the 20-foot diameter blue steel icon, making it visible at night all the way to the Eastern Shore. Folks downtown needn't consult their pocket watches either for the Seth Thomas gravity clock had four large faces with the letters B-R-O-M-O-S-E-L-T-Z-E-R encircling the dials.

The bottle stopped spinning in 1936 when engineers discovered cracks in the yellow brick tower and hauled Baltimore's blue monument to hangovers away for scrap metal. Eventually, Warner-Lambert Pharmaceuticals, which had bought out the company, shifted operations to Pennsylvania. Today the Mayor's Advisory Committee on Art and Culture, which redubbed the building the Baltimore Arts Tower, administers a host of public art programs from the city landmark. Not open to public.

Gone but not Forgotten

They were built over a period of a mere 50 years, yet iron-front buildings with their innovative facades and frames ornamented with columns and beams were the precursors to our modern age of steel skeleton sky scrapers. Baltimore once boasted over a hundred of these magnificent cast-iron facades. Today only nine of them exist, of which two have been restored, the Marsh and McLennan building and Blaustein building (see *Camden Yards* and *Jonestown*). More plentiful are storefronts, where only the ground level frontage is of cast-iron.

The iron-fronts presented a major breakthrough in the construction of large, commercial buildings industrialized cities needed to house their businesses, wares, and employees. Although two times the weight of granite, cast-iron possessed ten times the strength, was faster to build with and capable of fine detailing—all factors increasingly attractive to architects. By the late 1840s, the Sun Iron Building was under construction as the first major commercial cast-iron structure in the nation, and the era of the iron-front buildings was underway (see ``Sun Iron Building'' in *City Hall*).

University Center has the highest concentration of cast-iron full-front buildings remaining in the city. Unfortunately, most have not yet undergone restoration. Full iron-fronts: On W. Baltimore Street numbers 307-309, 322, and 407-409 and 121 N. Howard Street. For more information on iron-facade buildings here, read *Baltimore's Cast-Iron Buildings and Architectural Ironwork*, edited by James Dilts and Catharine Black.

HIPPODROME THEATRE

12 N. Eutaw St.

This once-elegant, grand dame of vaudeville and playhouse to mid-century crooners and comedians is getting a face lift. The University of Maryland, which currently owns the 1914 theater, hopes the renovated facility will spark commercial redevelopment in the Eutaw Street corridor. Once completed, the Hippodrome will host large Broadway road productions.

FIRE MUSEUM OF THE BALTIMORE EQUITABLE SOCIETY

21 N. Eutaw St. 410-727-1794

Since the first colonists erected buildings in old Baltimore Town, flames have brought them down despite fire ordinances and building codes. This small museum above one of the oldest insurance societies in Baltimore is packed with the history of the city's fires and the men and equipment that battled them. The Baltimore Equitable Society, founded in 1794, was one of the early fire insurance companies modeled after the system founded by Benjamin Franklin in 1752 in Philadelphia. As more insurance firms sprung up, each had its own fire mark, or emblem, to identify its privately operated fire company as well as the buildings it insured. When the klaxon alarm sounded, competing brigades would race to the scene of the fire, often battling each other to get there first, only to stand aside or leave if the burning building wasn't one of their insured properties. This mayhem continued until 1858 when Baltimore established a municipal fire department.

Located on the second floor of the Society, the Fire Museum houses the largest collection of fire marks in the city, along with an array of fire fighting equipment including early 1800s pumpers. There are also dozens of artifacts on display, many of which can be handled or tested, such as the watchman's klaxon, a larger version of a child's rattle used as a fire alarm, as well as ceremonial and working helmets, fire trumpets and engine models. In addition to memorabilia, there is an extensive collection of photographs, articles, and drawings depicting the history of fire fighting in Baltimore, including sheet music of firemen's ballads. Weekdays 10-4. Free.

ST. JUDE SHRINE

308 N. Paca St. 410-685-6026

At 6:30 in the morning, life in the Market Center of Baltimore is already stirring. While trucks unload at Lexington Market down the street, a steady trickle of people join the small group waiting on the steps of a church. When the doors to the St. Jude Shrine swing open, spilling a glow of lights and candles into North Paca Street, the worshippers file in to pray. All through the day and into the evening, people of all faiths throng to this national shrine dedicated to St. Jude Thaddeus, patron saint of desperate and hopeless cases. They come for hope, solace, or just a brief respite from everyday life. At a time when so many urban churches suffer diminished congregations, the St. Jude Shrine, which has no specified parish, keeps its doors open to a constant stream of worshippers from around the globe.

The church, in the Greek Revival style, was built in 1847 as the Seventh Baptist Church and sold to the Roman Catholic Archdiocese in 1904. Prior to its designation as the national shrine to St. Jude, the church served a local parish of Lithuanian Catholics, but over the years the congregation became predominately Sicilian. Several renovations of the interior have softened the austere lines of the initial design, and the original clear windows were replaced in 1917 with stained glass imported from Germany. Among the rich marble accents and statuary are elegant wall mosaics in the sanctuary and in the alcove housing the St. Jude Shrine.

The sanctuary remains open all day and provides, upon request, audio packs and services written in Braille. The Shrine offers a free concert series twice during the year in late fall and in the spring as well as visual arts shows in December and spring. It also celebrates the feast day of St. Jude on October 28th. Open daily; hours varied. Masses daily. Perpetual novena services Sun & Wed. Visitors' center, gift shop, and offices at 512 W. Saratoga Street.

Did You Know?

According to legend dating to the 1300s, three Sicilian men were awaiting execution for insurrection against the Holy Roman Empire, which then ruled the island. When an unknown woman with a baby in her arms appeared before them, the shackles fell off the prisoners. The governor of Sicily quickly freed the men, saying he was not one to interfere with God's will. In the early 1900s, the Sicilian parishioners commissioned a statue of a woman holding an infant and a length of chain to commemorate this miracle. The statue is located at left front wall of St Jude's sanctuary. A mosaic of the same theme is in the shrine alcove.

LEXINGTON MARKET
400 W. Lexington St. 410-685-6169
The market's 130 stalls offer a smorgasbord of culinary plenty from raw ingredients to an international array of prepared foods ranging from soul food, to deli, to international, to hamburgers. Eat your enchilada or spanakopita standing at a counter or find a table in the market's upstairs gallery. There are even stalls to buy greeting cards, tobacco, kitchen wares, and get shoes repaired. The market can be noisy and crowded especially if you come on one of its festival days, but that's part of the experience. Don't miss Lunch with the

Elephants in March when those mega-ton stars from Ringling Brothers and Barnum & Bailey Circus lumber up Eutaw Street to dine at a groaning board of bananas, carrots, apples, and other pachydermish delights.

In 1782 General John Eager Howard, in yet another one of his benevolent gestures, donated the land for an open-air market, named after the Revolutionary War's Battle of Lexington. In 1803, a large shed was erected to house the stalls. Business continued to boom over the next half century as Baltimore's population swelled. More sheds went up and street vendors or arabbers plied the areas around Lexington with their horse-drawn produce carts (see below). It was around this time that Oliver Wendell Holmes, in homage to the Market, pronounced Baltimore "the gastronomic metropolis of the union."

As immigrants swarmed into the city at the end of the 1800s, market demographics changed and stalls feeding the influx of Italians, Poles, and other nationalities sprung up. By this time the sheds were showing their age and debates over replacing them raged. A six-alarm fire in 1949 finally settled the argument. Within a week a temporary structure went up and three years later a brick marketplace arose. Now, more than 200 years old, the renowned food emporium sports a renovated West Market to go with the larger East Market and Arcade. Mon-Sat 8:30-6.

Did You Know?

If you're not from here, you might find yourself blinking as you come across this interesting Baltimore phenomena—for there in the middle of a neighborhood street is a pony, its ears poking through a flower-decorated straw hat, drawing behind it a colorful wooden cart piled high with fresh fruits and vegetables. It's real. "Hee-up," orders the elderly black man, flapping the reins. And the anachronistic apparition plods east on Lexington headed for downtown.

Arabbers, pronounced "Aaaa-rabbers," have been hawking fresh produce on the streets of Baltimore neighborhoods since before the Civil War. These hardworking seasonal street vendors, now down to two dozen and operating out of three remaining stables, hustle their goodies from mid-March through mid-October. But their a-rabbing days may be numbered. Animal control officers and public health officials pressure the street vendors with rules and regulations from animal rights to stable care and, well, pony poop. The Arabber Preservation Society is fighting back, so maybe Baltimore will have the arabbers' colorful tradition around a few more years.

FAIDLEY'S

Lexington Market. 410-727-4898

Faidley's crab cake has been called one of the ten best foods in the world. And who's to argue? Deep fried or broiled, these all lump crab cakes, made with just enough cracked saltines to bind the meat, have been sending Baltimoreans into gustatory ecstasy since 1886. Eat them standing at the market stall, carry them out, or ship them home. Other Maryland eat-on-the run specialities include hush puppies, fish steak sandwiches, coddies,  gumbo, crab soup, and steamed shrimp. Slurp down oysters on the half shell at the raw bar or have the counterman filet a rockfish or whiting (a lake trout) to cook for dinner. Those with down-home tastes and no time to hunt can buy rabbit, quail, pheasant, raccoon, and muskrat in season. $

CAFE ON THE SQUARE

11 S. Paca St. 410-625-1441

Want to grab a fast bite on the go? Not only is the service quick here but the sandwiches are fat and tasty. Take in the rays along with your lunch in the small park in front of University Hospital. The cafe offers a few tables for eating in, too. B, L, D weekdays. $

DONNA'S

22 S. Greene St. 410-328-1962

Who said all hospital food is lousy? Located in the atrium of the University Hospital, this mini-branch of the local restaurants serves the same delicious lunch menu we've come to expect from its larger siblings. Adapting to the ways of hospitals, self-service pastries and sandwiches are available most of the day, with at-table service from 11:30 to 4. B, L, D weekdays until 7 pm. $½

PENN RESTAURANT

663 Pratt St. 410-752-3606

This family restaurant serves hearty, down-home food of generous portions at reasonable prices. Both restaurant and the carry-out offer American fare mixed with a few Greek standards. B, L, D. $

"You having readings, Hon?" the waitress at the Palmer House on Eutaw Street would ask, pencil poised to take an order. For $15 plus the cost of lunch or dinner, you could have your tarot cards read by a psychic. Twenty-five bucks bought you a palm reading. Going to Palmer House was like entering a time-warp; the food was red sauce Italian and the decor included worn vinyl booths with imitation wood grain tables, threadbare plaid rug, and leftover Christmas roping. A schoolroom portrait of George Washington looked out over the assortment of ladies, lawyers, students, true believers, and gawkers who sought spiritual advice with their

spaghetti. Lauren Bacall, Trini Lopez, Carol Channing, and even Sinatra himself crossed those palms with cash.

The first umbrella in the United States was unfurled by a merchant on the streets of Baltimore in 1772. Legend has it the sight caused women to scream and horses to bolt, but children were thrilled and followed the bearer of the peculiar thingamajig through the streets. The first umbrella factory in the US opened here in 1828.

The first stage coach route in the country was established between Baltimore and Philadelphia in 1773, followed by the first post office system (by William Goddard) the next year.

The first American in flight took place in 1784 when Baltimorean Edward Warren ascended in a hot air balloon from what is now Mt. Vernon Place.

The first electric refrigerator (1803) paved the way for the first ice cream freezer (1848), followed by the first ice cream factory in 1851.

The J. S. Young candy company produced the first licorice in 1869.

Ottmar Mergenthaler invented the first typesetting machine in the world in 1884.

Baltimore Magazine became the country's first city magazine in 1906.

The first revolving restaurant in the US sat on top of the Holiday Inn from 1964 to 1977.

University Center

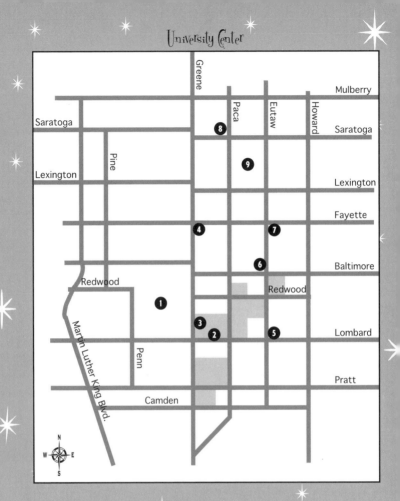

1. University of Maryland, Baltimore
2. Davidge Hall, School of Medicine
3. Dr. Samuel D. Harris National Museum of Dentistry
4. Westminster Hall and Burying Ground
5. Bromo Seltzer Tower
6. Hippodrome Theatre
7. Fire Museum of the Baltimore Equitable Society
8. St. Jude Shrine
9. Lexington Market

(Shaded area = Historic Loft District)

Neighborhoods

Camden Yards to Pigtown

Steam whistles shriek as metal train wheels grind to a halt on steel tracks. Men wrench boxcars apart, then couple new ones with cursing and clanging. Fire roars in the foundries where steel rail ties burn red hot and squealing pigs are herded through a dank alley near the railroad stockyards where lowing cattle mill. In the 1800s, this hellish cacophony greeted the ears of men who worked the train yards, foundries, machine shops, brick kilns, and slaughterhouses between the Camden and Mount Clare rail yards. Despite the continuous clamor and rank odors, this area of southwest Baltimore became home to recently arrived immigrants and freed slaves searching for new lives.

Beginning in the 1830s, and continuing well into the 20th century, the corridor from Howard Street west along Pratt and Lombard to Monroe, north to Baltimore Street and south to Washington Boulevard, was dominated by the almighty B&O Railroad and its attendant industries. B&O investors like John Work Garrett or Robert Oliver grew wealthy off the train system. Laborers lost fingers, hands, and often lives in its service, yet managed to scrape a livelihood out of the grimy, tough work on the rails. Meanwhile workers' neighborhoods grew up in the smoke and shadows of the giant railroad company.

By the mid-1870s Camden Station and the rail yards behind it were the busiest in the city and the star of the B&O line. Indeed, their legacy remains with the city today, although now Camden Yards has become synonymous with Baltimore baseball. But the streets around the yards were not thronged with happy people in the summer of 1877. Hundreds of angry rail workers crowded about, muttering their discontent, waiting for news of striking co-workers in Martinsburg, West Virginia, and Cumberland, Maryland. The year had seen a continuation of the economic depression shackling the nation, hitting the working classes hard. To add insult, B&O president John Work Garrett had just cut workers' pay for the second time in eight months—while simultaneously raising his stockholders' dividends. Rail employees in Martinsburg and Cumberland had put up picket lines four days before, on July 16, and Garrett, fearing a strike in Baltimore would bring his great railway to a halt, had asked the govenor to call up the Maryland National Guard.

As crowds gathered that Friday evening on July 20, the militia commander panicked and pulled the riot alarm. The Maryland Guard's Fifth Regiment reluctantly marched toward Camden Station from their barracks on Howard Street. The swelling masses surrounding the station—estimated at 15,000—erupted, pelting the militia with bricks and stones. A second mob of thousands, in the vicinity of City Hall, similarly attacked soldiers of the Sixth Regiment as they marched from their barracks near the Shot Tower in East Baltimore. As of Saturday evening, several people had been killed, and at the governor's request, President Hayes declared Maryland under martial law and mobilized federal troops toward the city. By Sunday, federal troops were entrenched in camps around Baltimore and the riots fizzled out. However, strike fever spread to other cities and railroad lines, sparking a national protest against miserable working conditions and pay. Ultimately, though Garrett had won this skirmish with his Baltimore employees, the B&O was forced to institute overdue reforms and benefits, including the first pension plan in the country.

Today little of the area resembles the booming industrialization of yesteryear, although occasional freight trains rumble along the southern edges of Pigtown, a remnant of the past dominance of the railroad. Yet some of the neighborhoods retain their old monikers: Ridgely's Delight, Pigtown, Mount Clare, Hollins Market, and Union Square, to name a few, although Little Lithuania has all but vanished now. And, of course, Camden Yards is no longer a railroad hub but the home of the "Birds"—as in the Baltimore Orioles—and another bird-team, the Ravens, the city's NFL football team now roosting in their brand new stadium. Even with this area's historical dominance by the B&O, it does have old ties to baseball, for none other than "Babe" George Herman Ruth, one of baseball's legends, was born in Ridgely's Delight, a long pitch from Oriole Park at Camden Yards.

Sights & *Sites*

RIDGELY'S DELIGHT

A plantation was the dowry John Eager Howard gave away along with his daughter's hand in marriage to Charles Ridgely, who conferred his name on the tract. By the early 19th century, the plantation had given way to simple, two and three-story rowhouses inhabited by laborers and craftsmen. As the century progressed, homes grew larger and more decorative in the styles of the day. Like many parts of the city, however, the vicinity fell prey to suburban flight in the mid-20th century. Luckily, urban homesteading and gentrification have helped revive and maintain this racially and economically mixed neighborhood over the last 20 years. Today it is a quiet enclave, tucked away into a pocket of the city, with most of the houses charmingly restored.

BABE RUTH BIRTHPLACE AND MUSEUM

216 Emory St. 410-727-1539

This narrow rowhouse, so typical of the early 19th century homes of Ridgely's Delight, is where one of baseball's giants was born in 1895. The museum (spread out over four buildings) focuses on the Babe's youth and early baseball years, including his half-season with the Baltimore Orioles in 1914, then a minor league team. The collection includes many items from the Ruth family and Babe himself, a video presentation, and a re-creation of the room in which young George was born. Memorabilia and exhibits from Ruth's professional career with the Red Sox and Yankees will be housed in the new Babe Ruth Baseball Center at Camden Station. Daily, seasonal hours. Admission.

ORIOLE PARK AT CAMDEN YARDS

Camden and Eutaw Sts. 410-685-9800
Tours: 410-547-6234

At the Eutaw Street entrance to Oriole Park, just west of Camden Station, stands a bronze statue of the young Babe Ruth with what appears at first a major league error. The legendary pitcher is holding a right-hander's glove, when, in fact, the Babe was a southpaw. However, as an impoverished 18 year old, fresh from St. Mary's Industrial School for Boys, a reform school, Ruth could not afford to purchase a proper lefthander's mitt and made do with available equipment on loan from the Orioles. A few feet from the statue stand four large aluminum numbers: #4 for Earl Weaver, former manager of the O's, and the remaining three for retired players Jim Palmer (#22), Frank Robinson (#20), and Brooks Robinson (#5). The stretch of Camden Street in front of the Eutaw Street entrance is named "Leon Day Way" in honor of the Baltimore native considered one of the best pitchers of the Negro Baseball Leagues and a member of the Baseball Hall of Fame.

The east side of the ballpark, incorporating the former B&O Railroad Warehouse, resembles a giant box car, running more than 1,000 feet long yet only 52 feet wide. Baseball fans may remember banners unfurled from the windows of the warehouse in 1995, enumerating each game Cal Ripken, Jr. appeared in as he zeroed in on Lou Gehrig's record for the most consecutive games played (2,130).

The alley between the 1905 warehouse and 1992 Oriole Park, a closed-in portion of Eutaw Street, is a hawkers' paradise of food stands and Orioles' paraphernalia. Follow your nose to find Boog Powell's barbecue stand, where the former Oriole often dishes up his famous BBQ along with autographs.

The third floor of the warehouse connects by a bridge to the stadium itself at the luxurious Club Level, where the box owners' plaques read like a "Who's Who" of Baltimore and where spectators can get seat-side waiter

179

service. The bleachers of Oriole Park are by far some of the best in the country, as all but a handful of seats give a full and unobstructed view of the ball field. Two orange seats in the bleachers mark significant Orioles' achievements. The seat in left center field commemorates Cal Ripken's 278th home run, which broke the record for home runs by a shortstop. Although Iron Man Cal now plays third base, he still holds that record. At right center field, another orange seat signifies where Eddie Murray hit his 500th home run and landed himself into the prestigious 500 Homer Club. Also of note, when the Orioles moved from Memorial Stadium to Oriole Park, they brought with them the right field foul pole and home plate. Tours daily during season; off season, variable hours.

"O-R-I-O-L-E-S," the crowd at the old Memorial Stadium would shout as a large bearded man from Section 34 began limning the letters with his beer-bellied body from the top of the Orioles' dugout. It was Wild Bill Hagy, fan and cheerleader extraordinaire, whose ritual dance drove the crowds wild for many seasons until the beefy cab driver dropped out of sight in 1983.

The Lords Baltimore, Baltimore's first African American baseball team, played in a small league in 1887 which included New York, Philadelphia, and Boston. The Baltimore Black Sox won the 1929 championship in the Negro Eastern League. Nine years later, the Elite Giants moved to Baltimore from Washington and carried off the 1939 pennant in the Negro National League and the 1949 Negro League World Series.

Leon Day, who grew up in West Baltimore and pitched for the championship Elite Giants in '49, is considered one of the best, if unsung, all-round players of baseball. In addition to a .300 batting average, Day bested the legendary Satchel Paige in three of the four recorded encounters between the two pitchers, and holds several strikeout records. Day passed away in Baltimore in March, 1995, shortly after his election to the Baseball Hall of Fame.

BABE RUTH BASEBALL CENTER
Camden and Howard Sts.
Long awaited and overdue, this latest museum to baseball will open sometime in 2000. The museum plans to follow the Babe's career from his brief stint with the minor league Orioles through his move to the Red Sox in 1914 to his glory days with the New York Yankees. The museum will also showcase several exhibits on the former Negro and women's leagues, minor leagues, ball parks, and the general history of baseball, and will have a gift shop and restaurant. The museum will be housed in the former Camden Station.

It was an old brewery turned rock emporium, tucked beneath the I-395 overpass on S. Howard St. amid warehouses and factories. Billed as the East Coast's largest night club, Hammerjacks blared out its presence with a big neon sign visible from the highway. Home of wet T-shirt contests, beer swilling kids, and singles on the prowl, music acts ranged from heavy metal to hip-hop to Waylon Jennings. Crazed suburban housewife Beverly Sutphin, alias ``Serial Mom,'' was arrested here in John Waters' 1994 movie. Alas, the cavernous rock palace fell victim to the Ravens' new stadium need for a parking lot. On May 12, 1997, the wrecking ball smashed into the two-story brick building, reducing it to rubble.

PSINET STADIUM AT CAMDEN YARDS

Hamburg and Russell Sts. 410-261-RAVE (7283)
or 410-261-FANS (3267)

One of the great debates of the '90s revolved around (1) would Baltimore get an NFL team? Then after the Ravens flew into town, (2) what kind of football stadium could possibly be compatible with the grand Oriole Park at Camden Yards? Architects HOK Sports Facilities Group, flush from their success with Oriole Park, found themselves in the unique position of designing a stadium which had to blend in with the city and the beauty of their earlier creation. Thankfully, they succeeded in building a state-of-the-art facility incorporating modern technology with a bit of the old. Think of PSINet Stadium as a compilation of the old ditty, "Something old, something new, something borrowed, something blue."

For something old, rich, burgundy-colored bricks provide a burnished arched facade reminiscent of 1920s-era college football stadiums and the historic industrial area south of Oriole Park. For something new, the architects sliced out the four corners of the upper seating deck, allowing the outside world to peek in and giving fans city vistas, making upper deck spectators feel like part of the skyscape. In the borrowed category, the designers used the same sports grass, a mixture of astro turf and natural grass formerly utilized at old Memorial Stadium. And the something blue? Well, those purple seats all over the stadium will just have to do. After all, purple is one of the Ravens' colors.

The seven-level, 69,000 seat facility with its curved, 100-foot long video screens at either endzone, offers dozens of restaurants and concession stands featuring snacks and meals from gourmet hot dogs to crab cakes. The Club Level with its roomy seats, and luxurious sky suites, offers additional watering holes and upscale food vendors. By the way, non-football fans need not despair for the stadium hosts concerts and other big happenings off season. Tours daily.

Did You Know?

Once the greatest team in football, the Colts were lassoed out of town in the dead of night by owner Bob Irsay in March, 1984. Mourning the loss of their beloved Colts for years, Baltimoreans never forgot nor forgave. Just the name, the "Indianapolis Colts" raised a fan's bile. The Baltimore Colts Band, however, gamely played on at events here in Baltimore and at games and parades around the country. In 1998, the proud, high-stepping, cymbalic band members donned new uniforms, picked up their instruments and debuted in the first pre-season game in the new downtown stadium as Baltimore's Marching Ravens. Fans cheered and the stadium rocked.

MARSH AND McLENNAN BUILDING

300 W. Pratt St.

The only completely restored iron-front structure in the city, the Marsh and McLennan building, named for its major tenant, an insurance firm, stands as a superb example of the Renaissance Revival architecture so popular among the cast-iron facades of the late 1800s. In addition to restoring the 1871 building's front, the architects added two set-back flanks which showcase the detailed ornamentation of the Corinthian columns and four stories of arches. At night, strategic illumination highlights the facade (see "Iron-front Buildings" in *University Center*).

HOLLINS STREET NEIGHBORHOOD

LITHUANIAN HALL

851 Hollins St. 410-685-5787

During the 1920s and '30s you could stand in the 800 block of Hollins Street and never hear an English word spoken. This neighborhood didn't earn the moniker "Little Lithuania" for nothing. However, the majority of the second and third generations of Lithuanians began moving out after World War II, and only a handful still live here today. Nevertheless, the Hall retains its traditional spot here in the old community, as does St. Alphonsus Church (see *Downtown*). Although the Lithuanian Festival is no longer held here, the Hall still hosts ethnic celebrations, bazaars, and, not to be missed, The Night of 100 Elvises every December.

HOLLINS MARKET

Hollins and S. Carrollton Sts.

The Hollins Street Market's Italianate building, constructed in 1865, stands as the oldest market building still in use in the city (although the market itself has been in existence since 1835). The Civil War-era building was renovated in the late 1970s, and the center has resurged in popularity the last few years, so that market days bring a plethora of seafood and produce vendors, butchers, and general grocers hawking their wares. Hollins Hall, above the Market, is not in use at this writing, although the local preservation society hopes to obtain funds to renovate it for community use.

The SoWeBo (Southwest Baltimore) Bohemian Arts Festival, a free-wheeling, offbeat celebration of the arts, is held in and around Hollins Market every year in late May. Market hours: Tue-Thurs 7-6 and Fri-Sat 6-6.

UNION SQUARE

Newspaper reporter, author, and editor H.L. Mencken and Union Square are inevitably linked together. Indeed, the "Sage of Baltimore" lived here most of his life, save for the few years he and his wife Sara rented an apartment at 704 Cathedral Street in Mt. Vernon. After she died, he returned to his 1524 Hollins Street home. When Mencken was growing up in the late 19th century most of the neighborhood, like his family, was German. However, by the early 1900s residents from Little Lithuania had spread west into this section of Hollins Street.

In the late 1790s wealthy merchant Thorowgood Smith built an elegant country villa called Willow Brook on several acres of land in what is now Union Square. Smith, however, never lived here. Bankrupted when French raiders hijacked his cargo ships, Smith was forced to sell off the estate at auction. His fortunes soon rebounded and in 1802 he was appointed Baltimore's second mayor (see *Jonestown*).

Following the construction boom of the B&O Railroad in the early 1830s along with successive waves of immigration, inexpensive housing sprang up in pockets around the yards and industrial zone. What had been countryside quickly turned into the sprawling outskirts of the city. The entire southwest section thrived during the second half of the 19th century and into the next. Post-World War II saw many residents desert Union Square for the suburbs, a pattern repeated all over America. But several devotees stayed on and others moved in, and by the late '60s the Union Square Association organized to restore the neighborhood to its genteel Victorian aura. Members contributed funds to replicate the park's original cast-iron fountain. Embedded in its rim are brass plaques representing Mencken's books. Thanks to this civic-minded group, many of the surrounding rowhouses have been renovated, adding 19th century frills such as gaslights and cast-iron grill work. Union Square Park stood in for 19th century New York's Washington Square in the movie of the same title and Barry Levinson's television series *Homicide* has filmed here. *Avalon*, Levinson's tale of Jewish immigration to the city, also used the Hollins Market as a location.

MENCKEN HOUSE
1524 W. Hollins St.

Henry Louis Mencken lived most of his 75 years in this modest, three story 19th century rowhouse. In his memoirs, the crusty author speaks of happy childhood days spent reading here or at the Hollins branch of the Enoch Pratt Library and playing with his younger siblings in the narrow backyard garden. Mencken's study on the second floor of the house, overlooking Union Square Park, was his lair—a man's library, with leather chairs, cigars, and even a spittoon. As a child he first read *Huckleberry Finn*, a lifelong favorite, here and as an adult he wrote at the desk and dozed on the sofa. Unfortunately, the house, a casualty of the closing of the Baltimore City Life Museums, is not open at this time, but residents and city officials are exploring options for reopening it as an independent museum or some related use.

Mencken's father and uncle ran a cigar factory in the late 1800s, but after his father's death in 1899, Mencken felt no compulsion to continue working in the family business. Instead he turned to newspaper work, landing his first job as a police reporter with the former *Baltimore Morning Herald* and later joining the *Baltimore Sun* in 1906. All told, most of Mencken's life was devoted to words. To wit: he spent 43 years as a newspaperman, during which time he penned more than 3,000 columns, authored 30 books (and reviewed other writers' efforts for 25 years), and edited several magazines, of which *The Smart Set* is the best known.

In recent years Mencken has received much criticism, particularly for comments and phrases in his diaries that while politically incorrect today, were part of the *lingua franca* of his time. Yet he encouraged African Americans to do stories for his magazine, suggesting they write honestly about their experiences rather than emulate the white writers of the day. Noted black author Richard Wright was heavily influenced by Mencken, and while not always agreeing with all he wrote, admired the wordsmith for his "surly, funny, and uncompromisingly honest" style.

Did You Know?

The Smart Set, a popular literary magazine from 1900 to 1930, may have discovered and published more unknown talent than any magazine of its era, thanks to editor H.L. Mencken. Literary pieces by authors like F. Scott Fitzgerald, Dorothy Parker, James Joyce, Upton Sinclair, James M. Cain, Dashiell Hammett, and Anatole France filled the magazine. Many of these young authors became better known nationally than Mencken, who preferred Baltimore's slower pace of life to New York and greater literary fame. Instead, Mencken made only occasional train trips to New York to work on the magazine with fellow editor George Jean Nathan.

Mencken and Nathan also collaborated in developing two pulp magazines, *The Black Mask*, for which Mencken tapped budding author and Baltimorean Dashiell Hammett, already a *Smart Set* contributor, and *Saucy Stories*, a romance pulp. The two found screening incoming manuscripts overwhelming and soon turned the pulps over for a profit, but not before establishing *The Black Mask* as the leading mystery magazine of the day.

Hammett went on to write *The Maltese Falcon* (1930) and *The Thin Man* (1934), although he was most fond of *The Glass Key* (1931), a novel based on political corruption in Baltimore, although the city is never specifically indentified.

EDGAR ALLAN POE HOUSE AND MUSEUM

203 N. Amity St. 410-396-7932
http://raven.ubalt.edu/features/poe

Poe lived in this tiny house with his aunt, Maria Poe Clemm, her mother, and her daughter Virginia, who Poe married in 1836 when she was a mere 14. This is not the only dwelling that housed the poverty-stricken Poe and Clemm family in Baltimore, but is the only one left. Today this small house stands among dilapidated public housing as a museum to the father of the mystery novel.

Period furniture and a brief video presentation offer impressions of how Poe lived and wrote. Almost incongruous among the simple furnishings is a fancy china set owned by the author's stepfather, John Allan, which Poe used during his youth in Richmond. The second floor houses Poe memorabilia, including reproductions of Gustave Doré's illustrations for "The Raven," the nefarious obituary written by Rufus Griswold in which he posthumously defamed his former friend, and a lap desk and telescope owned by Poe.

A frequently asked question is whether the house is haunted by Poe. While he won't go so far as to name the father of mysteries himself as a ghostly visitor, the curator does admit that several psychics have claimed a presence haunts the building. And there has been at least one curious incident. A few years ago as an actress dressed for a theatrical presentation of "Berenice," the lower portion of the window in the small second-floor bedroom blew out and crashed to the floor. The pane of glass had moved as if pushed inward from outside, although the window itself was locked and the exterior shutters latched shut. Convinced an angry spirit wanted her out of the house, the shaken actress quickly complied. Despite the fright, dramatic enactments of Poe's stories continue on at the Poe House, usually the second weekend before Halloween. Seasonal hours. Closed Jan-Mar and major holidays. Admission.

Did You Know?

A few blocks northwest of Union Square sits a blighted area of drug dealing, violence, and wasted lives. Journalist David Simon and Baltimore ex-homicide detective Edward Burns have written *The Corner*, a chilling account of the destruction wrought by the crack cocaine and heroin epidemic on people living in this poor section of West Baltimore. Simon's previous bestseller *Homicide: A Year on the Killing Streets* provided an inside look at the city's homicide investigation squad and was made into an acclaimed television show by Baltimore-born Barry Levinson.

PIGTOWN AND MOUNT CLARE

Like Ridgely's Delight, their quieter neighbor to the northeast, Pigtown and Mount Clare developed as 19th century workers' housing around the industries spawned from the B&O Railroad. Pigtown's ignominious name supposedly derives from the pigs that were herded through the streets on their way to the slaughterhouses of South Baltimore from stockyards at the train depots. Cattle were also driven through these same streets, but somehow the older, German nickname of "Kuh Viertel" (Cow Quarter) never stuck like "Pigtown." Newer residents now genteelly refer to their neighborhood as Washington Village, although old-time Baltimoreans prefer the former appellation.

Mount Clare owes its name, like its development, to the old Mount Clare Station, rail yards and shops which the residential area bordered. The yards, in turn, were named for the nearby Georgian manor house of a branch of the Carroll family, which gave a sizable chunk of land to the railroad for their yards.

Pigtown has always been a brew of immigrant workers since its earliest days as the city's southwestern outskirts in the late 18th century. Irishman Alexander Russell established his kilns and brick works here, which soon became the largest in the country. Other industry and businesses followed the railroads, and newcomers flocked to the area for jobs and homes. Germans dominated the mix of immigrants through much of the 19th century, but Irish, Lithuanians, and African Americans filled out the melting pot. And while some old Pigtowners went the way of the 1950s suburban flight, many more have stayed in this racially and economically mixed community, thus preserving its original working class character. In the past decade, Vietnamese workers from the few remaining factories here have started buying homes, thus adding to the colorful ethnic blend.

Did You Know?

Despite having a sprawling environs named "Pigtown," Baltimore is also known as "Charm City," a nickname often attributed to that staunch booster of everything Bawlmer, H.L. Mencken. Alas, research doesn't support this (nor could the curator of the Mencken Room at the Enoch Pratt Library). Here's the deal: In July 1974 two local ad agencies created the moniker while working on a joint community service project for the city. The Baltimore Promotion Council didn't fall over itself bandying this alias about. Instead, it prudently waited to launch the advertising campaign until the simultaneous trash strike and summer heat wave were over.

B&O RAILROAD MUSEUM

901 W. Pratt St. 410-752-2490

Railroad fans will delight in the B&O's topnotch displays, document, and artifacts—not to mention the Roundhouse full of those iron horses of yesteryear. The B&O, the nation's first successful commercial and passenger railroad played a crucial role in the phenomenal development of 19th century Baltimore industry and trade. The Mount Clare Station, built in 1829, was not only the first rail depot in America, but also the terminal to which Samuel Morse sent the first telegraph message in 1844. The main exhibit areas in the new station, an 1851 replacement of the original, and the Annex Building trace the history of the B&O from its conception, to the laying of the cornerstone of the original station by Declaration of Independence signer Charles Carroll, to the investors in this risky enterprise such as Johns Hopkins, Robert Oliver, George Brown, Enoch Pratt, and George Peabody. Other notables mentioned include John Work Garrett, president of the B&O, and Peter Cooper, creator of the Tom Thumb, America's first steam locomotive, built in Baltimore in 1829. Exhibits also cover workers who laid the tracks, maintained and served on the B&O, and the engineers who helped design and operate the massive locomotives. Be sure to take a peek at the second floor of the Annex where miniature-scaled trains puff about on a large model railroad display.

The Roundhouse, built in 1884, remains the largest "circular" (although it actually sports 22 sides) industrial building in the world at 123 feet high and 235 feet in diameter. Originally a passenger car shop, the Roundhouse now displays rail cars and locomotives from the experimental Tom Thumb and stagecoach-style passenger cars of the early years, to troop cars, a rail post office car, and 20th century engines, some of which can be entered. The staff are knowledgeable, long-time rail buffs, so be sure to ask questions.

Behind and to the southwest side of the Roundhouse, just a fraction of the old yards that once stretched behind Mount Clare for several blocks remain. Many cars and engines are on exhibit, such as the old work-horse locomotive the Chessie Allegheny, which hauled coal up and down the Allegheny mountains in the 1940s until the newer diesel engines retired these behe-moths a decade later. The Chessie, the largest steam locomotive at 7500 horsepower and 389 tons, is as tall as the one-and-a-half-story townhouses built for the rail workers, and almost as wide. Climb on up inside the control room where you can see the original valves and levers manned by the engineers, as well as the immense coal hopper and furnace that fueled this monster train engine. At the southeast end of the yard you can catch a glimpse of former rail workers' houses, most restored and still in use, shouldering right up to the old, recent-ly renovated Passenger Car Shop where visitors can see how a working repair shop operates.

The museum conducts excursions throughout the year, as well as Halloween and Christmas special events and activities. The B&O also participates in December's Dollar Day, where several attractions in the city are open all day for one buck admission. Two-mile train rides offered seasonally and on weekends. Teachers and senior citizens discounts available. The museum and Roundhouse also rent out for parties. Daily, 10-5. Closed Thanksgiving and Christmas. Admission.

Did You Know?

Although the B&O began rail service in January, 1830, few Americans today would consider it a railroad by today's definition. The 1830 system consisted of stagecoach-like cars drawn by horses along iron rails. Although the celebrated Tom Thumb puffed its vaporous breath in its debut just a few months later, steam locomotives did not come into regular use on B&O for passenger or commercial service until 1832.

MOUNT CLARE MUSEUM HOUSE

1500 Washington Blvd. 410- 837-3262

Mount Clare, built in 1760 by Charles Carroll, the Barrister (not to be confused with Charles Carroll of Carrollton), is Baltimore's oldest residence and considered Maryland's first museum house. The majority of period furnishings and original paintings in this elegant Georgian mansion belonged to the Carroll family, with many pieces dating to Charles Carroll and his wife, Margaret Tilghman Carroll. The house is flanked by two wings added in the early 1900s as public bath houses and which now contain offices and a reproduction colonial kitchen. Archeological digs are being conducted on plots surrounding the main house where earlier additions once stood.

Charles Carroll contributed to young Charles Willson Peale's art education in London, thus helping to launch the multi-generational painting careers of the Peale family. In return, Peale painted several portraits of the Carrolls, which hang in their original locations in the manor house.

The museum portrays many artifacts of colonial and post-revolutionary history from displays of china, silver, and crystal, to pairs of Margaret Tilghman Carroll's fancy slippers and gowns. Members of the Carroll family lived at Mount Clare until 1850, and the property remained in the family until 1890 when it was sold to the City of Baltimore. During the Civil War, Union officers were quartered in the mansion while troops camped on the property, forming Camp Carroll.

"Christmas at Mount Clare," held the second weekend of December, finds the mansion resplendent with period holiday decorations, music, and refreshments. Closed January and most major holidays. Tours scheduled on the hour, Tues-Fri, 11-3; Sat-Sun, 1-3. Admission.

2600 BLOCK OF WILKENS AVENUE

Drive down this block to see the longest uninterrupted strip (1,800 feet long) of Baltimore rowhouses, complete with marble steps, and designated a city historic district. The houses, constructed in 1912, follow the popular, late 19th century Italianate style. You may even see a housewife or two on her knees scrubbing the stoop. You may also glimpse other Baltimore traditions: folks sitting in front of their houses in aluminum folding chairs, or even a tire planter or two.

Browse and Buy

ORIOLES' BASEBALL STORE

B&O Warehouse, Camden and Howard Sts.
410-332-4633 x158
What would a visit to Oriole Park be without some souvenir of the Birds? Fans can find official Baltimore Orioles merchandise to suit their taste and budget from T-shirts to key chains. Daily.

LUNCH BREAK

NATES AND LEON'S

300 W. Pratt St. 410-234-8100
Try fat slices of Challah French toast or a malted waffle for breakfast, a hefty corned beef sandwich, or a spicy Romanian pastrami sandwich at this nouveau-style diner, or splurge on entrees from grilled salmon to the Blue Plate Special. Floor-to-ceiling windows provide panoramic views of Oriole Park or the opportunity to

just people-watch. Upstairs seating includes a gallery of autographed photos of old-time celebrities like Pinky Lee, Milton Berle, and Jerry Lewis, while downstairs displays decades of Orioles memorabilia and photographs. Outdoor grill on the patio for Orioles and Ravens game day/nights. B, L, D. $½

PASTIMES CAFE

B&O Warehouse, Camden and Howard Sts.
410-332-4633 x155
This cafeteria-style lunch room can be a welcome stop after touring Oriole Park. Homemade soups and a hot order grill add rib-stickers to the standard offerings of sandwiches, subs, and salad bar. Stroll to the back wall and check out the old-time baseball photographs and memorabilia. Can accommodate large tour groups with advance notice. L. $

WATERING HOLES

A number of sports bars are within a reasonable amble to the Camden Yards stadiums, many of which offer specials or parties for both Orioles and Ravens games. Across from Oriole Park on Washington Boulevard are Pickles Pub (410-752-1785), a neighborhood bar with a sports theme, and Sliders Bar & Grill (410-547-8891) which caters its pregame parties towards the under 35 crowd. If you're looking for a friendly, old fashioned bar, stroll west to Ridgely's Delight and check out the cozy Strike Three (410-539-9052), a neighborhood hangout for over 40 years at 633 Portland Street. On Pratt Street is the Camden Pub (410-547-1280) with tailgate parties before Ravens games and menu specials for both teams' events. The Downtown Sports Exchange further east on Pratt features a pre-game barbecue pit as well as a full dining menu. El Bambino's (410-332-4633 x156) inside the Camden Yards Warehouse operates only during Orioles games. The "official" Orioles' Sports Bar in the Sheraton Inner Harbor Hotel (410-962-8300 x7168) features pre- and post-game revelry as well as occasional appearances by past and current players.

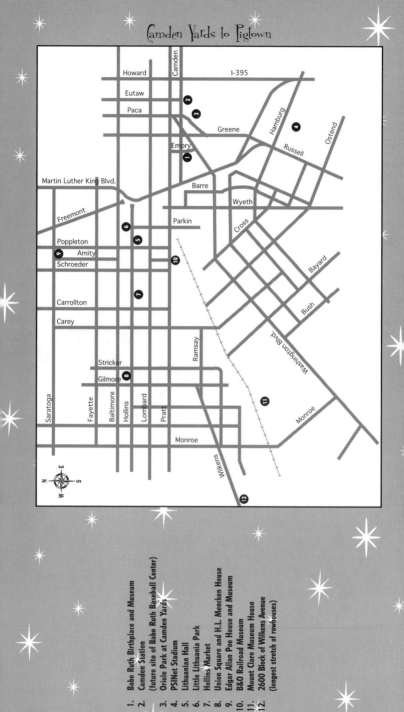

Camden Yards to Pigtown

1. Babe Ruth Birthplace and Museum
2. Camden Station
   (future site of Babe Ruth Baseball Center)
3. Oriole Park at Camden Yards
4. PSINet Stadium
5. Lithuanian Hall
6. Little Lithuania Park
7. Hollins Market
8. Union Square and H.L. Mencken House
9. Edgar Allan Poe House and Museum
10. B&O Railroad Museum
11. Mount Clare Museum House
12. 2600 Block of Wilkens Avenue
    (longest stretch of rowhouses)

Federal Hill and Otterbein

A view from the top of Federal Hill takes in a sweep of the Inner Harbor from Camden Yards on the west, to the red tower of Harbor Court Hotel, past the glass pavilions of Harborplace, the pentagonal World Trade Center, and National Aquarium in the middle, east to the Domino Sugars sign down the Patapsco toward the Chesapeake. Back in 1608, when explorer John Smith sailed into the bay, he wrote in his journal of red clay banks "flanking a natural harbor basin." In less than two centuries, a clay mound further along the harbor would become Federal Hill, but at the time Smith made his observation, the area served as hunting grounds for the Susquehannocks who lived farther north along a river that would carry their name.

The Federal Hill district began with four land grants in the 17th century. By 1782 when the city annexed the site, John Eager Howard had already absorbed most of the acreage into his massive estate. Streets were soon laid out and Federal Hill became a neighborhood.

Shipping industries started filling in the edge of the harbor beneath the mound known as John Smith's hill. Houses for sea captains, merchants, and port laborers went up, and in 1797 the hill became an observatory to watch for incoming ships laden with cargo for local merchants. The hill also served as a community meeting ground for rallies, festivities, and other historic events. In 1788, upon the Maryland General Assembly's ratification of the new Federal Constitution, celebrants partied on its top, giving the area its present name. During the War of 1812, when the British threatened the city and many residents fled north, those that remained watched the British bombardment of Fort McHenry from the hill top, witnessing the "rockets' red glare" that Francis Scott Key wrote about in his "Star-Spangled Banner," composed during that siege. And when the Civil War erupted, Union troops took the hill, training cannons on rebel hot spots in the city.

During the 19th century canneries, breweries, oyster packing houses, shipworks, steamboat building companies, fertilizer and chemical plants, and iron and steel mills moved in. So did pollution. Processing plants fouled the water and perfumed the air with the stench of their by-products. Immigrants came to work the factories, braving long hours, filthy worksites, and frequent injuries. In 1921 Bethlehem Shipbuilding Corporation bought a local shipyard off Key Highway, expanding and stepping up ship repair and refitting operations during the two world wars. Up until recent years, Federal Hill residents could hear the sound of hammers coming from the South Baltimore yards.

By the 1960s the first of the urban homesteaders moved into what was then a down-at-the-heels blue-collar enclave. Then the proposed Interstate 83 threatened to drive an expressway through the heart of Federal Hill, Fells Point, and Canton. Then-neighborhood activist Barbara Mikulski later said in a speech, "They were going to give us a snazzy turn-off into the Inner Harbor so that when you rode through you could kind of look at the dead fish." The commuters never got that view because Mikulski and a cadre of community groups battled the road and won. In the aftermath, preservationists won Federal Hill a spot on the National Register of Historic Places, giving restoration efforts a boost.

Stand atop the west side of Federal Hill today and you'll see rows of gentrified houses sporting sun decks and freshened up brick facades. Now go down and walk around the Hill's 20 blocks and you'll find a charming, livable neighborhood. Much of the Formstone, faux stone facades popular in the '40s and '50s, have been stripped off and the underlying brick repointed and cleaned.

Rows of older houses with their Flemish bond brick and gabled roofs with dormers share streets with their later more ornate Victorian neighbors. The commercial district, with its Federal Hill banners flying from lampposts, centers around South Charles and Light Streets. Charles, the livelier of the two, has more stores and restaurants but with more businesses opening on Light, it, too, should catch up.

Sights & Sites

The Baltimore Architecture Foundation (410-625-2585) presents monthly walking tours of Federal Hill and The Preservation Society (410-675-6750) offers occasional walking and house tours during the year.

AMERICAN VISIONARY ARTS MUSEUM

800 Key Hwy. 410-244-1900

How can you not love a museum that at one point posted a 14-foot statue of Baltimore's late great drag queen and John Waters' diva Divine at the entrance to the first floor galleries? Even better, when visitors tapped her head, she bobbed her Marilyn Monroe coiffure in welcome.

No matter what the theme of the current exhibit—be it apocryphal "The End is Near!" or the lovelorn "Love: Error and Eros"—this outsider art museum celebrates the wacky, the witty, the poignant, and the just plain weird. Visionary art encompasses works produced by self-taught artists who've never dipped a toe into the world of mainstream art (or if they have, they've whipped it right out again). Among their ranks are religious Don Quixotes, the politically disenfranchised, the homeless, the mentally ill, and just plain folks who march to their own drummer. Once a year, the show changes and another parade of these fabulous works, wrung from their creators' passionate obsessions, catapults visitors into yet another unexplored universe. (The captions, by the way, are often as entertaining as the art.)

The driving force behind this museum is founder-director Rebecca A. Hoffberger who began collecting outsider art in the mid 1980s. Like her visionary artists, she, too, pursued her dream—a great canvas of a museum filled with quirky works that offer windows on the minds of their creators. The museum opened in November 1995 to great national applause.

Main Building—This 35,000-square-foot building, sculpted around the curved wedge of the Baltimore Copper Paint Company, is every bit as visionary as the work it holds. Taking the rhythm of the 1913 shell, architects Rebecca B. Swanston and Alex Castro incorporated it into their spiraling concrete vision of galleries, offices, restaurant, and gift shop. Multi-media artist David Hess' staircase, iron fencing with bronze hand-cast balustrades, spans the three levels of galleries devoted to each specially-themed exhibit. Castings of discarded objects are caught up in its bars, like debris from a whirlwind as Hess explains it.

A small gallery of permanent exhibits sits on the main floor. Among its many treasures are the intricate matchstick jewel boxes and a replica of a ship, constructed by Baltimorean Gerald Hawkes whose art career, he claimed, stemmed from a bad mugging. The most moving piece, however, is Mryllen's Coat, a garment embroidered by a young schizophrenic in 1940. Using rags torn from old hospital bed sheets, she covered it with scenes from her life. However, after shock treatments and Thorazine, she could no longer work or even remember creating her masterpiece.

Library—In addition to its collection of scholarship, slides, and books about visionary art, the library also houses the archives of Dr. Otto Billig, Zelda Fitzgerald's psychiatrist and an expert on psychiatric art. The library is open by appointment.

Central Sculpture Plaza and Giant Whirligig—On the central plaza stands Vollis Simpson's 45-foot whirligig, a wind-dri-  ven giant horizontal pin- wheel made of bicycle wheels, car parts, cables, and other discarded objects. This "Calder of the South" con- structed it and others like it in a mule pasture on his North Carolina farm.

Tall Sculpture Barn—The former Four Roses whiskey warehouse (built circa 1900) now houses large sculptures, car shows, and is also used for lectures and parties.

Wildflower Sculpture Garden and Wedding Chapel—In a field of wildflowers sits Ben Wilson's wedding chapel, a rough hewn sculpture made from tree limbs. People do tie the knot here or just walk around contemplating the infinite.

Museum Shop—Elvis and Barbie do-it-yourself car shrines, jewelry fashioned from old typewriter keys, toys from tin cans—you get the picture. Lots of odd stuff fills this small shop in addition to a selection of books and postcards on visionary art.

Joy America Cafe—With its panoramic view and creative culinary entrees, this sophisticated eatery is a good place to sustain the stomach as well as the soul (see Epicurean Bites).

Visionary Village and Center For Visionary Thought—The museum recently won a $5 million dol- lar grant to convert a whiskey barrel warehouse into a "Visionary Village" featuring entire "environments" cre- ated by visionaries with large-minded ideas. A top floor think tank will provide space for movers and shakers to brainstorm creative ways to improve urban life.

Museum open Tues-Sun 10 am-6 pm. Admission.

FEDERAL HILL PARK

Between Battery Ave. and Covington St.
Warren Ave. and Key Hwy.

In 1797 and in the century to follow, whenever ships entered the harbor, lookouts armed with telescopes atop a wooden observer's tower here hoisted the private flags of vessels to alert merchants who had arriving goods. A new observatory complete with a ground-floor ice cream concession replaced the old landmark in 1888. Alas, high winds toppled the tower 14 years later much to the dismay of merchants and butterfat devotees.

The hill also saw its share of dramatic events. Upon ratification of the US Constitution by the Maryland General Assembly, 4,000 Baltimoreans celebrated with a parade to the hill—complete with a wagon pulling a 15-foot replica of a fully rigged ship called *The Federalist* on whose deck stood Revolutionary War hero Commodore Joshua Barney. Revelry, fireworks, and a feast at the top punctuated a grand finale. As the Civil War erupted, just days after the attack on Fort Sumter, a mob of Southern sympathizers hoisted a Confederate flag on the hill and fired a cannon in salute to the rebels. Union supporters, clearly not amused, chased them off. Then in May 1861 General Benjamin Butler marched into town and installed barracks, breastworks, and canons at the heights, training the weapons on suspected hotbeds of Southern radicalism. A 19th century mining operation for silica, used in making glass, created tunnels beneath the park. Some folks say Union troops stowed their beer and ammunition in these underground passages while others insist moonshiners and their customers used them for hiding bathtub brews.

Today dog walkers, people watchers, kids playing ball, and folks out for fresh air climb the steps to the top. Among the memorials scattered on the hill are Civil War canons and statues of War of 1812 heroes General Sam Smith, who directed the city's defense, and Major George Armistead who commanded Fort McHenry.

Despite attempts at stabilizing the hill and controlling drainage over the years, erosion is still a problem.

In 1996 big winter snows and heavy downpours caused a giant fissure to erupt on the northern slope, forcing city engineers and contractors to renew their efforts.

Battery Avenue

This street may look as if Tinkerbell sprinkled fairy dust on it, but it's glasphalt, a mixture of asphalt, slag, limestone dust, and broken glass that provides the sparkle. Back in the early '70s then-City Council President William Donald Schaefer heard about the substance and thought it would solve some of the city's solid-waste problems. The experiment proved expensive, costing nearly twice as much as ordinary paving, so only a few stretches of road in the city ever got this glittery surface.

Montgomery Street and Surrounding Neighborhood

Several years back, in the fever of historic rehabilitation, the residents of this street rolled up their sleeves, tore up the blacktop, and restored the roadbed of 100 E. Montgomery Street to its original stone block. Such enthusiasm shows up in the fine restorations of Montgomery's gold coast of 18th and 19th century houses undertaken in the last few decades. As you walk around Montgomery and its neighboring streets, look for some of the following:

"Incomplete Houses"—Architect and Federal Hill resident Walter Schamu calls these dwellings that sit back from the street along the 100-200 blocks of E. Montgomery "incomplete houses." Today they appear as pleasant little abodes with landscaped front yards, but most likely they were only partial buildings, built in a measure of economy. Penny-strapped owners, architects theorize, constructed back portions of the house with their kitchens and bedrooms, forgoing public rooms or parlors until their fortunes improved. Obviously, for some it never happened.

Hidden roof top decks—Nowhere to go but up. Several homeowners have installed wooden decks atop their houses, many affording great harbor views. In keeping with the district's strict historic guidelines, the decks have been cleverly concealed in front from the view of bystanders.

Narrow row houses—Some houses are only 12-16 feet wide and one at 200½ Montgomery is a mere 87 inches.

Wooden house—Leftover from the days before fire codes outlawed wooden houses, this late 18th century survivor at 130 E. Montgomery stands out among its brick neighbors.

Storefronts—In the 1300 and 700 block of S. Charles a few first floor display windows remain from the old shops located here in the days before this section turned totally residential.

One-and-a-half-story houses—The only one-and-a-half-story rowhouses circa 1800 left in Baltimore stand at 1124 and 1126 Riverside Avenue south of the park. Each of the mirror-image brick dwellings has one center dormer in a gabled roof.

In-fill houses—In place of old warehouses and on lots left vacant by the city's ill-fated I-83 venture, when buildings were torn down to make way for the highway, developers have built traditional housing on S. Charles and elsewhere to fit in with the neighborhood.

CROSS STREET MARKET

Cross St. at S. Charles and Light Sts.

The first of the city's district markets opened in 1764 at Gay and Baltimore Streets. In 1846, Federal Hill got its own when peddlers set out produce and meats in stalls beneath a long open-air shed on Henrietta Street. Workers, housewives, and the occasional servant could pick up fresh fixings for dinner. In 1873, the market moved to its present site. Today's one-story Italianate market building opened in 1952 after a 12-alarm fire destroyed its predecessor. The high-ceilinged room is lined with stands and deli cases displaying meats, cheeses, vegetables, and fruits, baked goods, flowers, tobacco, and a variety of take-out foods.

SCHOOL 33 ART CENTER

1427 Light St. 410-396-4641

Sculptor and painter Susan Lowe works the clay, transforming it into a fertility goddess with 20 breasts while all around her students fashion their own visions. Meanwhile, Susan Hecker demonstrates dry point to a class of print makers. Upstairs, a watercolorist asks about studio space. If you're an artist wanting inspiration, information, or a new skill, this visual arts center, housed in an old brick elementary school, can steer you in the right direction. Aside from classes for adults and children, the city-administered organization sponsors gallery talks and shows, and provides exhibition and studio space for emerging artists. Not to be missed is the annual April Open Studio tour where, like a progressive dinner, art lovers travel from studio to studio throughout the city, feasting on paintings, pottery, sculpture, and other fine works from local artists. Gallery Tues-Sat 11-4. Office Tues-Sat 8:30-4:30.

OTTERBEIN

Back in the 1960s Otterbein's future looked hopeless. Its 19th century rowhouses were crumbling and the prospect of that neighborhood nemesis I-83 hung over its head like the sword of Damocles. Luckily, Housing Commissioner Robert C. Embry, Jr. rode in like a white knight with a proposal that would rescue this tiny enclave—"dollar housing." He and then-mayor William Donald Schaefer threw an open house, inviting prospective home owners to tour 110 dwellings offered by the program and enter a lottery held in August 1975. The winners became instant urban homesteaders, garnering low interest loans and lots of technical advice, along with new addresses. Today the area is a showplace of restored Federal row houses and new compatibly styled residences.

Named after Old Otterbein Church on Conway Street, the neighborhood began a little over two decades before the Civil War. Because of its proximity to the harbor, the tiny district attracted merchants, ship workers, mechanics, and others associated with the port industries. While the middle class lived in brick rowhouses with cornices or with gabled roofs and dormers, blacks and poor whites crammed into alley houses. Later, three-story Victorian era residences with ornate cornices and shops with storefront windows joined the ensemble. The Fire of 1904 spared Otterbein and immigrants from Italy, Germany, and Eastern Europe moved in. Today the community is populated by folks with an active interest in maintaining the historical character of the neighborhood.

OLD OTTERBEIN UNITED METHODIST CHURCH

112 W. Conway St. 410-685-4703

Dwarfed by the hulking concrete and steel Convention Center next door, the city's oldest church in continual use by its congregation sits in quiet dignity. Built in 1785, the small Georgian building started off as a German Evangelical Reformed Church. In 1800 its pastor, Prussian-born Philip Wilhelm Otterbein, fired with the zeal of spiritual renewal, "converted" his German-speaking congregation to the Church of United Brethren in Christ, a denomination he helped found. Otterbein remained a bishop until his death in 1813 and perhaps because of his four decades of service, the church later took on Otterbein's name. The Church was eventually folded into the United Methodist Church in 1968.

Unlike many of the city's old churches, Otterbein has retained its plain glass arched windows, allowing sunlight to bounce off its white walls and brighten the small plain interior. The balconies that once rimmed the south and east walls were removed in 1840, leaving only the west gallery. The exterior, executed in bricks purportedly brought over as ship ballast, is topped by a low, broad steeple. As the oft told story goes, when the congregation groused about its skimpy height, the builder retorted, "When you see the bill, you'll think it's high enough." Otterbein's grave is located on the Conway Street side of the building. Tours following Sun 11 am service.

LITTLE MONTGOMERY HISTORIC DISTRICT

100 block W. Montgomery St.
and 800 block Leadenhall St.

A remnant of South Baltimore's old Sharp-Leadenhall neighborhood, this historic district of pre-Civil War dwellings housed Irish and German immigrants and freed blacks who worked in port or railroad jobs. 117 W. Montgomery Street (circa 1820), one of nine half-houses in the district, is the oldest of these one-room deep structures. Numbers 113 and 109 served as combination shops and residences. In the mid-1830s the semi-detached houses on the north side of the street were built for freed slaves. An arabber (see *University Center*) stable once stood in the neighborhood.

EBENEZER AME CHURCH

20 W. Montgomery St. 410-783-0190
For over 150 years the Ebenezer AME, South Baltimore's oldest African American congregation, has ministered to the needs of the community. Among its pastors was Bishop Daniel Payne, noted minister and educator who established a school for black youths at Ebenezer and went on to become the first African American college president in the nation at Wilburforce University in Ohio. (Wilburforce, founded in 1856, was the second college in the nation established for blacks.) Unfortunately, this once thriving congregation has dwindled due to changing demographics and an overall decline in church attendance. The original facade of the church was replaced with the current Romanesque Revival front and the interior was modified. However, the original marble pulpit remains along with the diamond-shaped stained glass windows. Sun service 11 am.

LEADENHALL BAPTIST CHURCH

1021 Leadenhall St. 410-539-9334
Not all newcomers to Baltimore in the late 1800s were European. Thousands of African Americans fled the deep South in the aftermath of the Civil War and subsequent Jim Crow laws. Reverend Ananias Brown, pastor here from 1875-1919, used to stand at the docks of Locust Point, welcoming the bedraggled travelers as they poured out of ships' steerage and offering them shelter in the homes of his congregation until they found housing and jobs.

Freed slaves formed the Leadenhall congregation in 1849. The present church, dating from 1870, was refurbished in 1995, with much of the detailed interior gold stenciling and painting done by hand. Sun service 11 am; Wed prayer service noon and 6 pm.

Browse and Buy

There's still a handful of pawn shops, but these days retailing is looking up. Old-timers like Shofer's—the Lexus of furniture stores—and Herb's Bargain Center—a veritable grab bag of cheap stuff—are sharing Federal Hill with newer specialty shops.

CHARLES TILES

801 Light St. 410-332-1500

This showroom inspires fantasies of opulent bathrooms and *Architectural Digest*-caliber kitchens. Pick from an international selection of stone or handmade ceramic tiles as well as custom-painted ones with designs of your own choosing.

A COOK'S TABLE

717 Light St. 410-539-8600
www.acookstable.com

Gourmet chefs as well as those who don't know a frying pan from a tea kettle will find practical items like cookbooks and cooking utensils intermingled with the exceptional—patterned Portuguese ceramics, hand-painted glasses customized to your decor, designer salsas. From the kitchen at the back, local chefs give demonstrations and teach courses like French cooking for two and sushi-making.

GAINES McHALE ANTIQUES AND HOME

836 Leadenhall St. 410-625-1900

Gaines McHale has transformed this old box manufacturing warehouse into a 32,000-square-foot showroom of 18th and 19th century Irish, English, and French antiques. The dealer, one of the mid-Atlantic's largest, also offers a compatible selection of old and reproduction paintings, lamps, and other home accessories and will customize old armoires or custom build new ones (using wood salvaged from flooring and walls of demolished English houses) to house computers, televisions, and other technological necessities.

GALLERY ELIZABETH

1448 Light St. 410-752-3466

Betty Branson wields her paintbrush to transform old furniture and miscellaneous pieces into functional *objets d'art*. A dresser becomes the canvas for a southern landscape and mansion. An old leather doctor's bag sports a scene with a surrey out for a country ride.

KEN-ZO'S YOGI MAGIC MART

1025 S. Charles St. 410-727-5811

Here's those jumbo clip-on ears you've been wanting for your Prince Charles getup. Not to mention those form-fitting rotten teeth that make you look like a junkie on a candy binge. Along with costume trappings, professional and would-be Houdinis alike can find rubber rats, disappearing ink, ventriloquist dolls, and how-to books and videos at Baltimore's own mecca for magicians. The store's salespeople are always happy to teach tricks, but do keep in mind that their policy is "the secret is told when the magic is sold."

RESURGAM GALLERY

910 S. Charles St. 410-962-0513

Resurgam, Latin for "I shall rise again," is a fitting name for this 19th century house-turned-gallery featuring month-long exhibits by local photographers, painters, and sculptors.

VANESSA VINTAGE TREASURES

1132 S. Charles St. 410-752-3224

Vanessa's overflows with old clothing, dishes, linens, and costume jewelry. Pull open a dresser drawer to find hundreds of buttons and trims. If you're in the market for a vintage wedding dress, call Vanessa for a private showing.

WARRIOR EMPORIUM
1027 Light St. 410-625-9278
No one messes with this store's customers. Martial arts enthusiasts will find uniforms, sparring equipment, self protection devices, and weapons here. Collectors will want to check out the Samurai and Ninja swords and knives, Egyptian mummy daggers, and antique guns.

Epicurean Bites

BANDALOOPS RESTAURANT AND TAVERN
1024 S. Charles St. 410-727-1355
The name Bandaloops, borrowed from Tom Robbin's novel *Jitterbug Perfume*, refers to a group of Tibetans who discovered the secret of eternal life from food, drink, and sex. Bandaloops provides the first two-thirds of the recipe with its eclectic menu "specializing in specials" like spring rolls, veal Oscar, quesadillas, and other global dishes. A brick-walled dining room hung with local art and a smaller upper room provide a cozy atmosphere. L, D. ☽ $$

BOOMERANG PUB
1110 S. Charles St. 410-727-2333
Brash, bold, and noisy, Boomerang celebrates Australia from its colorful two-story murals of the Great Barrier Reef and Outback to the boomerang alcoves in the mezzanine dining area. For a taste of down under try filet of kangaroo or grilled emu accompanied by Aussie wine or beer. The less adventurous can order prime rib

or barbecued ribs. An enclosed bar draws pool players and sports TV fans. D. Open late weekends 🌙 $$

JOY AMERICA CAFE
800 Key Hwy. 410-244-6500
This sleek top-floor cafe offers a panoramic eye on the Harbor and creative American cuisine worthy of its Visionary Arts Museum home. Menus of brown craft paper bound with beads, twigs, and leather list entrees like cinnamon-and-chocolate grilled chicken and leek-and-scallion smoked duck. Even the presentations display an artist's touch. Long, skinny twists of crackers snake up out of an organic green salad and spun sugar swirls high over steel head salmon sashimi. L, D. Br, Sun. $$½

MATSURI
1105 S. Charles St. 410-752-8561
Matsuri has garnered accolades for its traditional Japanese cuisine, featuring sushi and robata (grilled vegetables, fish, and meat), as well as noodle and teriyaki dishes. Sit at the sushi bar or at small blonde wood tables. L, D. Open until 11 weekends. 🌙 $$

ONE WORLD CAFE
904 S. Charles St. 410-234-0235
The light vegetarian fare has an international scope—black bean burritos, eggplant gyros, hummus, and even organic peanut butter and jelly sandwiches. Get wheat grass and other healthy concoctions at the juice bar or live it up with microbrews, wine, espresso, and Irish coffee-type drinks. B, L, D. 🌙 $

SISSON'S
36 E. Cross St. 410-539-2093
Quaff a stockade amber ale with that spicy jambalya. Sisson's serves up Cajun, Southwest, and Southern chow along with its South Baltimore Brewing Company beers in its popular family-run brew pub. L, D. Br Sun. 🌙 $$

SOBO CAFE

6 W. Cross St. 410-752-1518

Mix paintings by local artists hung on bright yellow walls with background jazz and an ever-changing blackboard menu and you have the recipe for one of Federal Hill's artsiest eateries. The chef's main repertoire consists of pot pies, Cincinnati 5-way chili, salads, sandwiches, and soups followed by interesting desserts like strawberry-rhubarb pie and pear tarts. L, D. $

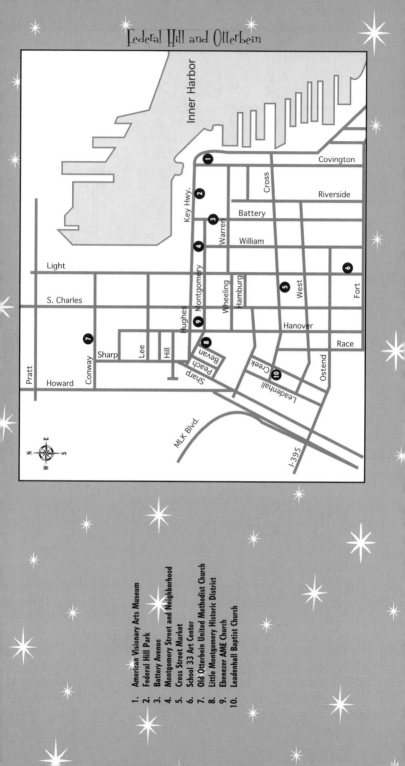

Federal Hill and Otterbein

Inner Harbor

1. American Visionary Arts Museum
2. Federal Hill Park
3. Battery Avenue
4. Montgomery Street and Neighborhood
5. Cross Street Market
6. School 33 Art Center
7. Old Otterbein United Methodist Church
8. Little Montgomery Historic District
9. Ebenezer AME Church
10. Leadenhall Baptist Church

South Baltimore

Imagine sailing up the mouth of the harbor in the late 1800s. On your right you'd see the Lazaretto Lighthouse and docks of Canton, and across the water on the left, the star-shaped earth embankments of Fort McHenry. Stretching past the old fort, the docks of Locust Point bustled as stevedores loaded and offloaded ships' cargoes into miles of waiting railroad cars. Nearby laborers hammered and painted vessels in ship repair yards. Then you'd notice the swelling mass of Federal Hill, and beyond, the church spires and rowhouses of the city. For the immigrants arriving at Piers 8 and 9 on Locust Point (our equivalent of Ellis Island), Baltimore was the first landfall in their new country. And while most continued on via rail to points west during this time period, many settled in Baltimore, further enriching the city's ethnic mix.

The Immigrants

In its earliest days Baltimore was settled primarily by immigrants from the British Isles, along with a number of Germans and French and both free African Americans and slaves. (One of the first men to set foot on Maryland soil from *The Ark* and *The Dove* was a free black man.) Because of several factors—a natural harbor further inland than others on the East coast, the rise of industry, commerce, and ship building, and the boom brought on by the Revolutionary War and War of 1812—Baltimore's port and commerce expanded rapidly. Beginning in the 1820s, and continuing until the Civil War, 250,000 Europeans, the majority German, followed by Irish fleeing the potato famines, settled here. By the end of the Civil War, Germans comprised the largest immigrant group in Baltimore and in Maryland, and state laws were published in both German and English. Private German schools, newspapers, and societies flourished, followed by the introduction of select public schools in which parallel courses in English and German were taught in order to accommodate the large number of immigrant children.

With the development of the railroad, Baltimore's commercial development boomed, making it the third largest city in the country. Additionally, its international trade patterns, most notably with German ports, helped set the stage for the immigrants who flooded to America in the late 1800s. In 1868, the North German Lloyd Line and the B&O Railroad signed an agreement that enabled Europeans to travel here by ship then transfer to westward bound trains. At first most of the takers were German, but soon Poles, Ukrainians, and East European and Russian Jews poured in, followed by Greeks and Italians. And though the majority of the immigrants fanned out to the mid-West and beyond, thousands stayed on, welcomed by churches or ethnic societies established by earlier compatriots. All in all, more than two million European immigrants entered the United States at Locust Point from 1868 until 1914, when the outbreak of World War I halted passenger shipping. Indeed, the Port of Baltimore was second only to New York as a point of entry, although its numbers were nowhere near those of its northern neighbor.

Most of the immigrants immediately sought work, a necessity for survival in this new land where so many arrived penniless, but soon found fierce competition from native-born Americans and more established ethnic groups who fought to retain the best paying jobs. With the additional barrier of an unfamiliar language, the most menial or dangerous and lowest paying jobs went to the newcomers or Baltimore's growing African American population. And, with each influx of white Europeans, blacks usually lost out in the struggle for steady employment.

Industry and the Labor Movement

During the 1700s, the Port of Baltimore shipped local products such as tobacco, iron ore, and grain to England and the West Indies. By the early 19th century, new technology had developed, allowing the region's food products to be processed or refined. Beginning first with canned oysters, a process developed here in 1820, the city's newest industry took off. By the 1830s, canneries ringed the harbor, packing oysters in fall and winter, fruits and vegetables in the spring and summer. In 1845, the B&O Railroad extended its tracks south from the harbor into Locust Point, building marine terminals and spawning further industrialization as slaughterhouses, meat packers, granaries, rail, and ship yards joined the packing houses. By the end of the century Baltimore, now the canning center of the country, was also a major national import and export center.

The seemingly endless flow of immigrants provided cheap labor for the industrial behemoths. Men flocked to the railroads, foundries, or slaughterhouses while women and children filled the bulk of low-skill jobs in the garment factories and canneries. In the smelly, damp, hazardous factories, laborers risked scalding, mutilated fingers, falls, rashes, and a host of other maladies, and young children labored for 12 hours or more, their pitiful wages necessary to help the family survive. Both European immigrants and African Americans relied upon neighborhood churches, benevolent societies, and charitable associations for help, and, increasingly in the 1870s, the growing labor union movement, to right the many social and economic wrongs.

The factories and businesses fought back and labor violence became a fact of life during the early decades of the movement. Laws protecting workers, especially children, were long in coming and implemented piecemeal. In 1906 Maryland's General Assembly enacted legislation prohibiting children under 12 from working in factories, and by 1912, most school-age children were required to be in school. Other laws limited women to working no more than ten hours per day whereas for male laborers 10-12 hour work days, along with hazardous working conditions, continued to be the norm. The weakened labor movement of the 1920s, and the Depression of the 1930s, hit Maryland workers hard, although President Franklin Delano Roosevelt's New Deal, followed by the ship building boom and the war buildup, helped refuel the city's economy. Bethlehem Steel alone set a national record of building 384 Liberty ships, more than any other single shipyard.

South Baltimore Today

Baltimore's harbor and industries spiraled into a post-war slump in the '40s, continuing into the late '60s as industrial plants and factories closed down or relocated. In the past 30 years, Baltimore's economy, like the harbor, has rebounded with new and diverse business and economic opportunities. And while a few old Baltimore stalwarts remain, the huge industrial and manufacturing plants of Locust Point and other parts of Baltimore are largely a memory. South Baltimore today is still a mix of blue-collar housing and industrial zones, although the latter is mainly concentrated on the south side of Locust Point. Interstate 95, part of the proposed highway project that galvanized protest from residents of Federal Hill, Canton, and Fells Point, now passes this industrial area before dipping under the harbor through the Fort McHenry Tunnel.

Sights & Sites

FORT McHENRY

Fort Ave., East End. 410-962-4290

In August 1814 the city was tense. The British had routed and burned the city of Washington, and were now headed north to lay waste to Baltimore. In the preceding years the fledgling United States had attempted to remain neutral as England and France battled. But as British ships increasingly impounded American vessels and conscripted their seamen, the United States felt forced to declare war. Baltimore, already renowned for its swift sailing ships, had been issuing marks of privateering to ships' captains, a dubiously legal authorization to pirate British ships and cargo. Now, after sacking Washington and burning the White House, the British had come to Baltimore to wipe out that "nest of pirates."

The British planned a two-prong attack upon the waiting city. On September 12, the land forces disembarked at North Point and skirmished with the Baltimore militia. The next day, English warships sailed up the Chesapeake and began their assault on Fort

McHenry just as their land forces pressed another attack a few miles to the east. For over 24 hours the British fleet bombarded the fort. Yet at dawn on September 14, the huge American flag sewn by Mary Pickersgill still waved in defiance over the fortification. Defeated, the British fleet hauled anchor and sailed away as their land forces retreated.

During the battle a young American lawyer stood on the deck of a truce ship within the British fleet where he had come to negotiate a prisoner exchange. The morning after the bombardment an awed Francis Scott Key saw the huge American flag still flying over the ramparts as the faint sound of "Yankee Doodle Dandy" played by the fort's band came over the waves. Inspired, Key jotted down the poem that would eventually become "The Star-Spangled Banner," the national anthem.

Later during the Civil War, Key's grandson, Frank Howard Key, one of several dozen pro-South Baltimoreans detained at Fort McHenry, held a less sanguine opinion of the fort. Shortly after the anti-Union riots of April 18-19, 1861, President Lincoln, fearing additional mobs would succeed in severing the railroad, the major link between the embattled capitol and the North, suspended the writ of habeas corpus in Maryland and placed Baltimore under Union military occupation. Dozens of prominent citizens, including Key, the mayor, newspaper publishers, and state legislators, were summarily arrested and imprisoned within these walls and at other federal installations. Fort McHenry, once a symbol of freedom, soon became known as the "American Bastille."

Baltimoreans tend to put a positive spin on their history so nowadays the old fort is lauded primarily for its role in defending the city in 1814 and distinguished as the nation's only park designated both a national monument and historic shrine. The visitors' center and park grounds are open free to the public, but there is an admission fee to the fort itself. Map and brochure available for self-guided tours. Schedules for Ranger-led tours of the fort are posted daily. Flag changing ceremonies occur twice a day. National Flag Day (June 14); Civil War reenactments of Fort McHenry as a prisoner of war camp (late April). Daily 8-5; June-Aug 8-8. Closed New Years and Christmas. Admission.

Did You Know?

Many of the defenders of Fort McHenry were not fully enfranchised citizens. The majority of the men manning the cannons were African American sailors who were skilled naval gunners and had been transferred from their ships to the fort's battlements. Several other defenders were Jewish. (Neither group held rights as citizens in that period.) The original manuscript of Francis Scott Key's "Star-Spangled Banner" is on display at the Maryland Historical Society. The home of the original flagmaker, Mary Young Pickersgill, is now a museum in Jonestown.

BALTIMORE MUSEUM OF INDUSTRY
1415 Key Hwy. 410-727-4808
Youngsters work the assembly line in the 1883 oyster cannery, sleeves rolled up, shucking oysters into the row of passing cans, while their friends are busy making more containers, gluing printed labels as the tins pass by. Nearby a third group stuff oysters with clay.

Canned oysters stuffed with clay? Children working in a factory? Welcome to the Museum of Industry, housed in an authentic 19th century oyster cannery, where children (and adults) learn first-hand—literally with their hands—about the jobs immigrants held in the era of the canning, printing, steelmaking, maritime, and garment industries. Kids can crank out their own handbills or build cardboard model replicas of 1914 trucks in the Children's Motorworks Assembly Line. (Unlike real auto workers, you can take the truck home with you.) Or they can tour the *SS Baltimore*, the last authentic steam tugboat on the East Coast, built in 1906 and salvaged from the deep by the museum.

Exhibits include photographs, artifacts, documents, and original machinery, and an Art Deco style Orientation Theater runs a short film on 200 years of manufacturing in Maryland. The newest permanent gallery, Garment Industry Workshop, provides an in-depth look at the industry that employed nearly a quarter of Baltimoreans in its heyday. Specialized tours are available to groups of ten or more.

The museum offers seasonal events throughout the year: Haunted Factory on the Harbor with its theme of re-enacted historic industrial accidents; the December Holiday Heritage Festival celebrating Baltimore's ethnic diversity; Thank You Day in April offering free admission; and Fathers' Day promoting family fun with model airplane construction. The museum's location on the north shore of Locust Point provides an excellent vantage point for viewing July 4th fireworks (reservations required). Special events priced separately from regular admission. Open Wed-Sun. Admission.

Did You Know?

You can buy a brick along Baltimore's waterfront promenade (410-347-5225). Immortalize your name along with those of celebrities and Baltimore boosters and help build the promenade at the same time. Join the thousands of Maryland citizens and visitors from around the world who have their name engraved on one of the bricks placed at selected spots around the harbor. Cost: $60 to $250, depending on location.

VIETNAM VETERANS MEMORIAL

Waterview and S. Hanover Sts.

The memorial is a quiet spot honoring the more than 1,000 Maryland men and women who died in the Vietnam War. The names are inscribed on the low, horseshoe-shaped stone bench which faces east toward the cranes and piers of Canton across the water.

Epicurean Bites

HULL STREET BLUES CAFE

1222 Hull St. 410-727-7476

You won't find the blues wailing here, but fresh seafood dishes and lighter fare in The Commodore Room and cafe next to the bar. The Sunday brunch with items like Italian quiches and banana pecan pancakes is one of the best in Baltimore. L, D. Sun Br. $½

LITTLE HAVANA

1325 Key Highway. 410-837-9903

With its purposely peeling ocher and cherry-colored walls and its mural depicting "the land of the eternal spring," this former pickle-warehouse-turned-cantina is about as close as Baltimore will get to Papa Hemingway's Cuba. The menu features black beans and rice, grilled fish, chicken and pork dishes spiced with mango, papaya, and salsa. And the bar attracts a 30-something crowd who favor beers like Magic Hat Blind Faith as well as old standbys like Corona. L, D. Open late Fri & Sat. ◯ $$

RALLO'S RESTAURANT

838 E. Fort Ave. 410-727-7067

This family-style restaurant, owned and operated by the Rallo family for nearly 60 years, offers American fare with regional specialties like soft shell crabs (in season), crab cakes, and perhaps the best codfish cake sandwiches in town. B, L ,D. $

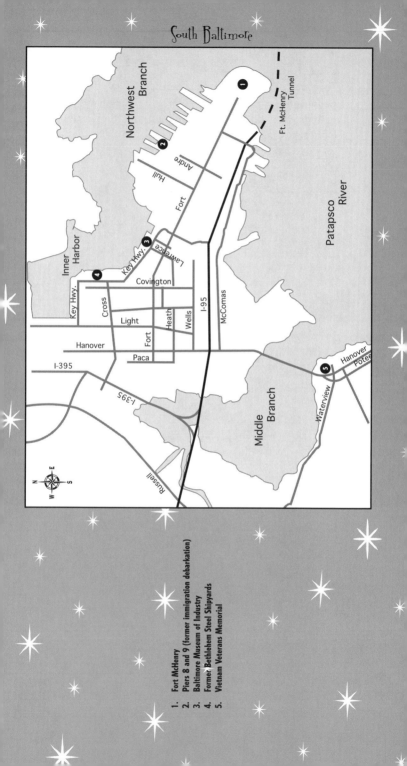

South Baltimore

Northwest Branch

Ft. McHenry Tunnel

Patapsco River

Inner Harbor

Andre

Hull

Fort

Lawrence

Key Hwy.

Covington

Key Hwy.

Cross

Light

Heath

Wells

Fort

Hanover

Paca

I-95

McComas

I-395

I-395

Middle Branch

Waterview

Hanover

Potee

Russell

N
E S W

1. **Fort McHenry**
2. **Piers 8 and 9 (former immigration debarkation)**
3. **Baltimore Museum of Industry**
4. **Former Bethlehem Steel Shipyards**
5. **Vietnam Veterans Memorial**

West Baltimore

A plaintive sax wails through the night air in response to a trumpet riff, then both merge in a crescendo against a staccato beat of drums. Cab Calloway's clear tenor trills "Hi-de-ho!" and the audience's response rolls past the open doors of the theater to the toe-tapping crowds on the sidewalk waiting their turn to enter. Soft jazz pulses from bars and juke joints lining both sides of the broad avenue while stylish women and men in zoot suits meander between the clubs, restaurants and cabarets, soaking in the music and camaraderie. Harlem in the '30s? Nope. West Baltimore. "The Avenue," Pennsylvania Avenue, to be exact.

In The Avenue's heyday from the 1930s through the '50s, West Baltimore was the entertainment mecca and the center of African American culture in the region, drawing thousands to its theaters, night clubs, and restaurants. All the black jazz greats played the Royal Theatre, including Baltimore's own Billie Holiday, Blanche and Cab Calloway, Eubie Blake, Chick Webb, and, somewhat later, Ethel Ennis. After shows at the Royal, stars could be seen in neighborhood eateries like homey Mom's Restaurant, just across Pennsylvania Avenue, or at Sess's, once the number one restaurant for black Baltimore, up on Division Street.

By day, Pennsylvania Avenue bustled as the shopping and business center for the neighborhoods radiating out from The Avenue. It also served as central byway for celebrations, boasting colorful parades at Halloween and Easter, or competing marching bands of fraternal orders, or simply serving as a place for families to take Sunday strolls.

Although the majority of businesses in West Baltimore were owned by whites, some black-owned businesses flourished such as the Murphy family's *Afro-American* newspaper chain, and, later, the Parks Sausage Company, founded by Henry Parks in 1951 in a former dairy off The Avenue. Many of the premier nightclubs, too, were owned by blacks. Often these African American-run concerns provided services not available to blacks in white-owned establishments. At Victorine Adam's tony "Charm Center," for example, young women could purchase ball gowns and learn proper etiquette.

Nor was success along The Avenue limited to entertainment and business, as West Baltimore was home to many African American leaders in the civil rights movement like Thurgood Marshall, the Mitchell family, the Murphys, and the grand dame of the NAACP, Lillie Mae Carroll Jackson.

Establishing a Community

Until the late 19th century, Baltimore's black population was scattered in pockets amid the white neighborhoods of the city, occupying the tiny, bleak alley houses behind the larger homes of whites for whom they worked or run-down tenements near the docks or rail yards. With the advent of Jim Crow laws, life in Baltimore for the average African American became even more restricted in terms of housing, education, and labor. For the vast majority of blacks, economic opportunities were almost as limited after emancipation as before for they had to struggle to compete for jobs with each new wave of immigrants entering the city.

Beginning in the mid-1880s, primarily because of the poor sanitation and dilapidated housing in South Baltimore, many African Americans began moving into West Baltimore, first into the area of what is now Martin Luther King, Jr. Boulevard, then spreading further uptown along Pennsylvania and Druid Hill Avenues. This migratory trend grew over the next two decades, initiating "white flight" out along the northwest corridors of the city, and by 1910, over half of the city's black population lived in West Baltimore.

Education for African Americans became a state function after the Civil War, but the black public schools of Baltimore were woefully inadequate and overcrowded. African American leaders for years fought for improvements, but it was not until 1925 that a modern school for black youths was opened, the Frederick Douglass High School. Despite many obstacles, approximately a third of Douglass graduates went on to college or "normal" (teaching) schools, and several returned to positions of leadership within their community.

And while the majority of African Americans continued to struggle against the degradations of racism, a thriving community radiated out along Pennsylvania and Druid Hill Avenues, even as many of its denizens began hammering at the barriers of segregation.

West Baltimore Today

It is ironic that the success of the civil rights movement in Baltimore contributed, in part, to the demise of old West Baltimore. As segregation's barriers started to tumble, blacks had more freedom of choice in where they lived, shopped, and sought entertainment—all of which they sought with increasing frequency outside the neighborhood. By the mid-'60s, for example, the Royal Theatre no longer booked live shows, and eventually closed in 1970. Many families moved either further west or northwest in Baltimore, or out of the city to the suburbs. However, it was the wide-scale riots following the assassination of Rev. Martin Luther King, Jr. that resulted in the worst destruction to West Baltimore. Kweisi Mfume, currently President of the NAACP, was raised in West Baltimore from the age of 12. As a young man he witnessed the riots, events he recounts in his autobiography. "The level of rage [in this country], spontaneity or pain has never been as far reaching as in those days following King's death," he wrote. Worst hit were entire blocks of Pennsylvania, Druid Hill, and North Avenues where businesses and homes owned by both blacks and whites were devastated. Families fled to the suburbs, never to return.

In recent years the city government has launched several initiatives to reclaim parts of West Baltimore from decay and blight, efforts aimed at both expanding the economic base as well as renovating or building new housing. While change is slow, the progress has been steady, as pockets of revitalized commercial zones and housing are making a comeback (see "The Avenue Market" below). Citizens' and business groups within the community, active participants in the area's rejuvenation, have proposed that Pennsylvania Avenue be designated a historic district. With continued city and private development, it is hoped that this once bustling section of the city can be revived to its former prosperity.

Did You Know?

Ethel Ennis—born, raised, and still living in Baltimore—is often referred to as the "reluctant" jazz star, only because she's chosen to spend most of her life here rather than pursue fame elsewhere. During her career, Ennis has performed with jazz and swing greats like Benny Goodman, with whom she toured as a young woman, Louis Armstrong, and fellow Baltimorean, Cab Calloway. For several years, she was the owner and featured singer at Ethel's Place, a night spot across from the Meyerhoff. Now in her late 60s and semi-retired, Ms. Ennis still sings on occasion in the Baltimore area, much to the delight of her fans.

The Murphy Family and the Afro-American

The *Afro-American* was a little-known church newsletter when John H. Murphy, Sr., a former slave, purchased the paper in 1892. By the time of his death in 1922, the newspaper was nationally recognized and the pinnacle of a successful publishing business. One of Murphy's sons, Carl, expanded the newspaper's reach by publishing editions of the *Afro-American* in Washington, Philadelphia, Newark, and Richmond, and led the business into other successful venues. Under Carl Murphy's leadership, the newspaper took on an even more active voice and role in the struggle for civil rights. John H. Murphy III, the third generation of the family to head the news publication, established ties to another prominent Baltimore family when he married Camay Calloway, one of Cab Calloway's daughters. Located for over eight decades at 628 N. Eutaw Street in West Baltimore, the *Afro-American* has relocated to N. Charles Street where it is still owned and operated by the fourth generation of the Murphy family.

Thurgood Marshall

Even before making history as the first African American appointed to the US Supreme Court, Thurgood Marshall had an established reputation as a champion for civil rights. Born and raised in West Baltimore, Marshall was forced to attend law school outside of Maryland because of his race. In 1936 he joined the NAACP's Legal Defense and Education Fund and was soon handling virtually all cases involving the constitutional rights of African Americans. In all, he argued 32 cases before the US Supreme Court, of which he won 29. His most notable success was the 1954 decision on *Brown v. Board of Education*, which set the stage for the desegregation of public schools across the country. Despite the city's strong history of racial discrimination in all facets of life, Baltimore's public school system was the first to begin to dismantle its segregated schools after the Supreme Court decision. Marshall was appointed an Associate Supreme Court Justice in 1967 by President Lyndon B. Johnson and served until his retirement in 1991. Thurgood Marshall died at 84 in 1993. A bronze statue on the corner of Pratt Street and Hopkins Plaza honors him.

The Jacksons, the Mitchells, and Other Activists

Often called "the black Joan of Arc," Lillie Mae Carroll Jackson's indomitable strength and will took her to the forefront in the battle against segregation. As head of the Baltimore chapter of the NAACP from the 1935 until 1969, Mrs. Jackson whittled away at racial discrimination in the workplace, shopping districts, schools, and restaurants.

Her daughter, Juanita Jackson, was the first African American woman to graduate from the University of Maryland Law School and to be admitted to the Maryland bar. (Etta Maddox of Baltimore became the first licensed female lawyer in 1902 when legislation was passed to admit women to the bar.) When Juanita Jackson married fellow Baltimorean Clarence Mitchell, Jr., head of the NAACP's Washington bureau, two major forces in civil rights were joined. Mitchell, reverently nicknamed "the 101st Senator" for his persuasiveness and influence on Capitol Hill, was an ardent lobbyist on behalf of civil rights legislation. In 1985, a year after Mitchell's death, the City of Baltimore renamed the courthouse in his honor (see *City Hall District*). Parren J. Mitchell, Clarence's brother, in 1970 became the first African American from Maryland elected to the US House of

Representatives, and Clarence Mitchell IV currently serves in the State legislature.

Several other Baltimore African Americans gained political ground during the years of struggling for equal rights: lawyer Henry S. Cummings, the first African American city councilman in 1890; Harry A. Cole, the first African American state senator; Verda Welcome, the first black female state senator; Victorine Quille Adams, first African American woman elected to City Council; and Kweisi Mfume, former Chairman of the Congressional Black Caucus, now President of the NAACP.

Did You Know?

Transplanted Atlantan-turned-Baltimorean Taylor Branch won the 1989 Pulitzer Prize for *Parting the Waters: America in the King Years, 1954-63*, the first volume in his scholarly yet readable history of the civil rights movement and the life of Rev. Martin Luther King, Jr. *Pillar of Fire*, the second of the planned trilogy, covers King and the movement during 1963 to 1965.

Sights & Sites

Up until the Civil War, Baltimore boasted the largest population of free blacks in the country, and, despite socioeconomic and political limitations, the African Americans of Baltimore flourished. The linchpin to the thriving black community during the 19th century was, as in most African American societies, the church. There are dozens of African American churches throughout the city, but it is in this quadrant where several significant inroads took place that affected the religious, political, and social institutions of Baltimore.

ORCHARD STREET CHURCH

512 Orchard St.

One of two documented stops in Baltimore on the Underground Railroad, the Orchard Street Church congregation began as a prayer meeting held by former slave Truman Pratt. Pratt along with other free blacks and slaves built the first structure, an African Methodist Episcopal Church, in 1837 on land donated by a Quaker abolitionist. The current 1887 Victorian Italian Renaissance building, the third church on this site, is now owned by the Baltimore Urban League.

Inside, sunlight illuminates the stained glass rosette at the back of the sanctuary, flooding the interior with light on its original wood stairs, floors, and molding. Heavy, rounded wooden beams, evoking the interior of a slave ship, brace the ceiling and two sets of columns support the interior balcony. The basement and lower walls of the church contain a warren of tunnels through which, it was once believed, slaves crawled to freedom. Recent research indicates most of these tunnels were constructed after the Civil War as part of an underground heating system, thus making it more likely that runaway slaves used some of the older burrows as hiding places. Although most of the tunnels are now closed, a few excavated by archaeologists are open for viewing. An exhibit of artifacts from the early days of the church and escaping slaves is planned. Interfaith services held Sun. Church and halls within the Baltimore Urban League are available for private and civic functions. Tours by appointment through African American Renaissance Tours (410-727-0755 or 410-728-3837).

SHARP STREET MEMORIAL UNITED METHODIST CHURCH

1206 Etting St. 410-523-7200

This imposing, granite church with its 85-foot granite bell tower, along with nearby Bethel African Methodist

Episcopal (AME) Church (see below), has the distinction of causing one of the greatest shake-ups in American religious history. The first Methodist meeting house in Maryland, at Lovely Lane in 1774, was quickly followed by a second meeting house at Strawberry Alley in Fell's Point. Initially, the Methodists welcomed free blacks to join them in their services at both chapels, but in 1785, banished them to balcony seating and segregated communion. Two years later several black members, as a means of protest, began holding prayer meetings in their homes or in rooms lent by sympathetic whites. The group eventually formed the Colored Methodist Society, building their first church, Sharp Street Methodist in 1802, near where Pratt and Sharp Streets intersect today.

Sharp Street quickly became a landmark for early African American accomplishments, including assuming control of the African Academy, the first school for black children in the city, established by the Quakers in 1797. Morgan State University traces its roots to the Centenary Biblical Institute, begun in 1867 by Sharp Street Church to train youths for leadership and the cloth. Later the church founded Mount Auburn Cemetery, now the oldest existing black cemetery in Baltimore, and in 1921, the first community house for African Americans. Sharp Street also stood at the forefront of the civil rights movement, with prominent Baltimoreans such as Lillie Mae Carroll Jackson and the Mitchell family among its congregants.

Having outgrown its original facility, the congregation built its present Gothic Revival church in 1898. The original wooden pews, arranged in amphitheater style, and a second floor balcony provide seating for over 1,200 people. The stained glass windows are of Italian cathedral glass and wall murals and statues of angels extend from overhead ceiling vaults. The church maintains an active role in the community with youth groups, a weekly soup kitchen, the N.M. Carroll Home for the Aged, and an Archival Center with church papers, artifacts, and occasional special exhibits. Tours of the church and Archival Center by appointment. Donations accepted.

BETHEL AME CHURCH

1300 Druid Hill Ave. 410-523-4273
The Bethel AME Church, like Sharp Street Methodist, traces its roots to the black Methodists' 1787 protest of racial discrimination. In 1815 part of the congregation split off from Sharp Street and under the leadership of Rev. Daniel Coker, a former slave born on the Eastern Shore, formed Bethel Church in Baltimore. A year later, Coker and other black church leaders started the Bethel African Methodist Episcopal Church movement in Philadelphia. Coker was elected the first bishop, but resigned the next day in deference to Rev. Richard Allen who had spear-headed the new denomination. As with other historic black churches, Bethel has championed causes for African Americans from the abolition of slavery to the continuing fight for equal rights. Today, the church carries on its history of community outreach and service with religious and social programs.

The Bethel AME Church, now a congregation of 12,000, purchased its current Gothic Revival facility from St. Peter's Episcopal Church in 1910, and renovated it in 1978. The highlight of the sanctuary is a large, pyramidical mural behind the pulpit which depicts African American history using color to demarcate eras. The people's roots in Africa (green), blend into the blue and lavender misery of slavery. Orange-reds depict the strife of the Civil War and humiliation of the Jim Crow laws, then taper into the orange-yellow empowerment of the civil rights movement. Illuminated in gold are the husband and pregnant wife, posed before a cross, lifting the born child against a sunburst, representing the family as the hope of the future. Tours by appointment.

UNION BAPTIST CHURCH

1219 Druid Hill Ave. 410-523-6880
Union Baptist was established in 1852 by the Rev. Dr. Harvey James, later one of the founders of the Niagara Movement, the forerunner to the NAACP. The church's

pastors and congregation have been at the core of the civil rights movement for decades, and remain a potent, grassroots political force in the city. The church's rough stone exterior belies the beauty of the sanctuary with its diamond-paned side windows of earth tones against smooth stone walls, accented by stained glass windows at the front and rear of the church. Tours by appointment.

ST. PETER CLAVER ROMAN CATHOLIC CHURCH
1546 N. Fremont Ave. 410-669-0512
The first church in the world to be dedicated to St. Peter Claver, the apostle for the slaves, this is also the third African American Catholic church in Baltimore. In the mid-1880s Baltimore had only two black Catholic churches, both on the east side, and Catholics from West Baltimore either had to walk the long distances or suffer the indignities of being relegated to the balconies or rear of the white sanctuaries. The Josephites, who have ministered to the congregation since its inception, acquired this former Protestant church, which Cardinal Gibbons dedicated to St. Peter Claver in 1888. Father Charles Uncles, the first black priest both trained and ordained in the United States, assisted for several years at St. Peter Claver while teaching at nearby St. Joseph's preparatory college. In the 1960s, Father Phillip Berrigan began his career of social activism while serving as assistant pastor. Tours by appointment.

OLD ST. MARY'S SEMINARY CHAPEL
AND MOTHER SETON HOUSE
600 N. Paca St. 410-523-3443
The history of African American Catholicism in America begins here, in the basement of the old Chapel of St. Mary's Seminary, the first Roman Catholic seminary in the United States. Both black and white French-speaking refugees from Santo Domingo (now Haiti) flocked to this neighborhood after arriving in Baltimore in 1793, fleeing a brutal revolution. Two years earlier, the French Sulpician Fathers, themselves refugees from the French Revolution, had established the seminary in nearby One Mile Tavern until a permanent facility could be

built on this site. (The seminary is now located at 5400 Roland Avenue in North Baltimore.)

In the basement chapel, Mother Mary Elizabeth Lange took her vows and established the first order of African American nuns, the Oblate Sisters of Providence, in 1829. St. Francis Xavier Church, the first African American parish church in the nation, grew out of the black congregants of the St. Mary's Chapel. The upper chapel, designed by Maximilian Godefroy in the French Gothic Revival style, was dedicated in June, 1808, and contains a high, vaulted ceiling, tall graceful columns, and stained glass windows which replaced the original clear, diamond-paned windows. The upper chapel was reserved for seminarians while lay parishioners worshipped in the lower chapel where statues of Mother Seton and Mother Mary Elizabeth Lange flank the altar.

The Mother Seton House is where the newly-widowed Elizabeth Ann Seton and her children lived for a year after arriving in Baltimore in 1808. In 1975 Mother Seton, who converted to Catholicism as a young widow, was canonized by the Vatican as the first American-born saint. During her short lifetime (she died at age 42) she began first a school for Catholic girls, then the Sisters of Charity here in Baltimore. Later Mother Seton moved both the school and the order to Emmitsburg, Maryland, where she devoted her life to aiding the poor and the sick.

Today the Federal-style house is furnished with early 19th century pieces, but only one item in the house, a small lap trunk, is known to have belonged to Mother Seton. Weekends or by appointment. Donations accepted.

Did You Know?

The Oblate Sisters of Providence, founded in 1829 by Mother Mary Elizabeth Lange, was the first religious organization in the world for women of color. Born in Santo Domingo (Haiti) in 1784,

Mary Elizabeth Lange and her family escaped the bloody slave revolt, seeking refuge first in Cuba, then Baltimore. Prior to forming the Oblate Sisters, Mother Lange established a small school for immigrant children of color in her own home in West Baltimore. (The term "people of color" was first introduced to Baltimore by the French-speaking immigrants of Santo Domingo.) This school, the first Catholic school for black children in the country, continues today as St. Frances Academy in East Baltimore, and is still administered by the Oblate Sisters. In 1991, in recognition of her meritorious deeds, Cardinal William Keeler, Archbishop of Baltimore, proposed Mother Lange for sainthood, one of two African Americans so honored.

WALL OF PRIDE

The Elwood Brown Memorial Playfield,
N. Carey and Cumberland Sts.

Baltimore boxing champion Joe Gans, Billie Holiday, Frederick Douglass, Malcom X, and other historical African American figures look out from this colorful outdoor mural by Pontella Mason. The 1976 painting, commissioned by the Baltimore Mural Program of the Mayor's Advisory Committee on Art and Culture, overlooks a playground dedicated to the memory of Elwood Brown, a local activist who worked with youth in the area.

Did You Know?

Born in Baltimore in 1825 to free parents, Frances Ellen Watkins Harper attended her uncle's Watkins Academy, one of the preeminent schools for free blacks in Maryland. Considered one of the most influential women of her era, Harper became an eloquent, passionate orator for abolition and women's rights. A prolific writer of both prose and poetry, Harper was the first African American published novelist, making her debut in 1845. Unfortunately, no copy of the book exists. *Moses: A Story of the Nile* (1869) and *Iola Leroy* (1892) are considered her best works.

BILLIE HOLIDAY STATUE

Northwest corner of Pennsylvania Ave. and Lanvale St.
Billie Holiday moved to Baltimore as a small child and lived here until she turned 15. Although revered by Baltimoreans—there is an annual celebration in her honor in April—her childhood here was a lonely, painful time. She found solace in jazz and the blues, and often ran errands for a brothel madam so she would have a reason to hang about the bordello, listening to the gramophone in the parlor playing the music of favorites Kate Smith and Louis Armstrong. At the age of 15, Billie and her mother relocated to New York. Legend has it that Billie, seeking work in bars, auditioned as a dancer, but failed miserably. The piano player, pitying the young girl, asked if she could sing, Billie shrugged and tossed out, "How can you make a living singing?" Nevertheless she obligingly belted out a tune, wowing the pianist, and, ultimately, the world, with her unique voice and style.

Diagonally across from Billie Holiday's statue, where playing fields now exist, stood the historic Royal Theatre at 1329 Pennsylvania Avenue. The Royal, the best known entertainment showplace in Baltimore, was one of the obligatory stops for up-and-coming black performers on the "chitlins circuit," the network of white-controlled show halls called the "Theatre Owners' Booking Association." Black performers, however, joked that the initials "T.O.B.A." actually stood for "tough on black asses." This elite entertainment circuit included the Howard in Washington, D.C., the Earle in Philadelphia, and of course, the mecca of the entertainment world, the Apollo of Harlem. Many of the country's best entertainers got their shot at fame at the Royal or other establishments along the Avenue. Red Foxx got his start as a comedian at Willie Adams' Club Casino, and Ike Dixon's Comedy Club regularly featured black entertainers like Charlie Parker, Dinah Washington, and Della Reese. Then there was the exclusive, private Sphinx Club with its formal dances, annual Mardi Gras ball, and charity affairs, where the elite of the African American community rubbed shoulders for 46 years until the club closed in 1992.

Unfortunately, as with so many other live entertainment venues, the Royal faded in popularity with the ascent of television and films as sources of entertainment. Yet, before it was demolished in 1971, the theater had hosted all the major African American entertainers and bands of the century, from the early jazz greats to more recent performers such as Nat King Cole, the Temptations, the Platters and the Supremes.

Local citizen and business groups plan to erect a monument to the Royal Theatre at Pennsylvania Avenue and Lanvale Streets to serve as the gateway to The Avenue.

HENRY HIGHLAND GARNET PARK

Southeast corner of Druid Hill Ave. and Lafayette St.
Born a slave in Kent County, Maryland, in 1815, Henry Highland Garnet escaped as a child with his family to New York City and grew up to become a Presbyterian minister and fierce abolitionist. Garnet's famous 1843 speech, "Call to Rebellion," appealed to abolitionists and slaves alike to adopt a more militant stance against slavery, and helped fuel demands for emancipation. In 1865 Garnet was the first African American minister to deliver a sermon before Congress.

He first played drums and sax, then sang and danced. He wrote nonsensical, happy lyrics to snappy jazz and pranced about the stage as he belted them out. He'd holler, "Are you all reet?" and the band would bellow in return, "We're all reet!" He was the Professor of Jive, the Hi-de-ho Man, he ruled the Cotton Club. He was electric, talented, and possibly the best entertainer of the century.

Raised in Baltimore, Cab Calloway spent most of his life pursuing his career in New York, but never forgot his home town, to which he gives credit for much of his success. A prolific song writer, Calloway is credited with penning over 200 songs, one of which, "Minnie the Moocher," recorded in 1931, garnered him his "Hi-de-ho Man" moniker. According to Calloway, in the middle of a performance he forgot the lyrics, and hurriedly inserted nonsense syllables instead. The audience loved it.

George Gershwin modeled the role of "Sportin' Life" in *Porgy and Bess* on Calloway, but the entertainer couldn't perform in the musical when it opened in 1935 due to his commitments at the Cotton Club. Eventually Calloway did take on the role in the musical's 1952 revival with Leontyne Price. The great Gershwin was apparently more than impressed with the virtuosity of Baltimore progeny, as he rewrote and expanded the role of Bess for Anne Brown, another Douglass High School graduate, whom he picked to play the title role in the show's debut. (Brown, the first black student at New York's Julliard, had been rejected by the Peabody in Baltimore because of her race. The singer eventually emigrated to Europe, where she remains an expatriate.)

THE AVENUE MARKET

1700 Pennsylvania Ave. 410-728-1012

Friday nights the Avenue Market swings to "Cool Jazz on the Avenue," a free concert with live jazz and rhythm and blues from local artists. Join the throngs while eating crab cakes, fried shrimp, or hoagies. By day this neighborhood market, located in the heart of the old African American entertainment district, sells groceries, fresh produce, meats, seafood, carry-out meals, and a variety of Afrocentric accessories, many handmade by local residents. A mural near the raised dais for the bands reflects the community's musical heritage, with pictures of the Royal Theatre, Billie Holiday, Cab Calloway, and others. Hanging from the exposed, colorful pipes overhead, banners display flags and facts about African countries. Formerly known as The Lafayette Market, the building opened in 1871 to serve the burgeoning post-Civil War community. The recently refurbished Avenue Market is the cornerstone for economic rejuvenation in the community.

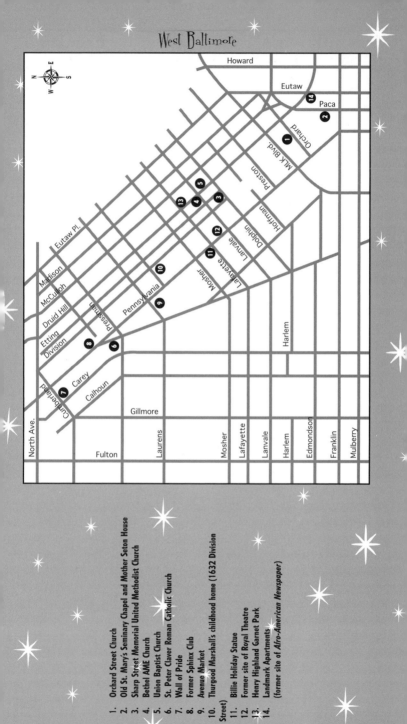

West Baltimore

1. Orchard Street Church
2. Old St. Mary's Seminary Chapel and Mother Seton House
3. Sharp Street Memorial United Methodist Church
4. Bethel AME Church
5. Union Baptist Church
6. St. Peter Claver Roman Catholic Church
7. Wall of Pride
8. Former Sphinx Club
9. Avenue Market
10. Thurgood Marshall's childhood home (1632 Division Street)
11. Billie Holiday Statue
12. Former site of Royal Theatre
13. Henry Highland Garnet Park
14. Landmark Apartments (former site of Afro-American Newspaper)

Jonestown
and Shot Tower Vicinity

Two tall cylinders thrust up into the sky along the east side of President Street, the domed steeple of St. Vincent de Paul Roman Catholic Church and the old Shot Tower, from which this area gets its modern-day sobriquet. The original settlement in this neighborhood, called Jones' Town, dates to the late 17th century, when David Jones set up a trading post at the mouth of a broad, vigorous stream which became known as Jones Falls, now much diminished and paved over in this section of the city.

By 1828, the year the Shot Tower was erected, Jonestown was an established Baltimore suburb of merchants and gentry wishing to escape the bustle and stench of the harbor and the docks of Fells Point. The home of Baltimore's second mayor, Thorowgood Smith, stood with other elegant brick houses of the merchant class along Front Street; Charles Carroll, last surviving signer of the Declaration of Independence, wintered at his married daughter's home on the corner of Lombard and Front; and Widow Mary Pickersgill ran a respected flag-making business from her home on Pratt Street. But change was in the wind as Europeans flocked to Baltimore beginning in the 1840s, escaping famine or political and religious oppression in their native lands. The vast majority of immigrants were English, Irish, and German-speaking Christians and Jews, with some Italians by way of New York. By 1850, an estimated 70% of the state's foreign-born population resided in the city.

While all of these ethnic groups left their mark, no one group is more closely associated with this area of the city than the Jews, first the German-speaking Jews of the early to mid-19th century, then the Russian and East European Jews who flocked in from the 1880s until the outbreak of World War I.

Early Jewish Settlers
The first Jew to settle permanently in Baltimore was Benjamin Levy, a merchant from Philadelphia, who

re-established himself here in 1773. During and after the Revolutionary War, more Jewish merchants were attracted to the city, which was developing into a major commercial hub and port. The Etting and the Cohen families, both headed by enterprising widows, arrived in 1780 and 1805, respectively, and members of both soon became prominent leaders not only in the growing Jewish community, but in the city's business and civic affairs, as well. When the "Jew Bill" was enacted in 1826, finally extending religious freedom and political participation to Jews, businessmen Solomon Etting and Jacob Cohen promptly won election to the City Council.

The growing number of German Jews in the mid-1800s helped shape much of Baltimore's character well into the next century. Many worked as peddlers or tailors, occupations relegated to them in Europe. Of the new immigrants who became itinerant peddlers in the city and rural areas, some were able to save and open small shops. Eventually, some of these retail businesses prospered and developed into the big department stores of downtown Baltimore in the late 1800s, virtually all of which were owned by German Jews. Many others entered the incipient needle trades, thus setting the stage for the massive garment industry of the late 19th century, also dominated by German Jews. Unlike their religious compatriots from Eastern Europe and Russia, the German Jews regarded themselves German first, both culturally and linguistically, and Jewish second. While they strove toward assimilation into American culture, they nevertheless placed a Germanic emphasis on educational attainment, cultural activities, and financial acumen. As their population grew, they naturally established places of worship: the first, the Baltimore Hebrew Congregation's synagogue on Lloyd Street in 1845, now part of the Jewish Museum of Maryland, followed in 1847 by a second synagogue in Fells Point, and several others soon after.

The German Jews, for the most part, settled in East Baltimore between the Shot Tower and Lloyd Street. Beginning in the early 1880s, the most affluent followed the lead of the Christian merchants and businessmen of Baltimore and moved to newer neighborhoods west and northwest in the city. Many synagogues followed the shifting population. This migration became even more pronounced with the arrival in the late 1880s of thousands of East European Jews fleeing starvation and persecution.

The East European Jews

The new immigrants crowded into the housing vacated by the German Jews and soon the neighborhood spread eastward past Jonestown as far as Patterson Park. While some German Jews, like Henrietta Szold and her father, Rabbi Benjamin Szold of Oheb Shalom, welcomed the new immigrants, helping them settle in, the two groups had little in common, even in the practice of their shared religion. They soon entered into an uneasy co-existence which lasted for decades.

The German Jews, predominantly Reform, held services in English, and were relatively affluent, well educated, and assimilated into American life. The East European Jews, on the other hand, were strictly Orthodox in their religious practice. Moreover, the majority were poor, uneducated, and spoke only Yiddish, which put them at disadvantage in obtaining jobs especially amid the flood of other immigrants. As the garment industry in Baltimore grew in the latter part of the 19th century, East European Jews provided a disproportionate amount of the labor force in both the downtown factories and the infamous sweat shops of East Baltimore, the majority owned by German Jews.

By the turn of the century, the needle trade had mushroomed and was second in the country only to New York. Although several large factories were built in Baltimore (see "The Loft District" in *University Center*), a great deal of piece work remained contracted out to the sweat shops. Though laws were passed to minimize the brutal working conditions of these worksites, they were largely unenforced. The working conditions in the factories, not much better than in the wretched sweat shops, spawned intense unionization efforts, and by the end of World War I, over 60% of the needle workers were unionized. Due to sharp decreases in government clothing contracts after World War I, production fell and the industry entered a slump from which it never fully recovered. The Depression, labor unrest and the poor economy of the thirties further stunted production; by the mid-1950s many of the factories had closed or relocated and the heyday of the needle trade was long gone.

Jonestown After World War I

The Jonestown area remained heavily Jewish through the turn of the century, but by the 1920s, half of the Jewish population had left East Baltimore, following the German Jews' earlier northwest migration, settling in large numbers along lower Park Heights Avenue and Forest Park. (Few East European Jews settled in Eutaw Place, a stronghold of wealthy German Jews.) With growing affluence and the dominance of the automobile in the post-World War II era, Baltimore's Jews, as many other whites, began the great suburban exodus. As before, the synagogues and the majority of the Jewish small businesses followed the shifting population. The abandoned synagogue buildings, for the most part, were either sold and converted to other uses or demolished. Since the 1960s Baltimore's Jewish population has been centered mostly in Upper Park Heights Avenue and Pikesville in Baltimore County and the newer northwest suburbs around Owings Mills.

Jonestown Today

As the Jews moved out of Jonestown, other ethnic groups moved in, primarily African Americans migrating from the South after World War II. Today, The Jewish Museum of Maryland, flanked by two historic synagogues, serves as the main reminder of the former Jewish character and history of the neighborhood. Even East Lombard Street, once bustling with groceries, delis, and commerce, is greatly diminished. Of the many delicatessens that drew daily crowds on Corned Beef Row, only three remain.

The city intends to demolish and replace most of the dilapidated public housing in the neighborhood, and is encouraging private revitalization of the commercial zones. And, despite the much-lamented 1997 closing of the Baltimore City Life Museums, new attractions and small businesses are opening or expanding in the area.

SHOT TOWER

Front and Fayette Sts.

Originally named the Phoenix Shot Tower, this 215-foot landmark has stood at this corner since 1828. Charles Carroll of Carrollton, signer of the Declaration of Independence and winter resident of Jonestown, laid the cornerstone in the base, which is over 40 feet wide. Approximately 1.1 million bricks were used in its construction, which was all done by hand and without use of a scaffold. The shot was made by pouring molten led through sieves at the top of the tower. Small balls of lead formed as the lead fell and solidified upon hitting cold water tanks at the bottom of the tower. The tower produced 500,000 25-pound bags of lead shot annually until it closed in 1892.

9 NORTH FRONT STREET

410-837-5424

Once home to Thorowgood Smith, Baltimore's second mayor, this 1790s Federal style house is the only survivor of several homes built for Baltimore's wealthier denizens in this old Jonestown neighborhood. Today, the restored Federal style house serves as the headquarters for the Women's Civic League. Among the antique pieces are artifacts owned by Smith, including the distinctive eye-glasses he wore suspended from a silk band tied around his forehead. Apparently quite vain about his long, aquiline nose, Smith did not wish to hide his magnifi-cent proboscis behind ordinary spectacles. A reproduc-tion of his portrait hangs in the parlor. Tues-Fri, 10-2.

Baltimore City Life Museums

In the mid-'80s, the Baltimore City Life Museums, for-merly the Municipal Museum of Baltimore, embarked upon an ambitious effort to gather several historic buildings and collections in east Baltimore under one umbrella. Within a decade, the now private BCLM had amassed an impressive array of Baltimorana and added new facilities to its Museum Row along Front Street, albeit incurring debt that would force its closure in 1997. Fortunately, the Maryland Historical Society now owns the BCLM's collection and the University of Baltimore has assumed the Urban Archaeology Center. The city-owned buildings have been offered for sale to local developers, with the exception of the Peale Museum and the H.L. Mencken House, in hopes that the private sec-tor can maintain the facilities in the future (see *City Hall District* and *Camden Yards*). However, it is unclear at this time if the remaining buildings, the Shot Tower, Brewers Park, the 1840 House, the Carroll Mansion, and the Blaustein Building will be reopened to the public as attrac-tions or will be converted to commercial use. Because of the historic nature of two of these buildings, we've included a brief mention below.

CARROLL MANSION
E. Lombard and Front Sts.
Charles Carroll of Carrollton, the last surviving signer of the Declaration of Independence, died in this house in 1832 at age 95. Contrary to popular belief, Carroll did not own this house, but simply wintered here dur-ing his elder years. The house, in fact, belonged to his daughter, Polly Caton, and her husband. While under the care of the BCLM, the mansion was restored and refurbished with period antiques, a living memorial to an old patriot and bygone era.

MORTON K. BLAUSTEIN BUILDING

33 S. Front St.

This striking cast-iron-front once adorned the old G. Fava Fruit Company building on West Pratt Street, approximately where the Convention Center now stands. The facade was dissembled in 1976, then restored and reassembled as the facade to the main exhibition building of the former BCLM. The Blaustein family, for whom the structure was named, founded an empire which began with door-to-door kerosene sales, then mushroomed into the American Oil Company, which, among Baltimore's many firsts, came up with the idea of drive-in gas stations.

Did You Know?

Henrietta Szold was born in Baltimore in 1860, the eldest of five daughters of Benjamin Szold, rabbi of the prestigious, German-Jewish Oheb Shalom Synagogue. As waves of East European Jews poured into Baltimore in the 1880s, she and her father found shelter and employment for hundreds of immigrants. In 1889, Szold raised funds to establish a Russian Night School on East Baltimore Street, one of the first in the country.

On a tour of Palestine in 1909, Szold was shocked at the unsanitary and impoverished living conditions of both Jews and Arabs. Upon her return to America, Szold founded Hadassah in 1913 as a national Jewish women's philanthropic organization that established clinics and hospitals in Palestine. Of her many accomplishments, Szold was most proud of her role in the relocation of 11,000 Jewish youths from Germany to *kibbutzim* in Palestine, thus saving thousands from certain death in the Nazi camps. Szold died in 1945 in Palestine, where she had lived for 20 years, and was buried in Jerusalem.

JEWISH MUSEUM OF MARYLAND

15 Lloyd St. 410-732-6400
www.jhsm.org

The newly renovated and expanded Jewish Museum of Maryland includes several components: The Jewish Historical Society of Maryland; the Lloyd Street Synagogue, the first synagogue built in Maryland; and the B'nai Israel Synagogue, the oldest continuously operating Orthodox temple in Maryland.

The Lloyd Street Synagogue was built in 1845 by the Baltimore Hebrew Congregation, then sold to a Lithuanian Roman Catholic Church when the assembly moved uptown near Eutaw Place in 1890. The Greek Revival synagogue, designed by Robert Carey Long, Jr., has a distinctive Doric columnade on the facade. The interior features a women's balcony and a reproduction of the original Torah ark. The stained glass window over the ark dates to the original structure and is thought to be the earliest architectural use of the Star of David in America. The remaining stained glass windows were added in 1871, and ritual baths and ovens for baking Passover matzah were installed in the basement after the turn of the century. The Jewish Historical Society ran a campaign to save the synagogue when it was slated for demolition in the late '50s, and after acquiring it in 1962, embarked on extensive efforts to restore the temple to its 1871 splendor. The first ordained rabbi in the country, Rabbi Abraham Rice, led the congregation for its first 11 years.

The B'nai Israel Synagogue, with its elegant Moorish Revival architecture embellished with intricately detailed woodwork and brass, was built in 1876. Unlike that at the Lloyd Street Synagogue, the women's balcony here is enclosed by solid wood in keeping with Orthodox practice. Of particular interest are the gas lights on the exterior walls of the sanctuary, as well as the chandeliers which contain both gas and electric bulbs, and a hand-carved wooden ark. Despite its earlier neglect, the synagogue has undergone a successful restoration, winning several awards.

The Jewish Museum has two spacious galleries, displaying both temporary and permanent exhibits of the history and culture of Jews in Maryland and America. The museum's collection totals more than one million photographs, papers, objects, and artifacts, and the expanded library is now housed in new facilities. An interactive children's museum, The Golden Land: A Jewish Family Learning Place, enables youth between 5 and 11 years to explore the world of Jewish immigrants in Baltimore between 1880 and 1920 with hands-on experience. With the purchase of a self-guided walking tour booklet, visitors can get a flavor of the teeming Jewish neighborhood of bygone days. The Museum occasionally offers guided bus tours of various old Jewish neighborhoods and synagogues throughout the year. Tours of both synagogues Sun 1-4. Museum galleries, Tues-Thurs and Sun 12-4. Admission.

Did You Know?

Following World War II, Baltimore businessmen secretly bought and converted a Chesapeake Bay steamer for a secret mission. In July, 1947, the ship picked up more than 4,000 Jewish refugees from southern France with the intention of smuggling them into Palestine. As the refugee ship approached the Palestinian coast, the British warship blockade surrounded her. The Haganah soldiers on board promptly raised the Zionist flag and unfurled a banner with the new name of the ship, *Exodus 1947*. A battle ensued and when the *Exodus 1947* surrendered, the refugees were forcibly returned to displaced persons camps in Europe. World-wide outrage following the incident ultimately swayed the United Nations' November 1947 vote to partition Palestine and create the new state of Israel. Baltimore-born Leon Uris' somewhat fictionalized account of the event became a 1958 bestseller that led to the acclaimed movie, *Exodus*.

McKIM CENTER

1120 E. Baltimore St. 410-276-5519

Around the corner from the Jewish Museum of Maryland stands another fine example of Greek Revival architecture, the McKim Center. A re-creation of the north section of the Acropolis in Athens, this building has been hailed the most perfect example of pure Doric architecture in the United States. The McKim Free School, as it was originally named, was one of the first private schools in the country built to provide free education for indigent youth regardless of ethnic or religious background. Quaker John McKim, son of Irish immigrants and a successful local businessman who founded one of the country's first cotton factories, bequeathed funds and directions for building the school near the Friends Meeting House. Incorporated in 1821, the school moved to the present site in 1835.

Today, the McKim Community Association, a private non-profit, continues McKim's mission by providing tutoring, counseling, after school care, and athletic programs for local underprivileged children. The Center also provides kids' summer camps and adult evening classes.

FRIENDS MEETING HOUSE

Fayette and Aisquith Sts.

The modest brick building behind the McKim Center is the oldest religious building in the city. Built in 1781 and renovated in 1995, the former Friends Meeting House serves as an annex to the McKim Center and as the home for the New Covenant Tabernacle Church.

The renovations returned the interior to its original state, including a small balcony and the vertical doors used to separate the men and women during the services. During renovations when the former flooring was removed, small compartments were discovered in the sub-floor walls, leading to speculation that the Meeting House may have been a stop on the Underground Railroad. However likely the possibility—Quakers in Baltimore, as everywhere, were fierce abolitionists—this theory as yet has not been verified. Ask at the McKim Center for permission to see the Meeting House.

STAR SPANGLED BANNER FLAG HOUSE

844 E. Pratt St. 410-837-1793

When the threat of a British attack on Baltimore seemed imminent the summer of 1813, Major George Armistead, Commander of Fort McHenry,  reported his troops were at the ready but had no suitable ensign for display. He stated his wish "to have a flag so large that the British will have no difficulty seeing it from a distance." Out of Armistead's wish came not only a monumental flag, but the inspiration for our national anthem.

The story behind the making of the Star-Spangled Banner and the War of 1812 are documented at The Flag House, the home of Mary Young Pickersgill, the woman commissioned to make the flag that flew over Fort McHenry during the British bombardment. The house, built in 1793, has been restored and furnished with Federal period furniture. A museum detailing Pickersgill's story and her life-long work making ships' flags also displays uniforms worn by American and British combatants, actual canon balls shot into Fort McHenry, and other war related memorabilia. It also features an audio-visual presentation depicting the battle and the story of the flag. While the original 30-foot by 42-foot flag is on display at the Smithsonian Institution in Washington, D.C., a replica can be seen flying over Fort McHenry.

The Flag House offers monthly educational programs for children as well as special events, the largest of which is Flag Day, June 14. Tues-Sat 10-4. Closed major holidays. Admission.

MARYLAND MUSEUM OF AFRICAN AMERICAN HISTORY AND CULTURE

Pratt and President Sts.

Scheduled to open in the fall of 2001, the museum will house both permanent and temporary exhibits reflecting the historical and cultural experience of Maryland's African Americans, and will feature an interactive learning center, classrooms, meeting rooms, a gift shop, and cafe.

Did You Know?

As a teenager, Eubie Blake sneaked out to play ragtime and jazz piano in local brothels—the only venue where such "unrespectable" music could be heard in turn-of-the-century Baltimore. It was here that Blake developed the distinctive boogie-woogie bass that became his trademark sound. In fact, Blake's large hands had such a wide spread and speed, he was able to perform technical feats that few rag or jazz piano players could duplicate. His bass chord structure, combined with his intricate and often independent melodic right hand, often required two pianists to perform the music he created.

It was in Baltimore that Blake met and teamed with singer-songwriter Noble Sissle in 1915, and began churning out popular songs. In 1921 the two made history when their musical *Shuffle Along* opened on Broadway, the first all-African American Broadway production from its composers down to its producers, performers, and orchestra. Blake remained a prolific composer during his long life, writing more than 350 piano pieces, songs, and musicals. The Eubie Blake Cultural Center maintains a small museum of his musical legacy (see *Cultural Center*).

Born William Henry Webb in 1909, Chick Webb got his nickname from childhood taunts of "Chicken Back" after a severe fall at age four that left him partially crippled and hunched.

As a young child Webb developed a passion for drumming, and by age 11 was playing in local bands. Five years later, Webb left for Harlem, where Duke Ellington became his mentor and encouraged Webb to form his own band. Webb soon achieved national fame as

"King of the Drums," elevating percussion from time-keeping status to a solo, musical art form. At age 30, Chick Webb contracted spinal tuberculosis and died in Baltimore.

ST. VINCENT DE PAUL ROMAN CATHOLIC CHURCH

120 N. Front St. 410-962-5078.
Dedicated in 1841, St. Vincent's lays claim to being the oldest Catholic parish church in continuous operation in the city. (Two older churches, the Basilica and St. Mary's, did not have parishes, and St. Patrick's, the oldest existing parish, is not in its original facility.) With its 150-foot domed tower and Neoclassical architecture, the building is a prominent landmark east of President Street. The interior has undergone several renovations, the most extensive in 1941, which restored the sanctuary to its original, simpler beauty.

Founded to serve the wealthy Catholics of Jonestown, St. Vincent's found itself buffeted by the tides of immigration that swept the city in the 19th century. Nevertheless, the church has managed to adapt and attract parishioners in creative ways. Probably the most famous was the 2:30 a.m. printers' mass first instituted in 1914 for newspaper workers as they left the presses. The mass became a favorite of Baltimore Catholics of all job descriptions, even drawing late night revelers as they wound down from partying. No longer an immigrant parish, the church has evolved into a metropolitan congregation with a social ministry focusing on the poor and young of Jonestown with a variety of educational programs. Weekday noon services; Sat 7:15 and 12:15 am (Printers' Mass); Sun 9:30 and 11:45.

BALTIMORE CITY FIRE MUSEUM

Gay, Ensor, and Orleans Sts. 410-727-2414
The Baltimore City Fire Museum is housed, most appropriately, in the Old No. 6 Engine House, the last volunteer firehouse in Baltimore before the city established a municipal fire department in 1858. The wedge-shaped structure, in continuous use since its construction in 1853, was one of successive firehouses owned by the Independent Fire Company. A 117-foot landmark

Gothic tower resembling Giotto's Tower in Florence was added in 1874 as a fire look-out post.

On display in the old firehouse are several engines and pumps, from the 1917 "Rolls-Royce of engines" (which still runs) to hand-drawn pumps dating to the 1700s. Mixed among the display cases are apparatus and gear, along with the 1920s brass slide poles. In addition, the museum offers exhibits on the history of fire fighting in Baltimore, with special focus on the Great Fire of 1904. Of great interest is the demonstration of the old fire box and communications system, which relied heavily on the telegraph, and operated city-wide until 1980. The private, nonprofit Box 414 Association, named after the box that sounded the first alarm for the Fire of 1904, operates the museum for the city. Sun 1-4. Free.

Browse and Buy

THE COP SHOP, INC.
803 E. Baltimore St. 410-837-5757 or 1-800-776-5717
Step onto the chalk outline on the floor and you will be surrounded by uniforms, detectives, feds, soldiers, and bail bondsmen—all shopping, of course. While you've got to be in law enforcement to buy anything with police insignia, civilians can purchase items like guns, chemical sprays, boots, knives, leather goods, sunglasses, tee shirts, and handgun magazines. Closed Sun.

PATISSERIE POUPON
820 E. Baltimore St. 410-332-0390
While you are sleeping, the pastry chefs at Patisserie Poupon are firing up their baking ovens, preparing to create traditional eclairs, mixed tarts, rich shortbread cake, and other special French pastries. The affable

owner Joseph Poupon, who hails from Brittany, and his staff arrive each morning around 3 am to bake their goodies.

ATTMAN'S DELICATESSEN
1019 E. Lombard St. 410-563-2666
One of the last and best of the delis on Corned Beef Row, Attman's offers a full range of New York fare with a few Maryland specialties like crab cakes and coddies thrown in. In keeping with the times, Attman's also serves low-fat pastrami, corned beef, and chicken selections. But go ahead and splurge your calories on old-fashioned stuff and eat it in the adjoining Kibbitz Room to experience Bawlmer lingo first hand. B, L. $

WEISS' DELICATESSEN
1127 E. Lombard St. 410-276-7910
A small deli with excellent cold cuts and deli-style sandwiches. Burgers, ribs, fried chicken, and other hot lunch dishes are also available. In-house seating or carry out. B, L. $

LENNY'S DELICATESSEN
1150 E. Lombard St. 410-327-1177
This large deli offers not only New York style sandwiches and both hot and cold lunch fare, but also has a counter where you can stock up on meats, cheeses, pickles, and deli fare. B, L. $

Jonestown and Shot Tower Vicinity

1. **Shot Tower**
2. **9 North Front Street**
3. **Former Baltimore City Life Museums**
3A **Carroll Mansion**
3B **Morton K. Blaustein Building**
4. **Jewish Museum of Maryland and Lloyd Street and B'nai Israel Synagogues**
5. **McKim Center**
6. **Friends Meeting House**
7. **Corned Beef Row**
8. **Star Spangled Banner Flag House**
9. **St. Vincent de Paul Roman Catholic Church**
10. **Main Post Office**
11. **Baltimore City Fire Museum**

Little Italy

A warm summer night in Little Italy. A bocce player rolls his ball across the court on Stiles Street while three other players talk politics. Two boys, students at Father Kolbe's in Canton, whiz by on bikes, waving to seniors, who, hoping to beat the heat, have set up lawn chairs on the sidewalk in front of their house. A Volvo in from the suburbs cruises past, looking for an elusive parking space. Meanwhile the restaurants are filled with customers happily dining, depending on their tastes and wallets, on tortellini, risotto, or ossobuco.

While other ethnic communities have disappeared, Little Italy has clung to its 12 blocks or so of 19th century rowhouses. St. Leo's Roman Catholic Church, the focal point of the neighborhood, still holds spaghetti dinners and fills the streets with festive throngs on St. Anthony's and St. Gabriel's feast days. Even those who've left for less urban climes often return for Sunday mass. Although much of Little Italy's population is aging and many small shops shut down when their elderly owners died, younger generations, perhaps nostalgic for their ethnic roots, have started moving back.

Little Italy began in a crush of broken dreams. Gold had been discovered at Sutter's Mill in 1848, kicking off a rush of fortune-seekers who swarmed to California. Genoese adventurers, lured by the promise of wealth, came to America intent on hopping a train to the rich California fields. While waiting for their train and dreams to come in, they rented rooms by the waterfront near President Street Station. Some, their fantasies evaporating, ran out of money and never left. They took jobs at the local hotels and restaurants or went to work for the railroads.

By the late 1800s immigrants arrived from Naples, Sicily, and Abruzzi, driven by poverty. Many of the newcomers established fruit vending businesses, selling from pushcarts and market stalls. Others labored as masons, barbers, tailors, common workers, and tradesmen. Even street musicians—fiddlers, harpists, hurdy-gurdy men with red caped and coated monkeys—joined the brew. And a mix it was. Late 19th century Italy, although unified geographically, spanned cultural divides which were reflected in the developing ethnic

255

village. Different dialects, with distinct vocabularies, along with societal differences spurred the growth of mutual aid societies, groups organized around home territories like Abruzzi or Naples that lent immigrants money and helped them adjust to life in this grimy industrial city.

The area which grew into Little Italy had originally started off with German, Irish, then Jewish residents. In 1880, Cardinal Gibbons, taking note of the burgeoning Italian population, had authorized the building of St. Leo the Great and by the 1920s the little community of rowhouses was solidly  Italian. As the neighborhood prospered, its residents moved on to higher education and more skilled jobs. Some opened businesses, among them Little Italy's famous restaurants. The community, too, gained more political clout, especially with the election of Thomas D'Alesandro, Jr., an immigrant's son who became a Maryland state delegate in 1926, then a US congressman and Baltimore City Mayor in the '40s and '50s. His son, Thomas D'Alesandro III, followed him to the mayor's office in 1967.

Over the years, the deterioration of neighborhoods north of the enclave could have sent Little Italy spiraling downward. But the tight-knit community with its foot patrolmen and family-based values has prevented serious crime from getting a foothold.

To get the flavor of the tiny neighborhood, take a walk before lunch or dinner. Note the occasional window shrine with its Mary nesting in artificial flowers and visit the bocce ball court on Stiles Street.

Recently much of Little Italy's notorious parking hassles have been eliminated thanks to the cadres of valet parking attendants willing to drive your car to a lot for a five spot. Of course, you can always opt for parking at the surface lots of

President Street (bring one-dollar bills), walking from the Harbor, or taking a water taxi.

CHRISTOPHER COLUMBUS STATUE
200 block S. President St.

On the edge of Little Italy, across President Street, stands the statue of Christopher Columbus sculpted by Bigarani Anuro in 1984. Surrounded by flags and with reliefs of the Niña, the Pinta, and the Santa Maria in its base, the statue honors a fellow Genoese, the forerunner of all those adventurers who arrived here in the mid-1800s. To Columbus' south is the Museum of Public Works and to his north, Scarlett Place, a condominium built around the core of the 19th century Scarlett Seed Company. With its staggered roofline, the post-modern structure has been designed to resemble a Tuscan hillside.

BALTIMORE CIVIL WAR MUSEUM
President Street Station, 601 S. President St.
410-385-5188

Baltimore, true to form, lived up to its reputation as "Mobtown" during the early years of the Civil War. The city's pro-Southern population and geographic location on the major north-south railroad route primed it into dual roles as a hotbed of protest and as a major linchpin in the Underground Railroad.

The President Street Station, the southernmost depot of the Philadelphia, Wilmington & Baltimore Railroad, was one of the few depots actually used on the Underground Railroad on which hundreds of African Americans fled slavery to freedom in the North.

Frederick Douglass escaped to Philadelphia from here, boarding the northbound train with "borrowed" seaman's papers. Another slave, Henry "Box" Brown, was shipped from Richmond to Camden Station in a wooden box, transferred to the President Street Station, then onward to freedom in Philadelphia. (The unwitting shipping agency, Adams Express Co., still maintains an office in Baltimore although it no longer is in the delivery business.)

The station was also where travelers from the north disembarked and transferred to Camden Station, less than a mile away, to continue their journey south. Among the thousands of travelers who passed this way was the newly elected Abraham Lincoln, who crept through Baltimore in the dead of the night to escape the wrath of the city's Confederate sympathizers. The President managed to slip through undetected but arrived in Washington to face Confederate troops on the Virginia side of the Potomac River, with a decidedly unfriendly Maryland at his back door. Five days after South Carolina seceded from the Union, the beleaguered President summoned northern troops to Washington. On April 18, 1861, when the four called-up companies of the 25th Pennsylvania Infantry Regiment stopped in Baltimore, mobs of pro-Southerners attacked, pelting the soldiers with paving stones, bricks, and other missiles. The first blood was shed when Nickoles Biddle, a free black man in the employ of a Union officer, was struck in the head by one of the paving stones and severely wounded.

The events of the next day, however, caught national attention when the first lives were lost—with no military engagement. That morning, the 6th Regiment Massachusetts Volunteer Militia and the "Washington Brigade," ten companies of the 26th and 27th Pennsylvania Infantry, disembarked at the President Street Station and marched down Pratt Street to make their southbound connection at the Camden Street Station. Southern sympathizers again went on the attack, throwing bricks, bottles, and stones and firing shots into the air. Despite intervention by the mayor and police chief, the outcome was inevitable. Gunfire was exchanged at several points along the route, and by day's end, nearly two dozen soldiers and civilians lay dead with many more wounded.

The Civil War Museum, housed in the President Street Station, presents an array of compact exhibits detailing local events leading up to and through the Civil War. Of particular interest are displays on the Union occupation, the railroads during the war, the history of the Underground Railroad, and the role of African Americans during the war and afterwards.

For information about additional Civil War sites in the region ask at the museum or call The Civil War Discovery Trail at 1-800-CW-TRUST (www.civilwar.org). Daily 10-5, closed Thanksgiving and Christmas. Admission.

Did You Know?

The April 1861 Pratt Street Riot became headline news all over the country within days. James Ryder Randall, a native of Baltimore with strong Southern sentiments, heard about it while teaching school in Louisiana. He dashed off a poem titled "My Maryland," expressing his patriotic outrage. The poem, published widely, quickly gained popularity. Two Baltimore sisters, Hettie and Jennie Cary, set the pro-Southern poem to the very northern Yale college song "Lauriger Horatius" and changed the title to "Maryland, My Maryland." However, at the printing press, the poem was reset to the German music of "O Tannenbaum." The song became a rallying cry among pro-states' righters. The Cary sisters often performed it at parties and Confederate soldiers reportedly sang it in battle. In 1939 "Maryland, My Maryland" became the state song.

ST. LEO THE GREAT ROMAN CATHOLIC CHURCH
227 S. Exeter St. 410-675-7275
As the Great Fire of 1904 rolled eastward, the people of Little Italy knelt before St. Anthony. "Spare us," they prayed, "and we'll hold a celebration in your honor."

Miraculously, the flames stopped at the Jones Falls, saving the little community. From that time on, the parishioners of St. Leo's have thrown St. Anthony a fabulous fête on the weekend closest to the saint's June 13th birthday.

Sunday morning, after mass, a procession carries the statue of St. Anthony through the narrow streets as the devout reach out to pin dollars onto his robes. Afterwards, in front of the church, Exeter and Stiles Streets bustle with crowds devouring pizza, pasta, sausage and peppers, and homemade *pizzelle*. Children play games while grownups browse through the flea market booths. And the music! Al Baitch blows his sax. The Balli D' Italia break into a tarantella and the Monaldi Brothers rock out pop tunes as the block fills with dancing folks of all ages. In late August, parishioners throw a similar party for St. Gabriel of Abruzzi, where many residents' ancestors hailed from. On the second Sunday in December a special mass is held for St. Lucy, patron saint of Sicily and Syracuse, who, years ago, restored one troubled parishioner's eyesight.

The old brick church, built in 1881, draws not only from the neighborhood but even from those who long departed Little Italy for the suburbs. It holds spaghetti suppers, youth groups, summer camps, and serves as a social hub for the community. In 1998 the interior got a new paint job along with kneelers which had been absent since a previous priest removed them in a fit of reform back in the 1980s. Mass: Sat 5:30 pm; Sun 9:30, 10:30 (in Italian), 11:30 am; Weekdays at 8 am.

BOCCE BALL COURT

902-904 Stiles St.
Contact Gia Blattermann or Joe Scalia at 410-367-3482
Friday night. A man tosses the wooden ball down the sandy court and it rolls within an inch of its target, the smaller pallino. His fellow players, two gray-headed men and a dark-haired woman offer congratulations. On the second court, a young boy takes his shot. Not so lucky. Over on the bench, a grandma in a baseball

cap and her neighbors smile. He'll improve with practice. Meanwhile, a handful of patrons from local restaurants, stomachs filled with pasta, watch the action. For a look at cream of the crop players, stop by during the annual bocce tournaments held during the Bocce Ball in May, St. Anthony's feast day in June, the July wheelchair competition, or the Christopher Columbus Classic in October (weekend of Columbus Day) when players from all over the East Coast compete.

Browse and Buy

WATER FROM THE MOON GALLERY

217 Albemarle St. 410-727-6380

In 1996 Rosanna Williams, a Little Italy native and welder, put down her blow torch and opened up this delightful gallery. The shop, whose name is derived from an Asian saying meaning "something you desire that's really hard to get," is filled with objects of desire— Venetian glass vases, hand painted marbleized pottery, silk weavings, and other fine crafts by nationally known artists.

Epicurean Bites

Nearly two dozen restaurants—red sauce spaghetti houses and elegant gourmet restaurants alike—cater to Baltimore's appetite for good Italian cooking.

ALDO'S RISTORANTE ITALIANO
306 S. High St. 410-727-0700
Step inside and you could be in a small Italian villa. Aldo's mauve walls with tapestry inserts and its white columned courtyard room with a second story loggia make a splendid backdrop for a dinner of *frutti di mare*, a Florentine-style grilled sirloin, or a simple dish of gnocchi. D. $$

AMICCI'S
231 S. High St. 410-528-1096
Eat your "comfort food" Italian to reggae, top 40, classic rock, or whatever beat of the day is playing in this popular trattoria. Favorites include chicken marsala, gnocchi and *pane rotundo*—a round of hollowed out garlic-and-butter glazed Italian loaf filled with shrimp in creamy garlic sauce—guaranteed to delight taste buds and drive away vampires. L, D. Open until 11 weekends. $½

BOCCACCIO
925 Eastern Ave. 410-234-1322
That 14th century Florentine author would have supped well had he dipped a fork into his Little Italy namesake's veal chop stuffed with ham and fontina, and followed it with a chaser of strawberries *zabaione*. Certainly over wine from the Piedmont, Trentino, or any of the 200 plus selections from the rest of Italy, he'd have a good tale to tell. For a post-dinner guessing

game, he could play "who's eating risotto behind the big wood wine cellar door?" Sarah Ferguson? Cal Ripken? Or maybe just plain folks celebrating an anniversary. L, D. Open until 11 nightly except Sun. Reservations highly recommended. ☽ $$$

CAESAR'S DEN

223 S. High St. 410-547-0820

Since 1970 families and romantic couples alike have come to this Southern Italian ristorante for classics like veal saltimbocca, grilled fresh fish, as well as the more sophisticated black fettucine with arugola. The simple, yet formal dining room, with paintings of Italian village scenes, makes diners feel like they're in Naples. L, D. ☽ $$$

CHIAPPARELLI'S

237 S. High St. 410-837-0309.

Sinatra sings while Mom, Dad, and the kids dig into the antipasto. Meanwhile, the Chiapparelli family tablehops, greeting customers just as they've done since the 1940s. There have been a few changes over the years: panini on the menu, several more dining rooms, and, of course, a price hike. (Spaghetti cost a dollar according to the 1950 menu on the wall.) But Chiapparelli's remains an old reliable. L, D. Open late Fri and Sat. ☽ $$

CIAO BELLA

236 S. High St. 410-685-7733

Tony Gambino is describing the veal *ciao bella*, his hands re-enacting each step that goes into rolling of the veal with proscuitto and provolone. Bravo for the little tableside drama and bravo again for the seafood, meat, poultry, and pasta dishes that follow. No wonder so many Little Italy customers come back for repeat performances. Complimentary shuttle service to and from local hotels. L, D. Open until 11 weekends. ☽ $$

DA MIMMO RISTORANTE

217 S. High St. 410-727-6876

Pavarotti ate here. So did Nureyev and James Earl Jones. Baltimoreans, too, applaud Da Mimmo's pasta *alla dente*, red snapper *Adriatico*, and thick succulent veal chops accompanied by an international wine list. Enjoy live music in the lounge while sipping a pre-dinner drink, then dine by candlelight in the elegant green dining room, one of Little Italy's most romantic. L, D. Fri & Sat open until 1 am. Reservations recommended. $$$

DALESIO'S
829 Eastern Ave. 410-539-1965
Dalesio's brick and ironwork grill facade is the entry to Florentine-style dining rooms graced by murals of Florence and Tuscany. The menu, Northern Italian with a dash of California and France, centers on pastas, veal, chicken, and beef dishes accompanied by an award-winning wine list. Cigar aficionados head up to the third-floor lounge for an after dinner smoke. L, D. Open until 11 pm Fri & Sat. Reservations recommended. $$$

LA SCALA
411 S. High St. 410-783-9209
If you're lucky enough to eat here when co-owner Nino Germano's Sicilian mother has been around to bake, you'll get to eat Baltimore's best and lightest cannolis. However, even if she's off in her native Italy, this small eatery serves up a menu that encompasses the best of "The Boot" like *pomodori freschi* (plump tomatoes with olive oil and basil), an Abruzzese chicken topped with sundried tomatoes, and a 16-ounce veal chop succulent with fontina and prosciutto. D. Open late Fri & Sat. $$

LA TAVOLA
248 Albemarle St. 410-685-1859
Step into the black granite foyer for La Tavola's innovative Italian cuisine. Grilled fish and fresh homemade pastas, veal dishes paired with marvelous bread, at moderate prices have made this a Little Italy favorite. L, D. $$

LUIGI PETTI
1002 Eastern Ave. 410-685-0055.
This restaurant is best in summer months when you can eat your lobster *fra diavolo* or veal chop on the outdoor

terrace and watch Little Italy go by.   L, D. Open late weekends. 🌙 $$

SABATINO'S

901 Fawn St. 410-727-9414

A long-standing Little Italy "red sauce" restaurant, Sabatino's offers basic Italian, big salads, and late late hours for midnight snackers. Big on the tourist trade and popular with the locals, too, this eatery was a favorite of Spiro Agnew's who reportedly nursed his wounds here after resigning the vice-presidency. L, D. Open nightly until 3 am. 🌙 $$

VACCARO'S

222 Albemarle St. 410-685-4905

This is no place for dieters. Oh, sure you could stick to cappuccino, but first you've got to walk past a case filled with incredible concoctions—pine nut cookies, cannolis, rum cakes, tiramisu, eclairs—just to name a few. Then there's the Schwarzenegger-sized portions of gelati. Daily from 7:30 am. 🌙 $

Restauranteur Maria Allori liked to brag that she put Little Italy on the map. Maria's, she boasted, was the first to put dishes like lasagna and fettucine Bolognese on the menu and to draw celebrities like Rocky Marciano and Max Baer. When cowboy movie star Gene Autry rode into town, he hitched his horse outside the popular Depression-era eatery at 300 Albemarle Street and went in for Italian chow. Another regular, H.L. Mencken, stopped in for Crabs Sorrento, a dish Maria claimed she invented for him. After World War II when the Formstone craze hit town, Maria, with an eye to pro-motion, insisted her new faux stone facade be tinted red and green— the colors of the Italian flag. Alas, the popular restaurant owner died in 1974 and so did Maria's.

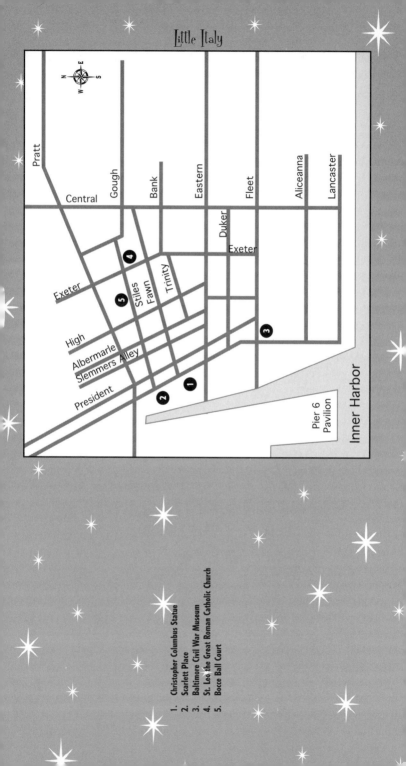

Little Italy

1. Christopher Columbus Statue
2. Scarlett Place
3. Baltimore Civil War Museum
4. St. Leo the Great Roman Catholic Church
5. Bocce Ball Court

Inner Harbor

Pier 6 Pavilion

Pratt
Central
Gough
Bank
Eastern
Fleet
Aliceanna
Lancaster
Duker
Exeter
Exeter
High
Albermarle
Slemmers Alley
President
Stiles
Fawn
Trinity

Fell's Point

Fells Point has been called Baltimore's Greenwich Village. But look beneath the trendy veneer. Boutiques, gourmet restaurants, and yuppie nightclubs coexist with second-hand stores, Mom-and-Pop carry-outs, and scruffy biker bars. Nineteenth century rowhomes gussied up with Formstone stand next to immaculately restored brick neighbors. BMWs, fancy 4x4s, and stretch limos roll across ship-ballast-paved roads right along with the occasional junker. On Shakespeare Street a movie crew films the line of red row-houses that is standing in for Old New York. Over by the waterfront a modern TV cop drama, *Homicide*, unfolds on the City Recreation Pier. All in all, though modern day Fells Point may be spiffier, it still embraces its seafaring and blue-collar roots.

In 1730 William Fell, his head filled with dreams of shipping, sailed over from his native Lancashire, England, and bought a 100-acre tract on Long Island Point called "Copus Harbor." He'd embarked on this risky venture on the advice of his brother Edward, a Jones' Town merchant and land speculator. Putting his carpentry trade to task, William built a house and began constructing two-masted ships in a yard

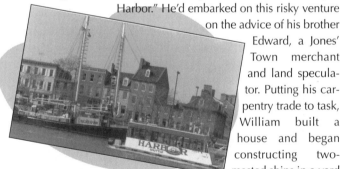

at what is now Lancaster Street. Thanks to abundant local timber, the harbor's depth, and his thrifty Quaker heritage, Fell prospered, expanding his holdings to more than 1,100 acres.

By 1763 son Edward was laying out streets, bestowing them with English names like Shakespeare and Thames. He gave alleys colorful monikers like "Strawberry" and "Petticoat." Fell's Point or Fell's Prospect, as the elder Fell called it, boomed. Sounds of hammering filled the air as small frame houses for mariners and merchants sprang up and shipyards and related enterprises moved in. Rooming houses and taverns where sailors could lift a tankard of grog and get a decent meal bustled. The Revolution spurred business further when the Continental Navy ships *Wasp* and *Hornet* were refitted here.

With the legions of men came brothels, brawling, and drunkenness, earning Fells Point a rowdy reputation. Political tiffs were particularly hazardous as one Captain Ramsdell found out when he protested a Congressional embargo on foreign trade by lowering his ship's flag at half-mast. Captain David Stodder, a boat yard owner, and his cronies expressed their opposition by dressing him and a companion in a coat of tar and feathers.

By the turn of the century, Fells Point had incorporated with Baltimore Town and Jones' Town to form Baltimore City. Sheds for the market on Broadway had already gone up on land donated by the Fell family. Newer houses were brick now, sometimes with offices or shops on the first floor and living quarters on the second and in the attic. Unfortunately, sanitation was minimal and yellow fever epidemics swept through killing hundreds.

It was the Baltimore clippers, two masted schooner-style boats, streamlined and fast, that boosted Fells Point's reputation. With names like *Comet*, these swift crafts plied the Caribbean, dodging pirates and bringing cargoes home safely. Privateers favored them, and in the War of 1812 the British, smarting from the new city's enterprising raiders, vowed "to wipe out that nest of pirates." The most famous clipper was the *Chasseur*, nicknamed "Pride of Baltimore," which much to English chagrin and annoyance outmaneuvered their warships along their own coastline. Later in 1832, one of the prototypes for clipper ships or Yankee clippers, the square-rigged and roomier *Ann McKim*, sailed off for the China trade, armed with a battery of 12 brass guns.

A depression followed along with more yellow fever outbreaks. Ignoring the 1808 Federal ban on importation of slaves, several shipyards began building and converting clippers for the slave trade. However, by the 1840s, coffee had revived local trade as ships swapped their cargoes of flour for beans in Brazil. Boatloads of tobacco, wheat, and sugar also left Baltimore wharves bound for Europe, returning with South American gold and silver as well as guano, used as fertilizer by local farmers. As commerce increased, German and then Irish immigrants arrived to work the docks and shipyards.

Along with the newcomers, African Americans, both free and slave, toiled as stevedores, laborers, and caulkers. Competition for jobs between immigrants and blacks was fierce and ship owners could hire at low wages, often dismissing workers expeditiously whenever business dropped. Frederick Douglass, as a slave, became an apprentice caulker at Gardner's Shipyard on Lancaster and Wolfe Streets in the 1830s and found himself the butt of violent racism from white fellow apprentices. He fled north in 1838 where he later wrote his influential autobiographies. After the Civil War, Isaac Myers, a free-born caulker, and other African Americans would raise $10,000 dollars to start the Chesapeake Marine Railway and Dry Dock Company near Willis Street, a business that lasted nearly two decades.

With the advent of steamboats following the Civil War, shipping companies began shifting their terminals to the deeper waters at Locust Point. Canneries and packaging companies, which had first appeared around the harbor in the 1830s, expanded and Eastern European immigrants took jobs in the vegetable and fish processing plants (see *South Baltimore*).

The turbulent Depression years intensified maritime workers' frustration with wages and job opportunities. Unions were formed and broken, and thugs from both sides bashed heads of anyone who disagreed with them. The culmination was the Midnight March of the Baltimore Brigade led by organizer Paddy Whelan in 1937. Hundreds of protesters trooped to the US Department of Commerce and the Capitol in Washington, D.C., to publicize their cause. Out of the demonstrations came the National Maritime Union and a more equitable agreement with the shippers.

A death knell sounded for Fells Point in the 1960s when plans were announced to route an expressway link to Interstate 95 through the waterfront of Fells Point, Federal

Hill, and Canton. Citizen activists, social worker Barbara Mikulski among them, rallied with a grassroots "Stop the Road" campaign. Borrowing a mimeograph machine from the Holy Rosary Holy Name Society, they formed several groups, including the colorfully named SCAR (Southeast Council Against the Road). They held bake sales to raise battle funds and lobbied Annapolis and Washington. In the end, David slew Goliath and the highway plans were withdrawn. Fells Point got a spot on the National Register of Historic Places in 1969 and Mikulski eventually went on to become a US Senator.

But times do change. As industry declined, immigrants' children left behind the Formstone and brick rowhouses for the ranchers and colonials of suburbia. In recent years artists, empty nesters, young couples, and singles have moved in, establishing stores, restaurants, and bars that cater to younger and/or more upscale clientele. The old ethnic enclaves are disappearing, but vestiges remain and immigrants from Latin America and other parts of the globe have drifted in. With care, a new generation will continue to preserve and cherish Fells Point's marine and ethnic heritage.

Stroll down Shakespeare Street where some members of the peninsula's founding family, the Fells, are buried. This block of 18th and 19th century rowhouses was designated a slum in the early 1900s, at one point held a squalid sweatshop which turned out postal uniforms. Over the years, homeowners have prettied up the row and a glance at the upper stories of some of the houses reveals different color brick where renovations have been done. During the filming of *Washington Square* a few years back, the two-block long street was transformed into Old New York. To get an authentic look, a crew covered over the roadbed with dirt and had modern effects like utility poles temporarily removed.

Sights & Sites

ALONG THE WATERFRONT

ADMIRAL FELL INN

888 S. Broadway. 410-522-7377

Built in 1892 to rescue seamen from the clutches of fleabag innkeepers who plied the homesick lads with liquor and loose women, the Anchorage (as the hotel was then called) offered "a home away from home." Nicknamed "The Dog House" by its salt-crusted guests, the project was run by the Women's Auxiliary of the Port Mission, a Christian organization, who charged 35¢ for a night's rest on a cot. Despite the ladies' genteel influence, the hotel boiled over with political activity and in 1929 the YMCA took over. After the YMCA left, the building became a vinegar factory. Today the Admiral Fell Inn is a spiffy hotel with 80 elegantly appointed rooms.

Did You Know?

Fells Point came to be known as Nickel Town because sailors' spare change went a long way in this shipbuilding, seafaring community.

BROWN'S WHARF

1600 block Thames St.

In the 19th century boats picked up flour stored in these warehouses for export to Europe. On return trips they unloaded their cargoes of Brazilian coffee beans. In the

1880s bales of cotton were stored in the warehouses. The wharf is named after early owner George Brown, son of financier Alexander Brown. Today a row of brick buildings has made a comeback as a complex of shops, offices, and restaurants.

BROADWAY PIER

Foot of Broadway at Thames St.

No Statue of Liberty greeted immigrants coming into Locust Point, Baltimore's version of Ellis Island in the late 19th century. But like their New York counterparts, thousands of European immigrants took a ferry to their future home. The Locust Point Ferry deposited newcomers here until 1917 but continued regular passenger services into 1937. The restored wharf is paved with bricks paid for by donations and engraved with donors' names, including celebrities like Dionne Warwick. Movie buffs may want to rest their bottoms on the same bench (although not in the same spot) where Meg Ryan contemplated a better life in *Sleepless in Seattle*. Number 904 S. Broadway, incidentally, is the rowhouse where Ryan's "Annie" character lived.

CITY RECREATION PIER

1700 Block Thames St.

Couples once danced in the moonlight on the roof of this 1914 old municipal pier. On cooler nights they waltzed inside across the polished floor of the ballroom on the top floor, while eager lads lost their virginity in the arched tunnel below.

In 1992, a "Baltimore City Police" sign went up on the door and cruisers started parking beneath the arches. Hollywood filmmaker and hometown guy Barry Levinson had taken over the old building for the TV show *Homicide* and transformed the interior into the investigative team's offices and interrogation rooms. Peer inside the door for a glimpse of the steps where Pembleton, Bayliss, Munch, and their fellow detectives tossed fleeting conversations at one another as they rushed off to a murder scene. Outside, the flat roof in back provided a spot for many a philosophical conversation or introspective moment when the grisliness of crime and complexities of life burdened their souls.

Fiction has bumped into reality many a time over the past few years. When the *Homicide* crew drove the newly departed Detective Crosetti's coffin to St. Stanislaus Church in a U-haul, some locals unaware it was all show shook their fists and cursed "the family" for not hiring a proper hearse. At another point, a real thief, absconding with stolen goods, ran on to the *Homicide* set. "Please, don't shoot," he cried as the actor cops made a real life collar. Not open to the public.

Concierge Plus' Hollywood on the Harbor Tours (410-580-0350) gives guided walks around Fells Point, complete with anecdotes about *Homicide* and other movies and TV productions filmed in the area.

WATERFRONT HOTEL RESTAURANT

1710 Thames St. 410-327-4886
On *Homicide*, this is the bar Munch, Meldrick, and Bayliss own. In former incarnations it's been a private home (for the Howard Long family in the 1770s), produce store, Prohibition-era bookie joint, tavern, and a hotel. Today, when it's not starring as a TV set, The Waterfront is a real bar and restaurant.

ORPHEUM CINEMA

1724 Thames St. 410-732-4614
www.charm.net/~orpheum
This art and revival movie house shows everything from silent films like the 1928 *The Passion of Joan of Arc* to newer talkies (from Hitchcock to Ed Wood) to foreign films like the Danish 1964 *Gertrud*. Not familiar with the movie? No problem. Give the theater a call. Owner George Figgs provides recorded capsule descriptions along with personal commentaries on current features. Double features nightly except on weeks when new films are playing. Matinees on Sat and Sun.

Did You Know?

Black Jacks, African American sailors, comprised one-fifth of the country's sailors in the early 19th century. Black seamen were such a common sight in the port of Baltimore that in 1838 future civil rights activist Frederick Douglass, disguised as a sailor and carrying papers borrowed from a former seaman, was able to board a train at President Street Station and escape from slavery to Philadelphia.

Marylander Matthew Henson began his adventurous life shipping out of Baltimore, first as a teenaged cabin boy then as an able seaman. The ship's captain took a liking to Henson and taught him reading, mathematics, and navigation skills that Henson would later use in his polar explorations with Admiral Robert E. Peary. To this day many believe that it was Henson, not Peary, who was the first man to reach the North Pole.

THE MARYLAND MARITIME CENTER

This complex of historic houses and a visitors' center (the next four entries) was founded by the Preservation Society, an organization that grew out of the 1960s battle to stop the highway from cutting through the waterfront. The society also sponsors walking tours and house tours of Fells Point and Federal Hill. 410-675-6750.

ROBERT LONG HOUSE

812 S. Ann St. 410-675-6750
Built in 1765, this tidy small house once owned by Quaker merchant Robert Long is the oldest existing residential building in Fells Point. The house, an excellent example of well-preserved 18th century architecture, is furnished with pre-revolutionary artifacts and furniture. The adjoining garden also replicates plants and herbs used in colonial times for food, dyes, and seasonings or medicinal purposes. The house is currently the headquarters for the Preservation Society. Self-guided tours. Call for hours. Groups by appointment.

MARYLAND MARITIME VISITORS' CENTER

810 S. Ann St.
The center, opening late spring 1999, will feature an information and exhibit center to introduce visitors to Fells Point. It will be housed in the renovated shell of a house dating from 1775. An interpretive program will include a video, exhibits, and hands-on presentations.

EARLY MERCHANT'S HOUSE

1732 Thames St.
This Federal style building (circa 1800) is now undergoing renovation. The three-and-a-half-story brick house, with its period furnishings, will offer a glimpse into the life of an early merchant family. Included in the museum will be a gift shop, bookstore, and meeting rooms.

MARYLAND MARITIME MUSEUM

1726 Thames St. 410-675-6750
Currently under development, this new museum will feature items from the Maryland Historical Society's maritime collection.

WILLIAM PRICE'S HOUSE

910 Fell St.
Shipyard owner William Price, who in 1805 built the famous sloop of war the *US Hornet*, lived here. Across the street at 909 stands the residence of his son John, also a shipwright. Today the latter building houses Margaret's Cafe. Price's house not open to public.

CAPTAIN JOHN STEELE'S HOUSE

931 Fell St.
In the late 19th century shipbuilder John Steele could keep an eye on his shipyard across the street from the windows of his Federal-era residence. In his first floor offices, he could count his fortune, then adjourn to the second for a good meal or a game of whist before climbing up to bed on the third. The 1786 house is done in Flemish bond with alternating brick headers and stretchers. The attic dormer rooms probably served as sleeping quarters for children or servants. Later on, the

building was carved into a boarding house, but in recent years preservation-minded owners rescued and restored it back to a private residence. Not open to the public.

BELT'S WHARF
960 Fell St.
The C. Morton Stewart Company's former coffee warehouse, built in 1877, now houses 104 luxury condominiums, nine of which are townhouses and ten of which are dockominiums.

HENDERSON'S WHARF
1000 Fell St.
In the 19th century, laborers loaded tobacco here on ships bound for Europe. The 1897 warehouse, built by the B&O Railroad for cargo storage and named after merchant John Henderson, is now home to a 38-room inn and luxury apartments. In 1984 a fire gutted the old structure. To appreciate the effort it took to salvage the remaining shell, take a look at the black and white photos on the lobby walls.

SWANN'S WHARF
1001 Fell St.
In the 1850s when Thomas Swann had his offices and warehouses here, the air was pungent with the odor of guano heaped in open piles behind the wharf. Swann, who became mayor and later governor of Maryland during the Civil War, also at one point headed the B&O Railroad. Bars on the second story windows are reputedly left over from the days the warehouse served as a temporary prison for Confederate soldiers. Today the building serves as headquarters for the Belt's Corporation, a warehousing and real estate development firm founded in 1845.

WOODEN HOUSES

Fire was a major problem in the days of wooden houses—not only did city dwellers have to worry about whole blocks burning, but they had to duck rowdy firefighters who'd just as soon swing their pick axes at rival companies as throw buckets of water on the flames. While wooden structures were common in the 18th and early 19th centuries, a 1799 fire law banned them and brick houses became the norm. Survivors stand at 533, 602, and 719 S. Ann Street, 1800 Fleet Street, and 614 Wolfe Street.

ST. STANISLAUS KOSTKA CHURCH

700 S. Ann St. 410-276-2849

Until recently St. Stanislaus gleamed like a lighthouse beacon. Around its steeples, four 20-foot aluminum and copper crosses were illuminated against the night sky. In the early 1900s so many Polish immigrants and their families joined the congregation that the parish built a second church on its upper floor, complete with pews and altar, to serve its burgeoning congregation. Adjacent to it, a big hall hosted religious gatherings and even wrestling and boxing matches, including a 1920s' bout between former world champions Strangler Lewis and the Great Zbyszko. The hall burned in 1978 and today with a dwindling membership, St. Stanislaus is facing closure. In recent years, *Homicide* has filmed several scenes here including the baptism of Frank Pembleton's baby and a scene on its steps where the angst-ridden detective faced a crisis of faith. Mass Sat 4 pm and Sun 10 am and noon.

ON BROADWAY

BROADWAY MARKET

600-700 Block S. Broadway

In the 1780s the Fell family donated land for a market here in the center of Fells Point. A series of sheds with stalls were built for merchants to hawk fresh produce and meats. Today the market is contained in two brick buildings. Along with fresh fruits and vegetables, flowers, fish, meats, and cheeses, you can pick up-a-taste-of Baltimore's ethnic heritage—Polish sausages, Greek spanakopita, and Italian subs and pizzas. Try Mrs. Parr's, located in the North Market, for homemade fudge and confections. This is also the place to buy Mrs. Berger's chocolate top  cookies, which the East Baltimore baking company has been turning out for more than three-quarters of a century. Open daily 9-6; closed Sun.

PORT MISSION
813-815 S. Broadway
Crummy food, fetid and cramped sleeping quarters were an 19th century sailor's lot at sea. On land, it wasn't much better. When innkeepers weren't gouging the boys for lousy meals and cheap gin, they were hustling the services of prostitutes. Appalled by the situation, the Leverings, a coffee merchant family, and others founded this charitable organization in 1881 to encourage church-going and provide room and board for homesick seamen. They set up a reading room filled with international magazines and newspapers, a writing room, post office, and space for church services. The mission also functioned as a community center with weekday night classes for boys and girls in industrial arts and manual training and religious instruction on weekends. Despite the Leverings' good intent, many sailors groused about the mission's paternalism.

VAGABOND PLAYERS

806 S. Broadway. 410-563-9135

In the early days of its existence, the Vagabond Players lived up to its name, roaming from "home to home" until it landed on Broadway in 1973. Back then the building, a former bar and perhaps brothel, sat among boarded up storefronts and crumbling sidewalks. Today the Victorian building has been renovated along with most of the block. Since its beginnings in 1916, the troupe has presented classics by Tennessee Williams and Eugene O'Neill, alternative pieces like Zelda Fitzgerald's *Scandalabra*, as well as contemporary fare.

THE WEST END

LONDON COFFEE HOUSE

854 S. Bond St.

In the late 1700s gentlemen gathered here to drink coffee and offer opinions on politics, patriotism, and any other subject on their minds. Threatened with demolition by its previous owner, Baltimore Gas and Electric subsidiary Constellation Real Estate, the remains have won a reprieve from the Preservation Society who plan to stabilize the building and seek proposals for its reuse.

GEORGE WELLS' HOUSE

1532-34 Thames St.

Historians are unsure whether this 1787 building was Wells' house, or an inn, or perhaps, at different times, served both functions. Wells' shipyard, located across the street, built the Continental Navy's first new frigate, the *Virginia* in 1777. The Preservation Society has performed a rescue operation on the shipbuilding owner's three-and-a-half-story brick structure and hopes to restore it for commercial use.

CHASE'S WHARF AND FUTURE MARITIME PARK

Philpot and Thames Sts.

Once part of a six-building complex named for merchant Thorndick Chase, who lived on this property until his death in 1838, this mid-19th century coffee and sugar warehouse will be undergoing restoration by the Living Classroom Foundation (see below) as part of The Frederick Douglass-Isaac Myers Maritime Park. The brick building with its waterside Flemish stepped roof will house a multi-cultural exhibit commemorating Douglass and Myers and their contributions to Baltimore's maritime industry. The park is located close to the site of the Chesapeake Marine Railway and Dry Dock Company, the 19th century Fells Point shipyard established by Myers, and will provide hands-on demonstrations in ship building. Plans call for reconstruction of a wooden marine railway (similar to one built by Myers, to haul wooden ships from the water for repair) by LCF students in ship-building job training programs.

Did You Know?

Some called him a charlatan; others, a cult leader. He was once tried in a court of law for lunacy for preaching equality and peace among people regardless of race, gender, or religion. He was born George Baker in Rockville, Maryland, and worked in Baltimore at the turn of the century as a gardener and dock laborer, where he experienced the racism and religious inspiration that would shape his philosophy. In fact, Baker's ministry began in a storefront Baptist church on Eden Street, long since lost to time. At the height of his influence in the 1920s through 1940s, he was known as "Father Divine," head of the nationwide Peace Mission headquartered in Harlem, and adored by thousands. After his death in 1965, the movement declined and has all but died out.

LIVING CLASSROOM FOUNDATION

802 S. Caroline St. 410-685-0295
www.livingclassrooms.org
One hundred students took hammers in hand and built the tall ship *Lady Maryland* in 1985. When it was done, the boat became a floating classroom for young

people to learn maritime skills while studying the ecology, economics, and history of the Chesapeake Bay. Originally a program directed at kids-at-risk, offering on-the-job training and hands-on learning as an alternative to traditional classroom study, today the non-profit Living Classroom Foundation is open to school children of all backgrounds. Applying skills in math, science, language arts, ecology, and other academic subjects, students work on projects such as tracking air and water quality, building and maintaining boats, operating navigational equipment, sailing vessels and re-oystering beds. Instead of standard issue four walls, schoolrooms are boats, docks, a lighthouse, island, oyster sanctuary, the submarine *Torsk*, and the Chesapeake itself. The Foundation's innovative programs reach more than 50,000 kids a year. The organization is also developing the Frederick Douglass-Isaac Myers Maritime Park, which will include exhibits on African American maritime history. LCF also runs The Baltimore Maritime Museum (see *Inner Harbor*) and tours on the *Minnie V.* (see *City Jaunts and Tours*).

Little did Isaac Tyson, Jr. realize when he discovered chromite on his Bare Hills estate north of the city in 1810 that his find would one day sire the world's largest chromium chemical plant—AlliedSignal at Block and Point Streets. Tyson did, however, recognize the strike's potential value and began exporting the ore to England for use in paints and ceramics. In 1845, he opened up his own chromite processing plant, The Baltimore Chrome Works, here. By the 1950s the plant, now owned by Allied Chemical, was the biggest chrominium processor on earth. When the factory shut down in the '80s, the huge gray corpse was dismantled and the hazardous material cleaned up. Lots of uses—a park, hotel, opera house, cruise ship docks—have been proposed for these 22 acres.

DOUGLASS PLACE AND STRAWBERRY ALLEY

516-524 Dallas St.

Frederick Douglass built these five brick rowhouses, known as Douglass Place, in 1891 on the site of the old Strawberry Alley Methodist Church. The church, founded by Francis Asbury, the father of the American Methodist movement, had been the first Methodist place of worship to begin construction in Baltimore, although it was not finished until several months after the Lovely Lane Meeting House opened in downtown in 1774. White Methodists gave Strawberry Alley to the black congregants in the early 1800s, which the latter renamed Bethel African Methodist Church. During his years in Fells Point, Douglass, who'd been a parishioner there, had been appalled at the living conditions of free blacks and slaves alike. Upon his acquisition of the old church building, Douglass razed it and built these five homes in 1895, using them as an investment and at the same time, providing decent housing for blacks living in the neighborhood.

Did You Know?

Born Frederick Augustus Washington Bailey on the Eastern Shore, he made his escape from slavery in Baltimore in 1838, settled in Massachusetts, then changed his name to Frederick Douglass to avoid identification and recapture. Having learned to read and write during his years as a slave in Fells Point, he used these skills to embark on a lifelong campaign against slavery and racial discrimination, and soon became one of the most renowned orators of his day. In 1845 he published the first of his three influential autobiographies, *Narrative of the Life of Frederick Douglass*, which brought him international attention and acclaim. With the help of supporters, Douglass bought his freedom in 1846, then his successful abolitionist newspaper, *North Star*, the next year. Although he lived his last years in Washington, D.C., Douglass always regarded Maryland as home and intended to buy land near his birthplace in Talbot County to be buried "in the soil which gave him birth." Unfortunately, this was one dream he did not realize.

POLISH NATIONAL ALLIANCE CLUB COUNCIL 21

1627 Eastern Ave. 410-732-1100

Since 1907, families have been gathering in Fells Point to focus on all things Polish: cultural events, language lessons, and lectures. Their grand hall is the site for weddings and other festivities. The building, purchased by the club in 1956, was originally the location of the Holy Rosary School, now housed on Chester Street.

KOSCIUSZKO PERMANENT LOAN AND SAVINGS ASSOCIATION

1635 Eastern Ave. 410-342-1384

In 1894 a cabinet maker, dentist, barber, shoemaker, lawyer, tavern owner, insurance agent, and grocer (Barbara Mikulski's grandfather Michael Kutz) pooled their money to open a bank so that Polish immigrants like themselves could borrow to buy a house, start a business, or finance whatever else they needed. The bank was named after Revolutionary war hero Thaddeus Kosciuszko, a Polish nobleman who helped the Continental Army fortify strategic military sites. George Washington rewarded him with an appointment to Brigadier General and the Cincinnati Order Medal in 1783. After a failed attempt to help Poland win its independence, Kosciuszko returned home to Philadelphia. When he died in Switzerland in 1817, he left money to buy American slaves freedom as well as to school and provide land for them to live on.

POLISH HOME CLUB

510-12 S. Broadway 410-276-0636

When it comes to having a good time, these folks know how to party—anniversaries, christenings, Valentine's Day, Christmas, any excuse for the over-40 crowd to take a turn across the ballroom beneath the chandeliers and disco ball. With all the calories burned, the dancers dig into chicken and Salisbury steak often cooked by the club women. The long narrow ground floor lounge is called Polska Wioska (Polish Home) and has a long bar overseen by photographs of Kazimierz Pulaski and Tadeusy (Thaddeus) Kosciuszko. Organized in 1906, the club was originally a social gathering spot for Polish immigrants.

BALTIMORE AMERICAN INDIAN CENTER

113 S. Broadway 410-675-3535

For two dozen years the Baltimore American Indian Center has held its annual pow-wow the fourth weekend in August in the city or out in the county. The event provides an opportunity for the public to learn about Native American culture and about Baltimore's Lumbee Indians. The city's 5,000 Native Americans, most of whom are Lumbees, migrated from their native North Carolina from the late 1930s to the 1950s in search of jobs.

The Center was founded in 1968 to provide social, health, and economic assistance to the state's Native American population and today offers daycare, after-school and senior programs, and quarterly cultural events open to the public. Additionally, the organization runs classes in dance, drumming, songs, and cultural history. A youth dance troupe, the Soaring Eagles, performs in Baltimore and throughout the East Coast. A small, but growing museum displays a range of Native American artifacts such as stone arrow and spear points, tools and kachina dolls, as well as artwork and pottery by contemporary artists. Dioramas depict traditional dwellings and village life of tribes across North America. By appointment. Donations accepted.

FELLS POINT CORNER THEATRE

251 S. Ann St. 410-276-7837

Along with staging contemporary dramas like *Molly Sweeney* and rollicking comedies like *Room Service*, the company draws in the neighborhood with its directing, acting, and playwriting workshops and children's drama classes. Its volunteer program uses local help to build sets, make costumes, select props, and perform other theater-related duties. The shows are produced in a renovated 1859 firehouse outfitted with two stages, the lower one for regular productions and the upper for readings and other informal presentations.

NOTABLE QUOTABLE

"Living in Baltimore is like living in a cluster of small villages, each with its own distinct flavor. Baltimore is a great walking town. If you don't like the neighborhood you're in, just walk a couple of blocks and you're in another world."

Louise Titchener, author of mysteries set in Baltimore

Browse and Buy

Fells Point's funky boutiques, antique shops, second-hand and bargain stores draw folks of all ages and incomes. Like everything else in Baltimore, however, the landscape is subject to change. As the area heads more upscale, some of the old bargain basement shops and the iffier new establishments will undoubtedly seek lower rent districts. So far no Gaps or The Limiteds have moved in; thus for the moment, Mom-and-Pop businesses have Broadway and beyond to themselves. However, be warned, shops open, close, and relocate quickly in this shifting market.

Store hours and days of operation, too, fluctuate notoriously. Below is a sampling of shops to use as a starting point for exploration.

ANOTHER PERIOD IN TIME

1708-10 Fleet St. 410-675-4776

With a dozen dealers under one roof, serious collectors and browsers alike have lots to choose from. Furniture dating anywhere from 1770 to 1950, depression glass, stained glass, clocks, dolls, costume jewelry, advertising memorabilia, and art cover two floors.

THE ANTIQUE MAN

1806 Fleet St. 410-732-0932

Just when you think you've seen it all, owners Bob Gerber and Robert Jansen go and put on a sideshow. Sure, this former airplane and car repair warehouse is chock full of treasures: ceramic statuettes, stained glass, fine furniture, an ancient Coke machine. But then there's that taxidermied rooster. But what will really set this place apart is the planned mini-museum of oddities. Step right up to see the two-headed mummy, shrunken heads, a severed foot, four-legged chicken, and, as a bonus, memorabilia of Baltimore's own Johnny Eck, the carnival half-man on display.

FLASHBACK

728 S. Broadway 410-276-5086

In a past life, Bob Adams was John Waters' star Edith Massey's partner in her once-upon-a-time Fells Point second-hand store, Edith's Shopping Bag. Several incarnations later Adams and partner Robert Marsheck have Flashback—a rock 'n' roll-cum-hodgepodge store. Pick up a Jeff Beck or Kinks LP. And don't miss the chance to buy all those youthful memories your mother probably gave away—old magazines and books, the ubiquitous ceramic chicken knickknacks, costume jewelry, concert posters, and so on.

J & M ANTIQUES

1706 Fleet St. 410-732-5339

Along with a little bit of this 'n' that, Yosie Makias sells estate and collectable jewelry. He can also repair your

Aunt Sadie's broach or fashion it into something new. In addition, the Israeli-born Makias crafts menorahs and other Judaica.

SARATOGA TRUNK

1740 Aliceanna St. 410-327-6635
"The debris of my mind," is how owner Vicki McComas characterizes the front room of her shop. Indeed, browsing through the old furniture, jewelry, books, and curios is like rummaging through a favorite aunt's attic. Two cats, Rocky and Bear-Bear, lounge on the pillows, overseeing the wares. Step into the back room and you've entered McComas' pottery studio where whimsical cats, fishes, mermaids, and other clay creatures await.

ARTS AND CRAFTS

MINÁS

733 S. Ann St. 410-732-4258
Sunday afternoon poetry readings and changing exhibitions of art make it worth the short walk off the main tourist path to visit artist Minás Konsolas' shop. To clothe the poetic soul, there's worn-in Levis, vintage wear, discount silver jewelry, and hats by Spoon Popkin. To feed the soul, there's journals of poetry and a fine selection of arty photo postcards.

OFF BROADWAY CLAY

1725 Aliceanna St.410-522-1996
Buy a cup or bowl in potter Diana Levi's shop and you'll come away with a piece of local history at affordable prices. Levi incorporates clay impressions of wooden mold designs hand-carved by a 19th century Baltimore craftsmen. An opera buff, Levi owns two cockatiels named Carmen and Caruso who perch by the pots and sing along with Callas. In addition, Levi offers classes in wheel thrown pots and hand building.

ADRIAN'S BOOK CAFE

714 S. Broadway 410-732-1048

Upstairs browse through cookbooks, novels, or nonfiction while lounging on a couch and sipping an Italian cream soda. Or sit at a table and enjoy veggie chili, Thai peanut noodles, or killer carrot cake. Weekend evenings live music encourages even more lingering. Downstairs, along with more books, Adrian's offers an interesting selection of cards, journals, and postcards.

BLACK PLANET BOOKS

718 S. Broadway 410-563-2008
www.blackplanetdirect.com
Radical is the operative word here. Che Guevara, Marcus Garvey, and Kafka share quarters with Zippy the Pinhead, the occult, and other counter culture subjects in this small store tucked in back of Black & White Chess.

MYSTERY LOVES COMPANY

1730 Fleet St. 410-276-6708 or 800-538-0042

Mystery enthusiasts find Baltimore authors like David Simon, Laura Lippman, Sujata Massey, Louise Titchener, Barbara Lee, Helen Chappell, and Edgar Allan Poe here alongside new and used books by hundreds of other American and British writers. Along with signed first editions, the shop sells custom-made gift baskets filled with mugs, T-shirts, books, and other mystery-themed presents. Don't miss the annual "Mystery Loves Company Conversations with Mystery Writers," talks co-sponsored with Johns Hopkins University's Odyssey program.

REPTILIAN RECORDS

403 S. Broadway 410-327-6853

A string of skeleton lights in the window is a tipoff that this is not your typical record store. Underground and independent labels—punk rock, ska, hardcore, and so on—dominate the CDs and vinyl sold here. Proprietor Chris X even has a house record label. In the back of

288

the shop there are more than 1,400 weirdo videos you'll want to keep out of kiddies' views. Rent classics like *Hot Rod Girls* and *Jail Bait*, '60s driver education films, Japanese animation, performance art, and the ever intriguing Survival Research Lab films of fighting robots.

CLOTHING

AFTER MIDNIGHT
819 S. Broadway 410-563-3870
Dancers and other trendy dressers come here for dark body conscious clothes. While the gals look around, men can browse the selection of Jerry Garcia and Nicole Miller ties. As a bonus, the Horner family doles out treats to dogs who shop with their owners.

KARMIC CONNECTION
508 S. Broadway 410-558-0428
Like wow! Plaid polyester pants. Didn't you throw out a pair like that in the '70s? And whoa, those tie-dye tapestries—not to mention the herbal smokes—are bringing on acid flashbacks. Trendy dressers and nostalgia buffs alike will find enough retro in this clothes store-head shop to make the late Divine swoon.

KILLER TRASH
1929 Eastern Ave. 410-675-2449
Doll yourself up like a real Hon with killer second hand clothes—*de rigueur* leopard vest ($35), blue sequin shoes ($9.95), black bustier ($12), and gold lamé pants ($10). For more sedate moments, pick up jeans, dresses, and shirts. Stop by the emporium next door for fuzzy dice, ceramic kitties, and kitsch.

ROMANCE STUDIOS
1714 Fleet St. 410-675-2595
Jennifer Brown hand-crafts millinery, jewelry, fantasy gowns, and accessories for brides or "anyone with a yen for glamor." Stop in for tiaras, sunglasses, bags, and other dress up items.

STIKKY FINGERS

802 S. Broadway 410-675-7588

Like the Rolling Stones' album of the same name, this store is baaaaad. The pierced and tattooed staff sport pink and purple hair. The walls are dark as a raven's wing. The merchandise ranges from black leather getups to streetwalker bustiers to Clockwork Orange-style boots. Body piercing available.

HOME ACCESSORIES AND GIFTS

BAY AND COUNTRY CRAFTS

1635 Lancaster St. 410-342-3317

Become one with Baltimore. Take home a screen painting or a brick painted to resemble the Cat's Eye Pub or other Baltimore-themed crafts by local artists.

BLACK & WHITE CHESS AND GIFTS

718 S. Broadway 410-534-5747

Join a tournament, play a game, or take a lesson at this chess arcade-cum-game store. Chess sets range from $15 to $1,200 for a steel cast ensemble sculpted by Kenneth Kuhn. Other chess-related items like ties, boxes, and books are for sale.

TEN THOUSAND VILLAGES

1621 Thames St. 410-342-5568

Shopping in Ten Thousand Villages is like visiting a Third World bazaar with items like handmade marbleized paper from Bangladesh, rice patterned dishes from Vietnam, and red kissi stone checkers from Kenya. The store itself is part of an alternative trading organization that buys crafts from impoverished artisans in Asia, Latin America, Africa, as well as the United States, enabling them to afford food, shelter, and health care.

Sea shanties played as macaws, Saigon and Singapore, perched on co-owners Captain Steve Bunker and Sharon Bondroff's shoulders. For years their store—China Sea Trading Company on South Ann Street— offered portholes, navy uniforms, lanterns, telescopes, antique weaponry, navigational instruments, and other stuff salvaged from old ships crammed the high- ceilinged warehouse. The African art scattered throughout the store recalled the days when Bunker's father had a trading post on the West Coast of the continent. Alas, Bunker and Bondroff will be bidding their store bon voyage sometime in 1999.

Epicurean Bites

BERTHA'S
734 S. Broadway 410-327-5795
For nearly three decades countless cars have sported green-and-white "Eat Bertha's Mussels" bumper stick-

ers. But just who was Bertha? When Laura and Tony Norris purchased this former scruffy old seamen's bar in 1972, they lifted the moniker from a stained glass memorial window inscribed with the name of

Bertha E. Bartholomew, a local piano and elocution teacher. Today, step into the tunnel of a lounge, its ceiling adorned with Christmas lights, a dingy, a grotesque clad in a wet suit, and other curiosities. Tuesday through Friday listen to jazz, blues, swing, and Dixieland musicians who cram into the front corner. The restaurant, a warren of rooms in the back, serves mussel specialties, along with steaks, chicken, and other seafood. Trifles, coconut-damson tarts, and afternoon tea (served daily except Sundays) reflect the owners' Scottish heritage. L, D. Br, Sun. Reservations recommended for tea. $$

THE BLACK OLIVE
814 S. Bond St. 410-276-7141

The Spiliadis family has transformed this former general store into a charming Greek taverna. Aegean blue tablecloths, white washed brick walls, and old pottery provide the backdrop for *kakavia* (a forerunner of bouillabaisse), grilled lamb with polenta, and grilled octopus. Step up to the deli case and choose from a selection of bronzini, Dover sole, rockfish, or whatever fresh catch has come in. Greek, French, and Israeli wines complement a memorable meal. D. Reservations recommended. $$$

Did You Know?

Since 1919 Victor Ostrowski and Son's has been making sausage for Baltimore. Kielbasa conossieurs also flock here for homemade Polish specialties like horseradish with red beets, and Krakowska (Polish garlic bologna), liver sausage, noodles, and pantry basics imported from Poland. Eastertime Polish families purchase sausage here to put in baskets with eggs, wine, bread, and butter for the Traditional Blessing of the Easter items at Holy Rosary and St. Stanislaus churches. Wed-Sat. 524 S. Washington St. 410-327-8935.

BLUE MOON CAFE

1621 Aliceanna St. 410-522-3940

The cafe's pale yellow interior with blue moldings evoke moon and sky. Even the art work on the walls is themed to heavenly bodies. Late risers can order omelets, cinnamon buns, and eggs Benedict all day, while those up with the sun can opt for lunchtime sandwiches, salads, and crab cakes. Fri & Sat the restaurant re-opens at 11 pm and stays open all night. ☽ $

CHARLESTON

1000 Lancaster St. (Sylvan Learning Center bldg.)
410-332-7373

Chef Cindy Wolf's latest venture, all pastels, palm-patterned wallpaper, and lattice work, sprawls over several rooms including a "wine library." Sit at the chef's tables facing the open kitchen where amid the sizzle and steam Wolf turns out grilled salmon with pomegranate sauce, juniper-scented grilled loin of pork, and other Southern culinary masterpieces. An impressive wine list accompanies her ever-changing menu. D. Reservations recommended. Open until 11 weekends. ☽ $$$

EL TAQUITO MEXICANA

1744 Eastern Ave. 410-563-7840

Bring your own *cerveza* and chow down on real Mexican food at this red checker tablecloth eatery. Beneath piñatas, customers chat in Spanish or watch Hispanic TV news programs. Order burritos, enchiladas, or tacos or try out the more exotic *chuletas en mole roja o verde* (pork chops in red or green sauce) or *conejo adobado* (seasoned rabbit). L, D. $

FUNK'S DEMOCRATIC COFFEE SPOT

1818 Eastern Ave. 410-276-3865

Yep, Funk's is funky. First there's the name—a legacy of the Polish Democratic Club and the Confectionery that once occupied the row house. Then there's the crash pad decor. But the food's cheap and plentiful—bean burritos, potato knishes, hearty soups and stews, homemade cheesecakes. Tuesday nights feature poetry readings. And there's always the stray composer ready to tap out his latest creation on the old upright piano. B (lite fare) L, D. $

HAMILTON'S
Admiral Fell Inn, 888 S. Broadway. 410-522-2195
With an eye to color and texture, Hamilton's presents its New American cuisine, an ever-changing menu of game, veal, scallops, and Angus tenderloins with fresh seasonal produce, in one of Fells Point's more elegant and historic settings. D. Reservations recommended. $$$

HENNINGER'S TAVERN
1812 Bank St. 410-342-2172
Once a speakeasy and then a Polish VFW hall, Henninger's Tavern has a two-decade old following. Both the lounge and dining room decor are notable for their collection of disaster photographs, glossies of old "showgirls," and prize fighters. A changing menu features great crab cakes and other top-notch American and Continental dishes. D. Open until 11 weekends. $$$

JIMMY'S RESTAURANT
801 S. Broadway 410-327-3273
A cast of Bawlmer characters from politicians to businesspeople to sailors to common laborers dine on cheap eats at this old-fashioned grazing spot. Eavesdrop on verbal political brawls, some encouraged by proprietor Nick Filipidis, while dining on subs, burgers, seafood, steaks, and eggs at red checker vinyl-clad tables. B, L, D. $

JOHN STEVEN, LTD
1800 Thames St. 410-327-5561
At the front bar the young and tattooed compete with middle-aged couples for counter space, micro brews, sushi, and steamers. To the rear, diners pack informal sea captainish dining rooms to sup on crab soup and dishes like crab cakes, Cajun crawfish pie, mussels, and fettucine with pesto. L, D. Sushi bar until 1:30 am. $$

MARGARET'S CAFE

909 Fell St. 410-276-5605

A local artists' hangout and vegetarian's delight, this cozy cafe offers health and fruit shakes, veggie specials, and meat dishes along with seafood delivered fresh from the Eastern shore by Margaret's dad. The Halcyon Gallery upstairs showcases paintings, sculptures, and multi-media installations, and hosts poetry readings, lectures, and wine tastings. L, D. Br, Sat & Sun. Open until 11 Fri & Sat. $½

OBRYCKI'S

1727 E. Pratt St. 410-732-6399
www.obryckis.com

Since 1944 customers have been greeted with the sound of mallets tapping against crustacean as diners indulge in the Maryland ritual of eating steamed crabs. Don't want to get your hands messy? There's crab cakes, meat, pasta, and fish you can eat with a fork. Between courses, stroll around the arched brick dining room and look at late *Baltimore Sun* photographer A. Aubrey Bodine's 1930s prints of the city. And if you want to share the bounty with faraway friends, Obrycki's will ship by FedEx. L, D. Open mid Mar-Nov. $$½

PIERPOINT

1822 Aliceanna St. 410-675-2080

Sit at a table near the open kitchen if you want to watch renowned chef Nancy Longo create her culinary takes on Maryland cuisine. Appetizers like smoked duck quesadillas and eggplant layer cake lead into entrees like Maryland style cioppino, poussin, and cornfried oysters. L, D. Br, Sun. Reservations recommended. Open until 11 weekends. $$$

RESTAURANTE SAN LUIS

246 S. Broadway 410-327-0266 or 0267

Hispanic news station provides background music and folks at neighboring tables chat in Spanish. A good sign. Now open the menu. *Pupusas*, shrimp in sour cream, flank steak with fried plantains. No Tex-Mex here, but authentic Salvadorian food. And at bargain prices. L, D. Open until 11 weekends. ☾ $

THE DAILY GRIND

1722 Thames St. 410-558-0399

Munch and his fellow *Homicide* detectives got their caffeine fixes here. Along with the *latte*, The Grind serves bagels, sandwiches, and pastries. Play chess, read *City Paper*, or just hang out in the back room. Lite fare daily from 7 am until midnight. Open until 1 am weekends. ☾ $

LIQUID EARTH

1626 Aliceanna St. 410-276-6606

This cozy coffee and juice shop features java, desserts, and vegetarian sandwiches along with exotic concoctions like Rabbit Test—a blend of organic carrots and loads of other veggies. In keeping with the natural theme, the bar of this former dairy building is decorated with embedded stones. Light fare from 7 am weekdays; from 8 am weekends. ☾ $

A June Saturday night in Fells Point. Taxis, cars, motorcycles, and limos prowl bumper to bumper past the market on narrow, cobble-stoned streets. Swarms of college kids and young professionals head for Rodos and Moby's wending around food vendors, the occasional homeless guy, and older folks out for a walk. Along Broadway and Thames music spills out of clubs and bars, and in front of Leadbetter's folks are dancing on the sidewalk. Away from the main event, dozens of pubs scattered throughout quiet residential neighborhoods cater to locals. At the other extreme, toward downtown, concertgoers flood Fletcher's and Bohager's, while Parrot Island's DJs entertain the masses beneath rustling, and very unindigenous, palms. Listed below are a few of Fells Point's saloons and clubs.

BOHAGER'S

515 S. Eden St. 410-563-7220
TicketMaster 410-481-SEAT
Bohager's books acts like Los Lobos, The Black Crowes, Aaron Neville, and the Dave Matthews Band, drawing sold-out crowds. Friday and Saturday nights DJs rule as dancers take to the floor. Light fare available.

CAT'S EYE PUB

1730 Thames St. 410-276-9866
The band is rocking out Hendrix as the crowd, crammed shoulder to shoulder in the small, narrow front room, boogie along. Above them hang a United Nations of flags, including one from The Conch Republic, Jimmy Buffet's home country. The Cat's Eye offers blues and zydeco to jazz and acoustic nightly at 9. Saturday nights are devoted to Irish music with bands playing at 4 and 9 pm. Weekends in the back bar, Kitty's Cookin' offers homemade specialities like coddies, shepherd's pie, and jambalaya at pub prices.

FLETCHER'S

701 S. Bond St. 410-880-8124
TicketMaster 410-481-SEAT
Fletcher's cramped second floor space regularly features alternative rock, but electronic, acid jazz, solo acoustic, blues, New Orleans funk, and swing acts often perform on its small raised stage. Plan on standing, dancing (space permitting), or sitting on the floor (when the act inspires thoughtful listening). On the first floor is a noisy, smokey, dark bar with pool tables, foos ball, and cheap brews. Show nights vary. Tickets avail-

able from TicketMaster, The Sound Garden (1619 Thames), or occasionally at the door.

FULL MOON SALOON

1710 Aliceanna St. 410-276-6388 or 410-558-2873
Slash from Guns and Roses stopped by to jam. So did Bruce Willis when he was filming *12 Monkeys*. And the Beach Boy's sideman rolled in his own keyboard. Baltimore's "home of the blues" showcases local and national bands who play what co-owner Zeke Phillips calls "blues with teeth." Find a seat on a cracked vinyl bar stool or back in the blues pews, makeshift wooden booths facing the stage adorned with a mural of a wolf howling at the moon. Imports and micro brews compliment home-style chow like red beans and rice, gumbo, and hoppin' john. Jams on Mons. Nightly shows begin at 9:30.

THE HORSE YOU CAME IN ON

1626 Thames St. 410-327-8111
Peanut shells on the floor, live music, and a fumbling ghost named Edgar who's responsible for all broken glasses mark Fells Point's oldest pub (circa 1775), once a hangout for rowdy seamen. Today everyone from businesspeople to ex-hippies to old salts show up for drinks, music, and the occasional game of foos ball. The Horse got its 15 minutes of fame when writer Martha Grimes sent Melrose Plant and Richard Jury to puzzle out a mystery here in a novel titled after the bar. Live music nightly.

LEADBETTER'S 2 TAVERN

1639 Thames St. 410-675-4794
www.erols.com/fons1/leadbetters.htm
When John Waters went down Broadway in the '60s, he took a stool at the wooden bar here among scruffy sea-men and plotted *Pink Flamingos*. Named after leg-endary blues guitarist Leadbelly, the saloon, even with its sailor-era patina, has turned a bit more respectable. Today folks drop by to hear regional musicians play rock, jazz, blues, and progressive music. Music from 9:30. Open mike Mon.

PARROT ISLAND

701 S. Eden St. 410-522-1000

Palm trees and Tiki huts in Charm City? This tropical bar-and-restaurant-on-steroids contains five, mostly open air bars and sprawls across a chunk of Fells Point's warehousing area. Early in the day, families pile in for the all-you-can-eat lunch buffet and the inexpensive American food menu. By 10 pm, party animals take over, boogying beer in hand to the DJ's choice. Live acoustic music Thurs and Fri. Happy hours and island music Sun afternoon. L, D Wed-Sun. Open April-Oct.

WEE PETER'S PUB

706 S. Broadway 410-276-7870

A bell clangs as a customer slips off her bra from beneath her sweater. Cheers erupt and the bartender rewards the lady with a Jagermeister. The discarded lingerie gets a spot on the wall or ceiling amid Peter's autographed underwear collection. Most nights, aside from willing female patrons, the juke box provides entertainment, but first Tuesdays an acoustic guitarist performs. Closed Sun.

Did You Know?

Started in 1995 to promote the arts and humanities in Baltimore, the Fells Point Creative Alliance helps artists find exhibit, studio, and living spaces; offers a data base of press contacts, galleries, and clients; and holds bi-monthly forums for members to show and discuss works. A quarterly newsletter lists exhibits, lectures, classes, readings, music, and theatrical productions. The annual Big Show, a members-only exhibition, is held in October. In 1998 the Alliance was given a grant to transform the old Patterson Theater on Eastern Avenue in Highlandtown into a multi-use cultural center (see *Highlandtown*). 909 Fell St. 410-276-1651. www.charm.net~fpca.

Fells Point

1. Admiral Fell Inn
2. Brown's Wharf
3. Broadway Pier
4. City Recreation Pier and "*Homicide* Headquarters"
5. Waterfront Hotel Restaurant
6. Orpheum Cinema
7. Robert Long House
8. Maryland Maritime Visitor's Center
9. Early Merchant's House
10. Maryland Maritime Museum (future)
11. William Price's House
12. John Price's House (Margaret's Cafe)
13. Captain John Steele's House
14. Belt's Wharf
15. Henderson's Wharf
16. Swann's Wharf
17. Wooden Houses
18. St. Stanislaus Kostka Church
19. Broadway Market
20. Port Mission
21. Vagabond Players
22. Shakespeare Street and Fells Family Grave Marker
23. London Coffee House
24. George Wells' House
25. Chase's Wharf and future site of Frederick Douglass-Isaac Myers Maritime Park
26. Former AlliedSignal Site
27. Living Classroom Foundation
28. Douglass Place and Strawberry Alley
29. Polish National Alliance Club Council
30. Kosciuszko Permanent Loan and Savings Assoc.
31. Polish Home Club
32. Baltimore American Indian Center
33. Fells Point Corner Theatre

Washington Hill

Seamen and merchants lived here. Edgar Allan Poe died here. One of the country's great medical centers sits at its upper edge. Washington Hill is also a mirror reflecting the rise, demise, and renewal of many urban neighborhoods. Named for the old Washington Medical College, now Church Home and Hospital, the historic district of Washington Hill is bounded by Eden Street on the west, Ann Street to the east, and Fayette and Lombard Streets to the north and south, respectively.

Houses appeared on the Hill as early as 1812 when Fells Point began to expand north along Broadway, yet the area remained mostly farmland until the 1830s when immigrants pushed east from Jonestown and north from the Point. The mid-1800s found Washington Hill an ethnic mix of German, Irish, Polish, Russian, Jewish, and Bohemian immigrants. With the newcomers came their churches and culture.

The 1850s brought considerable residential construction, including many fashionable townhomes, the Jacob W. Hugg house among them (see below). The majority of the wealthier residences on the Hill lay to the east of Broadway, while to the west, the poorer neighborhoods sheltered successive waves of European newcomers. The area prospered as an ethnically diverse community until shortly after World War II when the great flight to suburbia hit the community hard. The remaining residents fought back against the ensuing decay, establishing the Citizens for Washington Hill in 1971. Today, this largely residential community is a mix of older renovated homes and new construction, including the first housing in Maryland exclusively developed for artists. The community impetus has also brought in both municipal and federal monies for revitalization of this historic neighborhood.

While a few of the attractions described below are outside of this district, they are included here due to their long association with this general area of East Baltimore.

CHURCH HOME AND HOSPITAL
(FORMERLY WASHINGTON MEDICAL COLLEGE)

N. Broadway and E. Fairmount Ave.

In October, 1849, when Edgar Allan Poe was found nearly comatose at a voting station in an E. Lombard Street tavern, he was carted off to this hospital. He died here a few days later without regaining consciousness. Ironically, his aunt and mother-in-law, Maria Poe Clemm, also died at Church Home several years later. The institution, founded in 1833 as the Washington Medical College, was later renamed Church Home and Hospital.

WILDEY AND LATROBE MONUMENTS

Broadway, btw. E. Baltimore St. and E. Fairmount Ave.

This wide median of Broadway contains two statues of historical interest. At the intersection with Fairmount Avenue stands a monument to Thomas Wildey who founded the first Oddfellows Lodge in America in 1819 at Fells Point. Atop the marble column, a statue of Charity with a child in one arm, another under her protective hand, symbolizes the mission of the Oddfellows to "visit the sick, relieve the distressed, bury the dead, and educate the orphan." A block south, seven-term mayor of Baltimore Ferdinand Latrobe, cousin to the family of architects, strikes a commanding pose in front of an obelisk bearing the dates of his service, 1875-1895.

ARTISANS' ROW

1400 Block of E. Baltimore St.

Local artists, community activists, and the municipal government collaborated to develop the first cooperatively owned housing for artists in Maryland. Named "Artisans' Row," the co-op consists of 32 residential units, some with studios, all occupied since the mid-1980s by artists and related arts professionals. The large communal gardens in the rear, designed by a resident landscaper, are maintained by residents. While there are no storefronts on the row, some artists sell out of their studios by appointment. Every two years or so resident-artists hold a group exhibit for the public.

BROADWAY PHARMACY

E. Baltimore St. and Broadway 410-563-2500

Reputed to be the oldest pharmacy in the city, the Broadway Pharmacy has been dispensing potions and prescriptions to area residents since 1867. The pharmacy, originally called "John Hancock's Apothecary," today includes a liquor store along with its pharmaceutical counter.

JACOB W. HUGG'S HOUSE

1701 E. Baltimore St.

Jacob W. Hugg, a former Fells Point seaman-risen-to-clipper-merchant, built this handsome house in 1846. Today a historic fixture in Washington Hill, it has been converted to co-op apartments. Note the intricate cast-iron grill work on the balconies along the side of the house on Broadway; much of this ornamentation is original. Not open to the public.

JOHNS HOPKINS HOSPITAL AND SCHOOL OF MEDICINE

600 N. Wolfe St. 410-955-5000

Financier Johns Hopkins bequeathed the bulk of his vast fortune for the establishment of three fine Baltimore institutions: Johns Hopkins University (at Homewood) and Johns Hopkins Hospital and School of Medicine, here at the top of Washington Hill. Although technically not a part of the historic district of Washington Hill, the Johns Hopkins medical complex and its affiliate, the Kennedy Krieger Institute, intertwine with the northern edge of the neighborhood.

Johns Hopkins Hospital opened in 1889, followed by the medical school in 1893. Part of the delay in opening the School of Medicine, surprisingly, was the lack of funds. Mary Elizabeth Garrett, daughter of the B&O magnate, and several of her friends organized the Women's Medical Fund Committee to raise the necessary cash on the two conditions that first, Hopkins would have to establish the highest standards for entry of any such school in the country, and second, they'd have to admit women to the medical school. The university trustees agreed, after some debate, and only one faculty member resigned in protest. Four prominent physicians were retained by the university to establish and run the hospital departments, and later the medical school: William Welch (pathology), William Osler (medicine), Howard Kelly (gynecology), and William Halstead (surgery). These medical pioneers were immortalized in a painting by John Singer Sargent, appropriately titled, "The Four Doctors," which still hangs in the Welch Medical Library at N. Wolf and Monuments Streets.

Although fairly young, compared to the University of Maryland Hospital and School of Medicine, Johns Hopkins has an international reputation for excellence in medical care and research. In 1995, Johns Hopkins Medicine was formed to unite Hopkins' research, teaching, clinical care, and businesses enterprises, along with several city and regional affiliated hospitals under one umbrella, making it one of the largest employers in Maryland.

Did You Know?

Dr. William Halstead, along with other Hopkins surgeons, ushered in the modern era of surgical garb in his attempts to establish antiseptic operating conditions. (Previously, surgeons operated resplendent in frock coats worn straight off the street.) When Halstead's fiancee, an operating room nurse, became allergic to the strong chemical solutions used to cleanse the surgical personnel's bare hands, the ingenious surgeon also developed rubber gloves for her to wear in the operating rooms. In addition, Halstead pioneered the use of nerve-blocking anesthesia in surgery.

KENNEDY KRIEGER INSTITUTE

707 N. Broadway 410-502-9262

Just north of Johns Hopkins lies one of the foremost centers in the country for diagnosis, treatment, and research of disorders of the brain in children. The Kennedy Krieger Institute, affiliated with Hopkins, provides both inpatient and outpatient services for more than 10,000 children annually, and operates a nationally recognized lower and middle day school for children with learning disabilities and/or neurological impairment. Baltimore surgeon Winthrop Phelps founded the Institute in 1837 for the treatment of children with cerebral palsy, the first such facility in the country. In 1992, the Institute was renamed in honor of assassinated President Kennedy and long time board member Zanvyl Krieger.

SOJOURNER-DOUGLASS COLLEGE

500 N. Caroline St. 410-276-0306
http://host.sdc.edu

In 1972, community leaders and a local council of churches together with Antioch College, opened an adult education center to serve the black community. In 1980 that institution blossomed into Sojourner-Douglass College, named after famous abolitionists Sojourner Truth and Frederick Douglass. Today the largely African American school operates on a tri-semester system, offering bachelor's degrees in administration, human and social resources, and human growth and development. The school, the only predominately black private college in Maryland, has additional campuses on the Eastern Shore and Annapolis, as well as in the Bahamas.

WELLS AND McCOMUS MONUMENT

Southeast corner of Monument and Aisquith Sts.

The future of the young republic looked grim on September 12, 1814, as Captain Edward Aisquith's sharp shooter battalion watched the British march up North Point Road. The redcoats had sacked Washington, burning the White House and Capitol, and were advancing on Baltimore to root out the privateers that so plagued the British fleet. Daniel Wells and Henry McComus—aged 19 and 18, respectively—friends and apprentice saddle makers but now comrades in the militia, spied General Robert Ross, the British land forces' commander, and took careful aim and shot him. When Ross died seconds later, his infantry retaliated with fire, instantly killing the boys. But the damage was done. Dispirited, the redcoats continued their march on Baltimore, but retreated hastily the next day when faced with the barrage of cannon and men along the ramparts of Hampstead Hill (now Patterson Park). The land portion of the two-prong attack on Baltimore was over, and as of dawn, September 14, the British naval forces withdrew from their failed attack on Fort McHenry.

DIVINE SITES

FIRST BAPTIST CHURCH

525 N. Caroline St. 410-675-2333

The First Colored People's Baptist Church, as it was initially named, was founded in 1836 by former slaves and the Reverend Moses Clayton, a free black who risked his life traveling here from his native Norfolk to establish the church. (The 1831 slave rebellion led by Nat Turner in Virginia had struck fear among whites in the south, and in response, Maryland, like many others, enacted laws prohibiting free blacks from traveling between states and teaching slaves to read or write.) Once in Baltimore, Moses Clayton waged a battle against the exclusion of blacks from public schools, petitioning the city to relieve African Americans from paying taxes for public education when they were not permitted to attend classes. When the city denied the petition, the church added secular courses to its children's Bible study curriculum.

The church, built in 1881, has a Memorial Room containing documents, Bibles, and other memorabilia of church history dating from the 1830s to present day. Service Sun 10:45 am.

ST. MICHAEL'S CHURCH
1900 E. Lombard St.
ST. PATRICK'S CHURCH
Broadway and Bank St.
Tours of both churches: 410-276-1646
St. Patrick's Church in Fells Point traces its roots to the city's second Roman Catholic parish, founded in 1792 by French Sulpician priests for a largely Irish congregation. (The first, St. Peter's Pro-Cathedral, no longer in existence, was started in 1770 by the Jesuits for French Acadians expelled from Canada.) In 1995, due to declining attendance and dearth of priests, St. Patrick's joined with nearby St. Michael's (originally a German immigrant church dating from 1857) to form a combined parish. St. Michael's-St. Patrick's serves an increasingly Hispanic population and offers bilingual, English, and Spanish masses. Tours by appointment. Donations.

HOLY TRINITY RUSSIAN ORTHODOX CHURCH
1723 E. Fairmount Ave. 410-276-6171
Since acquiring this former Lutheran church in 1919, Holy Trinity has served the once vibrant Russian immigrant community, now dwindling as families moved to the suburbs over the years. However, the annual Russian Festival in October draws crowds eager to sample traditional culture and crafts such as egg painting, and to enjoy a smorgasbord of old-country dishes. Throughout the year, Russian crafts are sold after Sunday 10 am service.

SITE OF THE EDEN STREET SYNAGOGUE

15-21 S. Eden St.

Built in 1848 as the city's third synagogue, Eden Street began as a congregation founded in Fells Point as early as 1838. When a new Torah was dedicated in 1851, it was the first Torah consecrated in the United States instead of Europe. When the synagogue closed at the turn of the century, the Aitz Chaim Congregation acquired the building and remained at the site until merging with another assembly to form the Liberty Jewish Center in 1961. The deteriorating building was razed in 1976.

ST. FRANCIS XAVIER CHURCH

Corner of E. Oliver and N. Caroline Sts. 410-727-3103

St. Francis Xavier, founded in 1864, was the first Roman Catholic parish church in the nation dedicated exclusively to African Americans. The congregants trace their roots to worshipping in the basement of St. Mary's Seminary Chapel, where the Oblate Sisters of Providence were formed in 1829 (see "Oblate Sisters" in *West Baltimore*). After a series of moves, the black Catholics of Baltimore were given the basement chapel of St. Ignatius for worship in 1857. When they outgrew this facility, the Jesuits established St. Francis Xavier, which was taken over in 1871 by the Josephites, who continue to administer the church today.

The congregation acquired its present building, the former St. Paul's church, in 1933. At 204 feet, the square bell tower is a neighborhood landmark, as is the church with its imposing granite exterior. The interior woodwork and pews are all original, as are the Italian marble altars. Note: Shortly after receiving her masters degree in Social Work from the University of Maryland, future US Senator Barbara Mikulski headed up the parish's social services office in 1965. Services Sun 7:30 & 10 am, 12:15 pm. Tours by appointment. Donations.

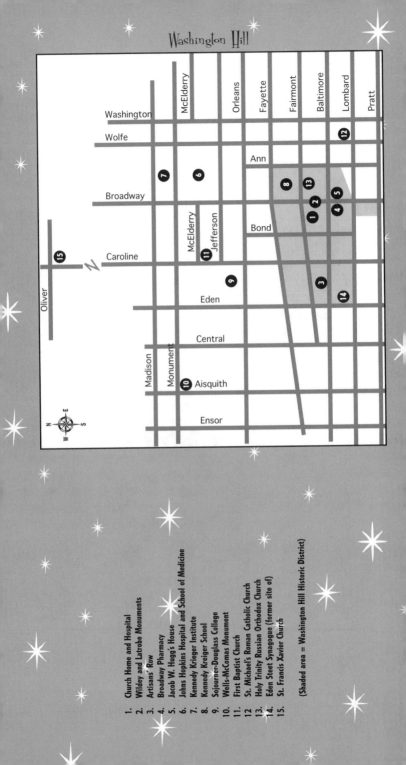

Washington Hill

1. Church Home and Hospital
2. Wildey and Latrobe Monuments
3. Artisans' Row
4. Broadway Pharmacy
5. Jacob W. Hugg's House
6. Johns Hopkins Hospital and School of Medicine
7. Kennedy Krieger Institute
8. Kennedy Kreiger School
9. Sojourner-Douglass College
10. Wells-McComas Monument
11. First Baptist Church
12. St. Michael's Roman Catholic Church
13. Holy Trinity Russian Orthodox Church
14. Eden Steet Synagogue (former site of)
15. St. Francis Xavier Church

(Shaded area = Washington Hill Historic District)

Canton

The sound of hammering fills the air as gentrification sweeps this former blue-collar enclave. Factories become artists' lofts or luxury condos. Formstone comes down; wooden decks go up. Around O'Donnell Square trendy saloons and restaurants cater to the professionals, artists, and empty nesters who've discovered this waterfront "small town." To top it off there's boat slips, a gourmet Safeway, and a brand-new Bibelot mega-bookstore.

But go beyond the waterfront and O'Donnell Square and you'll find the Canton of generations past—the small shops like Kurek's Hardware (3242 O'Donnell St.) with its personal service, Harry's Bakery (2400 Fleet St.) with its Polish baked goods, and of course, the people who kept the neighborhood alive, people who've grown up and stayed on to live and work in Canton. In warm weather you'll find these folks, sitting on their marble stoops watching kids play ball in the streets.

In August 1785, Captain John O'Donnell sailed into Baltimore on the *Pallas* carrying a shipload of china, silks, tea, and other wares from Canton, China. At that time the area east of Fells Point was owned by several large estates and O'Donnell, flush with money, soon joined the landed gentry, buying nearly  2,000 acres over a decade and building (near today's Boston Street between Clinton Street and Highland Avenue) a low East Indian style home named after his favorite port, Canton.

As the shipping industry crept eastward, the town's seafaring community developed. In 1797 the *Constellation* was launched from Major David Stodder's shipyard on Harris Creek. Some of the labor on that boat may have come from the slaves Stodder owned. Seeing the potential of the area, O'Donnell's son Columbus, along with a group of businessmen, founded the Canton Company in 1829.

They were granted the right to build a residential and industrial community of up to 10,000 acres and improve it with streets, wharves, shipworks, factories, stores, and dwellings.

Canton soon moved into the industrial age. In 1830 Peter Cooper—using a little engine, scrap iron, and musket barrels—pieced together the first successful steam locomotive, *The Tom Thumb*. Later, in the 1860s, armor plates for the iron-clad *Monitor*, which battled the *Merrimac* at Hampton Roads, were forged in the Canton Iron Works. Another local company, the Patapsco Bridge and Iron Works, built iron truss Bollman bridges that spanned waters in cities from here to Mexico. And by 1892, Standard Oil, which had bought out Canton's smaller refineries, was turning out 5,000 barrels of oil a day.

The area stepped into the national limelight when the Canton Racetrack hosted the Whig convention in 1840. Henry Clay, representing "Cotton Whigs," and Daniel Webster, the northern contingent, rallied the party around military hero William Henry Harrison for president. Enthusiasm and votes were garnered by offering hard cider to the citizenry. Harrison died one month into office and his successor John Tyler soon became estranged from the party. (In 1844 the Whigs met at the downtown Universalist church and handed the candidacy to Clay.)

Meanwhile around the waterfront, cargo piers and wharves arose along with more canneries, shipbuilding companies, copperworks, breweries, poultry feed, and fertilizer plants. From the 1870s through the 1920s, European immigrants filtered in. More brick rowhouses went up and elements so characteristic of East Baltimore residences—marble steps, stained glass door inserts, and painted screens—began to appear.

In the late 19th century, taverns and lunchrooms (35¢ a meal) fed factory workers and sailors alike. For recreation and an opportunity to bathe (most homes lacked bathtubs), residents headed to the 2nd Avenue beach (later Cardiff Avenue). Three cents got you soap, a bathing suit rental, and a swim. Sunday afternoons Baptists waded out into the waters to perform baptisms, hence earning the beach the nickname "Baptizing Shore."

In 1917 the army opened Camp Holabird, a quartermaster depot, on 225 acres of farmland to the east. By mid-century the post had expanded into Fort Holabird, a military equipment development center and a training site for its counterintelligence corps. It shut down in the early 1970s, its army intelligence school parceled out to Fort Huachuca, Arizona.

Much of Canton's history has been entwined with Fells Point, and the 1966 proposal to run Interstate 83 through the community proved no exception. Joining with their neighbors in Fells Point and Federal Hill, Canton residents fought against the expressway for more than a decade until the city re-routed the road. By then the Canton Company had grown into the largest privately held marine terminal on the East Coast. Exxon Corporation, which had closed its refineries and had become a storage and distribution facility, along with General Motors had stayed on, yet other industries were folding. Vacant factories and warehouses dotted the waterfront.

As Baltimore's Inner Harbor Renaissance flourished, entrepreneurs started eying Canton. In the 1980s the old Tin Decorating Company was fashioned into Tindeco Wharf's upscale apartments. Canton Cove, formerly a specialty canning company, was transformed into luxury condos. Other conversions followed. The American Can Company on Boston Street has been recently renovated into a business and shopping complex and the Harbor Enterprise Center at 1301 S. Baylis Street, popularly known as "The Broom Factory" because brooms were once manufactured here, now houses 75 artist studios and small businesses.

Nowadays, down by the waterfront, Boston Street looks spiffier thanks to a facelift that expanded its two lanes to four. The Promenade, a brick walkway along the harbor partially completed as of this writing, will one day link up to Fells Point, the Inner Harbor, and beyond.

O'DONNELL SQUARE

O'Donnell Square, on O'Donnell Street between Linwood Avenue and Potomac Street, was once the site of a 19th century farmers' market and Canton's business district. Today the park is a pleasant chunk of greenery with benches and flowers. Dog walkers and mothers with small children walk under the gaze of Captain John O'Donnell whose statue stands near the center. Across Linwood Avenue, Engine Company Number 22 anchors the west end of the square while the stone Messiah Lutheran Church looks out over the east. When the firehouse opened in June 1902, firemen used a 1891 LaFrance steam engine to battle flames that threatened Canton industries and homes.

ST. CASIMIR'S CHURCH

Kenwood Ave. and O'Donnell St. 410-276-1981
In the 1920s Father Ben Przemielewski had a dream to build a Renaissance-style church with a main altar like that of the Basilica of St. Anthony in Padua, Italy. For inspiration, he kept a postcard of the Italian church's sanctuary on his desk. In 1926, the church cornerstone was laid and many donations later, a 15-ton marble altar with bronze statues and life-sized crucifix, assembled in Florence, took its place in the sanctuary.

Outside, the Indiana limestone church's twin domed towers hold niches with statues of Saint Francis of Assisi and Saint Anthony of Padua. Inside, a series of vivid ceiling and wall murals, some by Baltimorean George Nowikoff and his students, depict the story of Catholicism in Poland (on the left) and in America (on the right). The stained glass windows in the nave portray Polish saints, and the church itself is named after a saintly young Polish prince. Masses Sat 5 pm; Sun 8 and 10 am.

MESSIAH LUTHERAN CHURCH

Potomac and O'Donnell Sts. 410-342-4543

The General Synod of the Evangelical Lutheran Church started a mission to minister to immigrants in Canton after the Civil War. The building, constructed of gray Port Deposit granite opened in 1900 and features a simple interior with a balcony, as well as a lower 100-seat chapel where summer services are held. Services Sun 10:30 am.

ENOCH PRATT FREE LIBRARY, CANTON BRANCH

1030 S. Ellwood St. 410-396-8548

Concerned that Canton's menfolk were spending too many after-work hours in bars and not enough time improving their minds, the Reverend J. Wynne Jones collected $800 from his neighbors in 1879 to establish the Workingmen's Institute, which offered a reading room filled with newspapers, magazines, and books. Impressed by Wynne's success, philanthropist Enoch Pratt gave the city funds to build the Romanesque brick library which opened in 1886. At the same time, he donated money to build three other libraries in the city. Today the Canton branch is the only one of the original four still in use. Closed Fri & Sun.

CANTON SQUARE

Between Elliot, Potomac, Boston, and Streeper Sts.

Just south of O'Donnell Square toward the water sits this development of recent townhouses. Now picture a six-lane highway with cars and trucks rumbling through it. That's what would have been here had citizen activists lost their battle with the proposed highway. As it happened, the houses originally on this site had already been demolished in preparation for the ill-fated road.

WATERFRONT

For a taste of old industrial and post-industrial Canton, stroll down the waterfront. Once "Canner's Row," this stretch has metamorphosed into the "Gold Coast." You'll find kids fishing, sunbathers, joggers, and walkers sharing the brick promenade. Across the river, huge tankers and freighters dwarf the cruisers and sailboats that pass by. The Promenade—which begins at the Korean War Memorial and skirts Canton Cove and Tindeco—will soon hook up to Fells Point. Meanwhile, docks lined with cruisers, sloops, ketches, and the occasional wave runner attest to the many weekend sailors who live in the area. During warm weather months, the patio of the Bay Cafe fills with boaters and landlubbers alike, catching the sunset.

KOREAN WAR MEMORIAL

Canton Cove Park at Boston and S. Ellwood Sts.

The centerpiece of this memorial is a flat stone circle carved with a map of Korea bisected at the 38th parallel. Surrounding the circle, a low granite wall on the south details events leading up to the outbreak of war in June 1950, the major battles, and final peace on July 27, 1953. The north wall, a somber reminder of the war's toll, lists names of the 525 Marylanders who died in action.

CANTON COVE CONDOMINIUM

2901 Boston St. 410-675-2560

This once specialty tin division of the American Can Company turned out containers for products like Lucky Strikes, Coca Cola, and imported teas. Now a spiffy 90-unit condominium complex, the building offers a small lobby display of cans that once rolled off its machinery. Buzz for entry or call ahead.

TINDECO WHARF APARTMENTS

2809 Boston St. 410-675-6664

During early 1800s many New Englanders emigrated down to work the canneries here. In a gesture of hospitality, the road was named "Boston." The Tin Decorating Company designed, manufactured, and decorated tins for cigarettes, bandages, and a variety of products. The company also made items like wastebaskets, cake pans, and other metal household goods. Redubbed Tindeco, today it is an apartment building. Among the lobby displays of old templates and products are novelties like Roly Poly cigarette tins shaped like a man with the lid as his head. Buzz to get in or call ahead.

Late 19th century Canton dwellers found their fun at Riverview Park, a large amusement center on the Patapsco in East Canton. A beer garden with picnic tables, and later brew-chugging bears, opened on that spot after the Civil War. In 1885 the first amusements were installed and 13 years later the City and Suburban Railroad, the park's new owners, expanded it into "The Coney Island of the South" with a roller rink, dance hall, shooting galleries, and tunnel of love. There was even a scream-inducing roller-coaster, the first south of the Mason-Dixon line. After a day's entertainment, parkgoers walked down to Sea Girt House for chicken, fish, and steak dinners costing less than a dollar. A series of fires and encroaching industrial development silenced the laughter and the park closed in 1929. The restaurant was torn down in 1949.

SS JOHN W. BROWN
Pier One. S. Boston St. 410-661-1550

Two or three times a year it seems as if the Japanese and Germans have once again joined forces and are attacking a lone ship at the lower end of the harbor. The vintage World War II planes dip and dodge return "fire" from the *SS John W. Brown*, one of two remaining Liberty ships built during that war. Relax, it's only a re-enactment, courtesy of Project Liberty Ship which has restored this famous Baltimore-built vessel to its original condition. In fact, the Bethlehem Fairfield shipyards turned out more Liberty ships (384 out of a total 2,700) in World War II than any other single facility in the country.

Launched in September 1942, the *Brown* made 13 wartime voyages, carrying supplies and troops to and from the theaters of war and America. Afterwards, the ship was used as a classroom by the New York City schools before returning to Baltimore in 1988 for restoration. Listed on the National Register of Historic Places, the *Brown* is a living tribute to those who lost their lives at sea in wartime. Now fully restored, the vessel provides a glimpse of shipboard life from the engine room to the galleys. On board is also a museum of the US Navy National Armed Guard and the largest collection of builder's plates from Liberty ships built during the '40s.

Battle re-enactments are held a few times each year and are open to the public along with other special events. Tours by appointment. Admission.

LAZARETTO LIGHTHOUSE AND POINT

Mertens Ave.

In 1831 expectant crowds gathered at the base of the brand new Lazaretto Lighthouse while two-and-a-half miles away, a similar group stood around the Shot Tower, their eyes glued to its top. The paper had announced that a man was to fly from the Shot Tower to the 34-foot lighthouse. Hours passed yet nothing happened. The would-be spectators grew restless. Eventually someone noted the date. April Fool. Shaking their heads, the crowds drifted home. And the prankster who placed the bogus announcement? None other than that strange writer with the weird sense of humor, Edgar Allan Poe. Later Poe would start a story "The Lighthouse," perhaps based on this prominent landmark, but, alas, he never finished it.

This first Lazaretto Lighthouse, a whitewashed brick structure, lit the way for ships entering the harbor for nearly 100 years. It stood on a vein of iron ore which contractors mined and carted off to nearby foundries throughout the post-Civil War years. As the surrounding skies blazed red from the increasing number of smelting fires, the tower's own red beacon grew indistinguishable. Eventually authorities were forced to replace it with a white one. More factories arrived and visibility grew even worse so in 1926 down went the old tower, up went the new, this time

317

closer to the water. In 1954 this lighthouse, too, suffered from encroaching industrialization and was decommissioned.

In 1801 Lazaretto Point, originally Gorsuch's Point, held a quarantine hospital for smallpox. Until the 1870s when quarantine operations shifted to Curtis Bay, immigrants coming off the boats with communicable illness also put in time here. During the War of 1812 the military placed a three-gun battery on its banks to shoot at British war ships. The attack on Fort McHenry came on September 12, 1814, and the Lazaretto guns fired away. When the British beat a retreat the morning of the 14th, the squadron let out a cheer. Today the Lehigh Portland Cement Company's storage towers dominate the historic point. Not open to the public.

NORTH CANTON

ST. MICHAEL THE ARCHANGEL UKRAINIAN CATHOLIC CHURCH
2410 Eastern Ave. 410-675-7557
It stands like a jewel—bright white even on the cloudiest day with its five golden domes reaching to heaven. Shaped like a Greek cross, the interior has angled rows of pews. Skylights illuminate the domed ceiling and the intricately carved *iconostas* or icon screen. Only a bishop, priest, or a deacon accompanied by a priest can enter the *iconostas'* Royal Doors, which join the sanctuary (heaven) to the nave (earth). These magnificent portals are topped by an icon of the Last Supper and above that a dove, symbolizing the Holy Spirit. Within the sanctuary itself sits the Holy Table or altar, representing the throne of God.

When Ukrainians first came to this area in the 1880s, the Divine Liturgy was celebrated in local homes by priests who traveled down from Pennsylvania. Then for a while, services were held at St. Stanislaus Church in

Fells Point. In 1913 the parish moved to a new home on S. Wolfe Street where it stayed until the present building opened in May 1991. Divine Liturgy Sat 5 pm (in English) and Sun 10:15 am (in Ukrainian with Gospel in both Ukrainian and English). Call for weekday times. Visitors always welcome.

NOTABLE QUOTABLE

"Living in Baltimore and working in D.C. gives me license for polygamy. Baltimore has lots of energy, vigor, and decency, whereas D.C. is sophisticated, racy, and occasionally cruel. It's like splitting my life between a good woman and a bad woman."

Stephen Hunter, *Washington Post* movie critic
and best selling author

Browse and Buy

BIBELOT AT THE AMERICAN CAN COMPANY
2400 Boston St. 410-276-9700

Bibelot has transformed this section of the former American Can Company into two light and airy floors of books and music. In addition, the home-grown family of bookstores offers a cornucopia of events—book readings, signings, clubs, talks, discussions, and live music. And if you need a little something to read before you hit the sheets, Bibelot stays open until midnight on Friday and Saturday.

CANTON GALLERY

2935 O'Donnell St. 410-342-6176
www.cantongallery.com

Joseph A. LaMastra focuses his gallery shows on contemporary regional art with a realistic point of view. A recent exhibit featured Carol Offutt's colorful paintings of the Block. Don't miss the gallery's annual painted screen show which offers the best of this unique Baltimore art form. In addition, LaMastra does conservation framing and matting.

JAPONAJI

1301 Baylis St.(The Broom Factory), Suite 210
410-675-4900 or 410-522-1087
www.japonaji.com

In her tiny shop, owner J. T. Orlinsky sells "the essence of Japan." Orlinsky, who lived in the Far East for four years, offers lanterns based on Noguchi designs, shibori pleated scarves, tea pots, rice bowls, lacquer boxes, kimonos, and other Asian pieces.

MODERN MUSIC

2919 O'Donnell St 410-675-2172
www.modernmusic.com

There's always something cool playing—jungle, house, club, acid jazz, techno—in this the area's largest underground electronic and dance music store. Rub shoulders with DJs while trying out the CDs or vinyl inventory. For vinyl fans, the shop sells turntables and needles.

TOUCH THE EARTH

2400 Boston St. (The Can Company) 410-522-1500

Call him the Alchemist of Boston Street. Stanford Lessans and his staff blend oils and essences to create lotions and potions for the mind, body, and spirit. Candles and incense stimulate the olfactory glands; New Age music relaxes the body; colorful greeting cards and dream catchers delight the eye. Complete the experience by putting yourself in Theresa Mueller and her staff's hands for massage therapy.

Epicurean Bites

CLADDAGH PUB

2918 O'Donnell St. 410-522-4220

The green shamrocks in the sidewalk lead to the Claddagh Pub where locals drink Killian's and Guinness and chow down on Black Angus steaks, crab cakes, and other pub fare. Saturday's eight-ounce Black Angus burger special is a bargain at $2.95. L, D. $$

HELEN'S GREAT FOOD AND WINE

2908 O'Donnell St. 410-276-2233

When Tom Looney's mother died and left him an inheritance, Looney decided to open a restaurant and name it in her honor. Together he and partner Ed Scherer have created a charming spot—all blonde wood and exposed brick with a generous dash of local art thrown in. The menu, accompanied by an outstanding wine list, is American eclectic, offering everything from homey Mom's pork chops to Greek shrimp to pecan-crusted brook trout. Keeping with the family theme, Scherer's mother Chotsie makes the baked goods. L, D. Br Sat & Sun. $½

LOONEY'S PUB

2900 O'Donnell St. 410-675-9235

Whether its the O's, the Ravens, the Indy 500, or Miss Fitness America, there will be a TV broadcasting within viewing distance of your table. With 27 brews on tap and pool tables, Looney's attracts a young crowd who chow down on pizza, subs, burgers, and quesadillas. On game days, Looney's runs a shuttle bus to and from the stadiums for patrons. L, D. $½

MANGIA! MANGIA!

834 S. Lucerne Ave.(at Hudson St.) 410-534-8999

A gigantic wooden fork with strands of dangling spaghetti punctuates the colorful Italian kitchen table mural covering the Hudson Street facade. Inside, this small eatery offers a menu of outstanding sauces which can be served over "nude" linguine or the *pasta di giorno* along with additional entrees, soups, salads, and sandwiches. The food's so good, no one's going to have to goad you with a *"Mangia! Mangia!"* L, D.
$½

NACHO MAMA'S

2907 O'Donnell St. 410-675-0898

Elvis Lives! It says so in neon in the window of this funky Mexican eatery. It wouldn't surprise us to see the King pull up to a wash bucket table to scarf down Mama's meatloaf or N'awlins' shrimp. Weekends he'd have to fight the crowds to get at the nachos and fajitas. The impatient can always opt for pizzas, subs, and salads at the Pizza and Wing Factory carry-out next door. L, D. Br Sun. $½

NEEDFUL THINGS COFFEE SHOP

2921 O'Donnell St. 410-675-0595

The name comes from a Stephen King book co-owner Debbie Brooks was reading, but never fear. The green and white decor is homey, the service friendly, and the coffee fresh-brewed. A painting of Ben, the pet yellow lab, above the fireplace oversees the daily fare of fruit-filled pancakes, omelets, sandwiches, and homemade scones. B, L. $

THE SURFIN' BULL RESTAURANT

2821 O'Donnell St. 410-675-9155

Located above a bar, this family-run restaurant offers Continental cuisine with a Latino flair. For meat eaters there's New York strip or *tournedos espanol*; for seafood fans, dishes like paella or seafood Miami— grilled fish topped with jumbo shrimp, finished with a mango cilantro *beurre blanc*. When time permits, the owners serenade with their guitars. D. Open late Fri & Sat.  $$

THE WILD MUSHROOM

641 S. Montford Ave. 410-675-4225

The Formstone facade may say "old Bawlmer," but inside this eatery is all cutting edge cuisine. Fungi fans can feast on wild mushroom ravioli or mushroom loaf—not to mention a grilled portobella appetizer with bourbon pecan smoked trout and gorgonzola. There's even dishes like pepper rubbed rib-eye for the non-veggie inclined. The oak bar up front provides a pleasant spot to wait before being ushered into the informal green-wallpapered dining room downstairs or the burgundy sponge-painted area upstairs. An all-you-can-eat gourmet lunchtime buffet on Fridays and Saturdays comes with a free martini. L, D. $$

BAR HARBOR

2239 Essex St. 410-327-0100

Look for the painted logo of the fish with the Blues Brothers-type hat on his head. Then step inside this small lounge for Friday and Saturday night live blues, jazz, and swing. A funky '50s-style side room complete with a patterned couch and co-owner Tara Sopher's artwork offers a homey addition to the front bar.

GOOD LOVE BAR

2322 Boston St. 410-558-2347

Fat candles in the windows and along ledges throughout the small three-story interior make this jazz lounge one of the sexiest spots in Baltimore. Listen to a DJ spin jazz, acid jazz, funk, swing, or rock while you sit at the bar or tables or lounge in chairs in the Good Love's three levels. Adding to the ambience handmade paper light fixtures and twisted metal mesh torchières throw interesting shadows against the exposed brick walls. DJs Thurs-Sat; live jazz Sun.

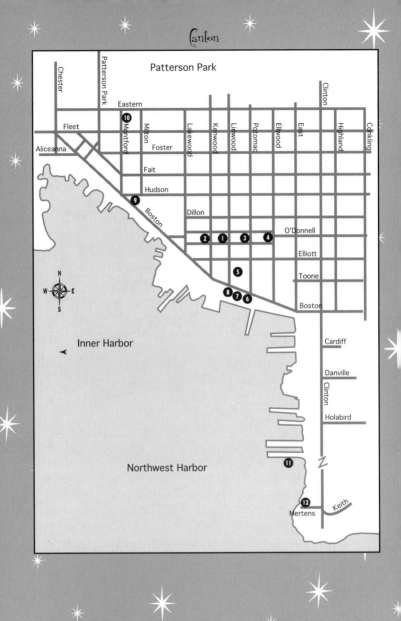

Canton

Patterson Park

Inner Harbor

Northwest Harbor

1. O'Donnell Square
2. St. Casimir's Church
3. Messiah Lutheran Church
4. Enoch Pratt Free Library, Canton Branch
5. Canton Square
6. Korean War Memorial
7. Canton Cove Condominiums
8. Tindeco Wharf Apartments
9. American Can Company
10. St. Michael the Archangel
    Ukrainian Catholic Church
11. SS *John W. Brown*
12. Lazaretto Lighthouse and Point

Highlandtown and Butcher's Hill

HIGHLANDTOWN

Drive through a typical Highlandtown neighborhood and you'll see blocks of Formstone and brick rowhouses with white marble steps, painted window screens, stained glass inserts, and window shrines. Along the commercial strip on Eastern Avenue you'll find discount stores, neighborhood bars...and boarded up buildings. Happily this stretch is cleaning up its act. A consortium of community and business groups, city and state agencies, institutions, and organizations like Southeast Development, Inc., and the South East Community Organization are working on a revitalization effort aimed at filling vacant spaces with shops, offices, galleries, a youth entrepreneurship center, a cinema, and other business ventures. Will Highlandtown be another Baltimore success story? If interest and determination have any say, it may very well happen.

Highlandtown began when a resourceful Irishman named Thomas McGuinness converted an old boat cabin into a makeshift house. He'd been sent by the Philadelphia Land Company to lay out roads after the Civil War. His work completed, he was followed by a German brewery and beer garden, a bowling alley, saloons, a lime kiln, and a butcher. Originally known as Snake Hill, the area adopted the name Highland Town in the 1870s capitalizing on the area's scenic water and city views. For several decades, the community remained a heavily Germanic village of mostly businesses and detached houses, but in 1918 when Baltimore expanded its borders, Highlandtown became a bonafide city neighborhood. Over the next decades rowhouses went up and the area's commercial core grew with shops, carts, and truck farmers. However, like other parts of the city, suburban malls in the '60s dealt a blow to the shopping district, a clobbering from which Highlandtown is still struggling to recover.

By Winter 2000 the Fells Point Creative Alliance should be finished with its renovation of the old Patterson Theater, which they'll have turned into the Patterson Cultural Center with art exhibition space, a 100-seat auditorium, cafe, and live-in artists' studios. Hopefully the renovation of The

Grand on Conkling Street won't be too far behind. Plans call for the old movie theater to be restored to its 1950s splendor. Along with the main screen which will show first-run art films, there will be two smaller auditoriums featuring first run foreign and micro-cinema motion pictures, as well as post-production facilities for film editing, and a cafe.

Meanwhile if you're visiting the area, take a drive around South Clinton, Bouldin, and Gough Streets for a glimpse of Bawlmer at its Formstoned best. With the imitation stone disappearing off houses in Federal Hill, Canton, and Fells Point, this may be the last outpost of that local mid-20th century home improvement craze. Don't forget to look for painted window screens and window shrines (see *What Makes Baltimore "Bawlmer"*).

PATTERSON PARK

Bordered by Patterson Park, Eastern, Linwood, and Ellwood Aves. and Baltimore St.

In the heart of East Baltimore stretching along Eastern Avenue sits the 155-acre Patterson Park, named after wealthy merchant William Patterson. Boston may have its tea party, but in 1808 Baltimore threw an anti-British gin fest that brought thousands of rabble rousers to this hill. The occasion was the incident of the brig *Sophia*, which had been seized by a British man o'war, hauled into an English port, and forced to pay tax on her cargo of Dutch liquor. When the *Sophia* finally sailed into Baltimore, a mob carted her 720 gallons of gin up here and set it afire on a gallows to the strains of "Yankee Doodle" as a protest against British strong-arming.

With anti-British sentiment at fever pitch, citizens worked against the clock on the eve of the Battle of Baltimore in the War of 1812 to build fortifications here to protect the city. Nowadays the Pagoda (see below) sits upon the site of Rodgers' Bastion where Commander John Rodgers and his naval force stood guard to defend the rise. A few years later the hill offered refuge for citizens escaping from one of the harbor's many yellow fever epidemics. In 1827 William Patterson gifted Baltimore with much of the acreage, although it was not officially dedicated as a public park until 26 years later. Then, during the Civil War, this spot, like Federal Hill, became a Union military stronghold designed to keep Southern sympathizers in line.

The Patterson Park Observatory, called the "Pagoda" by locals, was erected in 1891. The yellow-and-orange tower, designed by Charles H. Latrobe, is encircled by three tiers of balconies and ornamented with fantail windows, lattice work, and oriental designs. Presently the 60-foot tall octagon is closed because its balconies' supports and platforms are in need of rewelding. After it's repainted and repaired, visitors will once again be able to climb the spiral stairs to its top.

Today Patterson Park offers an Olympic-size swimming pool, basketball and tennis courts, baseball, football, and soccer fields, a recreation and a senior daycare center, and a 2.6 acre stocked pond where people fish and watch heron, ducks, and flocks of geese. For a minimal fee, gardeners can rent a small plot to plant vegetables. From October through April the bubble-covered ice rink is open for skating, hockey clinics, and games. Special events such as a fish rodeo, doll contests, and turtle derby are also held here. Summers the Polish community throws a festival in the park, near the Pulaski Monument which honors Revolutionary hero Count Casimir Pulaski. Currently the city is working on plans to spruce up and add a small art gallery, gift shop, and more restrooms.

HOLY ROSARY CHURCH
408 S. Chester St. 410-732-3960
The sounds of Polish echo through this Romanesque church during mass and on holy days. Indeed Holy Rosary Church is the only parish in Baltimore where Catholics hear daily masses in Polish as well as English. That's because almost half the 900 families at Holy Rosary are Polish-speaking immigrants. The 1928 Woodstock granite church seats 2,000 and is notable for the clear sight lines to its Italian and Spanish marble altar. Steel arches support the ceiling, and its only pillars are those holding up the choir. The magnificent interior with its paintings, statuary, and German stained glass features a picture of Christ above the sanctuary arch flanked by Polish holy men and women. During mass, the Moeller mahogany organ pumps its music out through 3,000 pipes. Pope John Paul II visited here when he was Cardinal Wojtyla.

Mass: Mon-Fri 6:45 am & 7:30 am (Polish). Sat 8 am and 5 pm. Sun 8, 10 (Polish) & noon.

SACRED HEART OF JESUS
600 S. Conkling St. 410-342-4336
Couples love to get married here because of the large outside stairway and the beautiful arched, columned, and gilt interior with its 100-foot long aisle. Founded in 1873 by German Redemptorists, the first Sacred Heart was built near old Fort Marshall, a quadrangular earthwork used by Union forces during the Civil War to guard Fort McHenry from enemy attack. As the number of parishioners swelled to 4,000, the church began construction on its present building in 1908. In the early years, German was taught at the church, but today English is the chosen tongue at all masses. Nowadays

parishioners include families of all nationalities and this ethnic mix is reflected in the annual Sacred Heart Carnival, featuring coddies, crab soup, barbecue, and Italian sausage, as well as carnival rides. A sour beef and oyster dinner held the first Sunday and Monday in November draws crowds. Mass: Mon-Fri 6:30 & 8 am; Sat 5 pm; Sun 8:30 & 11 am.

GREEKTOWN

4600-4800 block Eastern Ave. and surrounding area

The commercial section of Greektown is only a three-block strip on Eastern Avenue, but it's a world away. Men sit in coffee bars or *kaffeneion* where they play cards, read newspapers, and sip strong cups of brew while televisions blare Greek news or sports. The all-male clientele often break down by which island you or your father came from, so visitors who wander in, especially females, may feel like outsiders. But the homey restaurants are welcoming with souvlaki, charcoal-grilled lamb, eggplant, and other Hellenic specialties. Little grocery stores stack cans of olive oil and grape leaves in the window and the Greek Village Bakery (4711 Eastern Avenue) offers sesame-crusted bread, baklava, and other Greek pastries. On Greek Independence Day, March 25th, blue and white flags fly from the storefronts.

The first wave of Greeks, mostly from the mainland, came to Baltimore in the 1890s and settled around produce markets throughout the city where they got jobs. From the Depression years on more immigrants came, many from the islands, to work shipyards and steel plants in East Baltimore. Some opened small cafes serving homesick countrymen their favorite ethnic dishes.

Now even though many families have moved out to the suburbs, St. Nicholas Greek Orthodox Church (520 S. Ponca St.) remains the spiritual center of "Greektown." Recently there's been talk of building a new Byzantine church for St. Nick's to give the small community another toehold of stability. Meanwhile newcomers, this time from Latin America and the Middle East, have settled in, adding yet another layer of texture to this corner of Highlandtown.

NOTABLE QUOTABLE

"Baltimore breaks my heart. Only something you love can break your heart. Yet I find myself in a constant state of reconciliation."

Rafael Alvarez, author of *The Fountain of Highlandtown* and *Orlo and Leini*

BUTCHERS HILL

On the rise of Hampstead Hill sits this 19th century enclave of brick rowhouses with views of the harbor and downtown. In 1792 William Patterson bought this undeveloped tract of land located on the Philadelphia Road, a post route connecting Philadelphia and Baltimore. By the early 1800s German butchers, attracted by the highway's convenience and propelled by laws prohibiting slaughterhouses in other parts of the city, set up shop here. One road, Lamley Street, even garnered the moniker Blood Alley thanks to the abattoirs there.

In a show of public good will just before the Civil War, a group of butchers donated 30 acres to expand Patterson Park. When war did break out Union troops descended on the area, bringing prosperity to some of the meat processors who supplied the soldiers. As a result, several merchants could afford to build fine homes here.

By the end of the 19th century, as the slaughterhouses started leaving the area, Butchers Hill began turning fashionable with Queen Anne Style, Renaissance Revival, and Victorian residences. As the 1920s rolled in, the area became heavily Jewish as families moved in around a new temple built there. Two decades later as these Jews migrated to the northwest, houses were cut up into apartments and the area deteriorated. Over the past 20 years, preservation-minded newcomers have moved in, gentrifying the neighborhood and restoring old houses to their former elegance. Butchers Hill was placed on the National Register of Historic Places in 1982.

Browse and Buy

ATHENAIKON
4717 Eastern Ave. 410-342-6900
KENTRIKON
4704 Eastern Ave. 410-675-4100
These two stores help keep contemporary Greek culture alive here by offering Greek Orthodox shrines, statuary, and ceramics along with Greek language newspapers, magazines, videos, and music. In addition, both store owners host Greek radio shows weekends on WBMD.

Epicurean Bites

HAUSSNER'S
3242 Eastern Ave. 410-327-8365
Come to this Baltimore landmark to eat wiener schnitzel, hasenpfeffer, sauerbraten—and don't forget the strawberry shortcake. Sculptures, candelabras, urns, and glassware fill every nook and cranny, and the walls are blanketed with paintings amassed by founders William and Frances Haussner over seven decades. Veteran waitresses, a 100-plus entree menu, and a bar graced by nude paintings add to the old Bawlmer flavor. L, D. $$

NOTABLE QUOTABLE

"If you go to the bar at Haussner's, you don't need a drink or a prescription for Viagra."

Steve Rouse, WQSR radio personality and author,

Rouse & Co.: Booked!

IKAROS RESTAURANT

4805 Eastern Ave. 410-633-3750

Theodossios Kohilas came to America from his native island of Ikaria in 1968 and learned to cook in Baltimore restaurants. The following year he and his brother, Xenofon, opened Ikaros and everything on the menu was priced $1.90 or less. Today the menu is still written in Greek as well as English and you can still get moussaka, lamb Guvetzi, and just about anything Greek along with Maryland seafood, nowadays for under $16. L, D. Open until 11 weekends. ☽ $½

MATTHEW'S PIZZERIA

3131 Eastern Ave. 410-276-8755

Since 1943 Matthew's has been serving up some of Baltimore's best deep-dish pizzas. Along with the pizzas, made with hand-pressed crust topped with home-style tomato sauce and three cheeses, the tiny shop offers a simple menu of meatballs, subs, spaghetti, and meat dishes. L, D. Open until 11 weekends ☽ $

SAMOS

600 Oldham St. 410-675-5292

Pull up a folding chair to the blue vinyl checkered cloth tables in this tiny neighborhood eatery. Behind the counter, owner Nick Georgalas cooks up stuffed grape leaves, chicken souvlaki, and other tasty dishes from his native Samos. An expansion is planned for 1999. L, D. $

ZORBA'S

4710 Eastern Ave. 410-276-4484 or 4485

On a typical evening you're likely to find the regulars drinking metaxa at the oak bar up front while watching

Greek news on the big TV. Meanwhile at the window in back, the chef roasts hunks of pork and entire chickens on a spit. Charcoal-grilled lamb, served only on weekends, draws crowds from all over. D. Open until 1 am. $

TAPAS BAR

4700 Eastern Ave. 410-522-5092

Go to this lounge after 9 pm on weekends and you'll find a mini Latin America of customers eating tapas with their *cervezas* and *vino*. The DJ plays salsa, merengues, and sambas loud while handsome couples demonstrate their dancing skills. Fri & Sat, 8 pm-2 am.

Highlandtown and Butchers Hill

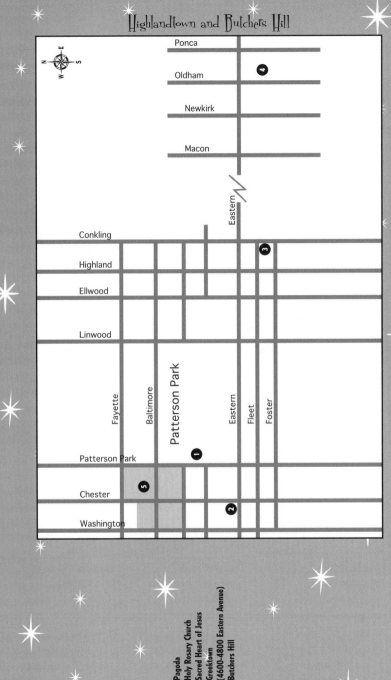

Ponca

Oldham

Newkirk

Macon

Eastern

Conkling

Highland

Ellwood

Linwood

Fayette

Baltimore

Patterson Park

Eastern

Fleet

Foster

Patterson Park

Chester

Washington

1. Pagoda
2. Holy Rosary Church
3. Sacred Heart of Jesus
4. Greektown
   (4600-4800 Eastern Avenue)
5. Butchers Hill

Hampden-Woodberry

This former mill town's past was defined by the force of the Jones Falls that rushed through the city. Near the end of the 18th century, Elisha Tyson built one of the first mills, Woodberry Flour Mill, on its banks. Wagons carted in the wheat from rural Maryland and hauled the processed grain down to ships bound for England and other foreign ports.

The miller's wheel gave way to carding machines, belts, and spinning frames as the Industrial Age rolled in. In the 1830s David Carroll and Horatio Gambrill jump-started the revolution by transforming several flour mills into textile plants which supplied Baltimore's shipbuilding industry with cotton duck for sails. More conversions followed and more manufacturing plants went up as a steam-powered railroad now rumbled in, bringing raw cotton from the port, exchanging it for finished sheeting. The hum of machinery grew louder when Poole and Hunt Union Works built a foundry next to the Northern Central Railroad tracks where, over the years, it would turn out mining, textile, and other manufacturing equipment along with boilers, railroad carriages, and steel girders.

After the Civil War Hampden acquired its name when the president of the Falls Road Turnpike Company, in admiration of 17th century English politician John Hampden, who'd lead the opposition to Charles I, bestowed that moniker on most of the area east of the Jones Falls. In 1888 Baltimore City embraced Hampden and its western neighbor, Woodberry, into its boundaries.

By the turn of the century the area had become the cotton duck center of the United States. Cheap labor recruited from Appalachia, kept happy with a knapsack of benefits, fueled the factories. In many ways Hampden was a comfortable place for these newcomers. It had hills, reminding them of home, and their neighbors were folks from the same region. Work was steady and the mill took care of them, providing inexpensive housing which they could stay in as long as one family member worked in the mill. The companies built schools, churches (mainly Methodist), libraries, and parks, and sponsored local baseball teams. Fraternal and service clubs and a small commercial district contributed to the insularity of the community.

While men often moved on to higher paying jobs, many of the lifetime employees of the mills were women. William E. Hooper & Sons, who hired single women from the mountains, built its Hooper Hotel on Clipper Mill Road to house and chaperone 250 of its female employees. Even children put in a day's work until the child labor laws cracked down on the practice in the early 1900s.

Wrapped in this fatherly embrace and its geographic isolation, the area was cushioned from the inner city by Druid Hill Park to the west and what would become Wyman Park to the east, resulting in what author D. Randall Beirne calls a "village of connected hamlets that were ruled paternalistically by the local industrialists." Even in 1885, when the Baltimore Union Passenger Railway Company opened the country's first commercial electric street railway, linking this area to the city at 25th Street, the little town remained a fortress against the slums and encroachment of immigrants northward. Nevertheless, its homogeneity and stability were also its weaknesses. Outsiders, particularly foreigners and blacks, were not welcome and unions discouraged.

As World War I flared up in Europe, however, company control began slipping. While canvas makers churned out knapsacks and tents for the battlefront, rumblings of discontent erupted. At Poole & Hunt, machinists and mill workers struck for higher wages and union representation. A strike in 1923 at Mount Vernon-Woodberry Mills, protesting an increased work week and small pay raise, eventually resulted in a portion of the firm packing up and moving south. The Depression brought a few more casualties with a brief rally during World War II. However, the rise of synthetics dealt another blow to the struggling mills and they folded, one after another, with Mount Vernon Mills, one of the last old-timers, shutting down completely here in 1972. Eventually groups of smaller companies moved into the old factories, but Hampden remained in a slump as residents sought work elsewhere. The Avenue, 36th Street's commercial district, grew emptier with boarded-up storefronts and litter.

Yet, sustained by its close knit community, Hampden-Woodberry endured. In recent years, entrepreneurs, artists, students, folks returning to their childhood roots, and those drawn by its safe neighborhoods have filtered into the old mill town and joined natives in boosting the area's economy. Pockets of poverty still exist by the mills, but on The Avenue the boards are starting to come down as more shops and restaurants move in and draw visitors. However, lest you think the area's getting too high-toned, Cafe Hon's annual Hon Festival—with awards for big hair and Bawlmer talk—gives the city a good-natured ribbing (see *What Makes Baltimore "Bawlmer"*).

Sights & Sites

MEADOW MILL
3600 Clipper Mill Rd.
On opening day in 1877 the officials of the William E. Hooper Company must have patted themselves on the back, for the four-story brick building with its tower and wooden cupola was destined to become a landmark of progress. For a long while it was. In the 1940s the company, mindful of the changing economic climate, switched from manufacturing cotton duck to producing synthetics, but eventually sold out around 1960 to the Londontown Manufacturing Company. When the London Fog raincoat maker left town in 1989, the mill was renovated and artists, guilds, shops, and small companies moved in. The Maryland Institute College of Art's Jewelry Center (410-235-5871) offers classes and certificates in jewelry making here and the Gem Cutters Guild (410-467-9838) holds workshops in gem cutting, design, jewelry fabrication, and other aspects of the craft. Also offering instruction is the Potters Guild (410-235-4884). A few doors away is the experimental playhouse Axis Theatre (410-243-5237).

BRICK HILL

Seneca and Oakington Sts. and Parkden Ave.

In the late 1870s workers from Meadow Mill began moving into this company-owned hilltop enclave of two and two-and-a-half-story brick duplexes. When Meadow Mill shut down, the houses were sold to private owners who over the years have modernized them. Brick Hill is now on the National Register of Historic Places.

SITE OF POOLE AND HUNT UNION WORKS

3300 Clipper Rd.

A simple memorial, a tiny roofed structure sheltering a photograph, faces away from the empty lot where the Poole and Hunt Foundry once stood. The picture is of a fireman who died fighting the blaze that ripped through the old complex in 1995. Back in 1853 Poole & Hunt had moved their foundry up from North Avenue into this brick complex. Here they turned out mining, textile, and milling machinery along with railroad cars, screw pile lighthouses, engines, and other machine products. During the renovation of the US Capitol building in the mid 1800s, the company cast the girders for the 288-foot high dome. Poole & Hunt failed in the 1920s and the site was taken over by Balmar Corporation Foundry and Machine Works, followed by a succession of light industries. Eventually artists moved in as did The Clipper City Gym, which used the walls for rock climbing training. The 1995 fire destroyed this portion of the mill, which has not been rebuilt.

AMARANTHINE MUSEUM

3500 Clipper Rd. 410-366-2368 or 410-366-0574

Artist Len Harris takes you on a trip from the Alpha to the Omega or sometimes in reverse, depending on his mood. Enter the labyrinth at the beginning (if that's where Harris has you starting this time), and walk through a cascade of tinsel into time before time. Multicolor phone wires and tinker toy sculptures heightened by eerie music launch us into a multi-media dance through history. Egyptian gods and Roman temples lead into cathedrals with mannequin saints martyred with lethal paint brushes. Room to room, era to era. The Impressionists loom into view, their chamber a floor to ceiling collage of paintings, spilling out of overlapping frames drifting into one another. On and on to the Space Age cluttered with mirrored chairs and tables with more tinker toy projectiles, this time protruding like satellite antennas placed where seats would be. Disco music, the roar of motorcycles and we are hurled out into the future. By appointment.

Clipper Road and Television Hill

Further north on Clipper Road sit 19th century mill-financed Greek Revival stone houses and the stone Woodberry United Methodist Church. Above it looms the transmission tower of Television Hill, which since 1959 has broadcast signals for local television stations. In 1987 a second TV tower and, ten years later, a police communications antenna were erected on an adjacent hill. From the road you can also catch glimpses of the Woodberry Mill (circa 1843) at 1760 Union Avenue. The plant, which started out as a cotton mill owned by Gambrill and Carroll, later became a William E. Hooper textile mill, then a tire company. Now the complex is part of Clipper Mill Industrial Park, which houses light industries.

PARK MILL

1750 Union Ave.

Horatio Nelson Gambrill expanded his empire with the building of this fishing net twine factory in 1855. Later the granite building housed an ice cone factory and then the Commercial Envelope Co., whose paper products got gummed up in a 1972 flood. Today it's part of Clipper Mill Industrial Park.

DRUID MILL

1600 Union Ave.

After selling off his share of the Mount Vernon Mills, Horatio Nelson Gambrill constructed this Italianate stone building, enlarging it in 1872 into the world's largest cotton duck factory. After the looms fell silent in 1917, Poole Engineering moved in, churning out washing machines. Other firms, too, took up residence, among them a rag processing plant and janitorial supply company. Today Life-Like Products manufactures plastic items like styrofoam ice coolers, toy trains, and racing car sets both here and in the old Mount Vernon Mill on Falls Road.

CLIPPER MILL

3300 Clipper Mill Rd.

Built in 1866 this long brick building replaced two mills which had burned down earlier. The new factory, named after Baltimore's famed clipper ships, made boat sails, mailbags for the post office, and other heavy cotton goods. The plant sat next to the Jones Falls and the tracks of the Northern Central Railroad not far from a village of mill workers' dwellings.

EVERGREEN-ON-THE-FALLS

3300 Falls Rd.

A succession of mill owners, among them Carrolls and Hoopers, who lived in this Italianate mansion must have enjoyed looking down on the valley and their profitable plants. Built circa 1860, the painted brick house once had a large cupola providing an even better view. In 1926 the SPCA bought the building for its offices and, after a fire in the 1970s, rebuilt it. Also on the property is a granite valve house (also circa 1860) for the now defunct Hampden Reservoir, which was filled in during the construction of the Jones Falls Expressway.

MOUNT VERNON MILLS

3000 Falls Rd.

Around a bend in Falls Road sits a collection of brick buildings that once made up part of Mount Vernon Mills, a cotton duck manufacturer. Like many of its competitors, Mount Vernon was plagued by fire and when the 1843 mill burned, it was replaced in 1873 by the current building. When the demand for cotton duck fell, the company switched to manufacturing synthetics. The mill's last gasp came in 1972 and then it was gone. Today Life-Like Products occupies the building (see "Druid Mill").

Facing Pacific Avenue, a short walk from the Mount Vernon Mills, is Stone Hill, a collection of 22 semi-detached stone houses built for company work- ers in the mid- 19th century. The houses today are privately owned. Below it another section of the mills, now renamed Mill

Centre (3000 Chestnut Ave.), was converted into artists' studios and other small business spaces in 1985. Among its tenants are artists and craftsmen, a martial arts and yoga center, and offices (See Browse and Buy). The artists of the Mill Centre also stage spring and fall open studio weekends. (For information call Lucinda Shaw at 410-467-4038.)

Browse and Buy

AROUND THE AVENUE

A mini-Renaissance is underway on and around 36th Street, also known as The Avenue, as boutiques, art gal- leries, and antique shops join the long-time bargain and used furniture stores here. More boards are being pried off vacant storefronts and new tenants are moving in. Some smaller shops only do business the latter part of the week, so if you're interested in a particular place, it's best to call ahead.

CHEAP CHIC INTERIORS

828 W. 36th St. 410-662-8383

What better bargain than lightly used furniture at affordable prices? Throw in a bit of owner Regi Elion's interior decorating advice and you'll end up with a room that's comfortable and beautiful, yet user-friendly to kids and dogs. For finishing touches, Elion carries a selection of home accessories, custom ottomans and pillows, and Vargas pinup prints as well.

FAT ELVIS

833 W. 36th St. 410-467-6030

There are NO Elvises at Fat Elvis. But there is plenty of kitsch. Say you collect butterfly shaped waffle irons from the '50s. There's probably one here. Or perhaps you have an urge to dress like the Queen Mother. Well, that pink peplumed suit will make you a dead ringer. How about a painting of Pope John XXIII, a nice vintage dresser, or a ceramic donkey? Look no further.

FRENCH ACCENTS ANTIQUES

3600 Roland Ave. 410-467-8957
www.faccents.com

When it comes to antiques, French Accents stands out like a Château Lafite-Rothschild Bordeaux in a rack of mid-priced Chablis. Daniel Garfink and Danetta Restivo sell the best of fine continental antiques like 16th century Italian *cassoni* and 18th century Dutch marquetry cabinets to dealers, interior designers, and knowledgeable customers from all over the East Coast and Chicago. Antique consulting and interior design service also available. By appointment.

GUSTAFSON'S

1006 W. 36th St. 410-235-4244

When Gustafson's partners couldn't decide on a name for their funky junque shop, they adopted Greta Garbo's family moniker instead. However when it came to their store inventory, no problem. In an inspired bit of "spring cleaning," the self-confessed pack rats initially stocked it with their own possessions, stuff like World War I veteran grave markers, silver candlesticks, an 18th century bed warmer, silk shawls, and even a Dukes of Hazard Game. Don't miss their humorous, and off-the-wall, window displays including the annual display of revolving Christmas trees.

HOMETOWN GIRL

1000 W. 36th St. 410-662-4438

Want a screen painting kit? Bawlmer Talk magnets? Colorful postcards and limited edition posters of city sights by Greg Otto? Hometown girl Mary Pat Andrea offers an eclectic array of gift items for every age including cards, Baltimore books, toys, and unusual souvenirs for the Baltimorean and visitor alike.

KOBERNICK'S USED FURNITURE

835 W. 36th St. 410-243-1432

Jerry Kobernick never knows what artifact will cross his threshold. One day it'll be a two-year-old office copy machine; another a pair of Eisenhower-era lamps. The quarter-of-a-century old store is two narrow rooms crammed with used furnishings. Paintings are piled to the ceiling and scads of chairs hang down from it. A basement bulges with washing machines, refrigerators, and other household appliances.

LA TERRA

4001 Falls Rd. 410-889-7562

Creative recycling and whimsy mark this gallery filled with eco-friendly purses made of out license plates, bottle top-rimmed mirrors, hubcap ashtrays, handmade ceramic dishes and tiles, and "Them"—insect specimens collected by children in Third World countries and mounted in hardwood frames. Mary DeMarco also makes her baroque-style La Contessa jewelry here.

MUD & METAL

813 W. 36th St. 410-467-8698

This showcase for local potters and metal workers features off-beat finds like handcrafted copper, ceramic, and bronze drawer pulls in whimsical shapes, artistic switch plates, mugs and mirrors, as well as other home accessories and gift items.

OH, SAID ROSE
840 W. 36th St. 410-235-5170
The store's name comes from one of those elusive Gertrude Stein passages. Forget puzzling over the meaning of it all and focus on the selection of handwoven jackets, hand painted purses, and other romantic women's clothing made of feel-good fabrics.

ORIN KENNEY
851 W. 36th St. 410-467-1763
Sort through the used clothing, silver, dishes, and household items in this former barbershop-residence for a glimpse of Hampden Past. Lace doilies, aprons, '30s tablecloths, and upholstery remnants abound.

THE PEARL GALLERY
815 W. 36th St. 410-467-2260
Mary Ellen Bronco has assembled a unique collection of art and crafted pieces including fine paintings, silver jewelry, handmade pillows and purses, and porcelain planters, and urban artifacts transformed into *objets d'art*. The shop also does custom framing.

PIECES OF OLDE
824 W. 36th St. 410-366-4949
Nancy Wertheimer sells vintage fabric pillows, stuffed animals, and other items made from old textiles along with collectable European travel and gallery posters. In addition, Jean Bartlett offers folk art and decorative accessories from emerging countries while Mary Steinke paints new life into old tables and chairs with scenes of Baltimore and other creative designs.

THE TURNOVER SHOP
3855 Roland Ave. 410-235-9585 and
3547 Chestnut Ave. 410-366-2988
Housed in a former pharmacy, Maryland's oldest consignment shop, along with its offshoot on Chestnut

Avenue, sells entire households of furniture—every-thing from fine antiques to silver to jewelry to the more practical like linens and small appliances.

WILD YAM POTTERY
1013 W. 36th St. 410-662-1123
While walking near St. Timothy's School, potter Nancy Brady came across a vine with beautiful heart-shaped leaves. Inspired, she began incorporating the vine's image into her clay pieces. Just before opening her shop, she discovered the vine was a wild yam, good for labor pains. So since she and her partners were labor-ing over the store name...well, the rest is obvious.

NOTABLE QUOTABLE

"The city didn't say, 'Let's do an urban renewal in Hampden.' Instead it's all happening with residents who've been part of the community fabric."

Mary Pat Andrea, owner of Hometown Girl

THE MILLS
Besides the galleries listed below, many artists' studios are open by appointment. For information about local artists studios, contact School 33 Art Center (410-396-4641) or The Maryland Art Place (410-962-8565), which maintains an artists' registry.

THE GLASSMAN
Suite 1404, The Mill Centre
3000 Chestnut Ave. 410-366-3171
Born Paul Darmafal in 1925, the Glassman now finds himself, after years of hospitalizations and unemploy-ment, a celebrity in the world of outsider art. Part street-artist, part-proselytizer, the maverick visionary shatters cracked bottles and glues them on his canvas—scraps of wood he's painted with soldiers, angels, liberty bells, George Washington, moon, stars, and whatever message he's lettered across its face. Much of the time he creates

his work at home, but step into his studio and you'll "hear" his voice.

GOMEZ GALLERY

Suite 100, Meadow Mill
3600 Clipper Mill Rd. 410-662-9510
www.gomezgallery.com
Walter Gomez's gallery entices with its top-notch exhibitions of contemporary art featuring artists like photographer Connie Imboden, painter Joan Erbe, and sculptor Hugo Marin. Along with an archival framing department, the gallery has opened The Gallery Cafe, serving global fare that reflects the current artists' exhibit (410-662-9513).

GOYA-GIRL PRESS

Suites 210 & 214, Mill Centre
3000 Chestnut Ave. 410-366-2001
An international slate of artists come to Martha Macks' studio to make high-quality prints. And if you're in the market for buying one, the press has an archive and gallery to look through. Among the inventory are works by poet Mark Strand and Baltimorean Joyce Scott.

THE POTTERS GUILD OF BALTIMORE

Suite 101, Meadow Mill
3600 Clipper Mill Rd. 410-235-4884
The fruits of Guild members labor are for sale in a gallery lined with shelves and cubby holes. If you'd like to try your hand at the craft, the Guild offers classes on plaster casting and other ceramic techniques for adults and children.

THE PURNELL GALLERIES

Suite 407, The Mill Centre
3000 Chestnut Ave. 410-662-7555
Old mill beams and brick walls provide a fitting space for this gallery of traditional 19th and 20th century American and English paintings. In addition, the century-old business carries sporting art and offers appraisals, conservation, and fine art framing. By appointment.

Coffee Break

THE COFFEE MILL

3549 Chestnut Ave. 410-243-1144

Located in a narrow old house, the Mill sells outstanding java to go along with chutneys, cheeses, breads, bulk spices, teas, and other packaged gourmet food. Daily.

Epicurean Bites

CAFE HON

1002 W. 36th St. 410-243-1230

Eat down-home food like chicken salad, gingerbread pancakes, meatloaf, pork chops, burgers, and fries—just like downey oshun ("down the ocean" to non-natives)—in a Grandma's kitchen atmosphere of wood floors, enamel and Formica tables, and mismatched chairs. Don't miss the homemade "hon" buns with cream cheese icing. B, L, D. Br Sat & Sun. $½

CAFE PANGEA

4007 Falls Rd. 410-662-0500

Victorian gingerbread outside, sleek cybercafe inside, Cafe Pangea caters to foodies, art lovers, and tekkies alike. "Pangea" refers to one supercontinent, and the global graphics on the floor, the international wine list, eclectic menu (Maryland curried crab to Italian panini and Moroccan chicken), along with Internet connections reflect that theme. Wine events, bi-monthly artists' shows, and catering. L, D. Br Sun. $$

GOLDEN WEST CAFE

842 W. 36th St. 410-889-8891

Owner Thomas Rudis hijacked the name from a closed bar in Albuquerque and headed east to serve up New Mexican-California cuisine including dishes like Vietnamese shrimp over rice noodles and huevos montuleños—corn cakes topped with eggs, pinto beans, chilies, fried bananas, feta, and salsa. Sit inside the tiny front room or on the outside porch in warm weather. B, L, D. $

HOLY FRIJOLES

908 W. 36th St. 410-235-2326

Expect a wait at suppertime, for this funky little Mexican eatery has only 36 seats—all mismatched—and a big following. There's lots of beans for vegetarians here and chicken, chorizo, and beef dishes for others. The sponge-painted walls are hung with an odd assortment of mirrors and strung with chili pepper and Day of the Dead skeleton lights. L, D. ☽ $

FRAZIER'S TAP ROOM

857 W. 33rd St. at Elm Ave. 410-889-1143

If you're a regular, the bartenders know your drink as well as your name. Bargain steak, crab cake, and steamed shrimp nights as well as a menu of old-fashioned entrees bring the locals to this 60-year-old plus basement taproom. L, D. Open late Fri & Sat. ☽ $

PINEBROOK RESTAURANT

1011 36th St. 410-467-2499

Ignore the aqua-tinted paneling, the molded booths, rec-room decor, and dig into generous portions of beef lo mein, moo goo gai pan, and other traditional Chinese dishes. Ten steamed or pan fried dumplings for a $1.50 is one of the city's best bargains. D. Open until 11 weekends. ☽ $

Did You Know?

During the winter holidays, don't miss Baltimore's own "Miracle on 34th Street," between Keswick Road and Chestnut Avenue, to be exact. Home owners along this pocket of 34th Street string an aurora borealis of lights from one end of the block to the other at Christmastime. Sure Santa's on the roof but so are hubcap Christmas trees and bicycle wheel snowmen. Giant candy canes line front steps, toy trains chug along porches, a carousel twirls on a light pole, and a miniature cable car performs a high wire act crossing the street. Of course there are illuminated angels, topiary deer, and more of those jolly fat men too. Lighting Ceremony: First Saturday evening after Thanksgiving. Decorations remain up through the first weekend in January. Free.

Hampden-Woodberry

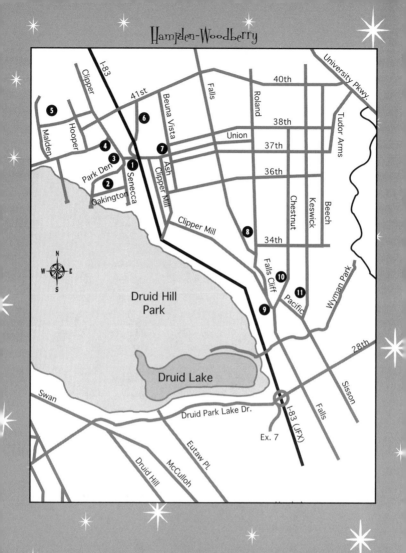

1. Meadow Mill
2. Brick Hill
3. Poole and Hunt Union Works
4. Amaranthine Museum
5. TV Hill
6. Park Mill
7. Druid Mill
8. Evergreen-on-the-Falls
9. Mount Vernon Mills
10. Mill Centre
11. Stone Hill

Roland Park, Guilford, and Homeland

Certainly one of the selling points of the new planned community of Roland Park had to be the laws banning pigs, privies, and other noxious nuisances. In 1891 the Roland Park Company had begun the venture with an eye to luring the wealthy away from Mount Vernon and the city's increasing congestion and poor sanitation. Promises of large homes on spacious lots with plenty of trees and clean air, sidewalks, lighting, and water and sewage systems conjured up visions of buyers living in their own private park. As their custom, Baltimoreans dragged their feet in skepticism, unwilling to venture so far from the city core. But when the Lake Roland Elevated Electric Railroad, established in 1893, started service to downtown, developer Edward H. Bouton built a country club with golf links and Baltimoreans headed uptown.

From the beginning the site, a ridge between the Jones Falls on the west and Stony Run on the east, offered challenges. Instead of fighting the rugged topography, the company hired landscape engineer George E. Kessler to lay out curved roads, protecting stands of mature trees and maintaining some natural vegetation. Later on the Olmsted Brothers, sons of Frederick Law Olmsted who designed New York's Central Park, wrestled Ridgewood Road's ridges and rises into a hillside village. Turreted Queen Anne style houses, half-timbered Tudors, Arts and Crafts homes, and gabled, shingled cottages dominated the development's landscape. Roland Park's familiar Tudor-style shopping center, one of the country's earliest, provided convenient shopping. Strict covenants, overseen by Bouton, maintained the harmony of the community. With it, however, came the unspoken edict that Jews, blacks, and immigrants need not apply.

Guilford, the Roland Park Company's next offspring, begun around 1907, wrapped itself in even more exclusivity. Naturally the piggies and privies were still *verboten*, but so were commercial buildings and pollution from coal fires. This time blacks, with the exception of servants, were restricted outright from living there—a situation civil rights laws of the '60s would eventually change.

The new tract was named after General William McDonald's Guilford estate, which got its name from a Revolutionary War battle where the general had been wounded. In 1857 his son built a 52-room Italianate villa here, also called Guilford, later owned by the *Baltimore Sun*'s Abell family. Along with amenities similar to those of its neighbor to the east, the company pitched the site's proximity to Johns Hopkins and other cultural institutions. Once again the Olmsted firm did the landscaping and this time a traditional mix of even more stately mansions arose.

Homeland, the company's third project, began with the merger of several estates. In 1694 Job Evans began buying up acreage along this ridge and, over the years, the land passed through a chain of owners leading to David Perine who eventually amassed 391 acres. Homeland, his two-story stone house, designed by Robert Cary Long, Jr., overlooked orchards, vegetable and grazing fields, and ornamental ponds. In 1843, when the house burned, an Italianate mansion, also by Long, replaced it. In 1924 the Roland Park Company purchased the property, razing the old buildings, subdividing the acreage, and selling lots to builders and prospective homeowners. Homeland's traditional-style stone and brick homes arose among the trees on roads named for Anglican saints and English towns. The result is a charming "suburban" enclave. (See map p. 370.)

Did You Know?

If her characters could walk off the pages of Anne Tyler's books, they'd blend in perfectly with the people on this city's streets. For the past 30 years Tyler has shunned the author-celebrity circuit and stayed home to pen her best-selling Baltimore novels, among them: *Morgan's Passing*, *The Accidental Tourist*, the Pulitzer Prize-winning *Breathing Lessons*, and her recent *A Patchwork Planet*.

Sights & Sites

SHERWOOD GARDENS

4200 Greenway and Stratford, Highfield,
and Underwood Rds.

"Come see my birds," invites a hand-lettered sign whose arrow points to a nearby house where a cluster of people gather round "Bird Man" Dr. Ed Johnston and his blue macaw Margaret. The object of attention hops from shoulder to shoulder pecking at his cheek. "Her beak strength is enough to take your finger clean off," he says, "but don't worry, she's a domesticated gentle bird." With that, she bows her head, pretending to sleep. The crowd "awwwhs." For her next trick, Margaret "challenges" a boy to stand in her cage, pick its lock, and escape from it faster than she can. Boy and bird compete. Bird wins. The crowd applauds and then visits with Johnston's 40 other feathered friends—ring-necked doves, cockatiels, and a parrot—who inhabit his sun porch. Such neighborliness is not unusual in Sherwood Gardens, particularly in the springtime when 80,000 tulips, complete with a sideshow of dazzling deep pink Sherwood Garden Tulips, burst into a rainbow of bloom.

For generations Baltimoreans have been making April and May pilgrimages to this seven-acre public park in the heart of Guilford. According to legend, the tradition evolved when oilman John Sherwood, owner of a brick mansion backing onto the then-smaller park, was told by his gardener that there were nearly a hundred people wandering around his tulip and azalea beds. "Let them look," Sherwood had said. And they did year after year. When he died, his heirs sold three of the estate's acres to the Guilford Association which maintains the grassy expanse. Nowadays after the spring blooms wither away, the association invites gardeners to dig up bulbs and buy them five for a $1. Following that, the annuals go in, providing carpets of blooms to carry into fall when next year's tulips are planted and Baltimoreans have yet another opportunity to stop and smell the flowers. Dr. Johnston's parrot lectures: 410-561-1500 x17.

Did You Know?

Ogden Nash's witty verses with their clever, convoluted rhymes tickled American funny bones for generations. The poet wrote some of these ditties while living in Guilford in the '30s and '40s. Later he packed up his family and went to New York for an interlude, before returning to winter at his Cross Keys townhouse from 1965 until his death six years later. His poems appeared in *I'm a Stranger Here Myself* (1938), *You Can't Get There from Here* (1957), *Bed Riddance* (1970), and other collections.

Browse and Buy

THE ROTUNDA
711 W. 40th St.
With its dome and medical insignia running across the parapet, this shopping center looks as if it belongs on the Johns Hopkins campus. Perhaps that's because the land was originally owned by the university, then sold to the Maryland Casualty Company who built their new headquarters here in 1922. When the firm outgrew the

space in 1970, the building was transformed into a shopping center containing 23 stores. Along with the stores listed below, there's a Giant Food, Rite Aid Pharmacy, bank, bookstore, eateries, and other shops and services. Loews Cineplex Rotunda (410-235-1800), a twin theaters arts house, offers first run independent and foreign films. Giant and Rite Aid open daily 24 hours.

THE BEAD

410-366-3808

The Bead is for women who like comfy but stylish clothes made from natural fibers. Since 1967, sisters Idy Harris and Anne Liner and their mother Belle Bashoff have been drawing customers from Baltimore and beyond with their mix of Ecuadoran sweaters, batik scarves, Mexican and Indonesian jewelry, and the Flax clothing line.

THE COOK'S CUPBOARD, INC.

410-467-2547

Stock a kitchen with everything from gourmet gadgets to practical pots and pans. Or have a gift basket made up for the bride or new homeowner. More unusual items include fancy ceramic dog dishes, decorative knobs, soap by the inch, and chocolate body paint.

TOMLINSON CRAFT COLLECTION

410-338-1572

Tomlinson offers the best of American made crafts. Chenille scarves woven in Appalachia, glassware ranging from whimsical to elegant, wooden toys and boxes, and gold and silver jewelry are among the standouts. Don't miss the back wall filled with shelves of pottery.

Epicurean Bites

ALONSO'S

415 W. Cold Spring Ln. 410-235-3433

Folks come to this old neighborhood watering hole for monster hamburgers—the kind you can't fit your mouth around. For more than 70 years Alonso's was dark and pubby but all that is changing now that Loco Hombre next door bought it out. Look for the same big burgers supplemented by a casual Italian menu. L, D. $

THE AMBASSADOR DINING ROOM

Ambassador Apartments, 3811 Canterbury Rd.
410-366-1484

Beneath a beamed Tudor ceiling, dine like the Raj on gourmet Indian fare like Bombay Lobster medallions sauteed with baby spinach leaves or spicy lamb vindaloo poached in curry sauce. In nice weather, try the outdoor terrace overlooking a garden. L, D. Br Sat & Sun. $½

LOCO HOMBRE

413 W. Cold Spring Ln. 410-889-2233

Loco Hombre doesn't take reservations, so on busy nights, you'll have to join the queue for grilled anchiote marinated flank steak burritos, adobo chicken with green chile sauce, and the hombre's gourmet take on tacos, fajitas, and enchiladas. The dining room, decorated with serapes and sombreros and cutout cactuses, can get noisy, but that's part of the fiesta spirit. L, D. Open until 11 pm on Fri & Sat. $$

MORGAN MILLARD

4800 Roland Ave. 410-889-0030

In 1906, Drs. Morgan and Millard opened up a pharmacy, tea room, and soda fountain. Among the specialties it served in its early years was a 35¢ peanut butter-and-ham sandwich, a hefty treat guaranteed to make Elvis smile. The pharmacy and the peanut-butter-and-pig are long gone, but Southern food like peppered pork chops and pecan crusted chicken still dominates the menu of this Arts and Craft style eatery. Located in one of the nation's first shopping centers, the "Morg" also showcases paintings and crafts from local artists. L, D. Br Sun. $$

POLO GRILL

Doubletree Inn at the Colonnade,
4 W. University Pkwy. 410-235-8200

Step into this favorite haunt of city power lunchers—a clubby room of hunter green walls, parquet floors, and horse prints. Famous for its fried lobster tail, reportedly a favorite of Oprah's, and its classy New American cuisine, this restaurant serves seafood and meats with a hefty portion of people-watching. B, L, D. Reservations recommended. Open until 11 weekends. $$$

STONE MILL BAKERY

5127 Roland Ave. 410-532-8669

Billy Himmelrich turned in his briefcase for a baker's pan and went off to France to learn the intricacies of baking baguettes and brioches. Take these Gallic goodies home along with sticky buns, scones, focaccia, and other specialty breads or eat them with coffee in the little side dining room. The shop also offers salads and sandwiches. Opens 7 am. $

NOTABLE QUOTABLE

"For me, Baltimore isn't just a locale, it's a character itself, full of grit and spunk and color."

Anne Tyler, author

Village of Cross Keys and Mount Washington

CROSS KEYS

Back in the 1800s, near today's junction of Cold Spring Lane and Falls Road, a tavern hung out the sign of two crossed keys to beckon drovers, teamsters, and travelers from the adjacent turnpike in for a brew. The crossed keys, a popular symbol of hospitality, had been derived from a papal emblem representing St. Peter's keys or authority. Over the centuries religious houses adopted the insignia as later did inns at pilgrimage sites. The custom spread to the New World where roadhouses, like the Baltimore tavern, as well as towns were called Cross Keys.

Renowned for its rowdy hospitality, the tavern attracted Irish quarrymen and Hampden-Woodberry mill workers who brawled and bet at the tavern's cockpit ring. Warmer months, city dwellers flocked to the inn's oak grove and pavilion to picnic, dance, and listen to brass bands. However, as the century drew to a close and railroads took away the wagon trade, Cross Keys lost its customers and became a private residence. Then in January 1909 it burned. Fire departments from the surrounding area fought to save the old building but the combination of wind and fire proved fatal.

Baltimore's claim to Cross Keys was resurrected in 1962 when the Rouse Company bought acreage off Falls Road, between Cold Spring Lane and Northern Parkway, not far from the site of the original tavern. The land, formerly part of a Baltimore Country Club golf course, was transformed into a planned community of 650 condominium residences with amenities like a tennis club, pools, hotel and restaurant, professional offices, and retail stores. The main attraction for visitors has always been the small village square surrounded by small shops and eateries. A 1995 renovation brought in chains like Talbots and Williams-Sonoma, but the center remains primarily boutiques. In warm months, outdoor art shows and concerts take place on the square.

Browse and Buy

To get to the shopping area, enter at the gate house (an old pumping station) at 5100 Falls Road (410-323-1000). The center's 26 shops include a Williams-Sonoma, Talbots, Bibelot, and optician along with shops selling upscale clothing, cosmetics, crafts, yarn, toys, stationery, and household accessories. Below is a small sampling.

BIBELOT AT CROSS KEYS

Open September 1999
Already a Baltimore institution after just four years, Bibelot is the place for books and music, meeting friends, or unwinding with a latte at Donna's. Bibelot's corporate offices are located above the store, the fourth in a family comprising Maryland's largest independent bookseller.

GAZELLE

69 Village Sq. 410-433-3305
This American handicraft store carries a unique collection of women's wearable art, knit sweaters, woven rugs, hand-crafted jewelry, and painted furniture.

GEORGE HOWARD LTD.

94 Village Sq. 410-532-3535
Cary Grant would have been at home here amid the mahogany counters and the racks of menswear featuring Italian-made suits and sportswear from designers like Ermenegildo Zegna and Luciano Barbera, and shoes by designers like Bruno Magli.

HEIRLOOM JEWELS LTD.

14 Village Sq. 410-323-0100

Heirloom offers one of the area's largest selections of one-of-a-kind estate jewelry and antique silver and crystal—all overseen by an attentive staff. Those with smaller budgets can check out the collectibles section featuring vintage jewelry, frames, and beaded purses.

JOANNA GRAY OF LONDON

23 Village Sq. 410-435-2233

Fashionable feet head for this small shop offering women's shoes, belts, and purses by Fendi, Stuart Weitzman, Richard Tyler, and other continental designers.

MANO SWARTZ

10 Village Sq. (Inside Octavia) 410-825-9000
www.manoswartz.com

This fourth-generation business sells shearlings, furs, hats, boas, and artwear such as braided beaver jackets. In addition the shop does fur alterations, repairs and remodeling, cleaning, and storing. Don't miss their December sale. Closed July.

OCTAVIA

10 Village Sq. 410-323-1652

Octavia carries the type of women's designer and bridge clothing lines you'd ordinarily have to travel outside the city for: St. John, Louis Feraud, CK, Nicole Miller, Chetta B to name a few. The Occasion Room, located in the back of the store, showcases evening wear including gowns and dresses by local designer Nicki Soble who will custom design as well. On-site alterations.

THE PIED PIPER

32 Village Sq. 410-435-2676

From Battenberg lace christening dresses to pre-teen clothing, The Pied Piper offers European and American labels for boys and girls. An assortment of toys—Madame Alexander dolls, stuffed animals, wooden toy trains—vie for space amid the store's packed racks.

RUTH SHAW

68 Village Sq. 410-532-7886

This is the only store in the city that carries top women's designers like Armani, Richard Tyler, Dolce & Gabbana, and Moschino. Because of its selection and customer service Ruth Shaw has been pulling in loyal customers sizes 2-10 for more than 27 years.

SUSAN KERSHAW DESIGN

Mid-square. 410-323-6600

Credit the lavish flowers in the *Washington Square* wedding scene to Susan Kershaw. When not decorating movie sets, she creates floral designs for weddings, parties, homes, and offices. She'll transform drab yards into mini-Edens, plan your fête, and decorate your house at Christmas. Drop by her little windowed shop for international fabrics and topiaries as well as majolica, French posters, and Venetian glass.

THE STORE LTD.

24 Village Sq. 410-323-2350

Like its no-nonsense name, The Store carries clean-lined merchandise—stainless cookware from Denmark and glass from Finland, along with other well-designed toys, housewares, china, leather goods, and gifts. Simply constructed women's silk and woven clothing is complemented by co-owner Betty Cooke's classic architectural silver jewelry. Cooke will also do custom settings "for anything from beach pebbles to diamonds."

The Bun Penny sandwich shop, Donna's in Bibelot, and The Crossroads restaurant at the Inn of Cross Keys are also options.

CRÊPE DU JOUR

Mid-square.

Baltimore takes a Parisian turn at this informal outdoor cafe. Beneath the cart's blue awning, the griddle sizzles as the chef pours batter on its hot plate. Maurice Chevalier serenades while diners at blue checked tablecloths sip lemonade or coffee and lunch on panini, croques monsieurs, baguette sandwiches, or crêpes. L. Until 8 concert nights. $

MOUNT WASHINGTON

As a boy H.L. Mencken summered at his parents' cottage here in the hills. The Mount Washington of the 1890s, the author remembered, "was a remote and beautiful place"— an escape from the sweltering city and its noxious smells. He and his brother Charlie roamed the woodland, fishing and setting traps for rabbits which they never caught.

Before the Mencken brothers ever walked its ridges, the area had been Washingtonville, a tiny mill town of brick houses owned by the Washington Cotton Manufacturing Company, which had begun operations at this confluence of the Jones Falls and Western Run in 1810. Two decades later the railroad chugged in, providing passenger service down to Baltimore as well as points north.

A dream rolled in with the rails. George Gelbach, Jr., noting the picturesque area's new accessibility to the city, joined with Reverend Elias Heiner to cook up one of Baltimore's first planned suburbs. A huckster in the tradition of Barnum, Gelbach sent out a fancy brochure touting the broad avenues, fountains, and promenades of this "Rural Retreat." The expansive amenities turned out to be mere soap bubbles, yet Mt. Washington's wooded charms drew in prospective homeowners. In the mid-1850s architect Thomas Dixon started building houses south of Smith Avenue. Two decades later, the ridge became known as Dixon's Hill. Before long the area north of Smith filled in with grand homes (some designed by Mount Washington resident Thomas C. Kennedy) and was named The Terraces.

By the time Mencken's father bought his cottage in 1892, the little village, although still a summer retreat, was garnering the attention of year-rounders. In his autobiography *Happy Days*, Mencken complained of the area attracting "the malignant notice of real-estate developers" and of the city "creeping out block by block." Baltimore did annex Mount Washington in 1918, but for the most part has left it to remain in its village state.

In the '50s an influx of doctors, perhaps heeding Gelbach's tonic for the good life, moved into the area west of Dixon Hill, which neighbors soon nicknamed "Pill Hill." No longer a summer retreat, Mount Washington now draws visitors to its tiny commercial district's small shops and eateries, and to the Northwest Family Sports Center Ice Rink (410-433-2307) on Cottonworth Avenue (see *Sports Shorts*).

Sights & Sites

MOUNT WASHINGTON OCTAGON

St. Paul Companies, Centennial Way.

On a hill overlooking the village, sits the most visible symbol of Gelbach and Heiner's dream rural retreat, a four-story octagon with wrap-around veranda and a cupola. The partners had hired architect Thomas Dixon to design the eight-sided building for the Mount Washington Female College. When it opened in 1856, the structure with its light-filled spaces was a success; the school was not. After it foundered following the Civil War, the Sisters of Mercy came to the rescue, purchasing the campus for their Mount Saint Agnes College. The United States Fidelity and Guaranty Company (now The St. Paul Companies) bought the campus in 1982, renovating the octagon's exterior and gutting its interior for a conference center. Along with its corporate functions, the center rents its eight suites, two dining rooms, and meeting space for private affairs.

MOUNT WASHINGTON PRESBYTERIAN CHURCH

1801 Thornbury Rd.

Tucked into the residential Dixon Hill, this white Stick-style church, built in 1878, stands in High Victorian Gothic glory with its wooden buttresses and spiky gables. Designed by Mount Washington resident Thomas Dixon and his partner Charles L. Carson, the building was purchased in 1968 by The Chimes, Inc., an organization providing services for the mentally and physically disabled. Today the old church serves as a home for six adults with developmental disabilities and the sanctuary, with its open arched ceiling and stained glass windows, functions as a great room. Not open to the public.

SAFFELL HALL

1619-21 Sulgrave Ave.

In 1867 William Saffell built this hall as a community center and general store. Seventeen years later the action moved down to the Casino, a larger meeting hall near St. John's Episcopal Church. The Casino was demolished in 1959, but over the years Saffell Hall has endured, serving as a theater, elementary school, political assembly hall, and today as a double house with shops.

Browse and Buy

MOUNT WASHINGTON CENTER

A handful of shops and restaurants make up the tiny, but charming, commercial district bordered by Sulgrave, Smith, and Greely Avenues and Newbury Street.

THE BEST GIFT
1609 Sulgrave Ave. 410-466-3300

Twins and ex-nuns Lynda Casserly and Lynne Sennett package gift "baskets" for their "bow-tique" customers in everything from colanders to birdcages to hat boxes. Choose from needlepoint pillows, painted furniture, jewelry, pottery, and other whimsical items. The sisters also offer a personal reminder service to keep track of birthdays and other important occasions.

CLAYWORKS
5706 Smith Ave. 410-578-1919

Look for the distinctive pottery collage in front of this branch library-turned-ceramic arts center. Inside, you'll find exhibitions of fine pottery by nationally known artisans and items for sale by resident studio artists. In addition, Clayworks offers classes in basic wheel, sculpture, raku, woodfire, and advanced techniques for adults and children, as well as resource help. Check out the seconds sale in June and the Christmas sale in early December.

JURUS LTD.
5618 Newbury St. 410-542-5227

Inspired by the Lascaux Cave petroglyphs dating from 15,000 years ago and artwork from other tribal societies, Philip Jurus fashions spirit guide pins and bold necklaces from materials like fossils, moonstone, tourmalines, diamonds, and silver. By contrast, Sandye Jurus "walks into little worlds" where she fuses tiny gold beads and inlays Gaudi-like mosaics into elegant and fanciful rings. The rest of the gallery features pottery, glassware, and other hand-crafted items from American artisans.

JUST A SECOND
5708 Newbury St. 410-542-4450

It may be the second time around for Just a Second's collection of ladies' career, evening, and casual clothing, but this consignment shop is choosy, selecting only items in excellent condition and current style. Prices run the gamut from a $2 belt to a $1800 fur coat.

OXOXO GALLERY

1617 Sulgrave Ave. 410-466-9696

The corrugated tin siding and yellow door serves as a fitting entrance to this gallery of beaded and metal work jewelry and art objects. Owner Judy Donald holds nine exhibitions a year spotlighting art jewelers like Martina Windel, who pleats metal into fan-like shapes, and Bob Ebendorf, who constructs necklaces out of found items like metal soy sauce containers.

SAVETTA'S ZODIAC SHOP

1615 Sulgrave Ave. 410-664-9154

Granddaughter of a famous Hungarian psychic, Savetta Stevens does tarot, palm, and crystal ball readings, and astrological charts. She also offers a tiny selection of crystals, spiritual candles, necklaces, and New Age books for sale.

SOMETHING ELSE

1611 Sulgrave Ave. 410-542-0444

Mexican Day of the Dead carvings and masks stare down over a kaleidoscope of colorful ethnic women's clothing and jewelry.

MOUNT WASHINGTON MILL

1300 Block Smith Ave.

A small upscale shopping center, including a Fresh Fields supermarket, a Starbucks Coffee, and a garden store has emerged from the ruins of the old Washington Cotton Manufacturing Company on Smith Avenue.

AMAZING GLAZE

1340 Smith Ave. 410-532-3144

Choose an unfinished pot, plate, or clay piece and play Picasso by painting, stenciling, or sponging a design of your heart's desire on it. The staff does the firing and *voilà*! The masterpiece is yours. Take a class or bring in the kids for a birthday party treat.

SMITH AND HAWKEN

1340 Smith Ave. 410-433-0119

Thoughts turn to summer when you stand in this catalogue store's open courtyard filled with pottery, plants, and outdoor tables. Inside, beneath the exposed beam ceiling, gardening tools and duds, cushions and topiary forms, and pots blanket the former cotton mill's floor.

Epicurean Bites

THE DESERT CAFE

1605 Sulgrave Ave. 410-367-5808

Spend a languid lunch hour on the tiny porch or dine in the very informal dining room. The food may be light Mid-Eastern, but calorie counters be forewarned. It will take enormous feats of will to pass up the chocolate macadamia tortes, mango custard tarts, and other delectables in the dessert case. BYO wine and beer. L, D. Open until midnight Fri & Sat. $½

ETHEL AND RAMONE'S CAFE

1615 Sulgrave Ave. 410-664-2971

First of all there is no Ethel and Ramone. But who cares? We'd rather focus our attention on the California-Italian pastas, fish and chicken dishes, and the not-to-be missed homemade desserts. Dine in the cozy downstairs parlor with its lace curtains and floral wallpaper or upstairs in a small, simpler front room. In sunny weather, try the tiny porch or sidewalk tables. BYOB. L, D. Br Sat and Sun. $½

HOANG'S SEAFOOD GRILL AND SUSHI BAR

1619 Sulgrave Ave. 410-466-1000

Hoang's menu is a mini-tour of Asia with Vietnamese spring rolls, Thai tom yum koong soup, Japanese sushi and sashimi, Szechuan shrimp, and a variety of curries, noodles, and fried rice. When the small lower dining room with its sushi bar fills up, there's a larger second story dining room to catch the overflow. L, D. $½

McCAFFERTY'S

1501 Sulgrave Ave. 410-664-2200

Named after late Colts coach Don McCafferty, this steakhouse is chock full of football memorabilia. The handsome dining room, appointed in mahogany with brass railings, boasts a gallery of caricaturist Rick Wright's work, featuring celebrities like Johnny Unitas, Brooks Robinson, and Clint Eastwood. (Yes, Clint ate here.) Needless to say with all this testosterone surging, the portions are man-sized—-slabs of steaks, mountains of mashed potatoes—and everyone goes home with a doggy bag. L, D. Open late Fri & Sat. ☽ $$$

MT. WASHINGTON TAVERN

5700 Newbury St. 410-367-6903

The Mt. Washington Tavern has a split personality these days. There's the century-old building with its rustic oak paneling and lodge-type atmosphere and its newest addition, the garden room, an enclosed glass dining area with a retractable roof that opens to the stars. The menu leans toward steak and seafood with chicken, burgers, and salads rounding it out. Weekly events like guest celebrity bartenders on Wednesdays and free oysters or shrimp during Thursday and Friday happy hour draws young professional crowds. L, D. BR Sun. ☽ $$

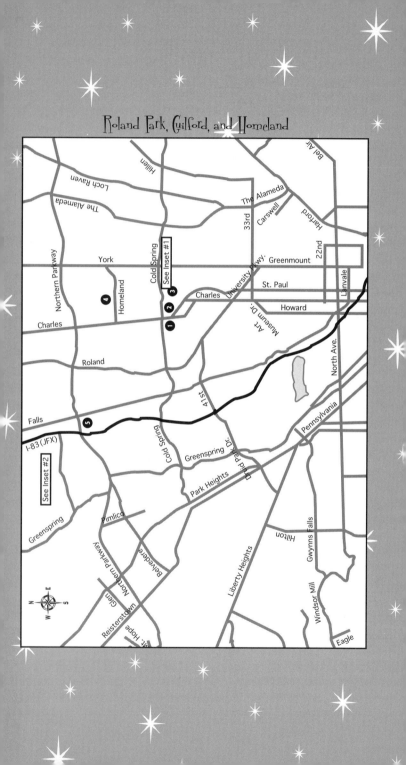

Roland Park, Guilford, and Homeland

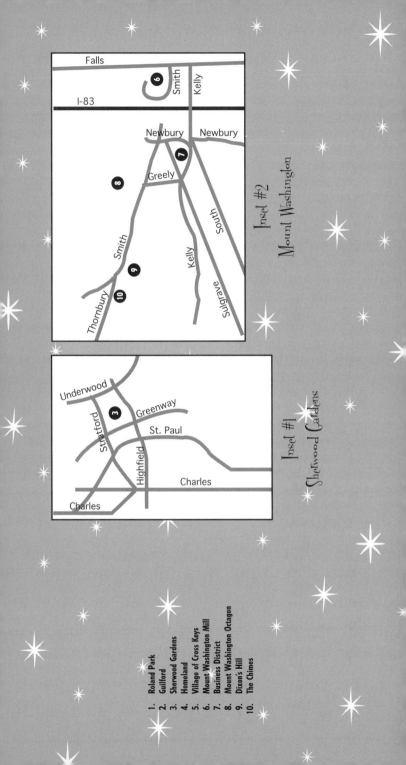

Inset #2
Mount Washington

Inset #1
Sherwood Gardens

Uptown

North Charles Street

We've used North Charles Street and North Avenue as a division point for our following three Uptown chapters. "North Charles" contains attractions bordering both sides of the north-south artery above North Avenue; and "West of Charles Street" and "East of Charles Street" cover attractions in the northwest and northeast sections of the city, respectively. The areas we'll be traveling through encompass a mixture of residential neighborhoods with parks, businesses, colleges, and other institutions.

NATURAL HISTORY SOCIETY OF MARYLAND MUSEUM
2643 N. Charles St. 410-235-6116

Jars of coiled snakes, a gorilla skull, ancient Native American pottery, fossils, rocks, arrowheads, taxidermied squirrels and eagles, bird eggs, and more fill this old rowhouse. Since 1929 Society members have donated their private collections and their time to maintaining this small museum. Exhibits are mostly unlabeled but guides will happily share their knowledge and even, in most cases, allow you to touch. Weds by appointment.

BALTIMORE MUSEUM OF ART
10 Art Museum Dr. 410-396-7100
www.artbma.org

On school days, groups of kids poke around the African and Native American exhibits, ooohing over masks and headdresses, and of course, giggling over well-endowed fertility gods. Upstairs a special Dale Chihuly exhibit featuring an illuminated glass mosaic ceiling finds visitors happily crouching to get different angles on the masterpiece. When the BMA opened in 1923, its founders insisted on creating a museum that was *not* "a mausoleum of art." Given the menu of special exhibits, concerts, films, lectures, and workshops, along with its fine art and artifacts, the museum has succeeded. Yet there's plenty of room for serious contemplation, too.

In 1929 the BMA moved from its original site at the old Garrett Mansion in Mount Vernon to this grand Classic Revival building designed by John Russell Pope, architect of Washington, D.C.'s, National Gallery. Over the years prominent Baltimoreans donated works, and art luminaries like Gertrude Stein and Le Corbusier gave lectures. The museum also launched cutting-edge exhibits, like its 1930s African and Contemporary Negro Art shows, displayed at a time when Baltimore was still a segregated city. The BMA's biggest coup, however, came in 1949 with the acquisition of the Cone collection—3,000 pieces of painting, sculpture, and works on paper by artists like van Gogh, Matisse, and Picasso—the bequest of a pair of wealthy sisters that catapulted the museum's reputation into the big leagues.

During the last two decades, the museum has added sculpture gardens, an east wing, and the West Wing for Contemporary Art. In addition to its permanent collection, the museum hosts 15 major exhibits a year, which have included shows like Edvard Munch prints, Sacred Arts of Haitian Vodou, and the Art of the Victoria and Albert Museum. Some highlights from the permanent collection:

African, Native American, Oceanic and Pre-Columbian Art—Among the items this gallery showcases are ceremonial headdresses, textiles, and reliquary boxes from Africa; ancestral figures and drums from the South Pacific; 19th century Native American blankets, baskets, and beadwork; Moche pottery and conquistador-era gold jewelry.

American and European Decorative Arts—Galleries of American furniture span the 18th to 20th centuries and include Baltimore's Finlay brothers' painted chairs and rooms re-created from historic Maryland houses.

The European exhibits feature porcelains and silver work, and other decorative pieces. A gallery of 12 miniature rooms offers peeks into spaces like a Georgian silver shop, Southern plantation entrance hall, and a Shaker dwelling.

Arts of Asia—This small gallery houses tomb guardians, funerary figures, and other ancient pottery.

Antioch Mosaics—The courtyard of the John Russell Pope building displays mosaics from an 1936-37 archeological digs in Antioch and Daphne.

Old Master Paintings—Rodin's "The Thinker" sits at the entrance to this gallery contemplating works by Raphael, Titian, Gainsborough, Hals, and other early European artists.

The Cone Wing—In 1901 Dr. Claribel Cone and her sister Etta embarked on a buying spree, amassing an amazing collection of works by artists like Picasso, Cézanne, van Gogh, Renoir, and Gauguin (see below). The sisters' legacy, left to the BMA in 1949, also resulted in the museum ending up with the largest holdings of Matisse in the Western Hemisphere.

West Wing for Contemporary Art—Many heavyweights of modern art reside here: Klee, Miró, Modrian, Kandinsky, Ernst, Chagall, Degas, O'Keeffe, Rothko, Pollock, de Kooning, Frankenthaler—and Andy Warhol. In fact, the BMA has the second largest collection of the Campbell's Soup portraitist on regular display.

Sculpture Gardens—Three acres of greenery feature contemporary and modern sculptors like Calder and Nevelson.

Along with the collections, the BMA has a library with more than 50,000 art books and periodicals which is open to the public by appointment. In addition The BMA Shop carries a good selection of art books along with gift items like postcards, jewelry, totes, and even art kits for the budding Picasso. At Gertrude's (410-889-3399) cookbook author and public television host Chef John Shields serves up the bounty of the Chesapeake at lunch, dinner, and Sunday brunch. Freestyle—free open houses featuring music, talks, and other activities—is held the first Thursday of the month from 5 pm to 9 pm.

Museum hours: Wed-Fri 11 am-5 pm; Sat & Sun 11 am-6 pm. Closed major holidays. Admission.

Did You Know?

Born in Tennessee, the seven-year-old Claribel Cone and her toddler sister Etta came to Baltimore in 1871 when their father, a German immigrant, embarked on a wholesale grocery business here. Two decades later, H. Cone & Sons expanded into textile manufacturing and distribution, building a fortune based, among other things, on denim. Along the way the sisters befriended the newly orphaned Gertrude and Leo Stein, who'd come from California to live with relatives here.

Claribel Cone, the more dynamic of the sisters, earned a medical degree from Johns Hopkins, the first woman to do so, while the reticent Miss Etta preferred housekeeping. The duo, now living in Marlborough Apartments on Eutaw Place, embarked on a series of trips to Europe. Over in France, they met up with the now Paris-based Steins who introduced them to a bold new group of artists—Matisse, Picasso, Cézanne, van Gogh, among them—who were turning the art establishment on end. Intrigued, the Cones became collectors amassing thousands of works which they displayed amid the clutter of oriental rugs, potted palms, and the Renaissance and Queen Anne furnishings in their triple apartment. Just before Dr. Claribel died in 1929, she confided to Etta that while she hoped their holdings would go to Baltimore, the city needed to show some improvement in their "spirit of appreciation of modern art." Soon New York's Museum of Modern Art, sure their southern neighbor wasn't worthy, was wooing Etta like a suitor. Luckily, the BMA won Miss Etta's affection and the collection became Baltimore's in 1949.

Civil War Monuments

Baltimore was a city divided during the Civil War. The majority of the citizens were pro-South, but the Union loyalists were quite vocal as well, and both groups chafed under the Federal-imposed martial law and the troops occupying the city. Yet when the war was over, the citizens and veterans alike honored the dead in a quite Baltimorean fashion by erecting memorials to the men and leaders of the warring factions. This section of the city contains three of the most beautiful and dramatic monuments to those who served in the War Between the States.

The Robert E. Lee and Stonewall Jackson Monument depicts the two Southern generals astride their horses the evening before the Battle of Chancellorsville where Jackson was accidentally killed by friendly fire. The monument, dedicated in 1948, was sculpted by Laura Gardin Fraser and stands to the right of the intersection of Howard Street and Art Museum Drive. The Union Soldiers and Sailors Monument, further east along Art Museum Drive, shows a farmer-turned-soldier buckling on his sword as he turns away from his plow and anvil, while twin angels, Victory and Bellona (War), stride after him, arms raised in benediction. All three figures project a sense of purposeful, forward momentum. The bronze sculpture was fashioned by Adolf Weinman and dedicated in 1909.

The Confederate Women memorial honors those intrepid women of the South who "held steadfast" throughout the war. Native Baltimorean J. Maxwell Miller's bronze sculpture which depicts one woman standing strong while another cradles a dying soldier in her arms is located at the intersection of Charles Street and University Parkway (see also "Confederate Soldiers and Sailors Monument" in *Cultural Center*).

JOHNS HOPKINS UNIVERSITY
3400 N. Charles St. 410-516-8000
www.jhu.edu

He had no formal schooling after age 12, yet by his early '20s he was on his way to becoming the richest man in town. Johns Hopkins quit school to help on his family's Anne Arundel estate when his parents, devout Quakers, decided to free their slaves. Later, in 1812 at age 17, the boy came to Baltimore to work for his uncle's wholesale grocery business. After expanding his uncle's fortunes, Hopkins joined his brothers in founding a wholesale provision venture, sending out fleets of wagons to the countryside with manufactured goods and products, returning with bounty from the farmlands, including corn whiskey. Hopkins, pragmatist and consummate entrepreneur, did not let his Quaker roots deter him from labeling the brew "Hopkins' Best" and turning a profit on its sales. As a result, the Society of Friends, prohibitionist to the core, banned him from meetings for a while.

Always quick to sniff out investment opportunities, Hopkins became the major stockholder of the B&O Railroad during its early years, landing himself a position on the board of directors. Hopkins' sphere of capitalist influence also spread to banking, where he helped maneuver the city's financial establishments into prominence in the region.

Hopkins never married. As a young man he fell in love with his cousin, but when his uncle refused to allow his daughter to marry him, the daughter dutifully broke the engagement. Thus, Hopkins reached his golden years with a bundle of money and no heirs. His friend and fellow merchant, George Peabody, encouraged Hopkins to use the bulk of his riches to establish a university in his name. And thus, the Johns Hopkins University, its school of medicine, and hospital came into being.

The Johns Hopkins University was founded in 1876, three years after Hopkins' death, and was the first in the Americas that followed the European model of a research institution. As such, Daniel Coit Gilman, the school's president, chose faculty for both the main campus (then located downtown) and medical campus (see *Washington Hill*) that emphasized excellence in research along with teaching. Hopkins moved to the present Homewood campus from downtown in 1915. In 1942 the school opened its Applied Physics Laboratory, which was devoted to defense efforts, in Silver Spring. The Lab, now in Howard County, is a research and development facility concentrating on telemedicine, space, and other peacetime pursuits. In 1977 the Peabody Institute Conservatory of Music became an affiliate. Today Hopkins, with its eight academic divisions, has more than 16,000 students on campuses in Baltimore, Washington, D.C., Italy, and China.

Did You Know?

What's that "S" doing at the end of "Johns"? The answer: "Johns" was Johns Hopkins' great-grandmother's maiden name, which was passed on to her grandson as his first. In turn, he passed it on to his offspring, who bequeathed it to the university.

Johns Hopkins University and its Famous Writers

Johns Hopkins University is famous for its writing seminars, once headed by novelist and guru John Barth, author of *The Floating Opera*, *The Sot-Weed Factor*, and other literary works. However, long before this program, other famous writers passed through the university's doors.

During the 1870s and early '80s southern poet Sidney Lanier lived in Baltimore where he lectured in English literature and played first flute in the Peabody Symphony Orchestra. Among his most famous poems are "Corn," "The Song of the Chattahoochee," and "The Symphony." A bust of the writer, who died at age 39 of tuberculosis, is in the Special Collections Department of the Milton S. Eisenhower Library and a statue sits on Charles Street between 34th Street and University Parkway.

Thorstein Veblen was once a graduate student at JHU. He wrote *The Theory of the Leisure Class* (1899) in which he coined the term "conspicuous consumption." One wonders, was he thinking of Baltimore's Gilded Age spendthrifts?

The peripatetic John Dos Passos spent several winters in the city, working on books like his 1957 *Men Who Made the Nation* at the Hopkins, Pratt, and Peabody libraries. He wrote about American life in a stream of consciousness style in which he employed a montage of narration, quotes, and biographies. Among Dos Passos' famous novels are *Manhattan Transfer* (1925) and his trilogy *U.S.A.* containing *The 42nd Parallel* (1930), *1919* (1932), and *The Big Money* (1936). Acclaimed writer Stephen Dixon and 1998 National Book Award-winner Alice McDermott are among Hopkins' current faculty.

NOTABLE QUOTABLE

"I could do everything I ever wanted to do in Baltimore except make a living."

P.J. O'Rourke, author of *The Parliment of Whores* and other books, *Rolling Stone* writer, and former Johns Hopkins student

HOMEWOOD

Johns Hopkins University campus,
3400 N. Charles St. 410-516-5589

At first glance the red brick mansion with its two wings and a white portico appears to be a classy administration building on the Johns Hopkins University campus, but in the early 1800s this Federal residence commanded 130 acres of lawns, forest, orchards, and fields. By 1803 Declaration of Independence signer Charles Carroll of Carrollton had spent more than $40,000, an enormous sum in those days, to construct this wedding gift for his prodigal son Charles and his bride Harriet Chew of Philadelphia. Within a few years the lad had drunk himself out of a marriage, and Carroll, resigned to his son's failings, told Harriet to take half the silver as she fled back to Philadelphia with the children. Eventually the signer's grandson (also named Charles—no originality in names here) sold the estate to merchant Samuel Wyman. The Wymans, finding the mansion too small, however, rented it out and built their own nearby. In 1897, the Country School for Boys (later renamed Gilman School), leased the mansion and in 1902 deeded the estate to Johns Hopkins University for their new uptown campus. After serving time as a faculty club, museum, and offices, Homewood re-opened as a historic home in 1987. Guided tours. Admission.

LACROSSE MUSEUM AND NATIONAL HALL OF FAME

113 W. University Pkwy. 410-235-6882

For those who think "faceoff" is nothing but a movie title, come see this lacrosse term in action. Baltimore is the international hotbed for lacrosse, a Native American game perfected for the next millennium at Johns

Hopkins and regional schools. The newly renovated Lacrosse Museum has self-guided exhibits which detail the history and development of the game. A 30-minute video features personal narratives from nationally known coaches and players, along with plenty of on-the-field play. The National Hall of Fame provides an interactive exhibit enabling the viewer to call up biographies of "Famers" whose pictures and plaques adorn the walls. Mon-Sat. Closed major holidays. Admission. School groups and US Lacrosse members, free.

LOYOLA COLLEGE

4501 N. Charles St. 410-617-2000
www.loyola.edu
Jesuits founded this liberal arts college, the first in the United States named after St. Ignatius Loyola, to provide an education "without the commitment of joining the priesthood." In 1852 the school began holding classes in a house on Holliday Street. As the number of students grew, the college moved into a new building on Calvert and Madison. In 1922 Loyola College relocated to its present 65-acre Evergreen campus. Up until 1971, when it merged with Mount Saint Agnes College, the student body was all men. Today this coed liberal arts university offers majors in 26 disciplines (see also "St. Ignatius Church" and "Center Stage" in *Mount Vernon* and "Mount Washington Octagon" in *Village of Cross Keys and Mount Washington*).

EVERGREEN

4545 N. Charles St. 410-516-0341
Up a long drive on the top of a hill, a magnificent yellow Italianate mansion with a massive white columned portico stands between the campuses of Notre Dame and Loyola colleges. Evergreen started out its life more modestly in 1858 as a Classic Revival home owned by the Broadbents, a merchant-broker family. After passing through a succession of owners, John Work Garrett, president of the B&O Railroad, purchased the estate in 1878 for his son T. Harrison Garrett and wife Alice. The new owners embarked on an ambitious renovation,

adding a huge wing housing a gymnasium, a bowling alley, billiard room, and schoolroom for their three sons. The renovations also included space for T. Harrison's growing collection of autographs, old coins, Asian porcelains, and rare books.

In 1920 Harrison's son John Work Garrett, a career diplomat, inherited the house. He, too, was married to an Alice, the former Alice Warder, whom he'd met during a diplomatic posting at the American Embassy in Berlin. (Note: To help keep the Alices and Johns straight, the staff at Evergreen hands out a Garrett family tree.) Once again, Baltimore's construction workers' wallets grew fat as this Alice, a painter and patron of the arts, expanded the mansion to 48 rooms and reshaped it to her creative bent. She transformed the gym into a fanciful Russian theater, designed and painted with folk motifs by Ballets Russes' costume and set designer Léon Baskt. Besides inviting others to perform, she sang and danced for her guests there. She also made the billiard and bowling rooms into a gallery, and added a magnificent walnut-paneled library which housed 8700 volumes including first editions of Chaucer and Milton, Shakespearean folios, and other prized books.

After the Garretts died, Johns Hopkins University inherited the house along with its furnishings and collections. Today Evergreen has been restored to its 1930s grandeur. The Garrett's fine collection of Japanese *inro* and *netsuke* is also on display. Guided one-hour tours. Admission.

COLLEGE OF NOTRE DAME OF MARYLAND
4701 N. Charles St. 410-435-0100
www.ndm.edu
This Catholic women's liberal arts school, located on a 58-acre wooded campus, offers both weekday and weekend college programs, the latter geared toward women and men with full-time jobs. In addition, the college has graduate studies (open to both sexes) in adulthood and aging, liberal studies, management, teaching, and leadership in teaching. Founded in 1873,

the 650-student college also encourages returning students with its continuing education program.

CATHEDRAL OF MARY OUR QUEEN
5300 N. Charles St. 410-433-8800

In 1904 as the Great Fire roared through downtown, legend has it that Thomas J. O'Neill prayed to the Virgin Mary that his North Charles Street department store would be spared. If it survived, the Irish-born merchant declared, he would build a grand cathedral. The wind shifted, the flames stopped short, and O'Neill kept his vow. On his death in 1919, the multi-millionaire's will stipulated that two-thirds of his estate would go to launching the project after his wife passed away. Church officials, however, hemmed and hawed. Baltimore already had a Basilica and the bequest, some reasoned, would be better spent on schools and other services. While the church hierarchy debated, the money sat until 1954 when the groundbreaking was finally held.

Angularity marks the 239-foot wide granite and brick structure whose architecture, with its interior buttresses and recessed stained glass, resembles an inside-out Gothic. Built in a cruciform with the altar at its head, the cathedral contains a wealth of ornamentation such as carved stone panels, French and American stained glass windows, and bronzes. Above the altar in the donor chapel memorializing Thomas O' Neill is a painting depicting the martyred Thomas Moore, Saint Francis of Assisi, Babe Ruth, and Al Jolson, the latter two having achieved part of their exalted status by attending St. Mary's Industrial School, a school for wayward boys in the city. To get a full appreciation of the architecture, buy a guidebook from the church office and, if you're in town during Easter, attend the 11 am mass. Mary Our Queen shares co-cathedral status with the Basilica, although major ceremonies like installations of bishops are held here. Mass daily. Church open daily 7 am-9 pm.

Epicurean Bites

LISA'S COFFEE HOUSE

2110 N. Charles St. 410-727-7081

American-Ukrainian food such as home made borscht, pierogies, and stuffed cabbage are staples at this tiny basement restaurant run by Lisa and her Ukrainian-born mother. B, L, D. Dinner reservations recommended. $

NAM KANG RESTAURANT

2126 Maryland Ave. 410-685-6237

This small basement restaurant has won acclaim for its authentic Korean cuisine. And best of news for insomniacs, the Nam Kang stays open until 4 am most days. The menu is predominantly Korean, with an offering of sushi and sashimi and Chinese cuisine. L, D ☽ $

NEW NO DA JI

2501 N. Charles St. 410-235-4846

A good bet for a fast lunch, the No Da Ji offers an inexpensive buffet for both take-out and eat-in. The buffet selection reflects the regular menu which emphasizes Korean cuisine with a fair amount of Chinese dishes and some sushi. L, D. $½

West of Charles Street

BALTIMORE STREET CAR MUSEUM

1901 Falls Rd. 410-547-0264

"What's in a streetcar?" one might ask. Actually, a lot, and the pictorial wall "descriptionary" in this small yet informative museum will prove it. A 20-minute video, a gallery of photographs, dioramas, and a car barn chock full of streetcars in various stages of rehabilitation detail the history of these mass transit vehicles in Baltimore from the original horse-drawn cars to cable and electric on up to today's Light Rail. Admission includes unlimited rides on a renovated streetcar traveling on a one-mile loop. Library open to public Sun by appointment. Museum hours: June-Oct: Sat & Sun 12-5; Nov & Jan: Sun 12-5. Closed Dec. Large groups must be booked in advance.

DRUID HILL PARK

2700 Madison Ave. 410-396-7931 (general information)

The jewel of Baltimore's parks, Druid Hill's rolling terrain, broad drives, and sparkling lake conjure up images of past leisure: matched pairs of horses drawing carriages, couples strolling along grassy paths, pink-cheeked skaters on the frozen lake. Today the park offers newer pastimes along with the old. The paths are now paved—to the delight of skateboarders and young bicyclists—and the basketball and tennis courts are much in demand. While the resident flock of sheep is long gone, the Baltimore Zoo pleases crowds with its array of animals from the Arctic to Africa.

The 600-acre park opened in October 1860 with a parade and military band, but its roots reach back to the 18th century when the Rogers and Buchanan families owned estates here. (Their family graveyards are still on the property.) Druid Hill, Colonel Nicholas Rogers' 1801 mansion which gave the park its name, serves as administrative headquarters for the zoo. In 1863 architect. John H.B. Latrobe radically altered the Federal-style structure when he tore out the center of the house, added Victorian arches, a main staircase, and cupola, and then tacked on 20-foot-wide porches around the perimeter.

Statues and old fountains dot the park. The fountains, from which the many natural springs of the area formerly flowed, once drew Baltimoreans for their pure drinking water. Formed by the construction of an immense earthen dam in 1871, then the largest in the country, the man-made Druid Lake was created primarily as a drinking water source for the city and performs that function even to this day. The park also contains a large swimming pool.

CONSERVATORY

Druid Hill Park. 410-396-0180

The 1888 Palm House resembles a giant Victorian birdhouse with a cupola sitting on the edge of Druid Hill Park. Step inside the 90 foot-tall yellow metal and glass structure and you've entered the tropics. A canopy of palms shields birds of Paradise, jasmine, banana trees, and other exotic plants. Over in a corner a

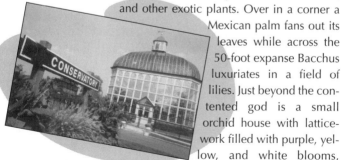

Mexican palm fans out its leaves while across the 50-foot expanse Bacchus luxuriates in a field of lilies. Just beyond the contented god is a small orchid house with latticework filled with purple, yellow, and white blooms, followed by three greenhouses and a side garden, including a rose patch dedicated to "John Cook, a renowned Rosicrucian worthy of his honor whose fame will never die." (Artists frequent the grounds and gardens searching for inspiration.) Thought to be the oldest extant public conservatory in the nation, the structure will soon be getting a mini-facelift. Plans call for the addition of small conservatories linking the Palm House to the greenhouses, which will be divided into three climates—tropics, Mediterranean, and desert, each displaying its indigenous plants. Finally, the gardens will be expanded and spruced up with native Maryland trees and plants. Thurs-Sun 10-4. Free.

BALTIMORE ZOO
Druid Hill Park. 410-366-LION or 410-396-7102
Most people don't think "zoo" when the air is frosty and full of Christmas carols, but coming to the Baltimore zoo is great fun in December. For starters, many zoo denizens like snow leopards, polar bears, and Arctic foxes favor cold weather, and Santa's reindeer hang out in the farmyard of the Children's Zoo waiting for St. Nick to round them up on December 24th. "ZooLights" is another reason to bundle up and head here. From late November through early January, Santa's helpers deck the grounds with a dazzling array of light sculptures and holiday decorations.

In warmer weather the zoo offers plenty of entertainment with the six-acre African Watering Hole, the Leopard Lair, Reptile House, Maryland Wilderness, and the award-winning Children's Zoo—to name just a few of the exhibits. And if any feathered or teeth-baring critter catches your fancy, you can "adopt" it and contribute to its continuing care at the zoo. (But you can't take it home with you!) If you tire of walking the zoo's 180 acres, hop the shuttle train to get to the next exhibit. There's also a carousel and miniature train, food concessions, and picnic tables. Closed Christmas Day. Admission.

BALTIMORE CITY COMMUNITY COLLEGE
2901 Liberty Heights Ave. 410-462-8300
Founded in 1947, BCCC was one of the first two-year colleges in the country and is the only state-sponsored community college in Maryland today. The school,

which offers associate degrees along with one-year certificates in more than 70 academic subjects, serves 6,000 credit and 8,000 non-credit students at its Liberty and Harbor (600 E. Lombard St.) campuses and at 40 off-campus sites. Among the nation's community colleges, BCCC ranks fifteenth in the number of AA degrees awarded to African American students.

COPPIN STATE COLLEGE

2500 W. North Ave. 410-383-5400
www.coppin.umd.edu
Originally an offshoot of Frederick Douglass High School, this college began as a training program for African American teachers of elementary school children at the turn of the century. In 1926, the program was named after Fanny Jackson Coppin, a former slave who graduated from Oberlin College in 1865, one of the first black women to earn a degree from a major US college. Afterwards she taught at the Institute for Colored Youth in Philadelphia where she later became principal and influenced black education in America. In 1938 the school became a four-year college and 25 years later expanded its curriculum to include a Bachelor of Science degree. Today Coppin also offers graduate studies.

MUSLIM AMERICAN SOCIETY OF BALTIMORE AND MUSLIM COMMUNITY CULTURAL CENTER

3401 W. North Ave. 410-945-0413
With approximately 1,500 members in the city, the Muslim American Society (MAS) of Baltimore is a bustling mosque and community center. Yet, despite its growing numbers, the MAS is often confused with other offshoot groups.

More than 50 years ago, the Muslim American Society originated as the Black Muslims under the largely self-appointed leader Elijah Mohammed. Eventually the Black Muslims evolved into the Nation of Islam and when Elijah Mohammed died in 1975, his son Wallace Deen Mohammed took over. Educated as an Imam or religious leader, Wallace Mohammed rejected the separatist views of his father and for a quarter of a century guided the movement, renamed "The Muslim American Society," toward Islam as traditionally practiced. Louis Farrakhan, meanwhile, re-established the Nation of Islam which, MAS is careful to explain, is more of a political than religious group. That the World Council of Mosques recognizes MAS is further substantiation of its legitimacy.

In addition to providing a place of worship, the Society and Cultural Center hold classes in Arabic and operate a weekend school and summer camp for youth, as well as a bookstore, second-hand shop, and a multi-cultural restaurant (open Wed-Sun) serving cuisine from Islamic countries around the world. The Imam and other leaders promote religious tolerance and peace and welcome non-Muslims to their center. Friday prayer service 1:30 pm. Prayer class Wed 7:30 pm.

DICKEYVILLE

Wetheredsville and Pickwick Rds. and Forest Park Dr.
At the city's western edge near Gwynns Falls Park sits Dickeyville, a small picturesque collection of 19th century stone and frame houses left from the area's mill town days. The white clapboard Dickey Memorial Presbyterian Church still stands with its red roof and stone fence on Wetheredsville Road. Ashland Chapel, the 1849 Greek Revival Methodist stone church still standing at the junction with Pickwick Road, as well as the old jail and mill office at 2435 Pickwick, have been converted into private residences.

The town's start dates from the 18th century when a series of mills and stone houses were erected. In 1829 the Wethereds, a Quaker family, bought out an old paper company, converted it into a woolen factory, and later built a cotton mill. Over the years the little village survived fire and floods but legend has it that during the Civil War when Union soldiers discovered the mills were turning out cloth for Confederate as well as Yankee uniforms, they forced a shutdown, hurting the town's economy. In 1872, Northern Irish immigrant William J. Dickey bought the village and added wood houses, a stone warehouse, and the Presbyterian church. Later in

1909 the Dickeys sold off their interests and the town's fortunes, under a succession of owners, took a tumble. In the 1950s the Dickeys returned, acquiring the surviving Ashland mill near Gwynns Falls and renaming it "Ballymena" after the patriarch's native city. Today the old mill houses small enterprises. Dickeyville is on the National Register of Historic Places.

STEAM TRAINS OF LEAKIN PARK

Eagle Dr. and Windsor Mill Rd. 410-448-0730

So you've seen the old, life-sized engines of yesteryear at the B&O Railroad Museum? Got a hankering to ride a real, albeit smaller version? Every second and fourth Sunday of the month, April through October, kids of all ages can ride these scaled "Live Steamers" around three miles of track in Leakin Park. In addition, volunteers will demonstrate how engines "steam up" and operate. Second and fourth Suns. April-Oct, 12-4 pm, weather permitting. Free parking and admission; donations accepted.

NATIONAL ASSOCIATION FOR THE ADVANCEMENT OF COLORED PEOPLE

4805 Mt. Hope Dr. 410-358-8900

The NAACP, representing Americans of color as the largest civil rights organization in the country, now has its headquarters here in Baltimore. Founded in 1901, the group spearheaded the push in Congress for enactment of voting and civil rights legislation, while its renowned legal department won significant court cases, including 35 in the Supreme Court. One of the cases argued by Baltimore lawyer Thurgood Marshall, *Brown v. Board of Education of Topeka, Kansas*, brought about the end of segregation in US public schools. Marshall later became the first African American appointed to the Supreme Court. Today the NAACP continues its support for equality for people of color in all aspects of American life. Tours by appointment.

Although Martin Luther King, Jr. never met Dorothy Parker, the famous writer bequeathed her estate—and her ashes—to the civil rights leader. Parker, a staunch defender of equal rights, died childless and wished whatever royalties or other monies accumulating after her death go to support King and the civil rights movement. After the civil rights leader's assassination in 1968, a year after Parker's demise, the writer's estate went to the NAACP. However, her cremated remains sat in a filing cabinet in her lawyers' offices in New York until 1988 when the NAACP brought them to their new headquarters in Baltimore. The organization has created a small memorial garden in honor of Parker, and along with a laudatory dedication on her plaque, the NAACP honored another one of the author's requests and included her suggested epitaph, "Excuse my dust."

BALTIMORE HEBREW UNIVERSITY

5800 Park Heights Ave. 410-578-6900
www.bhu.edu

Specializing in Jewish studies and scholarship, Baltimore Hebrew offers classes in the Bible, archeology, rabbinical literature, Jewish history and philosophy, Hebrew, and other related subjects. Along with graduate and undergraduate degrees, the school has a continuing education program (for credit or audit), Elderhostel, the English Language Skills Program, the Center for Jewish Communal Dialogue, and the Ulpan Modern Hebrew Department. In addition, BHU's Joseph Meyerhoff Library holds the largest academic collection of Judaica in the mid-Atlantic.

PIMLICO RACE COURSE

5201 Park Heights Ave. 410-542-9400

Home to the Preakness, the second jewel in the triple crown of thoroughbred horse racing, Pimlico's raceway, established in 1870, is the oldest track in continuous existence in the country. The Maryland Racing Exhibit on the second floor of the club house features artifacts, letters, and photos from the state's racing history. Among the more interesting pieces in the collection are a note from George Washington enumerating his losses at a horse race in Annapolis, and one of the first Parimutuel Wagering Machines which was pirated from its French inventor, reproduced widely in the United States, and used to place bets in the 1800s. Another item of note is the burnt, headless horse weather vane which survived the previous clubhouse's demise in a 1966 fire. (Per tradition, a likeness of each year's winner of the Preakness is fashioned into a weather vane and sits atop the clubhouse roof until the following year.) Exhibit open to the public racing days from 11:30-5:30 pm. Racing season mid-March to mid-June. Admission to the Club House (see also *Sports Shorts*).

CYLBURN ARBORETUM

4915 Greenspring Ave. 410-396-0180

Like so many grand mansions in the northern part of the city, Cylburn served as the summer home of a wealthy businessman. Jesse Tyson, who inherited his fortune from his father, chromium king Isaac Tyson (see "AlliedSignal" in *Fells Point*), moved into the Second Empire-style house in 1889. After his death, his very young widow Edythe remarried, kept the 180-acre estate, and hired the Olmsted Brothers to do the landscaping. When she died in 1942, the grounds were sold to the city for a park.

Along with the mansion, the Cylburn Arboretum has maintained and expanded many of the formal gardens laid out by the Olmsteds. Several trails on the grounds meander through woodlands and the gardens, and the house itself offers two small museums on birds and nature operated by the Maryland Ornithological Society. A Market Day fund-raiser held once a year, usually the Saturday before Mother's Day, offers herbs, trees, flowering plants, and crafts for sale. Grounds: Daily 6 am-9 pm. Mansion: Mon-Fri 7:30-3:30. Museums: Tues & Thurs 10-3.

ST. MARY'S SEMINARY AND UNIVERSITY
ECUMENICAL INSTITUTE OF THEOLOGY

5400 Roland Ave. 410-323-3200

In 1791 Father Charles Nagot and French priests from the Society of St. Sulpice founded St. Mary's, the country's first Roman Catholic seminary, at One-Mile Tavern in downtown Baltimore. Later, in 1929, the school moved to its present Roland Park campus into its long Italian Baroque building of Indiana lime-  stone. While the seminary trains men for the priesthood, the Ecumenical Institute is co-ed and offers graduate level evening classes in theology for students of all faiths. A retreat center which rents out to groups or individuals is also on the grounds.

Browse and Buy

MONDAWMIN MALL

2301 Liberty Heights Ave. 410-523-1534

Mondawmin offers a range of shops from a full service grocery to national clothes chains to specialty Afro-centric boutiques. Need a hat for a special occasion? Whether you want funky, elegant, conservative or just something to keep your head warm, you're sure to find one that fits your style at the mall's several millinery shops. One of the most popular stores is All That Gospel, specializing in bibles and other religious books and gospel music for African Americans. A smattering of booths inside the mall offer Afro-centric jewelry, crafts, and other wares.

Epicurean Bites

THE PAPERMOON DINER

227 W. 29th St. 410-889-4444
www.charm.net/~diner

Barbie with a burger. GI Joe with jambalaya. Pez dispensers with pasta primavera. If you're hungry for American bistro food or curious about how you might incorporate all those cast-off toys into your decor, this 24-hour eatery is the place to go. Popular with Hopkins folks. B, L, D. ☾ $

NIGHT LIFE

THE SPORTSMEN'S JAZZ LOUNGE

4723 Gwynn Oak Ave. 410-664-1041

The Sportsmen's Lounge rocks with live, local jazz bands Friday nights and opens the floor to jam sessions on Mondays. Located in northwest Baltimore off Liberty Heights Road, this cozy lounge attracts loyal fans who come to catch the latest hot jazz acts on the Baltimore scene or to gab around the scattered tables between acts. Drinks only. ☾.

East of Charles Street

Sights & Sites

TOWER CLOCK AT HISTORICAL INSTRUMENT RESTORATIONS

2100 St. Paul St. 410-752-4771

Along with concert orchestrions (self-programmed, perforated roll playing organs often used on old merry-go-rounds), Durward R. Center restores tower clocks, those immense timepieces found on old banks and public buildings. For an example of his work, drive by and look up to see two tower clocks dials powered by movements with a turn-of-the-century gravity escapement. The tower clock on the 21st Street side of the house features a dragon whose tail thumps a bell on the hour. House not open to the public. Restoration inquiries by appointment.

LOVELY LANE UNITED METHODIST CHURCH & MUSEUM

2200 St. Paul St. Church: 410-889-1512
Museum: 410-889-4458

The mother church of Methodism in the United States, this Romanesque church is one of architect Stanford White's masterpieces. A 186-foot granite bell tower, modeled after an eleventh century one on a church near Ferrara, Italy, dominates the corner of the 1887 stone building. Inside, a spacious double-tiered sanctuary in an elliptical auditorium offers marvelous acoustics with no seat more than 50 feet from the pulpit. The chairs themselves are equipped with original personally controlled heating and ventilation systems, as well as with individual under-the-seat hat racks.

Overhead a magnificent ceiling mural, based on a sky chart of the predawn sky on the morning of the building's dedication, depicts more than 700 stars and planets. Over the years the ceiling and roof have suffered severe water damage, but recently the church embarked on a campaign to repair them. The adjacent chapel, also of circular form, contains Tiffany windows and a gallery. In 1884 Lovely Lane's pastor John Franklin Goucher donated land next to this stone church for the establishment of the Women's College of Baltimore City (later Goucher College), also designed by White. Services Sun 11 am. Tours by appointment.

The Museum, run by the Historical Society of the United Methodist Church, has a collection of journals and letters by Francis Asbury, the first American Methodist bishop, and other early church figures. It also offers both permanent and changing exhibits on Methodism in the region and in the United States. The museum's non-circulating library contains church genealogy, history, biographies of clergy, as well as works of Asbury, John Wesley, and other prominent Methodists. Mon & Fri, 10-4.

GREEN MOUNT CEMETERY
Greenmount Ave. and Oliver St. 410-539-0641
An assassin, an art collector, statesmen, actors, poets, and generals are all buried here in the fourth oldest "garden cemetery" in the country. The rolling, monument-studded grounds abound with the names and accomplishments of many of Baltimore's finest citizens and leaders. And then there's John Wilkes Booth—although you won't be able to find a headstone. His remains lie in an unmarked grave so as to discourage vandals or defilement. But the tombstones of his distinguished acting family are readily seen.

Green Mount originated as yet another country estate, that of Robert Oliver, a shipping magnate and major investor in the B&O Railroad during the late 18th and early 19th centuries. Today a Gothic chapel stands on the home's former site near the entrance to the grounds. Oliver is buried here along with prominent business leaders Johns Hopkins, Enoch Pratt, Moses Sheppard, John Work Garrett, Ross Winans, and John McDonogh. Ferdinand C. Latrobe, seven times mayor of Baltimore, and Albert Ritchie, Maryland governor for 15 years, also lie here along with both Union and Confederate generals.

Representing arts and letters are: William and Henry Walters; Sidney Lanier, poet and flautist; Arunah Abell, *Baltimore Sun* newspaper founder; sculptor William Henry Rinehart; and photographer A. Aubrey Bodine. And three notable women rest in peace here: Betsy Patterson Bonaparte, who had little peace during her long life; Mary Elizabeth Garrett, who founded Bryn Mawr School and opened medical education to women at Johns Hopkins; and Mary Garrett Jacobs, the former's sister-in-law and doyenne of Baltimore society.

Green Mount staff can provide genealogical and burial research on a set fee schedule. Free maps and a list of the most visited grave sites in the cemetery are available from the office. Guided tours available in May and October (410-256-2180); fee. Grounds open Mon-Sat 9-3:45. (Office closes 11:45 Sats.) Closed Sun.

GREAT BLACKS IN WAX MUSEUM

1601-03 E. North Ave. 410-563-3404

Life-sized figures depict centuries of African American experiences from their African roots through slavery and hard-won liberty to their achievements in our nation's history. The museum was the first of its kind in the country when established by Drs. Elmer and Joanne Martin in 1983.

In addition to more than 100 historical figures, Great Blacks in Wax presents three major exhibits. "The Slave Ship Experience" is a chilling walk through the interior of a slave ship with murals, artifacts, eye witness accounts, and background sound tracks recreating a semblance of the terror and inhumanity of the ignominious trade. Even more overwhelming, "The Struggle Against Lynching" offers a painful reminder that lynch mobs are very much part of America's recent past. The Maryland Room depicts African Americans who've made significant contributions to state and national history. The museum plans a major expansion which will include theme pavilions honoring groups of African Americans such as physicians and nurses. Gift shop. Meeting facilities available for rental. Closed Jul-Aug and most Mons (except during Black History Month in Feb). Admission.

BALTIMORE'S ONLY BLACK AMERICAN MUSEUM
1765-69 Carswell Rd. 410-243-9600
Founded as a co-op to preserve, showcase, and sell African American art, Baltimore's Only Black American Museum (BAM) maintains a unique and varied collection of African artifacts and art from local and nationally known African Americans. Much of the artwork is for sale. In addition, the museum offers bimonthly exhibits, special museum events, and cultural activities for holidays like Martin Luther King Day and Kwanza. The museum holds free open houses Saturday evenings, and is open the first Sunday of each month for Family and Friends Day. Call in advance for information and to arrange group tours. Weekdays 9-5; weekends by appointment. Admission.

MEMORIAL STADIUM
33rd St. between Ellerslie Ave. and Ednor Rd.
The Orioles thrilled fans here before flying away to new digs at. Camden Yards and the Colts played here before owner Irsay pirated them away. Built on the same spot as the city's earlier Municipal Stadium and completed in 1954, Memorial Stadium now stands

silently awaiting its fate: conversion of parts or all of the structure for alternative uses, or destruction via the wrecking ball. The memorial urn—containing soil from the 100 plus cemeteries around the world where American soldiers are buried, and for which the stadium was named—may be relocated to the new PSINet Stadium at Camden Yards.

MORGAN STATE UNIVERSITY

1700 E. Coldspring La. 443-885-3333
www.morgan.edu
Morgan State began in 1867 as Centenary Biblical Institute with classes held at Sharp Street Methodist Church. After trustee Reverend Lyttleton F. Morgan gave the school a big bequest in 1890, the college was renamed for him. Following World War I, the campus moved to its current location, and in 1939 the state of Maryland bought the institution. Morgan became a university in 1975 and now offers undergraduate, masters, and doctorate programs in arts and sciences and professional fields. Today the school turns out the highest number of African Americans earning bachelor's degrees in the state. An eight-foot statue of abolitionist Frederick Douglass by Baltimore sculptor James E. Lewis stands on the campus.

JAMES E. LEWIS MUSEUM OF ART

Morgan State University, 1700 E. Coldspring Ln.
443-885-3030
Renowned sculptor, archeologist, and art historian Professor James E. Lewis amassed over 3,000 works of art from around the world which are now the basis of the museum. The collection includes paintings, sculpture, and other artwork of notable African Americans as well as of prominent European and American artists. Currently two small galleries feature traditional African and ethnic art and a rotating exhibit of contemporary black artists. Lewis also sculpted the Black Soldier Statue at Monument Square and a bronze relief of civil rights activist Clarence Mitchell, Jr. in the courthouse bearing his name (see *City Hall District*).

The university plans to open a new fine arts center by the end of 2000, which will more than double the current exhibit space. Mon-Fri, 9-5; Sat-Sun, 12-4. Free; donations accepted.

Did You Know?

Thirteen year old Zora Neale Hurston dropped out of school in 1916 to care for her brother's children. By age 16, after joining a traveling theatrical company, she found herself sick while on the road in Baltimore and decided to stay here for a while. She took a job as a maid and caretaker for a white minister who encouraged her to attend Morgan Academy, the high school division of Morgan College which she graduated from two years later. Hurston studied anthropology at Columbia University and went on to became an eminent African American novelist and folklorist. Her most famous works are *Dust Tracks on a Road*, her 1942 autobiography, and the 1937 novel *Their Eyes Were Watching God*.

SENATOR THEATRE
5904 York Rd. 410-435-8338
It's a treat to come to the 900-seat Art Deco Senator, the city's premier cinema showcase. Built in 1939 and listed on the National Register of Historic Places, this bonafide movie palace with its 40-foot wide screen has, in addition to playing first run films, hosted scores of world premieres including John Waters' *Cry-Baby*, *Hairspray*, and *Serial Mom* and Barry Levinson's *Diner*, *Tin Men*, and *Avalon*. Occasionally it holds special events like its past tribute to Ginger Rogers, attended by the grand lady of dance herself. Out front a "Sidewalk of the Stars" features signatures of actors with logos of their films. The Senator is adding two more auditoriums with cutting edge sound systems and, across the street, is building the Nibble & Clink diner, named after a long-ago favorite haunt of the theater's teenaged moviegoers.

Epicurean Bites

ANGELINA'S

7135 Harford Rd. 410-444-5545

If you're in the mood for crab cakes this northeast eatery serves up award-winners. While the dining rooms and pub may lack style, the crab cakes more than make up for it. The rest of the menu features old standbys like shrimp scampi and crab imperial. A trolley stocked with homemade goodies and an outstanding cheesecake make it hard to pass up dessert. L, D. Open until 11:30 weekends. ☽ $½

CAFE ZEN

438 E. Belvedere Ave. 410-532-0022

A convenient stop for Senator Theatre moviegoers, Cafe Zen offers generous portions of innovative Chinese dishes like Zen curry along with more traditional noodle and rice fare. There's a small sushi menu and, for the finale, tiny cups of lemon sherbet with fortune cookies. Classical music, plants, light wood tables and floors evoke an air of serenity. L, D. Open until 11 pm Fri & Sat. ☽ $$

EGYPTIAN PIZZA OF BELVEDERE SQUARE

542 E. Belvedere Ave. 410-323-7060

This shopping center eatery serves Middle Eastern platters and innovative pizzas with names that stretch from Fells Point to Monte Carlo to Giza. L, D. ☽ $

CAFE TATTOO

4825 Belair Rd. 410-325-RIBS

Inside the small dark lounge the Eubie Blake Jazz Orchestra is pumping out cool, sexy jazz as the folks at the counter and small tables groove along. Whether its blues, funk, bluegrass, jazz, rock, or rap, this no-frills bar serves up the best of local talent along with ribs, barbecue, and brews. And if you're feeling inspired, there's a tattoo parlor upstairs. For a real Bawlmer experience, come Sunday afternoons from Memorial to Labor Day for "Bullets and Brew" in the backyard, when pellet gun enthusiasts fire off shots between beers.

THE NEW HAVEN LOUNGE

1552 Havenwood Rd. 410-366-7416

The Haven earns kudos from many as one of the best jazz lounges in town, and certainly the only one that consistently books national acts on weekends. Located near Morgan State University, this narrow bar fills up quickly and stays packed through sets. Wednesdays feature Big Jesse Yawn, a local blues artist. DJs or jazz fills out the week. Drinks only.

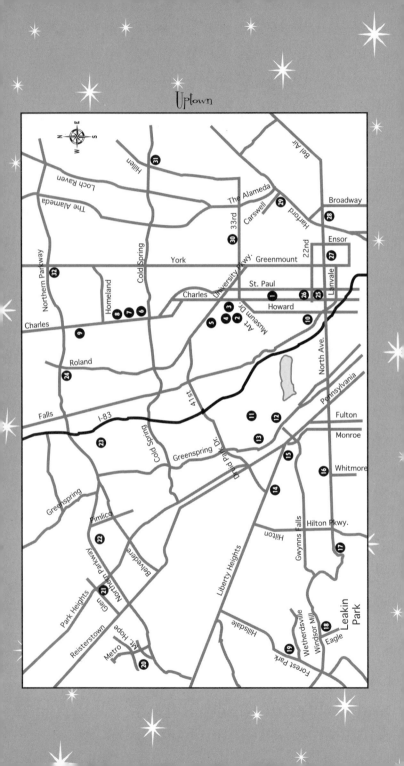

Uptown

Entertainment

City Jaunts and Tours

WATER TOURS OF THE INNER HARBOR

CLIPPER CITY

Inner Harbor. 410-539-6277
www.sailingship.com

Join Captain Rick on a replica of the original *Clipper City*, a 158-foot gaff-rigged topsail schooner. Set sail on a six-mile, two-hour trip around the harbor, party sails with live music, or a Sunday champagne brunch cruise. The clipper also hosts weddings, corporate outings, and other functions. Apr.-Oct. Reservations.

HARBOR CRUISES, LTD.

Inner Harbor. 410-727-3113
Twenty-four hour line: 800-695-2628
www.harborcruises.com

Since 1981, the *Bay Lady* and *Lady Baltimore* have been cruising the Inner Harbor with two enclosed climate-controlled decks and an open-air top observation deck. Come aboard for lunch and dinner cruises while a DJ spins popular music. Tours are narrated. The 300 plus-passenger blue-and-white vessels are available for private events as well. The company also runs cruises to Annapolis, kids' cruises, and crab feast cruises. Reservations recommended.

SCHOONER NIGHTHAWK CRUISES, INC.

1715 Thames St., Fells Point. 410-276-7447
www.a1nighthawkcruises.com

Tour the harbor by moonlight, solve a shipboard mystery, watch 4th of July fireworks from the water, or even get married "at sea." This 19th century-style gaff-rigged schooner, built in 1980, did stints in the Caribbean, Mexico, and South America before settling down in Fells Point in 1986. A century earlier the 82-foot boat would have hauled coffee, sugar, and tobacco. Today it totes folks who like live music, buffet dinners, and champagne brunches along with their water-going sightseeing. Reservations recommended.

SKIPJACK MINNIE V

Constellation Dock, Inner Harbor. 410-685-3750 x372
Weather permitting, the historic Minnie V. offers 90-minute narrated tours on one of the few remaining skipjacks under sail. All tours are walk-ons with no reservations in advance; tickets available on-board at the time of sailing or at the Visitors Center ticket booth. May-Sept: Sat, Sun, and holidays at 10:30 am and 1, 3, and 5 pm.

Did You Know?

In the 19th and early 20th century Baltimoreans escaped the sultry heat by boarding steamboats at the Inner Harbor bound for bay beaches. The boats also offered overnight runs to Norfolk and Richmond.

CITY JAUNTS

HARBOR CITY TOURS

Inner Harbor. 410-254-TOUR (8687)
Frances Zeller and her crew present Baltimore lore, history, and cultural insights as they tour visitors around the Inner Harbor, Fells Point, Mount Vernon, and other spots around town on small white-and-blue tour buses with wide windows. Twilight Tours of Baltimore include Phillips' Famous All-You-Can-Eat Seafood Buffet and a tour of the city's historic neighborhoods. Summers take "Make a Connection" aboard an authentic 1957 B&O transit bus, complete with sock hop music, to get to the B&O Railroad Museum. As a bonus, receive discount coupons to attractions and restaurants. Visitors who've taken Harbor City's regular city tours ride this "transit bus" free. Thurs-Sun.

HORSE DRAWN CARRIAGES 76 CARRIAGE COMPANY OF MARYLAND, INC.

Pier 4, Inner Harbor. 410-539-0626

Trot around the Inner Harbor with Sparky or Sugar or any of their fellow draft horses and view the sights. These narrated 30-minute round trip carriage rides loop around Pratt Street and the Inner Harbor. Hour-long trips go to Little Italy or Federal Hill. Twenty minute trips and hotel pick-up also available. Operates unless it's "pouring cats and dogs" or if it's sleeting and icy.

NEIGHBORHOOD TOURS

A TASTE OF LITTLE ITALY

Concierge Plus, Inc. 410-547-0479

Take a swing through Little Italy and learn the history of this popular eating neighborhood. Highlights include St. Leo's Church and the Star-Spangled Banner Flag House. Stop for a luncheon salad at Chiapparelli's, an entree at Da Mimmo, and a dessert that'll cost you a week's worth of calories at Vaccaro's. Walk it off on your way back.

BALTIMORE HERITAGE, INC.

11½ W. Chase St. 410-625-2585

Each spring this organization, dedicated to preserving Baltimore's architectural treasures, sponsors excellent walking tours of Baltimore neighborhoods led by architects, historians, and preservationists. A bookstore is also located on site.

HOLLYWOOD ON THE HARBOR

Concierge Plus, Inc. 410-580-0350

Meet at the Admiral Fell Inn for a two-hour walk around Fells Point to learn about the movies like *Sleepless in Seattle* that have been filmed in the area. Hear tidbits and tales, and visit locations where the Baltimore television series *Homicide* has been filmed. Tour concludes with lunch at Kooper's Tavern where the cast of the show hangs out.

BALTIMORE ARCHITECTURAL FOUNDATION WALKING TOURS

410-625-2585

Join these informative two-hour guided walking tours of Mount Vernon and Federal Hill and learn about Baltimore's history, its architecture, and its characters. Mount Vernon: first Saturday of month 10 am; Federal Hill, second Saturday 10 am.

LITERARY TOURS

410-605-0462

While you're perusing the wares at the Baltimore Book Festival in Mount Vernon in September, take a stroll through this historic neighborhood and see where H.L. Mencken, F. Scott Fitzgerald, Gertrude Stein, and other literary lights penned their masterpieces. Free.

MOUNT VERNON'S ROMANTIC LEGACY TOUR

410-605-0462

Hear the love stories of Edgar Allan Poe and Virginia Clemm, The Duke and Duchess of Windsor, Betsy Patterson and Jerome Bonaparte, and Henry and Sara Mencken. Free.

BALTIMORE RENT-A-TOUR

410-653-2998

www.baltimorerent-a-tour.com

Caters to groups of conventioneers, corporate meeting-goers, and other visiting groups. On its famous Insomniac Tour, nighttime sightseers prowl through the Streetcar Museum, Fells Point, Mt. Vernon, and the Harbor and attend a poetry reading at the tomb of Edgar Allan Poe. Other narrated offerings include a Stars and Stripes, an African American Heritage, a Catholic Heritage, and a "Roundhouse, Powerhouse, and Birdhouse" tour, as well as customized excursions of city neighborhoods.

ZIPPY LARSON'S SHOE LEATHER SAFARI

410-817-4141

Zippy creates 36 original themed tours for large groups on motorcoach or small to large groups on foot. Popular tours include: Wallis Warfield Simpson—The Woman He Loved: The Duchess, The King, and The Baltimore Connection; and Immigrant Tours exploring the cultural heritage of the city's ethnic neighborhoods.

BLACK HERITAGE TOURS

AFRICAN AMERICAN HERITAGE TOURS

P. O. Box 12528, Baltimore 21217. 410-728-8389
Offers small, personalized tours of black historical sites in Baltimore. Passengers also receive a set of postcards, photographed by Monroe S. Frederick II, depicting persons and sites they've visited. In addition, the company will arrange specialized outings such as the Sunday Church Tour, which includes attendance at a local church of choice, and a gospel brunch. Larger groups can be accommodated by bus with sufficient notice.

AFRICAN AMERICAN RENAISSANCE TOURS

P. O. Box 2402, Baltimore 21203. 410-728-3837
or 410-727-0755
Tours cover a wide range of historical and contemporary landmarks of Baltimore's African American culture. The Grand Tour, held each February in conjunction with Black History Month, offers costumed actors reenacting scenes and moments of African American history. Nightlife and other special tours are available, including catering, and visits to other destinations outside the city can also be arranged. Provides step-on guide service on buses. Customized excursions also available.

BALTIMORE BLACK HERITAGE TOURS

P. O. Box 3014, Baltimore 21229. 410-783-5469
Tours can accommodate all sizes of groups with step-on guides provided for each bus tour group. The company also offers personal and concierge services geared to African Americans. "Maryland Multicultural Tourism Guide" available on request.

ABOUT TOWN, INC.

700 N. Calvert St. 410-592-7770
www.abouttowninc.com

Specializes in group tours by mini-van or coach of Baltimore, Washington, Annapolis, Lancaster, PA, and Philadelphia. Tours can be personalized to accommodate children, military, and special interest groups. Professional guides also lead walking tours of the Inner Harbor and Fells Point.

BARGAIN HUNTING/UPSCALE SHOPPING SPREES

Concierge on Call. 410-484-4439 or 800-818-5484

Trawl for bargains with Livi in her Lincoln Town Car or van. Head to discount malls and Antique Row, Fells Point, Savage Mill and Tysons Corner in Virginia, too. Livi also offers transportation to and from airports and other destinations and can be hired as a personal chauffeur.

PRESENTING BALTIMORE

410-539-1344

Presenting Baltimore offers customized half-day and full-day group tours in the Baltimore, Annapolis, and Washington, D.C., region.

Standing Ovation

The curtain officially arose on Baltimore's legitimate theater in 1773 when Lewis Hallam set up a stage in a warehouse at Baltimore and Frederick Streets. After a brief intermission for the Revolutionary War, more playhouses opened, expanding their repertoires to dance, light opera, and concerts. Each June when yellow fever epidemics swept in, however, stages went dark until October. During the 19th century, notable actors like Edmund Kean, Junuis Brutus Booth, and his sons Edwin and John Wilkes stroked on greasepaint here. In an odd twist of fate, Baltimore theater owner John Ford opened his Ford's Theater in Washington, D.C., where three years later sometime-Baltimorean John Wilkes Booth would shout "*Sic Semper Tyrannis*" and shoot Lincoln.

At the cusp of the 20th century vaudeville became king. Singers like Al Jolson, jugglers, acrobats, animal acts, and tap dancers gamboled in the footlights until movies started bumping them off-stage in the '20s. In recent years Baltimore's live entertainment scene has made an astounding comeback. Listed below are some of the city's most active players.

THEATER

ACTION THEATER COMPANY

1616 Brevard St.410-523-6004

www.actiontheater.base.org

Action Theater likes to take chances on original work, staging them in clever, gutsy ways. Among its recent productions were: *The Cabinet of Dr. Caligari*, an original adaptation of the 1919 German movie, and *I Married A Fly*, a Kafkaesque look at relationships.

AXIS THEATRE MEADOW MILL

3600 Clipper Mill Rd. 410-243-5237

Located in a reconverted cotton mill, Axis challenges audiences to see life through other people's eyes with contemporary plays like Terrence McNally's *love! valour!*

compassion! and Tony Kushner's *Angels in America.* Axis also produces new plays by women and people of color.

ARENA PLAYERS

801 McCulloh St. 410-728-6500

Founded in 1953, the Arena Players are the country's oldest continually operating black theater company. This shoe-string operation stages a variety of mostly black-themed productions, ranging from musicals like *Carmen Jones* to dramas like *Livin' Right* (see also *Cultural Center*).

CENTER STAGE

410-332-0033

www.centerstage.org

Center Stage's recent Equity productions included the Pulitzer Prize-winning *How I Learned to Drive*, *The Glass Menagerie*, and Lorraine Hansberry's political epic *Les Blancs.* The Off Center Festival, an annual performance art series, showcases an extravaganza of song, storytelling, monologues, and heaven-knows-what-else (see also *Mount Vernon*).

ENCORE THEATRE

Forest Park Senior Center Complex

4801 Liberty Heights Ave. 410-466-2433

Set up cabaret-style with an elevated stage, this African American company produces black-themed plays with a pre-show buffet on most nights. A Day in Africa, sponsored by the Community Arts Project, celebrates the continent with dance, music, and lectures and sponsors a cultural series with acts like Morgan State University Big Band.

EVERYMAN THEATRE

1727 N. Charles St. 410-752-2208

This small Equity repertory company offers productions of classics like its acclaimed *Lion in Winter*, mainstream plays like *Amadeus*, and off-Broadway dramas like Pulitzer Prize-nominee *Voir Dire* (see also *Cultural Center*).

FELLS POINT CORNER THEATRE

251 S. Ann St. 410-276-7837 or 410-466-8341

This gutsy company, known for its avant-garde fare, produces everything from *Les Liaisons Dangereuses* to the Marx Brothers' old knee-slapper *Room Service*. Housed in an old firehouse, the theater also offers readings of original plays (see *Fells Point*).

LYRIC OPERA HOUSE

140 W. Mt Royal Ave. 410-685-5086

Home to the Baltimore Opera, this 1894 theater also features Broadway touring companies of musicals like *Cats*, *Jesus Christ Superstar*, and *Stomp* (see also *Cultural Center* and "Opera" below).

McMANUS THEATER LOYOLA COLLEGE

4501 N. Charles St. 410-617-5024

The Evergreen Players, Loyola's resident student troupe, presents classic and contemporary works like *Richard III*, *Guys and Dolls*, and *The Elephant Man* in this 300-seat theater.

MORRIS A. MECHANIC THEATRE

One N. Charles St. 1-800-343-3103
www.themechanic.org
TicketMaster: 410-752-1200
Group rates: 410-625-4251

When seats to see *Rent* or *Chicago* on Broadway prove elusive, you can take in their road companies here. The Mechanic also features shows in pre- and post-Broadway runs along with smaller productions like *Viva El Tango*.

PUMPKIN THEATRE

410-828-1814
www.vwenterprises.com/pumpkin

This storybook theater company presents plays and puppet shows for children ages 4-12. While most performance of its children's classics are staged at St. Timothy's School in Stevenson, the troupe also performs in area schools and for community organizations.

SPOTLIGHTERS THEATRE

817 St. Paul St. 410-752-1225

Tucked into the basement of an apartment building, the Spotlighters performs on a 13-square-foot stage with a house so small the feet of the folks in the front rows touch the stage. The company has mastered the skill of creative staging and for nearly 50 years has put on small productions like the four-character *Sylvia* and tackled Broadway blockbusters like *The King and I.*

Once upon a time there was an artist named Rick Shelley whose house was filled with his hand-crafted miniature churches, towers, and castles. Within this kingdom a diminutive Venetian theater with a gilt proscenium arose—Theatre Serenissima. When the curtain opened, it revealed a tableaux of paper dolls on sets fashioned from Oriental rugs and found-art items. The story, a tale of a monk who falls under the spell of a satyr, unfolded to Shelley's narration and synthesizer music. As the lights went up, the audience clapped happily thereafter. Performances at the creator's pleasure, 2000 Mount Royal Terrace. 410-225-3269.

THEATRE HOPKINS MERRICK BARN

Johns Hopkins Univ., 34th and Charles Sts.
410-516-7159

Shakespeare, Albee, Ibsen, O'Neill. Theatre Hopkins is synonymous with classics. Along with the heavy-weight line up, the company moves out to the lawns of Homewood mansion or Evergreen House every two years for informal summertime productions.

THEATRE PROJECT

45 W. Preston St. 410-752-8558

A comedy tonight, or maybe a post-modern opera, a drama on its way to off-Broadway, an international puppet show, dance works, performance art—in other words, if it's new, bold, and creative, the Theatre Project just may dish it up to Baltimore's more daring playgoers.

VAGABOND PLAYERS

806 S. Broadway. 410-563-9135

After wandering from stage to stage for 58 years the Vagabonds settled into their Fells Point digs in 1973. Now the only roaming they do is through a repertoire of classics like *Inherit the Wind* and *Sleuth* and more recent fare like *Moon Over Buffalo* (see *Fells Point*).

OPEN CALL

BALTIMORE PLAYWRIGHTS FESTIVAL

410-276-2153

An alliance of local theaters sponsor an annual playwriting contest for would-be Maryland Chekhovs and Mamets. Qualifying scripts get staged readings with winners earning a three-week run of full productions at participating venues.

BALTIMORE THEATRE ALLIANCE

410-783-0777

Along with promoting member theaters, this nonprofit offers an actors' registry and hotline for auditions.

OPERA

BALTIMORE OPERA COMPANY

Lyric Opera House, 140 W. Mount Royal Ave.
410-727-6000
www.baltimoreopera.com

In 1950 the curtain went up on *Aïda* and the Baltimore Opera Company made its debut. Today the BOC, offers a season of crowd-pleasers like *La Bohème* along with lesser known works like *The Pearl Fishers*. The use of surtitles has made BOC's opera more accessible to the public.

MUNICIPAL OPERA COMPANY OF BALTIMORE, INC.

410-785-2090

Frustrated by the lack of opportunity for minority performers, ten singers launched this African American opera company in 1991. Working on a tiny budget powered by volunteers, the troupe has produced works like Scott Joplin's *Treemonisha*, Mozart's *The Magic Flute*, and *Blake*, the story of an American slave and his journey to freedom.

Born in 1897, Rosa Melba Ponzillo was a child prodigy with a three octave range. Later she parlayed her talent into a vaudeville act with her sister. In May 1918 Rosa won an audition with the Metropolitan Opera and was soon playing Leonora to Caruso's Don Alvaro in *La Forza del Destino*. The diva, now billed as Rosa Ponselle went on to win accolades in *La Gioconda*, *Norma*, and other grand operas. In 1935 while touring in Baltimore with *Carmen*, she met Carle Jackson, the mayor's son. After an intense courtship and a falling out with the Met, Ponselle married him and retired to Villa Pace, an estate in Greenspring Valley. When the marriage broke up, she joined the Baltimore Civic Opera Company (now The Baltimore Opera Company), coaching singers, fund-raising, and coaxing the fledgling organization into a professional company.

CLASSICAL

BACH SOCIETY OF BALTIMORE

410-521-0209

The Society stages madrigal feasts attended by "Queen Elizabeth I" herself, Halloween requiems at Westminster Church, a Bach scholarship competition winners' concert, and a spring performance and tea featuring Haydn's patroness.

BALTIMORE SYMPHONY ORCHESTRA

Joseph Meyerhoff Symphony Hall
1212 Cathedral St. 410-783-8000
www.baltimoresymphony.org
Under the past direction of David Zinman, the BSO has won three Grammy Awards. A typical season offers several concerts series among them: a celebrity set, summer music fest, pops under the direction of Marvin Hamlisch, as well as a favorites, a concert-and-conversation, African American artists, and a family series (see *Cultural Center*).

BALTIMORE CHAMBER ORCHESTRA

410-998-1022
This chamber orchestra, under the baton of Anne Harrigan, offers performances from Bach to Vaughan-Williams at Goucher College and St. Mary's Seminary Chapel in Roland Park.

BALTIMORE CHORAL ARTS SOCIETY

410-523-7070
www.members.home.net/jcain/bcas.htm
In 1998-99 the Baltimore Choral Arts Society celebrated its 33rd season with works like Aaron Copland's *Old American Songs* and Handel's oratorio *Samson*. The 150-member Society's chorus and orchestra perform in the Meyerhoff and other area venues.

CONCERT ARTISTS OF BALTIMORE

410-625-3525
Edward Polochick conducts orchestral and vocal ensembles and chamber music at locations like Notre Dame, the Walters Art Gallery, and the Gordon Center for Performing Arts in Owings Mills. Past selections include Mendelssohn's *Violin Concerto* and Bach's *B Minor Mass*.

HANDEL CHOIR OF BALTIMORE

3807 N. Charles St. 410-366-6544
www.charm.net/~hcob
Along with its repertoire of Handel, the choir sings Bach and other baroque music. Concert venues like

Old St. Paul's Church and the Basilica of the Assumption add to the drama.

PEABODY INSTITUTE

1 E. Mount Vernon Pl. 410-659-8124
www.peabody.jhu.edu
The Peabody offers musical presentations ranging from operas, cabarets, cameratas, and ballets to the Sylvia Adalman Artist Recitals. Performances by the school's symphony and concert orchestras, wind and Renaissance ensembles, and chorus round out the playbill. Free Thursday noontime concerts at Friedberg Concert Hall.

PRO MUSICA RARA

410-433-0041
This group in-residence at the Baltimore Museum of Art plays Baroque music on authentic instruments.

SECOND PRESBYTERIAN CONCERT SERIES

4200 St. Paul St. 410-467-4210
The Second Presbyterian Concert Series include performances by a variety of artists like Herbert Greenberg, pianist Awadagin Pratt, and the Peabody Ragtime Ensemble. The free Chamber Music by Candlelight Series are performed by Baltimore Symphony members.

SHRIVER HALL CONCERT SERIES

Johns Hopkins Univ. 410-516-6542
This series offers artists like violinist Gil Shaham, the Tokyo String Quartet, and pianist Helene Grimaud.

ALSO OF NOTE

BALTIMORE BLUES SOCIETY

410-329-5825
This nonprofit promotes concerts by lesser-known blues artists from all over the country and hosts the Hot August Blues Picnic and the Alonzo's Eat the Rich Picnic held in September.

BALTIMORE CLASSICAL GUITAR SOCIETY

410-247-5320

The Society brings world renowned classical guitarists such as the Los Angeles Guitar Quartet and Marija Temo to the area.

BALTIMORE COMPOSERS FORUM

410-521-9811

www.ezonline.com/bcf

This organization provides an outlet for regional composers to present their music to the public in concerts. The Forum also sponsors seminars.

BALTIMORE FOLK MUSIC SOCIETY

410-366-0808

www.satelink.net/bfms

BFMS sponsors concerts, story-telling, and dances such as squares, contras, and English Country at Lovely Lane Church and other venues. Dance lessons included.

CHAMBER JAZZ SOCIETY

410-435-1985

Nationally known jazz musicians such as Barry Harris and Diva perform four times a year at the Baltimore Museum of Art.

JOSQUIN CHOIR OF BALTIMORE

410-484-0332

Under the direction of Clay Welch, Jr., Renaissance singers and musicians perform madrigals, fanfares, and other period works in churches and other venues around town.

LEFT BANK JAZZ SOCIETY

410-466-0600

www.baltmd.com/leftbank

In June cruise from the Inner Harbor to Annapolis and back to the strains of live jazz. The Left Bank hosts this event along with six or more concerts yearly featuring national acts.

NANCY ROMITA AND THE MOVING COMPANY

410-235-2678

This contemporary dance ensemble performs at the Baltimore Museum of Art and the Maryland Arts Festival, and offers classes to the public.

THE NEXT ICE AGE

410-685-4977

Whether it's Tchaikovsky or Mendelssohn or just good old rock 'n' roll, this 12-member dance company pirouettes, jetés, and kicks like Pavlova or Baryshnikov—except they do it on ice.

SANKOFA DANCE THEATER

410-528-5111

Sankofa, which means "reaching into the past to build the future," features dancers and drummers who present the traditions of Africa in historical context with dance and rhythm. The company also offers classes in traditional African dance and drum to the public.

COMEDY CLUBS

COMEDY FACTORY

36 Light St. 410-752-4189

People have been laughing above Burke's Restaurant since 1983. Robin Williams popped in and did a routine when he was in town filming an episode of *Homicide*.

WINCHESTER'S COMEDY CLUB

102 Water St. 410-576-8558

Head to the upper level of the Shamrock Pub for the area's only comedy-oriented open-mike night on Thursdays. Regular comedy acts Fri & Sat.

Sports Shorts

BALTIMORE ORIOLES

General info: 410-685-9800
Stadium tours: 410-547-6234
TicketMaster: 410-481-7328
Group ticket sales: 410-685-9800 x6601
Baltimore's pro baseball team in the Eastern Division of the American League, playing out of home field Oriole Park at Camden Yards.

BALTIMORE RAVENS

General info: 410-261-FANS (3267)
Stadium tours: 410-261-7238
Ticket info: 410-261-RAVE (7283)
TicketMaster: 410-481-7328
Out of town sales: 800-919-9797
Baltimore's pro football team playing at the PSINet Stadium at Camden Yards.

BALTIMORE THUNDER

General info: 410-321-1908
TicketMaster: 410-481-7328
Indoor lacrosse, or "box lacrosse," played by the National Lacrosse League's Baltimore Thunder at the Arena, 201 W. Baltimore St. Jan-Mar. The Baltimore area is major lacrosse territory with club and school games all through the fall and spring season. Call the Baltimore Chapter of **USLacrosse** for information on local events: 410-832-2855.

BALTIMORE BLAST

General Info: 410-732-5278
Tickets: 410-73BLAST
Baltimore's professional soccer team's indoor soccer season runs from Oct-Apr with home games at the Baltimore Arena.

TENNIS

TicketMaster: 410-481-7328

Native Baltimorean Pam Shriver's hosts the annual Tennis Challenge at the Baltimore Arena in November to benefit local children's charities. Local celebrities and professional athletes compete with Shriver and other tennis pros.

HORSE RACING

Pimlico Race Course
5201 Park Heights Ave. 410-542-9400

The top event in thoroughbred racing at Pimlico is, of course, the Preakness, the second jewel in the Triple Crown, held the third Saturday in May. The Preakness Week parade and celebrations (410-837-3030) kick off the weekend before the race. Pimlico flat racing season usually runs Mar 30-Jun 21 (schedule determined annually by Maryland Racing Commission).

STEEPLECHASE RACES

410-666-7777

The highlight of Maryland's spring steeplechase season is the Maryland Hunt Cup, held the last weekend in April.

CITY PARKS AND RECREATIONAL FACILITIES

One of the first municipalities to initiate a city-wide network of parks, Baltimore offers an array of public recreational facilities and activities.

General Information	410-396-7900
Golf Course Information	410-444-4933
Playfield Reservations	410-396-7015
Pool Information	410-396-3838

For listings of recreational activities and special events check *The Fun Book*, published each spring by the *Baltimore Sun*. You can purchase *The Fun Book* at Bibelot Books or by calling SunSource at 410-332-6800.

Catching Some zZZZZs

Catching Some ZZZZs

Baltimore has upscale hotels, cozy B&Bs, and many choices in between. When making reservations be sure to inquire about special deals and packages that include discounted meals and attractions. Also note that room tariffs vary widely depending on day of the week and season.

Ratings:
$$$$ Deluxe
$$$ Expensive
$$ Moderate
$ Inexpensive

HARBOR AREA HOTELS

BALTIMORE HILTON AND TOWERS

20 W. Baltimore St. 410-539-8400
www.hilton.com
This 1928 landmark hotel, formerly the Lord Baltimore, has splendid public rooms with original marble pillars and trim, carved moldings, and brass railings. Lobby bar, restaurant, and deli. Fitness room with whirlpool and sauna. 427 rooms and 12 suites. $$$

BALTIMORE MARRIOTT INNER HARBOR

110 S. Eutaw St. 410-962-0202
The Marriott is conveniently located within walking distance of Camden Yards, the Convention Center, and the Inner Harbor. Cafe and lounge. Business center. Fitness center, indoor pool, and sauna. Grand ballroom and meeting rooms. 525 guestrooms and 34 suites. $$$

BROOKSHIRE INNER HARBOR SUITE HOTEL

120 E. Lombard St. 410-625-1300 or 800-647-0013
Located one block from the Inner Harbor, this all-suite hotel has recently been renovated. Restaurant. Fitness center. Complimentary full breakfast. 97 suites. $$$

DAYS INN INNER HARBOR

100 Hopkins Pl. 410-576-1000

This basic hotel is just a jog across the street from the Convention Center and three blocks from the Inner Harbor. Bar, restaurant, outdoor heated pool, and business center. 250 rooms. $$

HARBOR COURT HOTEL

550 Light St. 410-234-0550 or 800-824-0076

This premier hotel exudes chic with its grand lobby and posh guestrooms, complete with oversized marble baths and harbor or courtyard views. Staffed fitness center and courts for racquet ball, squash, tennis, and croquet. Indoor swimming pool, whirlpool, tanning salon, and sauna. Restaurants, deli, lounge. Business center. 203 rooms including 23 suites. $$$$

HARBOR INN PIER 5

711 Eastern Ave. 410-539-2000 or 800-223-5652

Dock your boat and body at this elegant Art Nouveau hotel. Guestrooms feature oversized beds and marble bathrooms. Three restaurants, bar, and lounge. 64 rooms. $$$$

HOLIDAY INN INNER HARBOR

301 W. Lombard St. 410-685-3500 or 800-HOLIDAY

Baseball fans can get rooms with a view of Camden Yards in the recently renovated hotel. Restaurant, exercise room, and indoor pool. 375 rooms and two suites. $$$

HYATT REGENCY ON THE INNER HARBOR

300 Light St. 410-528-1234 or 800-233-1234

The Hyatt is known for its glass elevators with views of its six-story atrium lobby and the harbor beyond. Outdoor tennis, basketball courts, and pool. Fitness room, whirlpool, and sauna. Restaurants. Business center. 486 rooms, including 25 suites. $$$

OMNI INNER HARBOR HOTEL

101 W. Fayette St. 410-752-1100 or 800-THEOMNI
Elvis slept here. And so have a lot of others in Maryland's largest hotel. Sports-themed restaurants. Fitness club, outdoor pool, and business center. 707 rooms, including 25 suites. $$$

PARAMOUNT INNER HARBOR HOTEL

8 N. Howard St. 410-539-1188 or 800-537-8483
Built in 1888, The Paramount is the oldest continually operating hotel in the city. Not to worry, they've recently renovated the rooms. 90 rooms. $

RENAISSANCE HARBORPLACE HOTEL

202 E. Pratt St. 410-547-1200 or 800-HOTELS1
This first-class hotel offers spacious rooms and a rich paneled lobby with a Starbucks coffee bar. Connected to Harborplace via a skywalk and to The Gallery. Restaurant, fitness center, and indoor pool. 622 rooms, including 48 suites. $$$$

SHERATON INNER HARBOR HOTEL

300 S. Charles St. 410-962-8300 or 800-325-3535
This official headquarters hotel of the Baltimore Orioles and Baltimore Ravens makes some tickets available for guest purchase per game. Restaurants, indoor pool, exercise room, and sauna. Skywalk to Convention Center. 337 rooms, including 20 suites. $$$

FEDERAL HILL

SCARBOROUGH FAIR BED AND BREAKFAST

1 E. Montgomery St. 410-837-0010
www.scarborough-fair.com
The Scarboroughs offer country comfort with city convenience at this charming B&B within walking distance of the Inner Harbor. Spacious guestrooms filled with antiques and reproductions have private baths; four have gas fireplaces and two have whirlpools. Six rooms. $$

ADMIRAL FELL INN

888 S. Broadway. 410-522-7377 or 800-292-4667
www.admiralfell.com

Located across from the waterfront, this historic inn offers traditionally furnished rooms named after Baltimore historic figures like Mencken, Poe, Hopkins, and Peabody. Restaurants, bakery, and bar. Continental breakfast. 80 rooms (see also *Fells Point*). $$$

ANN STREET BED AND BREAKFAST

804 S. Ann St. 410-342-5883

A 1780s working person's home, today this small B&B, located on a residential street, is decorated in country colonial style. Full breakfast. Three rooms with private baths. $

CELIE'S WATERFRONT BED AND BREAKFAST

1714 Thames St. 410-522-2323 or 800-432-0184

This small, simple B&B in the heart of Fells Point can be a challenge to find for the entrance to Celie's is only a doorway in a sallyport or corridor between two buildings. Seven rooms with private baths. Continental breakfast. $$

INN AT HENDERSON'S WHARF

1000 Fell St. 410-522-7777 or 800-522-2088
www.hendersonswharft.com

Perched on a peninsula, this waterfront inn offers spacious rooms that face the harbor or the Wharf's marina. English courtyard garden. Continental breakfast. 38 rooms. $$$

DOWNTOWN

BALTIMORE CLARION HOTEL

612 Cathedral St. 410-727-7101 or 800-292-5500

This European boutique-style hotel, originally a 1930s apartment house, is located within walking distance to downtown museums. Deli. 103 rooms and five suites. $$

MT. VERNON HOTEL
24 W. Franklin St. 410-727-2000 or 800-245-5256
The Mt. Vernon Hotel and its Washington Cafe are operated by the Baltimore International College. 123 rooms, including seven loft rooms and five spa suites. $$

TREMONT HOTEL
8 E. Pleasant St. 410-576-1200 or 800-TREMONT
This low-key all suite hotel offers rooms with mini-kitchens, available for short and extended stays. Complimentary breakfast. Use of fitness center and outdoor pool at sister-hotel, the Tremont Plaza. Restaurant. 60 rooms. $$

TREMONT PLAZA HOTELS
222 St. Paul Pl. 410- 685-7777 or 800-TREMONT
A lobby with marble and mahogany accents leads to rooms with contemporary decor. Deli, fitness center, and outdoor pool. 230 suites with kitchens. $$$

DOWNTOWN-HOSTEL

BALTIMORE INTERNATIONAL HOSTEL
17 W. Mulberry St. 410-576-8880
www.hiayh.org
This 1880s brownstone offers a safe clean waystation for shoestring travellers. Common living area and kitchen, washer and dryer. Maximum three-night stay in large single-sex rooms. Part of Potomac Area Council of Hosteling International. Planned renovation Fall 1999.

DOWNTOWN-CULTURAL CENTER

ABACROMBIE BADGER BED AND BREAKFAST
58 W. Biddle St. 410-244-7227
Located right by the Meyerhoff Symphony Hall and Lyric, this romantic rowhome with small European hotel flavor has uniquely appointed rooms, some with canopy beds, and all with private bathrooms, phones, and televisions. Continental breakfast. 12 rooms. $$

BETSY'S BED AND BREAKFAST

1428 Park Ave. 410-383-1274

Betsy's is an 1870 Bolton Hill rowhome decorated with eclectic antiques. Convenient to Meyerhoff, Lyric, and Light Rail. Private baths. Full breakfast. Four rooms. $

INN AT GOVERNMENT HOUSE

1125 N. Calvert St. 410-539-0566

Once the home of bottle cap inventor William Painter and Olympic discus champion Robert Garrett, this 1889 Victorian is now an inn run by the city. The public rooms like the Japanese parlor, a library with stained glass windows, and a dining room with an amazing decoupage ceiling exude Gilded Age grandeur. The bedrooms are much simpler. Complimentary continental breakfast. $$

MR. MOLE BED AND BREAKFAST

1601 Bolton St. 410-728-1179

Yes, Mr. Mole is the "dude" in the Wind in the Willows, who hangs with Rat and Badger. This children's story is the origin for the name of this lovely inn with old English charm in a circa 1870 Bolton Hill rowhouse. Dutch-style breakfast. Five rooms with private baths. $

UPTOWN

DOUBLETREE INN AT THE COLONNADE

4 W. University Pkwy. 410-235-5400
www.doubletreehotels.com

Located near Johns Hopkins University this European style inn with Biedermeier-inspired furnishings welcomes guests with chocolate cookies upon arrival. Fitness center and domed indoor pool. Restaurant. 125 rooms, including 31 suites. $$$

HARGROVE HOUSE

2900 N. Calvert St. 410-366-6290
www.hargroveh.com

This Charles Village carriage house suite is within walking distance of the BMA. The first floor has a fully equipped kitchen, powder room, plus living and dining area. A spiral staircase leads to a king-sized bed, full bath, an extra bedroom and laundry room. $

HOPKINS INN

3404 St. Paul St. 410-235-8600

Antiques and original art fill this B&B's rooms decorated in various styles: Victorian, Federal, Art Deco, and Contemporary. Private baths. Continental breakfast. 25 rooms, including five suites. $

QUALITY INN AND SUITES AT THE CARLYLE

5 W. University Pkwy. 410-889-4500

This combination hotel and apartment building rents rooms nightly and long-term, and leases furnished apartments by the month. Hotel rooms and apartments have kitchen or kitchenettes. Restaurant, beauty salon, fitness center, and outdoor pool. 80 hotel rooms and 13 furnished apartments. $½

RADISON HOTEL AT CROSS KEYS

5100 Falls Rd. 410-532-6900 or 800-333-3333

Located on the village square in this planned community, Cross Keys offers French country decorated rooms. Restaurant. 146 rooms, including suites. $$

BED AND BREAKFAST RESERVATION SERVICE

AMANDA'S B&B RESERVATION SERVICE

410-225-0001
www.amandas-bbrs.com

Service covering MD, PA, DE, VA, WVA, NJ, and Washington, D.C.

B&B ASSOCIATION OF MARYLAND

202-518-6066

Just the Facts

GETTING HERE

Baltimore-Washington International Airport

General information and ground transportation: 410-859-7111 or 800-I-FLY BWI (800-435-9294). BWI is served by major domestic and international airlines. Located 15 minutes from downtown in non-rush hour traffic, the airport can be accessed by taxis, limo, and van service. Rates to or from the city vary by company, destination, and number of passengers.

Taxis—$20 and up
Shuttles—$16 to $25 and up
Limo service—$25 to $30

Listed below are some shuttle and limo services available from the airport.

The Airport Shuttle: 410-381-2772 or 800-776-0323
Baltimore Airport Shuttle: 410-821-5387
or 800-287-4227
Dan Transportation, Inc.: 410-418-4348
or 800-692-1700
Private Car: 410-519-0000 or 800-685-0888
SuperShuttle: 800-BLUE VAN
Triple Crown, Inc.: 410-732-7325

Amtrak 800

USA-RAIL 800-872-7245
Penn Station: 410-291-4265
BWI: 410-672-6167
Amtrak trains come in to Penn Station at 1500 N. Charles Street—just minutes from downtown and the Inner Harbor. Taxi service available.

MARC

800-325-RAIL (7245)
Maryland Rail Commuter's Camden Line operates between Baltimore's Camden Station and Washington, D.C.'s Union Station. The Penn Line operates between

Perryville in Cecil County, Penn Station in Baltimore, and Union Station in Washington, D.C.

Greyhound Bus Lines

800-231-2222

Terminal: 210 Fayette St. 410-752-1393

Greyhound provides service to East Coast cities and connects to many others throughout the United States and Canada.

GETTING AROUND TOWN

Charles Street divides the city east and west, and Baltimore Street divides the city north and south, with street addresses reflecting this division.

Taxis

Baltimore's streets do *not* abound with taxis. In the Inner Harbor you can pick up one in front of The Gallery and Harbor Renaissance Hotel, as well as in front of other area hotels.

Mass Transit

Light Rail, Metro subways, and buses offer one-way and roundtrip fares, as well as all-day, weekly, and monthly passes allowing unlimited travel on all three systems. Self-service fare machines at the stations accept $1, $5, $10, $20 bills. Discounts available for seniors and people with disabilities.

Light Rail

410-539-5000 or 800-543-9809

The Light Rail makes 28 stops from Hunt Valley in the north through Baltimore (including one at Oriole Park at Camden Yards) to Cromwell Station/Glen Burnie. The BWI line runs between BWI and Penn Station and connects with MARC and Amtrak there. Parking is available at most stations. Trains operate until 11 pm Mon-Sat and until 7 pm Sun.

Baltimore Metro

410-539-5000 or 800-543-9809

The Baltimore Metro subway system offers service through Baltimore between Johns Hopkins Hospital in the city to Owings Mills in Baltimore County with major stops in the downtown area at the Shot Tower, Charles Center, Lexington Market, and State Center. As a bonus, Baltimore's subway stations feature mosaics, montages, and sculptures done by local and national artists. Operates until midnight Mon-Sat. Note: Old Court and State Center Stations shut down at 8 pm.

MTA buses

410-539-5000

The MTA offers more than 60 bus routes throughout the Baltimore area, serving the city north to Hunt Valley and south to BWI Airport. Daily, weekly, and monthly passes are available. Schedule and routes are available by calling the above number. Exact fare is required.

POPULATION

Baltimore is the 14th largest city in the United States with a population of 657,256.

WEATHER

Baltimore springs and late autumns are comfortable with temperatures ranging from 55-70°F, more often on the warm side than not. January and February can be cold with frequent drops into the low 30s. Snow rarely amounts to a few inches, but infrequent storms can dump a foot or more. Summer months average 85°F with high humidity in July and August (410-936-1212). Time: 410-844-1212.

AREA CODES

All calls in the state of Maryland, including local calls, must be dialed with the area codes—410, 443, 240, and 301—with the exception of dialing 911 (emergency) or 311 (urgency, but not emergency).

BALTIMORE AREA VISITORS' CENTER
Next to Phillips at Light Street Pavilion, Harborplace
800-282-6632 or 888-BALTIMO
www.baltimore.org
Answers queries and fills requests for visitors' packets
filled with information and highlights of seasonal activities (see *Inner Harbor*).

BALTIMORE AFRICAN AMERICAN TOURISM COUNCIL, INC.
P. O. Box 3014, Baltimore 21229. 410-783-5469
The Council promotes Baltimore as a premier destination for African Americans and also local black-owned
businesses, cultural attractions, and tours. "The
Maryland Multi-Cultural Tourism Guide" is available
upon request.

WEBSITES
Listed below are useful general websites for the city.
Others are noted throughout the book.
www.encorebaltimore.org
www.ci.baltimore.md.us
www.baltimore.org
www.mdisfun.
http://home.digitalcity.com/baltimore

EMERGENCY NUMBERS
Police, fire, and ambulance: 911
Non-emergency: 311 (noise complaints, pothole repair,
parking violations, etc.)
Poison Control Center: 410-706-7701
Suicide Prevention Hotline: 410-531-6677
Alcoholics Anonymous: 410-663-1922
Narcotics Anonymous: 800-317-3222
First Call for Help: 800-492-0618 or 410-685-0525
24-hour health and human services information service
offering housing, health, and other referrals.

READ AND RECYCLE

For information about goings on in Baltimore and news in general, here are a few noteworthy publications. Many free publications can be picked up in stores, restaurants, and galleries around town.

BALTIMORE AFRO-AMERICAN
410-554-8200

BALTIMORE BUSINESS JOURNAL
410-576-1161
www.amcity.com/baltimore

BALTIMORE'S CHILD
410-367-5883

BALTIMORE GAY PAPER
410-837-7748

BALTIMORE JEWISH TIMES
410-332-1951

BALTIMORE MAGAZINE
410-752-4200

BALTIMORE SUN
410-332-6000

CITY PAPER
410-523-2300

DAILY RECORD
410-752-3849
www.mddailyrecord.com

STYLE MAGAZINE
410-332-1951

THE URBANITE
410-366-0574

Suggested Reading

Beirne, Francis F. *The Amiable Baltimoreans*. New York: E.P. Dutton & Co., Inc., 1951.

Dorsey, John, and Dilts, James, D. *Guide to Baltimore Architecture*. Third edition. Centreville, Maryland: Tidewater Publishers, 1997.

Fee, Elizabeth; Shopes, Linda; Zeidman, Linda, eds. *The Baltimore Book, New Views of Local History*. Philadelphia: Temple University Press, 1991.

Kahn, Philip, Jr. *Uncommon Threads, Threads That Wove the Fabric of Baltimore Jewish Life*. Baltimore: PECAN Publications, 1996.

Keith, Robert C. *Baltimore Harbor, A Picture History*. Baltimore: Ocean World Publishing Co., Inc., 1982.

Lewand, Karen. Beirne, D. Randall, ed. *North Baltimore, From Estate to Development*. Baltimore: Baltimore City Department of Planning and the University of Baltimore, 1989.

Phillips, Christopher. *Freedom's Port, the African American Community of Baltimore, 1790-1860*. Urbana: University of Illinois Press, 1997.

Sheads, Scott and Toomey, Daniel. *Baltimore During the Civil War*. Linthicum, MD: Toomey Press, 1997.

Shivers, Frank R., Jr. *Walking in Baltimore, An Intimate Guide to the Old City*. Baltimore: Johns Hopkins University Press, 1995.

Stockett, Letitia. Baltimore, *A Not Too Serious History*. Baltimore: Olympic Press, 1928.

I*ndex

A

B

F

G

H

M

Macht Building 60-61, 79

Marble Steps 10-11, 109, 131, 192, 311, 326

Marsh and McLennan Building 183

Marshall, Thurgood 57-58, 224, 226-227, 391

Maryland Art Place 40, 66, 79, 346

Maryland Club 104-105, 117

Maryland Historical Society 81, 96-97, 117, 244

Maryland Institute College of Art 118, 122-123, 140-142

Maryland Line, The 122, 125

Maryland Maritime Center 274-275

Maryland Museum of African American History and Culture 250

Maryland National Guard Museum 124-125

Maryland Science Center 24, 26, 29, 39-40, 49

Masonic Temple 62, 79

McKeldin Fountain 41

McKim Center 248, 254

Meadow Mill 338, 347, 351

Memorial Episcopal Church 136, 142

Memorial Stadium 182, 399-400, 405

Mencken House 185-186, 195, 244

Mencken, H.L. 25, 40, 63, 70, 88-89, 95, 105, 113, 116, 184-186, 265, 363, 411

Mercantile Safe Deposit and Trust building 55, 152

Mergenthaler, Ottmar 134, 172

Mfume, Kweisi 225, 228

Mikulski, Barbara 144, 197, 270, 308

Mills, Robert 82, 109-110

Mitchell, Clarence M., Jr. 149-150, 227-228, 400

Mobtown 159-160, 257

Monument Square 148-149

Morgan State University 230, 400, 405

Morris A. Mechanic Theatre 54, 57, 79, 416

Morton K. Blaustein Building 245, 254

Mother Seton House 232-233, 238

Mount Clare 177, 188-189

Mount Clare Museum House 192, 195

Mount Clare Station 176-177, 189-190

Mount Royal Station 118, 120, 122, 142

Mount Vernon 10, 53, 80-102, 116-117, 132, 409, 411

Mount Vernon Mills 337, 341-342, 351

Mount Vernon Museum of Incandescent Lighting 81, 85, 117

Mount Vernon Place United Methodist Church 84, 117

Mount Washington Octagon 364-365, 371

Murphy Family 224, 226

Muslim American Society of Baltimore 389-390, 405

Muslim Community Cultural Center 389

Myers, Isaac 269, 280-281

N

9 North Front Street 243, 254

NAACP 58, 225, 227-228, 231, 391-392

NAACP Headquarters 405

National Aquarium 24, 29-32, 49

National Historic Seaport of Baltimore 34

NationsBank Building 59-60, 79

Natural History Society of Maryland Museum 374, 405

New Refuge Deliverance Cathedral 107, 117

Nipper 96

North German Lloyd Line 58, 214

O

O'Donnell Square 310, 313, 325

Oblate Sisters of Providence 233-234

Old Otterbein United Methodist Church 205, 212

Z

Additions or Corrections?

Phone numbers change. Shops move. New sites and restaurants appear every day. For future editions of *Wish You Were Here!,* please send additions or corrections to

Baltimore Guide
c/o Woodholme House
1829 Reisterstown Road
#130
Baltimore, Maryland 21208